Hialeah Racetrack

Jewish Miami & Miami Beach circa 1960

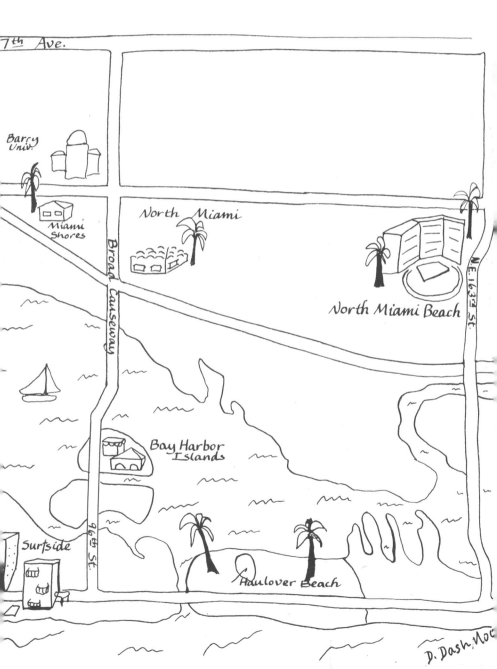

7th Ave.

Barry Univ.

Miami Shores

North Miami

Broad Causeway

North Miami Beach

N.E. 163rd St.

Bay Harbor Islands

96th St.

Surfside

Haulover Beach

D. Dash. '00

To the
Golden Cities

*Pursuing the American Jewish Dream
in Miami and L.A.*

Deborah Dash Moore

THE FREE PRESS
A Division of Macmillan, Inc.
NEW YORK

Maxwell Macmillan Canada
TORONTO

Maxwell Macmillan International
NEW YORK   OXFORD   SINGAPORE   SYDNEY

FOR MY MEN
MacDonald,
Mordecai, and Mikhael

Copyright © 1994 by Deborah Dash Moore

The Free Press
A Division of Macmillan, Inc.
866 Third Avenue, New York, N.Y. 10022

Maxwell Macmillan Canada, Inc.
1200 Eglinton Avenue East
Suite 200
Don Mills, Ontario M3C 3N1

Macmillan, Inc. is part of the Maxwell Communication Group of Companies.

Printed in the United States of America

printing number

1 2 3 4 5 6 7 8 9 10

Library of Congress Cataloging-in-Publication Data
Moore, Deborah Dash
   To the golden cities : pursuing the American Jewish dream in Miami
and L.A. / Deborah Dash Moore.
      p. cm.
   Includes bibliographical references and index.
   ISBN 0–02–922111–0
   1. Jews—Florida—Miami. 2. Jews—California—Los Angeles.
3. Jews—United States—Migrations. 4. Migration, Internal—United
States. 5. Miami (Fl.)—Ethnic Relations. 6. Los Angeles (Ca.)—
Ethnic Relations. I. Title.
F319.M6M824 1994
975.9'381004924—dc20   93–41775
                                                                        CIP

Contents

Preface and Acknowledgments

I don't remember the first time I saw Miami. My memories are imperfect vignettes, much like the faded photograph that sits on a bookcase in my parents' home. A hotel photographer captured my sister and me in the flouncy chiffon dresses of the era. I recall, of course, beautiful beaches with foaming waves, but I also remember the licentious pleasures of the children's dining room, where I ordered hot fudge sundaes with chocolate ice cream. Paradise on earth! And then there was the hotel porch with its white columns and comfortable chairs, where my sister and I—we billed ourselves as "The Dash Sisters"—performed "If You Knew Susie" to the delight and approval of my parents and grandparents. This was, I realize with an historian's hindsight, exactly the type of uninhibited behavior that worried the more zealous professionals working with some of the Jewish defense agencies.[1] "If You Knew Susie" belonged in the privacy of our room, not on the public porch where it might "generate" antisemitism among those who caught our act. Repeated visits to Miami added layers of impressions, a muddle of sensations.

I first saw Los Angeles on an early August morning in 1970. We were driving across the country on a trip to visit sites of historical interest and natural beauty, and approached the city from the east. Stopping at a roadside rest area on one of the mountains surrounding the city, we looked down on the sprawling streets that appeared to stretch limitlessly until they merged with a hazy horizon. Over us hung a heavy dull orange sky, the famous smog of L.A. Assuming L.A. offered neither historical interest nor natural beauty, we quickly drove through the city and headed north up the coast. Eight years later we returned to California. From our home in Santa Barbara we visited Los Angeles regularly, drawn not only by the pleasures of a big city but by friends, and friends of friends, who had moved there from the east. Then we saw another L.A.—one of promise, opportunity, the good life.

The idea of actually researching and writing about Jews in Miami and Los Angeles did not occur to me until 1984. That spring, George Pozzetta invited me down to Florida to participate in a conference on ethnicity in the Sunbelt. The conference members responded warmly to my paper on Jewish migration to the Sunbelt and encouraged me to research and write a book.[2] The idea planted in Florida blossomed in Jerusalem. On a Fulbright to the Hebrew University I had the good fortune to teach a course on American Jews since 1945 with Aryeh Goren. As we struggled to shape a syllabus, we realized that we had to create an historical overview of the era, developing a chronology and periodization, selecting key events and turning points. The postwar history of American Jews had not yet been told.

When I returned to the States, I recognized that migration to the Sunbelt provided an ideal prism through which to view American Jews' postwar history. Through migration, American Jews seized hold of their future and launched themselves on an odyssey into the postwar era. But they lived under the shadow of the destruction of European Jewry and in the euphoria, uncertainty, and demands that accompanied the birth of the State of Israel. Today we live in a world they shaped. Their choices redefined many components of American Jewish identity. Nowhere did the changes appear more vividly than in Miami and Los Angeles. The statistics confirmed my impressions: migration to the Sunbelt in the postwar decades translated into migration to Los Angeles and Miami. These were the pacemaker cities, the ones deserving an historian's attention.

I began my research in New York, a city blessed with a wealth of resources. At the Jewish Division of the New York Public Library, the librarians graciously expedited my many requests. At the American

Jewish Committee, Cima Horowitz in the library and Milton Krentz in the William E. Wiener Oral History Library provided valuable assistance. I also had the immense good fortune to meet Gladys Rosen, who shared with me her insights into Miami's Jewish history, the fruit of several years of research. Later she invited me to tour her basement and then generously gave me cartons of material she had accumulated. My research on Miami benefited enormously from her diligence and intelligence. I refer to these files as the Rosen files, after their archivist. At the YIVO Institute of Jewish Research, Zachary Baker and Dina Abramovicz in the library offered useful aid and Marek Web and Frume Mohrer in the Archives patiently helped as I scoured American Jewish Committee records. Marek's blend of professionalism and charm—who can resist being called *meydele*?—lifted my occasionally flagging spirits.

A Rapoport Fellowship in American Jewish Studies allowed me to visit the American Jewish Archives in Cincinnati. Abraham Peck and Fannie Zelcer facilitated my research there. Nathan M. Kaganoff [*z" l*] at the American Jewish Historical Society filled my mail and phone requests, making my brief visit exceptionally productive. Sharon Pucker Rivo at the National Center of Jewish Film accommodated my crowded schedule and guided me into the field of film research. A National Endowment for the Humanities fellowship supported research trips to Los Angeles and Miami, as well as a brief visit to the Library of Congress. In L.A. I had the good fortune to receive a warm welcome from Hannah Kuhn, the librarian at the Brandeis-Bardin Institute, and from Steven Lowenstein and Max Vorspan at the University of Judaism. The librarians and archivists at the Jewish Community Library of the Federation-Council, and the library of UCLA, including its Special Collections, assisted me. Several synagogue librarians and administrators also opened doors for me at the Stephen S. Wise Temple, as did Kala Ginsberg at Temple Adat Ari-El. A trip to Miami proved to be similarly productive. Henry Green at the University of Miami introduced me to the Mosaic project, while Beatrice Muskat at Temple Israel, Ruth Abelow and Helen Goldman at Temple Emanu-El, and Dori Goldman at Beth David offered generous assistance. In Israel I benefited from the expertise of archivists at the Central Zionist Archives and Steven Spielberg Jewish Film Archives.

Menaham Kaufman wisely encouraged me to consult the United Jewish Appeal oral histories at the Institute of Contemporary Jewry of the Hebrew University.

Researching a past within living memories challenges an historian. I am indebted to the many individuals who shared their memories of Miami and Los Angeles with me, in formal interviews and casual conversations. They are acknowledged in the notes, as are the oral histories I consulted. I would be remiss, however, not to single out an early interview with Wolfe Kelman [*z" l*], who shared with me his exceptional understanding of religious developments during the postwar era and an extraordinary series of interviews on a Friday in July 1989. Bud Hudson, reluctant to talk in much detail about his own migration from New York to Los Angeles, arranged for me to interview the Mavens, a wonderful group of guys who made new homes and lives for themselves and their families in the San Fernando Valley. Although I was able to use only a fraction of their stories, the book has benefited enormously from their generous spirit.

A similar generosity of spirit animated the many colleagues and friends who took time from busy schedules to read and critique chapters and work-in-progress. Miriam Cohen, Richard Cohen, Judith Goldstein, Eileen Leonard, Charles Liebman, Deborah Lipstadt, Peter Medding, Ezra Mendelsohn, Mary Shanley, Gerald Sorin, and Patricia Wallace gave me valuable criticisms. I also learned from opportunities to present material in public forums. I especially appreciate the comments of Selma Berrol, Michael Ebner, Marc Galanter, Robert Goldberg, Jeffrey Gurock, David Hollinger, Walter Nugent, Bruce Phillips, Riv-Ellen Prell, David Rothman, Martin Ridge, Moses Rischin, Joel Schwartz, Jan Shipps, and Alan Trachtenberg. Marc Stern urged me to examine the files of the Commission on Law and Social Action of the American Jewish Congress, and I am grateful for his prodding and insight.

Another type of vital help came from institutions and individuals who recognized the value of the project. Pamela Brumberg and William Frost at the Lucius N. Littauer Foundation encouraged me in spirit and substance. The foundation's support allowed me to write and helped in final preparation of the manuscript. Samuel Norich, executive director of the YIVO Institute for Jewish Research, very early expressed his enthusiasm and enabled me, during the year I served as research director, to devote myself to the book. My friends in the Department of Religion at Vassar College—especially Betsy Amaru, Robert Fortna, John Glasse, and Lawrence Mamiya—let me take what seemed to them like an endless number of leaves of absence required to research and write the book. Vassar College also generously supported me through several grants-in-aid, including a final grant from the Salmon Fund. I appreciate as well the University Seminars at Columbia University for assistance in the preparation of the manuscript for publication. Ideas presented here benefited from discussions in the University Seminar on The City.

Several research assistants speeded a long process. A former student and Vassar graduate, Cindy Sweet, first helped me determine the dimensions of the research. Elliott Gertel scoured newspapers for me. Jennifer Breen shared her research on *Exodus* as did Elizabeth Weaver on tourism to Israel. I was fortunate in having the aid of some competent Vassar students, especially Brian Sokol. Mikhael Moore transcribed tapes (a boring task). Roberta Newman did the photo research; her knowledge and skill translated my rather inchoate ideas into real pictures. Marcia Kerstein Zerivitz at Mosaic helped locate many photos of Miami.

When I thought that all was finished, I received unexpected and invaluable help from my editor, Joyce Seltzer. Her attention to argument, language, and coherence inspired me to tackle the text again, to clarify and condense. I learned from her and from her assistant, Cherie Weitzner, who peppered the manuscript with queries that sent me back to the computer to rethink and rewrite. Because of their care and skill, I have written a better book.

There is finally another kind of aid that I have constantly relied upon, but not without gratitude. My family truly made possible the research and writing. Trips to Los Angeles were affordable on fellowships because I could always count on sleeping on my cousin's couch. Glynnis Golden and her son, Gabriel, turned work into pleasure (and Glynnie's mastery of L.A. freeways and streets ensured that I never got lost). My grandmother, Bella Golden, never hesitated to give me the keys to her North Miami Beach apartment. My parents, Irene and Martin Dash, offered unfailing enthusiasm. Irene read and critiqued several chapters. Mordecai Moore did some research at crucial moments. Mikhael Moore surprisingly took up the challenge

of reading one chapter; his comments—both critical and praisewor-
thy—helped me see what still needed to be done. Both sons managed
as teenagers graciously to put up with a mother who appeared end-
lessly fascinated with what happened in two cities at a time before
their birth.

There are three people who did more. They read and critiqued
draft upon draft; they listened and argued over lunches and dinners
to ideas and interpretations; they managed somehow never to grow
bored, never to lose interest; they cheered me when I was discouraged; and they pointed out the work yet to be done when I thought
I was finished. Without them, the book might never have been written. Paula Hyman and Aryeh Goren shaped this book in ways they
cannot imagine. MacDonald probably can imagine his impact, but he
deserves to know how much it mattered to me. I am beholden in
gratitude and love. Needless to say, I am also solely responsible for
what lies between these covers.

WASHINGTON HEIGHTS, NEW YORK CITY
August 1993

1
On the Threshold

Modern consciousness entails a movement from fate to choice.

—PETER BERGER
The Heretical Imperative

Nineteen forty-five marks a turning point for American Jews. That year they crossed a threshold to embrace the fulfillment promised by America. Behind them lay the immigrant working-class world—their parents' world of passionate politics and a vibrant Yiddish culture, their childhood world indelibly associated with New York City and the other large cities of the Northeast and Midwest. Before them stretched the American century—their century. The future glittered most vividly in the opportunity America offered them to begin again, its tantalizing promise of a fresh start in new territory. As native-born Americans, Jews faced the future with anticipation and trepidation. Between the provincial past and boundless present loomed the horror of World War II. The war transformed American Jews, disrupting their ties to a familiar world and propelling many of them out of their homes into a mass migration across the continent.

1

The destruction of European Jewry ruptured American Jews' living link to their European past. The Holocaust shattered an era of European Jewish cultural innovation and religious renewal. The rich European Jewish community that had sustained American Jewish life through immigration and provided world Jewry with intellectual, moral, and religious leadership lay in ashes. The disaster left the New World as the remaining hope for a Jewish future in the diaspora. American Jews, long considered exotic provincials by their European brethren, now confronted an awesome burden of ensuring Jewish security and survival. This task they neither anticipated nor welcomed.[1] The end of World War II forced them to face their responsibility for world Jewry in a radically altered Jewish world. Having survived the war unscathed, American Jews forever lost their provincial isolation.

After the war American Jews began a journey that would rival the mass migration of their immigrant parents. The decision to abandon the big cities for a new frontier charted a course for the rest of the century. While many Jews chose to settle in suburbia, a significant minority opted for the open society of the emerging sunbelt. In the postwar era Jews discovered Houston and Dallas, Atlanta and Phoenix, and especially Miami and Los Angeles, cities on the verge of enormous growth. "Let me tell you, to me when I came here the first time, I had a feeling that I had come to Paradise," Isaac Bashevis Singer admitted. "First of all the palm trees. Where would I ever see a palm tree in my life?" Then there was the fresh orange juice. "That first sip was nothing less than ambrosia, especially after such a long journey."[2] Singer's initial impressions of Miami were far from unique. Jews thought Miami and Los Angeles possessed the earmarks of an earthly paradise: unending sunshine, the bluest of blue skies and the cleanest of clean air, an enormous expanse of ocean, miles of unspoiled sandy beaches, streets lined with tall palm trees, and a relaxed, easygoing style of life, a foretaste of eternal life itself.

Miami and Los Angeles present a peculiar perspective on postwar American Jewry. Preeminently cities of newcomers, they showcase American Jews unconnected to old routines. Jewish communities without long-established hierarchies and institutions flourished in the "land of young people looking for a future and retired folk reviewing the past."[3] Miami and Los Angeles lacked accepted patterns of deference to an entrenched leadership. Communal life was bland but also malleable and welcoming. These cities let Jews be whatever types of Jews they wanted to be. When they chose to be Jewish or liberal, to support the establishment of the State of Israel or the separation of church and state, Miami and Los Angeles Jews were not just fashioning an identity for themselves. Their decisions placed them in the vanguard of American Jewish life because they were freely taken. By migrating to Miami or Los Angeles, American Jews initiated a process of change. In typical American style they proposed to start anew.

Yet in their choices Miami and Los Angeles Jews drew upon childhood memories derived from an upbringing on the streets of a big American city like Chicago or New York. Memories of such rugged urban realities enhanced the beauty of Miami and Los Angeles. Recalling crowded, vertical, dark, and dirty cities, American Jews marveled at the clean, spacious, open, horizontal quality of Miami and L.A. In the daytime the cities were bathed in light, from the omnipresence of sunlight to the popularity of white and pastel-colored buildings. At night, streets were quiet and empty; in the morning, sounds of birds filled the air. Signs of prosperity abounded: almost everyone seemed to own an automobile—a luxury in the Northeast and Midwest—and most people lived in private, single-family houses with flowers and fruit-bearing trees in the gardens.[4] Even the sweet smells signaled a reality sharply at variance with the acrid fumes of coal-burning heaters and incinerators. The pace was more leisurely, less harried. The long train journey to reach these two cities helped set them apart from mundane America.

Los Angeles appeared more like clusters of small towns strung together along broad, straight streets than like the nation's third largest city. Visiting L.A. during the war, the French philosopher Jean-Paul Sartre compared it to "a big earthworm that might be chopped into twenty pieces without being killed. If you go through this enormous urban cluster," he wrote, ". . . you come upon twenty juxtaposed cities, strictly identical, each with its poor section, its business streets, night-clubs and smart suburb." Ironically, at the center of the city's structure stood the single-family detached suburban house, normally on the urban periphery. Miami barely made it into the ranks of big cities, so meager and dispersed was its population. "Miami, renowned as a gay, metropolitan playground, is also a quiet community of individual homes and gardens, and is rapidly recovering from its spectacular, adolescent growth," observed the WPA guide. "Wide stretches of vacant lots, overgrown with scrub palmettos, give these outlying sections a ragged, straggling appearance." Both Miami and Los Angeles devoted extensive acreage to farms within their county limits.[5] Seeing the external physical reality, American Jews imagined a corresponding internal one. The conspicuous absence of multistory slum tenements, for example, signaled a lack of poverty to American Jews. What made Miami and Los Angeles so attractive was their contrast with cities that most American Jews called home.[6]

Prior to World War II over 40 percent of American Jews lived in New York City, and another 10 percent lived in Chicago. With a handful of other big cities—Philadelphia, Boston, Cleveland—these accounted for the preponderance of American Jews. These cities shared much in common with such smaller industrial cities as Milwaukee, Detroit, St. Louis, Pittsburgh, Baltimore, and Newark. Ethnicity animated their neighborhoods, influenced occupational distribution, and dominated politics. Jews were one ethnic group among many. Jewish religion, culture, politics, and occupations stemmed from immigrant origins. "Down the street were Orthodox Jews, up the street were Zionists, in the middle of the street were shtetl Jews, get-rich-quick Jews, European humanist Jews," recalled the writer Vivian Gornick of her East Bronx neighborhood. Divisions among Jews—of class, birth, background, ideology, and religious observance—ultimately paled before differences separating Jews from other immigrants, mostly Catholics, many from peasant cultures. Their interaction with each other, and with the local, often Protestant, elites, shaped each city's character.[7]

Like their fellow city dwellers, Jews reckoned their ethnicity as part of the common coin of urban discourse. Those who grew up in the city, especially the children of immigrants, quickly acquired a streetwise savvy as they navigated patterns of daily life, walking from home to school, running errands at local stores, visiting relatives, playing games, meeting fathers returning from work at the subway or elevated stations. Occasional trips outside of the neighborhood reinforced through contrast a sense of the familiar.[8] Immigrants in the multiethnic metropolis each marked their separate turfs, defining both differences and shared aspects of urban culture. Where each group chose to settle influenced its perceptions of its collective identity.

In every city except New York, Jews were simply one minority struggling among others. Jews in New York City enjoyed the luxury of numbers and diversity. Almost two million strong and roughly 30 percent of the population, they were, in fact, the city's largest single ethnic group. Because of their critical mass, their internal differences did count. New York Jews could separate themselves from their fellow Jews on the grounds of ideology or religion, class or politics, and still find enough other similar Jews to fill an apartment house, an organization, or even a neighborhood. Gerson Cohen, the future chancellor of the Jewish Theological Seminary, grew up speaking Hebrew in an immigrant household, an unusual pattern of Jewish family culture. When he was a teenager, he met a Polish boy who had studied "within the Hebrew secular system of Poland. He and I played ball together, talking away in Hebrew, from which I drew the following inference: New York City was a place where people, however isolated they were from the mainstream, did not need to be alone."[9]

The diversity and numbers of New York Jews allowed them to settle large sections of the city and to endow those areas with a Jewish ambiance. Growing up in East Flatbush, Victor Gotbaum remembered that section of Brooklyn as "really insulated, wrapped in a false sense of security, what with Jews to the left of you and to the right of you and across the street from you." Although they shared the streets with other ethnics, New York Jews often were remarkably provincial. "Much later," the labor leader continued, "I was impressed when my Chicago friends told me that right across the street there might be a Polish family and a Polish gang ready to get you. I never had that problem. Neither did most Jews raised in Brooklyn. When you went to school the minority would be two or three non-Jews per class." The writer Grace Paley "grew up being very sorry for Christians. My idea was that there were very few of them in the world." Kate Simon knew that Italian immigrants lived on the east side of Lafontaine Street in the Bronx, but she considered them "just Jews who didn't talk Yiddish. They didn't go to synagogues, either, but a lot of Jews didn't. Most of them went to church only on their high holy days, like Jews." Comfortable in their own world, New York Jews rarely ventured outside of it. "The Jewish immigrant world branded upon its sons and daughters marks of separateness even while encouraging them to dreams of universalism."[10]

Living in New York, Jews understood the ineluctable quality of Jewishness. It dictated not only how one spoke, where one lived, the schools one attended, one's choice of job but even one's politics and friends. "The Jewish community enclosed one, not through choice as much as through experience and instinct, and often not very gently or with the most refined manners." The author Irving Howe's reminiscences ring true. "What you believed, or said you believed, did not matter nearly as much as what you were, and what you were was not nearly so much a matter of choice as you might care to suppose." Indeed, the flip side of ineluctability was naturalness. Being Jewish came naturally in New York; it required virtually no special effort. It was part of being a New Yorker, or to be more precise, of being from Brooklyn or the Bronx. "Growing up in the Bronx I didn't feel Jewish, nor did I *not* feel Jewish. 'Feeling Jewish' is something that occurs to people only when they already see some alternatives to being Jewish," Howe continues. "Growing up in a Jewish family that spoke Yiddish, as I did, made it all a natural environment. I had no distinctive consciousness that there was any choice or alternative."[11]

In Chicago and Philadelphia, Cleveland and Boston, Jews possessed a more acute awareness of their minority status. "It is no wonder, at least to me, that I was in my late teens before I dared go inside Brooks Brothers in Boston," the journalist Nat Hentoff admitted. "The name, the look of the place, the look of the salespeople I saw through the window, all signaled that they would smell the ghetto on me and not make me welcome." Hentoff grew up "in a three-story apartment house on Howland Street" in Roxbury, Boston, not far from Blue Hill Avenue, the main Jewish shopping thoroughfare. A substantial distance separated Jews from their Christian neighbors, both Catholic and Protestant. Irish Catholic Boston during the Depression revered Father Coughlin, the antisemitic radio priest. On Sunday excursions in the car, Hentoff listened to Coughlin's sermons with his family "and felt hunted too. None of us had the slightest doubt, on those Sunday afternoons, that pogroms could happen here too."[12]

In Philadelphia, most of the neighborhoods "were strictly segregated." Even Jewish builders were reluctant "to sell to Jews." One builder recalled that "as a kid in the models, I was told to warn any buyers coming in who happened to be Jewish that the rest of the neighborhood was all Gentile." Looking back, Marvin Orleans observed that the Jewish builders, including his father, "were not too crazy about selling to Jews for fear of what it would do to their market." In Chicago, as Jews left the West Side, the slum area that housed many different immigrant groups, they moved to sections of the city that rapidly acquired substantial Jewish populations.[13]

Although some Jews invested in single-family homes, many remained renters.[14] Renting facilitated mobility, and Jews moved often from one apartment to another depending upon their changing fortunes. To move to a new neighborhood—to change the view from the kitchen window—meant to exchange an old ethnic identity for a new one, to abandon tradition for modernity. Jews living on the Lower East Side of Manhattan looked out onto narrow, densely crowded streets, often filled with pushcarts. Wash hung from clotheslines strung across the rear yards. Yiddish and English signs adorned the tenement facades advertising the coexistence of workplace and residence. By contrast, Jews who moved to the Bronx saw from their windows wide, clean streets filled with criss-crossing patterns of fathers traveling to and from work, children heading to school or at play, and women making the rounds of shopping in local stores. Striped awnings covered windows in the summer, laundry often hung on the roof to dry, and pushcart markets cluttered only a handful of streets.[15]

In contrast to the new cities where Jews would soon move, the organized Jewish community in the northeastern and midwestern cities presented a picture of institutional completeness. Schools of all types—religious, congregational, communal, Zionist, Yiddishist, socialist, communist—and of all levels—elementary, secondary, vocational, college, teacher training, graduate—flourished or expected to flourish. Jews established hospitals, orphanages, old-age homes, homes for delinquents and for unwed mothers, community centers, settlement houses, and young men's and women's Hebrew associations. Gender provided a fulcrum for organization, and women's organizations represented a wide political and religious spectrum. Even occupational groups reflected ethnic background. There were organizations of Jewish public school teachers and policemen, unions of Jewish garment workers and bakers, of Yiddish writers and social workers. Most numerous were the small societies of Jews from the same hometowns in the old country, *landsmanshaftn*. These groups directly linked Jews with their European cousins. Religious activities increasingly fractured along denominational lines with growing distinctions among Reform, Conservative, and Orthodox. Finally, national Jewish organizations, from fraternal orders to Zionist groups, participated through their branches in local city life.[16]

From the individual club, synagogue, lodge, or union local, a network of coordinating groups extended up from the neighborhood to the city and often to the national level. Even many of the *landsmanshaftn* coordinated their activities through nationwide federations. Such organizational structures allowed individuals to rise to positions of leadership and to adopt a cosmopolitan perspective on the issues of the day. Growing up in a labor Zionist home in the Boston working-class suburb of Chelsea, the Jewish communal leader Jack Katzman remembered the many movement guests who regularly filled the house. "We were a part of something that was as big as the whole Jewish people, as wide as the world."[17]

Jews found in politics a broader sense of identity as well as a vision of a better American society. Franklin D. Roosevelt's liberal New Deal policies provided an ideology and a faith, along with practical proposals to solve pressing problems of the Depression. "Roosevelt, to many American Jews," writes the journalist Stephen Isaacs, "was the next thing to Moses. To many who had left religion, he was the new Moses." Roosevelt's coalition politics united Jews with their fellow urban ethnics, overcoming antagonisms that separated them in the cities and giving them a common stake in making a better America.[18]

Despite the influence of New Deal politics, local city elites held their power tightly. Any Jew aspiring to a leadership position faced discrimination. In Philadelphia, "in 1940, a class of WASP gentlemen still dominated the business and cultural life of the city as their ancestors had since colonial days." As Howe realized when he entered City College, "Authority and power in the city and the world were not Jewish." Denied access to leadership in metropolitan society, Jews developed their own parallel elites within the Jewish community. These wealthy men controlled most of the influential Jewish communal organizations, especially the citywide coordinating and fund-raising Jewish Federations.[19]

Although few Jews growing up in the big cities in the 1930s were aware of the extent and diversity of Jewish organizational activity, most participated in public expressions of Jewishness and many engaged in activities under Jewish auspices. Urban Jews knew about synagogues, even if they did not attend them, as most did not; indeed, they were as likely to walk by them on the streets as they were to pass a church. Similarly, Jews were conscious of the Yiddish dailies that shared the newsstands with the English papers, and they experienced the rhythm of the Jewish calendar because on Jewish holidays they refrained from school or work or shopping like other neighborhood kids. In the metropolitan milieu even the secular worlds of work, commerce, and recreation reflected Jewish associations. Special sales in local stores coincided with Jewish holidays like Rosh Hashanah or Passover, promoting patterns of consumption linked to Judaism. Strikes in Jewish industries, especially the garment trades, resonated throughout the streets of Jewish neighborhoods. Young Jews just might play basketball or attend a dance at the local Jewish community center; the lucky ones would spend summer vacations at Jewish country resorts, cottages, or camps; and all had some friends who became bar mitzvah at the age of thirteen.[20]

Just as young Jews were aware of a Jewish world, they were similarly conscious of limitations and discrimination. One didn't have to encounter antisemitism to know it existed, even to plan one's life and tailor one's aspirations so that one would avoid it. "I knew that I was a good student and that I was going to apply for graduate school," Maxwell Greenberg, a Harvard-educated lawyer recalled. "I knew that there were quotas in various graduate schools. I also knew that if I worked very hard and made good grades, and did everything that was expected of me by my parents and by society, . . . I would qualify for graduate school."[21] Jewish vocational patterns often reflected this reality. Few Jews tried to obtain engineering degrees, for example, because prospects for employment were slim. Some Jews changed their names to increase their chances at jobs in large firms.[22] But most navigated the prejudice and discrimination as facts of life. Compared to violent antisemitism in Europe, the American brand seemed tame.

Then the war came and uprooted Jews from their established routines, comfortable neighborhoods, and mundane affairs. Initially, however, the war didn't seem to change their lives. Jews read the papers, raised funds, and sent packages of food to help Polish Jews, the newest victims of Nazi attack. They protested and urged their political representatives to help rescue Jewish refugees desperately trying to leave Europe. They signed affidavits of support to assist near or distant relatives obtain visas. They helped the Yishuv, the Jewish settlement in Palestine, as it struggled against the encroaching reality of war. But at the same time they held banquets and dinners to raise money for their local synagogues and hospitals. They continued their intramural political struggles. They celebrated the ordinary rounds of holidays and family occasions, births and weddings, bar mitzvahs and confirmations.

When the United States declared war in December 1941 after the Japanese attack on Pearl Harbor, Jews threw themselves into the war effort together with their fellow citizens. Some young Jews did not wait to be drafted, but enlisted in the armed forces. Many shared Nathan Perlmutter's sentiments: When asked why he wanted to join the Marines, Perlmutter told a surprised recruiter, "I want to fight Fascism." But only a minority chose to leave college as Perlmutter left Georgetown University to enlist. The majority followed the more common track of continuing to work or remaining in school until called by their draft board. A few intrepid individuals battled American antisemitism just to enlist, the experience of one recent Yale graduate, Martin Dash. Rebuffed by biased New York recruiters who refused to enlist him in the Navy's officer corps, he went down to Baltimore to use his relatives' address to sign up. Seymour Graubard faced similar problems with Air Force Intelligence. A Columbia Law School graduate, Graubard had a deferral from the draft but "was insistent on getting into action. All my non-Jewish friends were accepted, but my application was lost three times running. I was finally informed by a sympathetic Air Corps officer that the Air Corps didn't want Jews." Graubard then pulled strings to get a commission in the Army. A handful of Jewish pacifists faced a different dilemma. Convinced that World War II "would be an imperialist one," committed Jewish socialists like Paul Jacobs had to decide: "Should we or should we not support the Allies against the Nazis and the Italian Fascists?"[23]

Approximately 550,000 Jewish men and women served in the United States armed forces during World War II, the equivalent of thirty seven divisions. The participation of 11 percent of the Jewish population in the service—50 percent of the men aged eighteen to forty-four—ensured that few Jewish families would not have a close relative in uniform.[24] Widespread involvement in the military turned

Jews into fighters. They became seasoned soldiers, competent in handling arms and comfortable in taking risks. The experience changed their lives, their perceptions of the world, and their self-understanding as Jews.

Military service lifted Jews out of their cities and sent them to bases located often in the rural areas of the country, especially the South and West. The first encounter produced a kind of culture shock. "I was in a strange land among people who hardly spoke my own language," wrote one GI from Brooklyn. "On this foreign soil one could not find lox or bagels or pumpernickel. Here Southern fried and grits were the popular delicacies." To many Jews' amazement, "this foreign soil" was indeed America. The United States turned out to be a Protestant nation, not a Catholic one. Jews in the armed services discovered a world beyond their provincial neighborhoods. "Most of us were kind of insulated," Abe Shalo remembered, ". . . we had very little knowledge of the rest of the country. Whatever we learned about the United States was for the most part from geography books . . . we knew very little about the people." And the geography books "didn't tell you how different the average American was." Jews acknowledged their surprise upon realizing how Protestant the United States was. They had mistaken the heavily Catholic cities of their childhoods for the entire country.[25]

The army introduced many Jews to racial discrimination and prejudice. One recruit stationed in Virginia observed a Jim Crow incident on a bus—a Negro soldier who refused to sit in the rear was forced to get off. Writing back home to Brooklyn, he described the matter and concluded: "It is about time that all JIM CROW laws were abolished in the South. . . . Such a move would prove how truly and genuinely we mean our war aims."[26] This awareness and anger at civil discrimination and its contradiction of clearly articulated American wartime ideals stimulated in many Jews a commitment to civil rights.

The armed forces gave Jews a new perspective on antisemitism. Greenberg remembered that the first time he was "labelled a Jew or a kike was in the Army." His experience was not uncommon. "You know, Dad, there is anti-Semitism. I have found it in the army," wrote Lillian Kimberg, a WAC. Although most Jewish soldiers encountered antisemitism in the service, many thought that daily living together reduced prejudice. Kimberg discovered that "many of the girls have never seen a Jew." But she felt that, as "a representative of my religion," she "showed them that Jews are people like all other in the world." Some were less sanguine about the impact an individual could make. Victor Gotbaum recalled many incidents and "statements about our cowardice and Jewish unwillingness to fight. I was deeply upset by it. Here we were fighting the Nazis, and then this madness in the United States Army!" Most contended that as they approached the battlefield, antisemitism declined and that it disappeared completely under the pressure of battle. Leon Uris wrote to his father in 1944 that he "fought beside Catholics, Protestants and Mormons, Indians, Irish, Italians, Poles. They liked me because I was a good man and a regular fellow." After two years of serving in the Marines in the Pacific, the future novelist was convinced that "it's not the religion we look at, but the man himself."[27]

Corresponding to this perception of a declining antisemitism came renewed respect for Judaism by Jewish GIs. Jews turned to religion in the armed forces to assert their identity. "It could only happen here," Albert Eisen wrote to his mother. "I went to Jewish Services tonight. I think I can count on the fingers of one hand the times I have gone before. However," he explained, "as a minority, it becomes necessary for us to declare ourselves to those who, unfortunately, are imbued with anti-Semitic sentiments." A few actually did find comfort in religion, despite a militantly secular and radical Jewish upbringing. Harold Paris grew up in Brooklyn within such a milieu and "was never religious. Now I somehow want to be very much. I go to services on Tuesday and Friday," the nineteen-year-old admitted to his immigrant parents, somewhat apologetically. "I feel better when I do. It gives hope for things to come." Surveying Jewish soldiers' attitudes to Judaism immediately after the war, Moses Kligsberg argued that they "perceived in it an imposing and powerful force." The war strengthened their identity as Jews.[28]

Chaplains, by contrast, marveled at how little Jews knew about their religion and culture and, correspondingly, how strong was the appeal of kosher salami and gefilte fish. Morris Adler concluded from his experience as chaplain what subsequent Jewish population surveys would confirm; namely, how the plethora of American Jewish organizations touch just a handful of American Jews. As a rabbi, he never realized "the extent and depth of the widespread, militant,

boundless ignorance of matters Jewish which characterize large sections of Jewry." Searching for an analogy, he suggested that "they are
Israelites of a pre-Sinaitic era. It is not that they have turned their
backs upon Judaism but that they have never faced it." Rabbis and
Jewish leaders "do not have to overcome a bitter opposition and
rejection. Culturally, we are presented with a *tabula rasa*," Adler
exclaimed.[29]

Fighting for their country empowered American Jews. In the
armed services they came to identify with America and its ideals.
"This feeling of affiliation with a great power and the sense that they
are symbolizing the principles for which this power went to battle"
made many of the same young Jewish men "begin to consider the
Jewish religion as a positive asset." A Jewish chaplain thought that
because the military "respects the heritage of the Jew and encour-
ages the active identification of every fighting man with his religious
civilization," Jews left the service with both components of their
identities as Jewish Americans enhanced. Kligsberg concluded that
almost all "came back from the war with a feeling of pride in their
Jewishness, with an awakened interest in Jewish life and with a
readiness to carry out actively certain Jewish responsibilities."[30]

Jews serving in the army in Europe experienced the liberation of
the Buchenwald concentration camp as a turning point where their
Jewish and American identities intersected. As American soldiers
they recognized the horror of antisemitism and their need to be Jews.
The distinctiveness of World War II for American Jews crystallized
then. "I came out of World War II with such a feeling of guilt that I
felt I had to do something," Marty Peppercorn admitted. Growing up
in the Bronx, "I had been a typical Jewish boy raised in a Jewish
home, accustomed to Jewish values, and certainly my friends were all
Jewish. Then, during World War II, after going into the DP camps
and observing what went on, I became ardently Jewish." As the
dimensions of the destruction of European Jewry unfolded, the war
took on new meaning for Jewish GIs. The war strengthened their
Jewish and American identities and produced an assertiveness that
contrasted with prewar patterns. "Something happened to me in the
Army of Occupation," Gotbaum mused. "The war was over, and soon
after we entered a little town in Germany I went to all possible religious services. . . . I had to go to a synagogue and be with other Jews."[31]

Even professional Jewish soldiers recognized how powerfully the revelations of the camps influenced their own behavior. Irving Heymont of the U.S. Third Army was placed in charge of the Landsberg displaced-persons camp in September 1945. In his first speech before the inmates, the twenty-seven-year-old major articulated his identification with the Jews forced to live there. "As I speak to you tonight, I can also be called a sort of DP," he told his audience. "We know what you suffered in the Nazi concentration camps—and not just through newspaper reports. My regiment liberated a concentration camp." Many years later Heymont concluded that "the few months I spent at Landsberg had a greater impact on my outlook on life than any other experience in my careers, including infantry combat in both World War II and the Korean War." Though he was unaware of it at the time, Heymont subsequently reflected that "Landsberg made me a conscious Jew again—not a religious Jew, seeking the ways of the Lord— but an affirmed member of the Jewish people."[32]

Jewish Socialists and Communists filtered the discovery of the death camps through their ideology. Jacobs, who never was sent overseas (perhaps, he speculated, because of his known Trotskyist background), remembered that when the German war crimes trials began, "I was not very much interested in them. My feelings of political ambivalence about the war were still fairly strong, although they had been shaken by the ghastly photos of the concentration-camp victims," he admitted. "But I couldn't help reflecting bitterly how neither the United States nor Britain had done very much to help either the Jews or the political victims of the Nazis until after Hitler marched into Poland." Despite his army service, Howe recalled that "at war's end we didn't know much about the Holocaust. . . . It took a couple of years for a horror of such immensity to sink in." Pondering his delayed reaction, he speculated, "It may be that by then I had become less ideological and more responsive morally." Kligsberg thought that "the greater the estrangement, the stronger was the blow and spiritual shock when they came face-to-face with the Jewish tragedy in Europe."[33]

For those who stayed at home, distance muted the horror of the extermination of European Jewry. Accounts appeared in the press, especially the Jewish papers, surrounded by descriptions of battles and the destruction of war. American Jews responded by contributing generously to the war effort. They purchased millions of dollars of war bonds; the working-class Brooklyn Jewish neighborhood of Brownsville bought fifteen million dollars' worth. Civilian defense volunteers wrote letters to servicemen and ran canteens for soldiers home on furlough. Jews participated in blood drives and scrap metal drives; they collected old clothing and books and magazines. In addition, Jews contributed to specifically Jewish organizations to rescue refugees, support the Yishuv, or save Jewish scholars and their students. They also raised substantial moneys for Russian War Relief; in Philadelphia thousands gave through *landsmanshaftn*, B'nai B'rith lodges, and women's auxiliaries and sisterhoods. Even such insular Jewish communities as the six thousand Syrian Jews in Bensonhurst, Brooklyn, enthusiastically supported the home front.[34]

News of the mass murder of European Jews touched some of the most prominent Jews working in Hollywood and on Broadway. Upon hearing of the Nazi extermination of the Jews, several luminaries pooled their talents in 1943 to create *We Will Never Die*, a memorial to the two million murdered Jews and a militant call for action to FDR. Written by Ben Hecht, directed by Moss Hart, produced by Billy Rose, with music by Kurt Weill, the pageant included a cast of a thousand led by such famous stars as Paul Muni, Edward G. Robinson, John Garfield, Claude Rains, Luther Adler, Burgess Meredith, and Jacob Ben-Ami. Hecht hastily wrote a script using eyewitness accounts of genocide smuggled out of Europe and given to him by the labor-Zionist intellectual Hayim Greenberg. The pageant involved the audience as a congregation in an act of faith.[35]

The pageant called upon its audience to mourn its dead and affirm its future. It presaged the birth of a new American Jewish popular culture willing to turn both history and politics into a mélange of drama, entertainment, and affirmation. As the ticket holders entered Madison Square Garden on March 9, 1943, they faced a stage draped in black with a giant *bima*, suggesting a synagogue interior. Above two forty-foot tablets of the law floated the Star of David, and above that flew the Stars and Stripes. The orchestra played Kol Nidre, the opening prayer of the Yom Kippur service; fifty rabbis and cantors chanted; then Muni and Robinson, the narrators, slowly called out the names of ancestors, linking them with the newly dead. The second episode depicted Jewish soldiers fighting under the flags of eighteen allied nations—all except their own. The militant message could not be mistaken. "We Jews of Europe are being killed as Jews. Give us the right to strike back as Jews." At one of the low points during the war, these Jews demanded: "Let the Star of David be one of the flags that enter Berlin." A long round of applause filled the hall.

The final section eerily anticipated the war's end. At a huge negotiation table sat representatives of the Axis and the Allies, but no Jews, because "they have no land to represent them at the table of judgment," because "there will be no Jews left in Europe for representation when the peace comes. They will have been reduced from a minority to a phantom." The phantoms themselves stood on the table, each telling its tale of atrocity, each pleading, "Remember us." Asking the audience to pray "for the voiceless and Jewish dead of Europe," the narrator closed the pageant with Kaddish, the prayer for the dead.[36]

In the spring of 1945, American Jews watched in shock and disbelief as the sweet fruits of allied victory turned bitter under the staggering revelations of the death camps. The Allies won the war against Hitler too late to rescue most European Jews. Not until General Dwight Eisenhower invited the press corps and politicians and moviemakers to tour Buchenwald did the horror strike home. Shepard Broad found it hard to believe the catastrophe until the Allies "actually physically entered the concentration camps and saw the disaster." Like Broad, Peppercorn knew what had happened, but it didn't really register. "My indignation was there but I never could visualize just how physical and malignant this whole thing had been. . . . And some of the things I'll never forget as long as I live. I guess I can still smell them." Only when they saw photographs and films of living human skeletons in striped uniforms, mountains of dead bodies, bulldozers pushing corpses into mass graves, piles of human hair, baby clothes, and eyeglasses, did American Jews realize, most for the first time, what had happened.[37] Susan Sontag calls it "a negative epiphany." She came across photographs of Bergen-Belsen and Dachau "by chance in a bookstore in Santa Monica in July 1945. Nothing I have seen—in photographs or in real life—ever cut me as sharply, deeply, instantaneously. Indeed," she writes, "it seems plausible to me to divide my life into two parts, before I saw those photographs (I was twelve) and after."[38]

American Jews reeled under their losses, trying to make sense of the disaster. The six million murdered during the six long years of war destroyed a third of the Jewish people and almost two-thirds of the Jews of Europe. "Our tiny people has sacrificed twenty-five times more lives in this war than Great Britain on all her battlefields, on the sea, under the sea, in the air and throughout the years of bombings. This is in absolute figures," wrote an anguished editorialist. Liberation not only came too late for European Jewry, but it also failed to liberate those who survived, the refugees or displaced persons, DPs for short.[39]

Aghast at the ravages of antisemitism, Zionists demanded free Jewish immigration to the Yishuv in Palestine and the establishment there of a Jewish commonwealth. Jews were losing patience with the politics of gestures. The Jews—"and they alone—are told to wait; to stand outside; to watch the remnants of their people ground to death in Europe . . . while the gates of Palestine, *where they would be welcome as nowhere else in the world*, are forcibly shut upon them," yelled the American Zionist Emergency Council. Frustrated at the continued unwillingness of the victorious United Nations to pay attention to the Jewish plight, American Zionists escalated their campaign to win converts to their cause among Americans of good will and among the rank and file of American Jews. "The ghosts of 5,000,000 dead already haunt the forthcoming Conference in San Francisco," that would establish a permanent international world organization. "We ask the world how great must this ghastly company grow before the voice of those still living will be heard?"[40]

If the Allies were reluctant to listen, especially Great Britain, which controlled immigration to Palestine, American Jews were ready to act. Convinced by the war of the virulence of antisemitism and the need to fight it vigorously, they swelled the membership rolls of American Zionist organizations and began to politick in earnest. "I became a Zionist after World War II, thinking that Jews, with their lives in jeopardy, must have a haven somewhere on this planet," the union leader Gus Tyler recalled. Others went further in their conversion to Zionism. Even when in recent years it became fashionable to attack Israel or criticize its shortcomings, many of these Zionists demurred. Talking at a casual gathering of fellow labor leaders with the Israeli consul many years after the establishment of the state,

Gotbaum refused to join in the friendly criticism. "I guess I'm an emotional party-liner in this case," he told his colleagues. "Since I helped to liberate Buchenwald, I feel Zionism as a *faith*. I can never be critical of Israel." In the war's aftermath American Jews transformed faith into politics.[41]

American Jews learned more than the bitter lessons of Jewish political impotence from the war. They acquired new perspectives on themselves and their country through their participation in the armed services of the United States. American wartime propaganda declared the struggle against the Axis to be one between democracy and fascism, between the values of equality and those of racism, between freedom and totalitarianism. Patriotic fervor also enlisted most American religious groups. Shortly after the war in Europe began, the president of the Jewish Theological Seminary incorporated the Conference on Science, Philosophy and Religion and Their Relation to the Democratic Way of Life. The conference included seventy-nine leading American thinkers and religious figures. Seeking "to create a framework for the preservation of democracy and intellectual freedom" in response to the rise of European totalitarianism, the conference proclaimed that American ideals were rooted in biblical tradition and sustained by the biblical religions of Christianity and Judaism.[42]

The concept of a Judeo-Christian tradition of democracy gained widespread currency as the American alternative to fascism. American fascist and antisemitic groups had preempted the term *Christian* in the 1930s. *Judeo-Christian* suggested an antifascist basis for democratic values. The idea "was to invoke a common faith for a united democratic front." The American way did not include prejudice and discrimination. Although the war failed to eradicate antisemitism in the United States, wartime propaganda discredited it.[43]

Even Jews remaining at home identified the American victory as a Jewish one, feeling strengthened by it. The legal scholar Robert Burt remembers how as a youngster he celebrated V-E day in Philadelphia with his maternal grandfather, a "relentlessly secular" Russian Jewish immigrant. When "the unconditional German surrender was announced" in May 1945, he writes, "my grandfather immediately went into his basement and returned arms filled with small American flags, party hats, horns, and other noisemakers and bags of paper confetti.

We dressed for the celebration and went out into the street, where he outfitted other neighborhood children." Burt's account would not be unusual, except that his grandfather later admitted that "on the day the war began . . . he had bought all of these supplies and stored them for the inevitable day when America would win the war. And the relevant triumph for him," Burt recognized, "was not the final end, not when the Japanese surrendered four months later. The victory was in Europe. It was also, as I think he saw it, a victory over Europe."[44] Over a Europe that had persecuted Jews for centuries.

Perhaps the war's mixed messages to American Jews complemented each other. If Jews could be targeted for destruction and could not rely upon the world's democracies for a timely rescue, then they had to rely upon themselves. The logic of the Jewish need for independent political power—a state of their own—pressed upon American Jews. A United Jewish Appeal activist after he left the service, Peppercorn thought that almost everyone was "motivated toward the creation of a Jewish state." He had no doubt that it was "the solution" to the DP camps.[45] The war gave American Jews a new self-confidence. As Americans, Jews could rely upon themselves; they could fight antisemitism and win. The American victory in the war was their victory as much as anyone else's. The dawn of the American century marked the start of their own self-confident era, American Jewry's era.

The war had disrupted American Jewish society, fueling new movements, releasing previously untapped energies, exploding the boundaries of a provincial urban world. Participation in the service interrupted the lives of many young Jews. Some found it impossible to return home to pick up the tangled threads of family, work, and education that had been attenuated during their military years. Their war experience had unsettled them; they had seen too much to resume their mundane lives where they had left them. "One quick furlough home" to Chicago's West Side convinced writer Clancy Sigal "that my beloved old neighborhood was a slummy shtetl, my hangout pals narrow-minded schlumps. Along with practically the entire West Side younger generation which fled either to Chicago's northern suburbs or to California, I took off without a backward glance."[46] Like Sigal, these footloose young men sought greener pastures, a fresh future filled with promise, a chance to try something new freed from familiar constraints. They remembered the other

America they had glimpsed during training, or en route to the Pacific war theater, or perhaps while recovering from a wound. With a brash self-confidence they decided to pioneer thousands of miles away from home. Eager for another adventure, they determined to take a chance, to rely upon themselves.

Nowhere did the possibilities to start afresh, unhampered by the mistakes and burdens of the past, appear as vividly as in the two American dream cities by the ocean. These vacation paradises, with their gentle ocean breezes and brilliant sunshine winter and summer, beckoned American Jews. Miami and Los Angeles, two cities of gold, promised newcomers a present and a future. The present was a glorious taste of heaven on earth. "Miami Beach is an unreal, six-year-old's dream of heaven," the historian Hyman Berman marveled on his first visit.[47] The future lay ahead, filled with whatever one wanted to make of it. Here was the perfect setting for American Jewry's new age.

2
Entering Heaven

Here I was in California where oranges were growing on
trees and the sun was pouring down like melted butter. . . .
I didn't know, I thought I was going to heaven.
                                        —MICHAEL KANIN
                    Oral history memoir, American Jewish Committee

During World War II Eddie Zwern, a second generation Jewish boy
from the Bronx, enlisted in the Army. Zwern was stationed briefly at
Fort Ord, California, before going overseas. Captivated by the California sunshine and lifestyle, Zwern told the Army that his wife,
Pauline, had moved to the state. He figured that his lie would get him
back to California when the war was over since he didn't have money
for a cross-country trip. So eager was he to reach California that he
didn't even call Pauline when he landed at Fort Dix, New Jersey, at
the end of the war. Discharged on the West Coast, Zwern took his
two hundred dollars mustering-out pay and invested in Army surplus
pants at fifty cents a pair. Going from door to door and from garage to
garage in Los Angeles, he quickly sold his supply. Only after accumu-
lating enough money to rent a furnished apartment did Eddie call
Pauline to tell her to come to Los Angeles. The Zwerns were a com-
patible couple: When Pauline arrived she, too, fell in love with the

21

City of Angels, and Eddie gladly went back to the Grand Concourse to close up their apartment on Fordham Road.

Their friends and family thought they were crazy: "Everybody said we'd be back in six months." Instead, gradually all five of Eddie's brothers as well as his sister and Pauline's three brothers and two sisters packed their bags and settled with their families in Los Angeles. "Relatives would come out to visit, next thing you know, they're making plans. You'd come out here in January, and you'd leave snow-filled streets in New York." Looking back, Eddie estimated that he and Pauline were responsible for the migration of over 250 Jews to Los Angeles. When Eddie brought his parents out to visit in 1948, they "didn't want to go home. My father had arthritis," he recalled, "here he is walking around in a T-shirt. That don't happen back East." One auspiciously scheduled winter visit usually was enough to convince any tourist to stay.[1]

Eddie Zwern was a postwar Jewish pioneer, and his story is a modern American frontier tale. His account contains elements critical to understanding the transformation of American Jews after World War II: growing up in a northeastern metropolis, marriage, military service, discovery of the West, the lure of sunny California, the ambition to succeed starting with very little money and no special training, and the reconstitution of family through chain migration. This postwar story harks back to classic tales of Jewish immigration to the United States. Leaving his wife back in the "old home," Zwern arrives alone with two hundred dollars in his pocket, equivalent to the twenty-five dollars sewn into many immigrants' coat linings. He builds himself up, rising from door-to-door sales of army surplus to a secondhand clothing store to a series of pawn shops. And during it all he is investing in real estate. Like his immigrant forbears, his prosperity comes with the prosperity of his city of choice, Los Angeles. Its booming economy and rapidly growing population provide a natural escalator for Zwern's ambition and hard work. Indeed, choosing the right city was an important ingredient in his subsequent economic success. "For New Yorkers," Eddie recalled, "Los Angeles was virgin territory."[2]

Zwern's life story typifies the experience of a significant segment of American Jews who left the old Jewish neighborhoods of the large cities of the Northeast and Midwest and created new urban Jewish centers in the South and West. Thousands of Jews came to Los

Angeles after the war. In the late forties, sixteen thousand new residents poured into Los Angeles each month. Jewish communal estimates suggested that during the peak year of 1946, five hundred Jews arrived each week, or over two thousand a month, making them roughly 13 percent of the incoming residents. Such large numbers unsettled the established Jewish community, a minority of less than 5 percent of the total county population prior to the war.[3] The steady streams of migrants to L.A. allowed it to overtake Chicago by the early 1960s to become the nation's second city.

Jewish enthusiasm for the City of Angels surpassed that of other Americans in the postwar era. Jewish migrants more than doubled the city's Jewish population, from 130,000 before the war to over 300,000 in 1951. Everyone, it seemed, was a newcomer: Only 8 percent of adult Jews in 1950 had been born in the city. By the end of the decade, only one Jewish household head out of six could be considered an old-timer, that is, a prewar resident. From the perspective of 1958, over half of all Jewish household heads had arrived in the thirteen years since the war's end and over half of that number had come during five brief years. Since Jews settled in Los Angeles at a more rapid rate than other Americans, Jews made up an increasing percentage of the local population. Communal estimates ranged widely, but all noted the increase. Some figures indicated a rise from 4 percent to 7 percent of the county population, while others suggested from 9 percent to 18 percent of the residents in many sections of L.A. Seventh among the nation's cities in numbers of Jews prior to the war, Los Angeles ranked second behind New York City within a decade after the war. By the 1960s only New York and Tel Aviv exceeded L.A. as the world's largest Jewish cities.[4]

Getting to Los Angeles wasn't that difficult, despite the thousands of miles separating it from established centers of Jewish settlement. Some came by car. In 1945 a "motorized hegira" of migrants swept the Southland. The *Los Angeles Times* described the new home seekers as former war-plant workers, discharged servicemen, and Easterners. Often newcomers took the train, especially those unlikely to own cars, a category that included many New York Jews. Ben Leftgoff discovered the train's advantages on his trip out. After finishing his stint in the Navy, he and his brother-in-law boarded the train back to the West Coast. "We had a layover in Chicago; we had to wait a day and a half," Leftgoff recalled. "I asked one of the gals who was handling the tickets at the time whether she couldn't possibly get us on a little sooner." His persistence paid off, and when the train pulled out of Chicago, Leftgoff got lucky. "The very next day, I was sitting in what they called a club car at the time. The seats faced the center. And this beautiful young lady came over, and she just sat opposite me. And I nudged my brother-in-law, and I said, 'you know Rich, believe it or not, but that's my wife.'" The "young lady" was traveling to visit relatives in Los Angeles. It was a long train ride but a short courtship. Three weeks later on the Fourth of July, Leftgoff married the woman from Chicago and they settled in L.A.[5]

A few migrants arrived with jobs or the promise of work, but most came on their own initiative, seeking employment. The boomtown, gold-in-the-streets image of Los Angeles in the minds of some Jews recalls the fantasies their parents and grandparents held of America, the *goldene medina*, as they prepared to leave their east European homes. The odyssey of Murray Getz, a second-generation Jew who grew up in Bensonhurst, Brooklyn, echoes the immigrant saga. Getz discovered California through his army service. After receiving his discharge, he "met a guy in New York who was there on a buying trip," Getz recalled. "He was in the costume jewelry business, and I was driving a laundry truck in New York City for the Brighton Laundry." When Getz said he was planning to go to California, the buyer told Getz to call once he arrived. Los Angeles's promise of opportunity attracted Getz. "I thought I could do better for myself than driving a laundry truck," he remarked. So he left New York with his wife for the "clean, nice town" that he remembered. When he got to L.A., he called the buyer and landed a job as a salesman. Getz hoped to earn a modest forty dollars per week selling women's accessories. On his first week out he made four hundred dollars. He was astounded. He found a furnished apartment in Hollywood on Kingsley Drive for twenty-three dollars a month and settled down with his job as a traveling salesman. Soon he was working for himself in his own wholesale accessories business.[6] Getz's L.A. experience, albeit not his substantial financial success, was typical.

The Army introduced Jews not only to California and Los Angeles but also to the American South. Although much of the South was rural and poor and not particularly attractive to urban Jews, many of those serving in the Army Air Forces Technical Training Command discovered Miami Beach when the corps decided to train its officers there. The first five hundred enlisted men arrived on February 21, 1942, and bunked at the Boulevard Hotel. The Army Air Corps leased the Miami Beach Municipal Golf Course for a dollar a year, setting it up as the school's headquarters and drill ground. Gradually the army took over 85 percent of the Miami Beach hotels. Twenty-five percent of the Air Force officer candidates and 20 percent of the enlisted men trained at Miami Beach. The Air Force transformed the vacation paradise. It stationed soldiers in hotel rooms and drilled them in the streets, on golf courses, and in Flamingo Park. Restaurants were converted into mess halls. A blackout darkened the city every night. "With night clubs closed and 'lights off' on the shoreline, with gasoline rationed and the races prohibited, Miami just did not attract the regular northern" vacationers, one wartime visitor observed. Nevertheless, the promise of life on the Beach captivated many soldiers who vowed to return. Family and sweethearts coming to visit their men in uniform also found the Beach appealing and thought of moving down.[7]

When the war ended and the Army gave the hotels back to their prewar owners, Miami Beach began to boom. One old-timer looked at the changes and quipped that the three A's built Miami: the army, airplanes, and air conditioning. Although far smaller than Los Angeles in 1940, Miami experienced an enormous influx of temporary residents during the war. Many "got sand in their shoes," that is, they decided to stay. Not only did former GIs and their families return to the paradise they remembered, but other northerners also sought out Miami's sunshine and clean air. The population of the city of Miami, 172,000 in 1940, increased to 249,000 by 1950. In the following decade it moved into the ranks of large cities, attaining a population of 325,000 by 1964. Miami Beach, a separately incorporated city, enjoyed an impressive growth rate of 65 percent. The number of permanent residents reached 46,000 in 1950, up from 28,000 before the war.[8]

Estimated at only eight thousand prior to the war, Miami's Jewish population mushroomed. The number of Jews doubled in five years to sixteen thousand. Then the rate of growth really soared. In the first five years after the war, the Jewish population increased over 300 percent to fifty-five thousand by 1950, far outstripping the solid 57 percent growth in the general Miami population. An average of 650 Jews arrived each month, and they came at the same rate for another five years. Within the brief span of the postwar decade, the migrants transformed Miami from a small provincial concentration of sixteen thousand Jews into a major urban Jewish center of 100,000 residents.

Although the phenomenal Jewish growth rate slowed after 1955, it continued to exceed the general influx. A small fraction of Miami's residents at the end of the war, Jews made up 15 percent by 1960. Then roughly 140,000 Jews lived in Miami, putting it in sixth place just behind Boston among the top American cities in Jewish population. Even more than Los Angeles, Miami was a city of newcomers. A mere 4 percent of the Jewish population had been born in the city. Virtually everyone had come from someplace else.[9]

Jewish migrants to Miami and Los Angeles not only came at a faster rate but they left homes different from their white counterparts'. Most non-Jewish white migrants came to Los Angeles from states west of the Mississippi River, earning L.A. the nickname "the capital of Kansas."[10] Mexicans, African Americans, and Japanese were the important visible minorities in Los Angeles, and like Jews, each group constituted a small fraction of the total population. The 1950 census reported 311,000 Hispanics (7 percent), 219,000 African Americans (5 percent), and 38,000 Japanese (less than 1 percent) in the Los Angeles metropolitan area. The majority population was white, Protestant, and native-born; in fact, 85 percent of the adults were native-born. Of the foreign-born whites, the largest numbers came from Mexico and Canada.[11]

Miami attracted many southern whites, largely from rural areas, and some Catholics. Not until 1958, however, were there enough Catholics to warrant establishing a Miami diocese, which included the sixteen southern Florida counties. At that time approximately 185,000 Catholics lived in the new diocese, "a missionary situation," according to one historian. Although the numbers of African Americans also increased, they remained 14 percent of the population, a relatively small minority for a southern city.[12]

Jewish migration represented a city-to-city movement rather than a shift from country (or small town) to city. Most of the Jewish newcomers left cities east of the Mississippi and brought to their new homes considerable social skills acquired from living in large metro-politan centers. Only a tiny fraction of Jews lived in rural areas in the mid-1950s, a pattern quite unlike the general U.S. population. A mere 3.5 percent of the American population, Jews made up 8 percent of the nation's urban residents. In fact, Jews lived almost exclusively in America's big cities. Migration did not change these patterns; most Jewish migrants settled in only a handful of southern and western cities.[13]

Jews moving to Los Angeles and Miami were participating in the postwar population shift to the South and West. The passion for moving gripped so many millions that observers feared Americans were becoming "a nation of strangers." But Jews were also following and developing their own migration networks. Not surprisingly, their mobility reproduced a pattern of concentrated dispersion. By 1960, as in the prewar period, 75 percent of American Jews lived in only five states. Jews remained significantly segregated from the general American population despite the impact of World War II and more than a decade of substantial internal mass migration. Alone among American religious groups, Jews maintained "one of the most distinctive" patterns of population distribution. Only 16 percent of all counties in the United States had more than one hundred Jewish residents.[14] However, given the urban choices, especially the rapid growth of such southwestern cities as Houston and such southern cities as Atlanta, the popularity of Miami and Los Angeles among Jews suggests the particular lure of a leisure lifestyle. Eighty percent of all Jews moving south after the war settled in Miami, and 70 percent of all Jews heading west landed in Los Angeles.[15]

The American ideal of living the good life—a vision of ease glamorized by Hollywood—attracted Jews to Miami and L.A. Jews loved the casualness and lack of formality of these resort cities. The possibility of living out of doors appealed to them. "Palm trees, the weather, the lifestyle," Leftgoff summed it up. "I thought it was casual, it was the type of lifestyle I've always dreamed I'd like to live in." The balmy weather, blue skies, and bright sunshine spelled a life of ease, more often associated with vacations than with the mundane reality of work. "I'd always wanted to go to California because I hated getting out of the subway in the wintertime," Mark Itelson confessed. The premium Jews placed on mobility, their desire to change the view from the kitchen window and thereby to change themselves, spurred them to pursue their American dream of paradise. "All ethnic and religious groups," noted the sociologist Erich Rosenthal, have "the moving spirit." However, he continued, "there is some indication that the Jews have a higher amount of this 'moving spirit.'" Jews saw in Miami and Los Angeles the chance to combine vacationing and daily living into a year-round package—a compelling vision. Nathan Perlmutter found it hard to resist. Initially reluctant to leave New York and his job with the Anti-Defamation League's main office, Perlmutter visited Miami "and of course I fell in love with it. I fell in love," he explained, "not with substantive issues, but with palm trees and with blue and green waters, with the climate, and with the Spanish style architecture in Coral Gables and Miami Beach."[16]

"The palm trees especially made a great impression on me," the Yiddish writer Isaac Bashevis Singer confessed. When he first arrived in Miami Beach in the winter of 1948, he stood on the balcony of his hotel room and stared at the palm trees for hours. Then he wrote articles about Miami Beach for the *Jewish Daily Forward*. "I had discovered the palm tree. I told them my impressions about the palm trees, how they are like trees and not like trees, how different they are. They created a mood in me, and maybe in other people, too," he speculated. More than anything, palm trees symbolized the American paradise. They grew only in that "strange land" beyond the gritty northeastern and midwestern cities. To live beneath one summoned up images of contentment inaccessible to those who stayed behind in New York or Chicago, Philadelphia or Boston. "In New York, I never saw a tree!" Getz exclaimed, describing his initial reaction to Los Angeles that enticed him to move. Trees grow in Brooklyn, of course, but not palm trees. Miami and Los Angeles tempted Jews with a vision of heaven on earth.[17]

The prospect of leisurely living that Jews found so alluring depended upon the urban economies of Miami and Los Angeles as well as their fabled setting. Both cities were boomtowns, and their urban metabolism a boom metabolism. After each boom the old Los Angeles "looked hopelessly ancient." In fact, each new economic spurt remade the city so that it was as if it were born anew. But none compared with the postwar one. "Prewar Los Angeles was a matter of ancient history; wartime Los Angeles was rapidly disappearing and a new city was rising," wrote one observer. In 1940 Los Angeles was the nation's leading agricultural county and eighth in industrial production, a collection of villages with citrus groves within sight of most homes. But postwar growth shattered this momentary equilibrium.[18]

The Federal government's hand could be seen in the wartime prosperity of Miami and Los Angeles, especially in the growth of their new economies. Plentiful jobs in booming industries attracted many Americans seeking work. The historian Gerald Nash describes what occurred in the West during the war years as "a metamorphosis." Ten percent of all federal moneys spent during World War II went to California, though it was only one of forty-eight states. These sums capitalized entire industries, including rubber, aluminum, and aircraft. Buoyed by $40 billion in Federal investments, Californians exuded "an unbounded optimism about their future based on the expectation of unlimited possibilities." Federal money also brought the technology that provided the basis for a postindustrial economy and the military installations that helped develop a service economy. Nash concluded that "by 1945 the war had transformed the West and made it the pace-setting region of the nation."[19]

Like Los Angeles, Dade County, "aptly called the Land of the Tomato Kings," led Florida in agricultural production in 1940. Unlike Los Angeles, building construction was Miami's leading industry, followed by dairying. Most of Miami's work force found employment in retailing that catered to the tourist trade. A small Southern city and pleasant vacation resort, Miami's transformation after the war was just as startling as L.A.'s. "Miami can best be described," wrote one new resident in 1955, "as a semi-dignified boom town. Since the close of World War II it has been the mecca for the rich and those who would be rich. It is simultaneously a health resort for cardiacs, asthmatics and arthritics and a haven for the confidence man, swindler and gambler." From a wartime port and training center, Miami became the convention capital of America, the gateway to Latin America, a major airplane hub, a modern city of a million inhabitants. Miami's growth drastically altered the character of Dade County. Dade became the state's leading manufacturing, commercial, and financial county as well as its most populous one.[20]

Florida and Miami also benefited from Federal investments, especially in aircraft and aluminum, and in military installations, although the dollar amounts never reached such large sums as in California. The federal government used military training centers and contracts for shipyards and aircraft plants to boost the South's economy. The Army built forty airfields throughout Florida during the war, and the Army and Navy operated a total of nine major airfields in Miami alone. The armed forces contributed significantly to Miami's record statistics that showed the city leading all world ports in international air travel from 1940 to 1946. Eventually the Federal government spent four billion dollars on military facilities in the South, or over one-third the national total. A comparable sum went to defense contracts awarded to public and private installations in the region.[21]

In transforming the economies of Miami and Los Angeles, the Federal government helped attract Jews to these cities because Jews sensed the heady optimism and openness of a boomtown. Both cities promised a life of leisure that blurred distinctions between work and play. Yet the City of Angels tempted Jews with a different vision of opportunity than did Miami. They saw an open city and a chance to make themselves over in their own image. Like their immigrant parents, Jews migrating to Los Angeles sought personal success and risked losing the nurturing ties of family and friends in the hope of finding prosperity. Their daring set them apart from their peers. The Jewish journey to Los Angeles took an unexpected turn: It became a postindustrial migration, primarily of young individuals. By contrast, those who set off for Miami remained within familiar categories of mobility. Jews heading south did not turn their backs upon past associations but attempted to extend them to embrace the pleasures of sun, sea, and sand. As I. B. Singer recognized, "Miami Beach was a continuation of the little town." Gradually two different types of migration streams flowed to L.A. and Miami.[22]

A promise of easy affluence complemented the vacation aura, setting Los Angeles apart from eastern and midwestern metropolises. Paul Sperry's parents had "talked for twenty years of moving to California," the singer recalled. "I think that my father sensed that the L.A. business was a wide open thing." In fact, there were whole industries in Los Angeles—petroleum refining, insurance, finance, and mining, for example—that were largely closed to Jews or in which Jews had little hope of rising beyond entry-level work. But most Jews saw opportunity in Los Angeles, not discrimination.[23]

Opportunity accompanied by ambition often proved more compelling than an actual job. Many migrants took up new lines of work, switching their occupation as they changed their home. Ben Perry, an engineer, worked for five years as an office manager after leaving the Bronx for Los Angeles in 1952. A year later Brooklyn-born Isidore Rosenthal arrived from Pennsylvania with a degree in economics. Rosenthal took what turned out to be a fourteen-year job as a furniture salesman at the May company, a large Jewish-owned department store. When Lenny Gottlieb left Manhattan's Washington Heights for Los Angeles after his war service, he answered an ad in the classified section of the newspaper and met his future business partner, a German Jewish refugee. "We got along great together," Gottlieb remarked. He stayed in the sportswear manufacturing business.[24]

Unlike relocations sponsored by large American companies, Jewish moves usually were self-motivated and unrelated to specific work requirements. Not until large, stable Jewish communities were established did substantial numbers of Jewish professionals follow the first ambitious migrants. Peter Antelyes recalled that when his dentist father arrived in Los Angeles in the late 1950s, an existing Jewish community afforded him a foothold in this new territory. Although the family was still living in temporary housing, his father knew he had to get started. So he walked into Cohen's jewelry store and introduced himself: "You're a Jew, I'm a Jew," he said, "send me people who need to have their teeth fixed." To both jeweler and dentist this seemed like a reasonable proposition.[25]

Initially many Jews came not as pioneers but as tourists. With money in their pockets from postwar prosperity, they sought a congenial vacation spot, not a new home. Tourist advertisements enticed Northerners and encouraged them to explore an exotic world. "Yes, Miami is orange juice, coconuts, stuffed alligators, flamingoes, palms and mangoes. It's everyone's dream come true—and it's yours for the taking!" exclaimed one ad in the *New York Times*. Southern California and Miami together accounted for over $700 million in tourist trade in 1949.[26] Many future settlers first tasted the pleasures and possibilities of Miami and Los Angeles on winter visits. Some became regular "snowbirds," living for three to six months under the Florida or California sun and then returning to the North and East for the remainder of the year. Others became "snowflakes" because they made several short trips each winter season. But many, especially parents with children, ultimately decided to stay. The striking contrast with the cold, snowy cities of the Northeast and Midwest, the relaxed and casual style of living outdoors, encouraged them to imagine they might live as if on an endless vacation were they to settle in Miami or Los Angeles. One contemporary observer thought that "the gap between work and play in Los Angeles must be narrower than in any other great city."[27]

"Florida is a figment of the imagination, with all of the qualities, beguiling and bizarre, of the best escape fiction," a reporter on the vacation scene concluded. Or as a woman visitor put it, "No other country has a Florida!" Upon closer inspection, this dream world possessed the easy familiarity of home. Working as a community relations professional for the Anti-Defamation League, Nathan Perlmutter preferred his vacations in places that were truly different, where he was in fact an outsider, but he thought Miami Beach "a wonderful place to live. With relatively low income, you can live luxuriously. There is a combination of urban convenience and suburban ease within twenty minutes of work. One is part of the community with a sense of community pride, a feeling of 'this is my town.' "[28]

Jewish hotel owners in Miami Beach actively courted Jewish customers with their cuisine. "Besides basking in the sun (the tourist rarely enters the nicely tempered water) the favorite sport of the Miami vacationist is eating," observed one columnist. "During the day, planes with long streamers flew over the beach advertising dinners with seven courses for $1.50 on Washington Avenue." Established Catskill resort owners began purchasing and building hotels on the Beach, seeing the opportunity to sell Miami Beach as a winter Catskills. Knowing what would appeal to Jews, one of the many ads placed in Jewish newspapers in the Northeast featured cheesecake flown in from New York. In 1945 Grossinger's bought the previously restricted Pancoast hotel. Paul Grossinger ended his predecessors' antisemitic policies with a vengeance. The renamed Grossinger Pancoast boasted a kosher kitchen and even advertised for the Passover holidays. Others soon followed. In 1951 the Levinsons of Tamarack Lodge in the Catskills built the luxury 258-room Algiers hotel on Collins Avenue and 26th Street. Jews dubbed Miami "the southern borscht belt" and joked that it had become a suburb of New York City.[29]

The hotel owners both catered to the tastes of their borscht belt customers and cultivated an ostentatious style of vacationing. The big Beach hotels not only sold luxuries to guests who were new to leisure, but they also showed their customers how to enjoy rich men's games. Many hotels employed social directors who approached their jobs with the enthusiasm of schoolteachers of leisure. One contemporary guidebook assured its readers that Miami Beach "crowds within its narrow limits the sophistication of a metropolitan city of a million. Flash and excitement hold the spotlight, and when things are in full swing the island city more closely resembles a spangled revue than a wealthy resort." Some scoffed at the nightly parade of mink coats despite the temperate weather, and others were equally appalled at both jewel-bedecked matrons lounging on the sand and the working-class male beach attire of choice: "long underwear and pants rolled up to the knee, the whole surmounted by a derby." But astute observers recognized that "Miami Beach is one of the many realizations of the American Dream. Like strawberries in January and wall-to-wall carpeting, it may not be the noblest of all possible rainbows' ends to which Americans aspire, but it appeals to the people."[30]

The sparkling success of the Miami Beach hotels attracted Jewish investors from New York and Chicago, both legitimate and illegitimate. In 1946 six new hotels went up on Miami Beach; the largest of them, the Martinique, had 137 rooms. The following year saw the construction of the first million-dollar hotel, the Sherry Frontenac, with 250 rooms, one of seven new hotels on the Beach. By 1948 the boom was in full swing. Gangsters from New York and Chicago, Detroit and Cleveland, got involved in building the Gold Coast, with greater Miami at its epicenter. Fortunes were to be made in these frontier towns. Under the tutelage of Meyer Lansky, one of the top figures in organized crime and the reputed brains behind the Mafia (which controlled such lucrative "rug joints" for gambling as the Colonial Inn and Club La Boheme), Miami's Gold Coast emerged as the provincial gangster capital of the United States. Kid Cann (Isadore Blumenfeld) became a snowbird together with his brothers and in-laws. They flocked to Miami from Minneapolis, buying homes and settling close to their flourishing gambling investments. The gamblers Louis Rothkopf and Sam Tucker of the Cleveland gang joined them, as did Nig Rosen from Philadelphia and Joe Linsey and

Hyman Abrams from Boston. "At noon, on the corner of Collins Avenue and Twenty-third Street, you could see half the underworld strolling about in flashy sports clothes and big black sunglasses, taking the air and exchanging the latest gossip." Jews seeking solid investments for their profits from illegal operations also set their sights on Miami. George Sax, the Windy City's "punchboard king," came down to build the Saxony, the most elegant of the seventeen Beach hotels erected in 1948, and acquired a reputation in Miami as a "Chicago banker."[31]

Each year brought a new rash of luxury hotels until Ben Novack reached a symbolic summit with his Fontainebleau Hotel. Born in the Bronx, Novack grew up in the resort business; his father owned Laurel-in-the-Pines, a Catskills hotel. Ben came to Miami Beach in 1940 and got started by leasing a small hotel. By 1949 he and his partner, Harry Mufson, were building a hotel of their own, the Sans Souci. Novack purchased the site of the Fontainebleau, the former fourteen-acre beachfront estate of Harvey Firestone, for $2.3 million to build what he called "the world's most pretentious hotel." Designed by Brooklyn-born Morris Lapidus, a showman who considered architecture a "broad form of merchandising," the fourteen-floor curved hotel took only eleven months to construct. When it opened in 1954, the Fontainebleau fulfilled Novack's expectations. It became "the most colossal, the most opulent, gaudy, outrageous and controversial of a generation of colossal, opulent, gaudy, outrageous and controversial Miami Beach resort hotels once collectively termed 'the nation's grossest national product' and designed, it was said, 'to convince a sucker spending $50 that he's actually spending $100.'" The main lobby offered a monumental showcase; its black and white marble columns echoed black-and-white-checked marble floors. French provincial antiques lined the corridors, and live tropical plants adorned the lobby. Outside, an immense pool abutted four acres of formal French gardens. At the dock there was room to moor fifty yachts. The huge ballroom held five thousand; three thousand could be accommodated for formal dinners. The Fontainebleau linked Hollywood and Miami Beach. Its lavish floor shows featured famous movie stars. Hollywood producers reciprocated by filming movies that used the hotel as a set. Amidst the palms and spectacles, few took notice of the hotel's *mikveh*, the ritual bath installed in 1958.[32]

These ostentatious and luxurious Miami Beach hotels—built, promoted, and managed by Jewish entrepreneurs—became a national
icon of American popular culture in the 1950s. Postcards featured
their extravagant elegance; movies like *A Hole in the Head* (the title
taken from a Yiddish expression) pictured the pleasures and gaiety of
vacations on the Beach. As more and more Jews vacationed in the
city that stamped its outgoing mail "The Closest Thing to Paradise
We Know," Americans increasingly associated the vulgarity and flam-
boyance of Miami Beach with an image of Jewish nouveau riche. The
Anti-Defamation League, concerned that Jewish behavior in public
places might provoke antisemitism, commissioned a short film in the
1940s to guide vacationers. Among the items criticized were
schmoozing on street corners (the movie recommended that conversations be held on the hotel porch), playing cards on hotel porches
(the movie preferred the game room), elbowing one's way to the front
rail in popular cafeterias (waiting in line was suggested), and engaging in loud arguments in hotel corridors (couples were urged to fight
in the privacy of their rooms behind closed doors). Most vacationers
ignored such strictures and relaxed without worrying about their image. As a result, Miami Beach became a synonym for popular indul-
gence in the American dream of luxury.[33]

Although many migrants to Miami and Los Angeles pursued occupations similar to Jews who stayed in the Northeast or Midwest, newcomers were most often attracted by each city's highly publicized and
glittery tourist and motion picture business. They interpreted a Jewish presence in these glamorous industries as indicative of America's
openness to Jewish entrepreneurship. Once settled down, in fact,
they gravitated to such typical Jewish occupations as retailing, real estate and construction, and the garment trades. Yet the glamour and
possibilities of the movies and hotels helped to lure Jews to Los Angeles and Miami. Of the two, the substantial wealth associated with motion pictures proved far more enticing than the hotels' glitter and
accounts in this period for the greater growth of L.A. than Miami.

The postwar Jewish migration gradually assumed a regional con-
figuration. Midwestern Jews more often migrated to Los Angeles
than did their northeastern relatives. In 1950 38 percent of the city's
Jewish newcomers hailed from homes in the Midwest compared to
32 percent from the Northeast. New York City, which held close to

half the American Jewish population in the 1940s, provided only one of every four migrants to Los Angeles. Yet Chicago, with less than 10 percent of the nation's Jews, sent one of every six of the newcomers. Nearly half of all the Midwesterners came from the Windy City. Miami drew a much more representative sample of Jews. Approximately 43 percent came from New York City and 13 percent from the Midwest, roughly corresponding to the Jewish national distribution. Unlike Los Angeles, Miami also attracted a sizable minority from the Southeast; approximately 10 percent of its new residents were southern Jews. These newcomers found Miami attractive because of its increasing prominence as the South's preeminent metropolis and gateway to Latin America.[34]

Whereas ethnic networks guided Jews to new homes in Miami and Los Angeles, the 1944 G.I. bill with its low-cost mortgages and generous college grants encouraged and enabled them to uproot themselves. Federal postwar benefits loosened the ties that bound individuals to networks of kin and friends and held them to familiar moorings.[35] No longer needing to rely upon relatives and neighbors to find work, to finance an education, or even to buy a house, Jews and other Americans were free to pursue their dreams of the good life without traditional supports. Determined to make their own way in new, even exotic territory two and three thousand miles from home, they cut loose.

Even when they reached L.A., Jews struck out on their own in choosing where to settle down. Relatives may have shared a common attraction to the city but not necessarily the same values, income, or desire to live near each other. Residential segregation by wealth in Los Angeles and the continuing upward climb of real estate values magnified the importance of time of arrival and income differences among relatives. Unlike earlier immigrants to northeastern cities who lived close together, families in L.A. were often forced to find homes in disparate sections of the city. Mike Singer came fifteen years after his sister, who had served as a WAC during World War II. Drawn to Los Angeles by her presence, he ended up buying a house at a distance from her. By contrast, David Moretzky initially bought a house in Porter Ranch near his sister, who had preceded him to Los Angeles. After eight years of living close to her in what he considered "a terrible area," Moretzky moved to Encino. When Alex Bratman left

Brooklyn to join his brother-in-law in business in L.A.—going from "smoked fish to smoked tires"—he bought a house in Van Nuys, ten miles away from his sister, who lived in Tarzana, a more affluent section of the San Fernando Valley. Arriving later, Bratman just couldn't afford to live near her.[36]

Because friendship often guided residential choices, it led to cluster patterns based upon city of previous residence. This was reminiscent of immigrant behavior. Surveys of Los Angeles after twenty years of continuing in-migration disclosed significant clusters of Jews from Cleveland, St. Louis, and Detroit concentrated in the northern and western San Fernando Valley. The wealth of former Chicago Jews registered in their visible presence in expensive sections of Beverly Hills, Brentwood, Westwood, and Pacific Palisades. Less affluent Chicago Jews lived in the more densely populated Wilshire-Fairfax and Beverly-Fairfax areas of western Los Angeles. Former New Yorkers, however, scattered throughout the city, exerting an influence in all sections of Los Angeles.[37]

For some Jews the leisure world of Miami and Los Angeles appealed to them less than the opportunity for a new start, a clean slate. They sought in migration a cure for their ills. Leah Naftali, a native New Yorker, fled the city and a "very unhappy marriage" by settling in Los Angeles with her daughter. Others came seeking the healthy climate, especially the clean air and strong sunshine. Both allergists and heart doctors often recommended to their patients a move to the salubrious Miami climate. Prevailing winds gave Miami an average temperature of sixty-eight degrees in the winter and eighty-two in the summer. Extreme heat or cold was as rare as a sunless day—and there was an average of only six of those per year. A young girl, Harriet Sadoff Kasow, moved to Miami with her family in 1945 when her sister contracted rheumatic fever. Her immigrant father, an ardent unionist, left his job as a designer and pattern maker in New York's garment industry and opened a small nonunion sportswear factory in Miami so that his daughter could benefit from the mild climate.[38]

Occasionally, poor health provided merely a final push to set migrants moving. Marty Rosenbaum arrived in Los Angeles as a child in 1943 when his mother, given a choice by the doctor, picked L.A. over Miami. "My mother was always family oriented and listened to everything my grandfather said," he explained. "He told my mother that he had heard good things about California. My mother, following her father's instructions, decided to travel to California." She was an avid fan of westerns as well, and that gave L.A. a special allure. Ben Perry spent time recuperating from a war injury at Fort Ord. Though he had always imagined that New York City was the only place to live, the injury and experience in California changed his thinking. He returned to Los Angeles in 1952. His wife, Florence, feared to leave the Bronx and her immediate family and friends but soon fell in love with California. Sy Bram, who was stationed down south during the war, joined his parents in Los Angeles in 1948. They left Jersey City for his father's health and settled in Santa Monica.[39]

Like many who had not initially intended to move, Bram was less than enthusiastic about the City of Angels when he first arrived. The distances disturbed him; he disliked the style of living, and he felt very isolated without a car. Bram saw Los Angeles as an extended village without a downtown, filled with ennui and alienation. Although he attended UCLA on the GI bill, he had difficulty making friends until he rejoined a Jewish fraternity, where he found again the camaraderie he had known in the East. Leonard Sperry moved to Los Angeles in middle age after raising most of his children in Chicago. He joined his older brother, an electromechanical engineer, who arrived during the war. Sperry decided to leave Chicago because of his own poor health. However his younger son, Paul, was not thrilled with the move. He disliked being uprooted and never enjoyed being dependent on automobiles and having to travel long distances all over the city—from Anaheim to Santa Monica—just to hear a community concert.[40]

Yet the old neighborhoods of the Northeast were changing and spurring many Jews to look elsewhere for a community of their own. Coming primarily from America's great metropolises, Jews witnessed the postwar social and demographic urban upheavals at close hand. The introduction of regular airplane flights from San Juan to New York City at the end of the war inaugurated a mass migration of Puerto Ricans that rivaled "the great population movements of the first two decades of the century." Thirteen thousand Puerto Ricans came in 1945, and almost forty thousand the following year. By 1950 the census showed over a quarter of a million Puerto Ricans and their children in New York City. But migration peaked in 1952 when 58,000 arrived. Puerto Ricans settled not just in Spanish Harlem but on the West Side, in Washington Heights, Chelsea, and the Lower East Side. In Brooklyn they moved near the downtown and Bedford-Stuyvesant sections; in the Bronx they found apartments in the Jewish neighborhood of Morrisania. "There was scarcely an area in the older boroughs in which Puerto Ricans were not to be found. Thus because of the housing shortage and slum clearance they rubbed shoulders with everybody in the city," noted the social scientists Nathan Glazer and Daniel Patrick Moynihan.[41]

In other cities, like Philadelphia, the movement of many Jews into suburban housing provided the pull, while the steady migration of blacks into old, established Jewish neighborhoods encouraged the remaining Jews to leave. In Cleveland, as African Americans moved into the Jewish neighborhood of East 105th Street, some Jews moved out to the suburbs on the heights while others moved south and west. In Chicago Jews abandoned Lawndale so quickly that it became an exclusively black section less than a decade after the war. Gottlieb insisted that of "my generation, 80 percent moved." As his parents had left the Lower East Side for Harlem and then abandoned Harlem for Washington Heights, so did Gottlieb's friends leave the Heights for New Jersey or Long Island, Los Angeles or Miami.[42]

The mobility of young people whose lives had been disrupted by the war and who were looking for fresh starts was complemented by their parents' similar need to move on. With social security benefits available, many faced the choice of retirement while they still had their health. Jewish tradition did not encourage elderly parents to depend upon children; many immigrants intended to rely upon themselves as they aged. "In Jewish we have a saying, 'When the father gives to the son, both are happy. When the son gives to the father, both weep.'" Under pressure from the changing demography of the large northeastern and midwestern cities, parents followed their children to Los Angeles or Miami when "they could no longer handle the winters in Brighton Beach." Others, given a choice between moving to Long Island to be near their children or to Miami Beach to be near their friends, chose Miami Beach. A survey noted: "These people came to Miami Beach with the expectation of completing their lives in a community of their peers where there would not be only the warmth of a semi-tropical climate, but better living conditions compared to that which they had in the northern and mid-western cities."

A few expressed "a feeling of alienation from the Americanized younger generation." Many realized that they were pioneers of a new frontier: the frontier of old age.[43]

Others chose early retirement while still in their fifties, moved, but then went to work again in Miami or L.A. David Moretzky sold his electrical factory in New York, after he could no longer endure the onerous daily commute from Long Island, and retired to Los Angeles where his parents and sister were living. But after settling down in 1964 with three teenage children, he gave up his retirement and went back to work in electrical supplies. So eager was Fred Burg to retire from his dry goods store in Cicero, Illinois, that he left for L.A., where his sister lived, right in the middle of the Christmas season. At age forty-seven, however, Burg had too much energy and ambition for retirement; within six months he returned to his real passion, making tools. He then started his own tool-making business, which rapidly proved to be a very successful enterprise that included his son and son-in-law as well. Seymour Hacken came to Los Angeles from Savannah after he sold his chain of pharmacies, Drug King, to Thrifty. The contract had a noncompete clause, and California was the only state exempt from it, so Hacken landed in Los Angeles. Before long, he was back in business.[44]

Federal policies encouraged mobility of the old as well as the young. The New Deal had transformed the realities of old age in America. The portability of social security benefits and union pensions facilitated migration in retirement as the GI bill helped young men leave home. Both Los Angeles and Miami initially attracted a comparable proportion of retirees. However, by the 1950s Miami was drawing an ever larger number, many of whom settled in south Miami Beach. By 1959 the median age of Jews in Miami had risen to forty-six from thirty-three while it had dropped to thirty-three from thirty-seven in Los Angeles.[45] In Miami Beach the median age skyrocketed, from forty-three in 1950 to fifty-four by the end of the decade. The mass migration of elderly Jews transplanted an entire way of life from the streets of New York City to those of Miami Beach. This change became visible particularly in the 1960s as word spread about the attractions of retiring in Miami, from warm breezes to cheaper prices, and the numbers of retirees soared. In 1960 those sixty-five years of age and older were 28 percent of the population of

Miami Beach; only five years later the same age cohort made up 38 percent of the total Beach population. Since newcomers continued to settle in Miami Beach and its residential population increased by over twelve thousand during those five years, the rapidly changing percentage of elderly confirms an extraordinary migration pattern.[46]

What began for many as a vacation lengthened into a permanent stay. The gradual transformation of older hotels into retirement residences eased the transition for some from the status of vacationers to that of residents. Jewish entrepreneurs were quick to enter this new field. Among the first was Michael Sossin. He purchased the once elegant Blackstone Hotel on Washington Avenue in Miami Beach and converted it into a retirement residence, offering weekly, monthly, seasonal, or yearly rates. Sossin recognized the reluctance of elderly Jews to enter institutional care and the profitable possibilities of modifying hotel living into a social form without the negative institutional associations of old-age homes. Like other hotel owners, he promoted his product. Sossin recruited customers through Jewish labor unions and fraternal associations. The initial success of the first retirement hotels spurred the conversion of many older, less profitable hotels in south Miami Beach and accelerated the migration of elderly Jews to Miami. Jewish black humor dubbed the Beach "God's waiting room."[47]

Distinctive migration streams of elderly Jews also emerged within Los Angeles. Retired couples and widows created these patterns by seeking residences in areas that did not appeal to young newcomers. During the 1950s the southeastern part of Hollywood between Western and Hoover Avenues south of Santa Monica attracted a substantial number of older Jews, many of them widows. Their presence doubled the proportion of Jews in the area from 12 percent to 25 percent and gave it some of the characteristics of a new Boyle Heights—L.A.'s immigrant Jewish neighborhood. Other elderly Jews migrated to Venice, attracted by the ocean and boardwalk. During the war social workers steered retired Jews on modest incomes to the Ocean Park section of Venice, recommending its mild weather, low rents, and high vacancy rate. When the amusement piers were torn down in 1945 and the games of chance closed, Venice became a haven for elderly Jewish immigrants. They were drawn by the cheap rents averaging less than twenty-five dollars per month for seasonal cottages built prior to

World War I and for apartments in multifamily buildings constructed before World War II.[48]

"Seeking a benign climate, fellow Jews, and moderately priced housing," writes the anthropologist Barbara Myerhoff, Jews from all over the country "brought their savings and small pensions and came to live near the ocean. Collective life was and still is especially intense in this community because there is no automobile traffic on the boardwalk," she observed. As in Miami Beach, Venice offered "a place where people may meet, gather, talk, and stroll, simple but basic and precious activities that the elderly in particular can enjoy here all year round." By 1950 Ocean Park emerged with a new identity as a Jewish area with a handful of synagogues and kosher bakeries and butcher shops. A survey that year revealed that over a quarter of the population had moved into their homes only within the last twelve months. By the end of the decade, the area had acquired the derisive nickname "Oshini Beach," from the antisemitic slur "sheeney."[49]

Most newcomers moved into new sections of the city as they were being built. In Los Angeles acres of farmland were laid out in lots and paved to make room for seemingly endless subdivisions. The agricultural San Fernando Valley, north of the Hollywood hills and separated by mountains from the rest of Los Angeles, particularly attracted Jews. Sparsely populated in 1944, the valley contained over a million residents after a decade and a half of frenzied construction of private homes. Developers turned over nine hundred square miles of agricultural land into single-family homes as Los Angeles built almost five hundred miles of freeways to connect its far-flung residents. Not only did fields of lima beans and citrus groves succumb to the developers, but even the studio backlot of Twentieth Century Fox in west Los Angeles was sold off to promoters of Century City. The steady upward spiral in real estate values amazed the city's hardiest boosters. Responding to an unending flow of newcomers, developers created a source of wealth that could compete successfully with the profits of the motion picture industry.[50]

As Jewish newcomers looked for homes in the San Fernando Valley, Jewish builders invested in extensive tract housing there. So many people purchased houses on extended terms that San Fernando was dubbed The Valley of the Shadow of Debt. Ellie and Bud Hudson, a young Jewish couple from New York, decided to buy a fourteen thousand dollar house in 1949 in Van Nuys because a friend told them "the air was sparkling." Wild flowers still bloomed in the Valley, though not for long. Given a choice between two neighboring subdivisions, they bought the cheaper house built by Leonard Chudacoff, an active leader in the Jewish community and head of the Federation of Jewish Welfare Organizations in 1946. Although neither Bud nor Ellie thought about Jewish matters when purchasing their home, they decided to buy from a Jewish builder. Chudacoff's Coronet Construction Company advertised its Economy Home in the local Jewish weekly. Veterans had to pay only a $350 down payment toward the $11,350 total cost. The 1,270-square-foot house boasted three bedrooms. "We do not give away refrigerators or kitchen ranges. We do give the most home for the money," the ad promised.[51]

Jewish builders were in fact replacing Jewish film magnates as the entrepreneurs par excellence in the postwar era. In 1944 builders like Chudacoff contributed 6 percent of the United Jewish Welfare Fund's budget. Ten years later their contribution had grown to represent 19 percent of the total moneys raised. One reporter characterized Chudacoff as "representative of the new-type of communal leadership being developed from the ranks of young, vigorous businessmen."[52]

The newcomers guaranteed that steady growth would replace the previous pattern of boom-and-bust cycles in construction. Michael Kanin recalled the arrival in Los Angeles of his father's friend from New York, a builder. "I want to get started," he announced. "Where do you buy?" Kanin's father replied, "Anywhere you can spit!" In New York, location and timing were the foundations of real estate success, but in Los Angeles, "it didn't matter, anywhere that you could build you would sell it. There were people coming in here all the time." Although he entered the industry relatively late after arriving from Philadelphia in 1961, Mike Singer found that building in Los Angeles was "good since day one." Jews went into construction in response to the mass internal postwar migrations. Their presence, in turn, helped to bring more Jews out to the Valley.[53]

However, Jews did not work in all levels of the construction industry as they did in New York City. Jewish involvement remained largely limited to real estate, building, some contracting, and engineering. There were few Jewish workers in the building trades and few Jewish banks that specialized in loans to builders, except for the Union

Bank, which expanded in the 1950s. One survey estimated that in 1959 only 7 percent of Los Angeles Jews worked in construction. These Jews, however, made up approximately 20 percent of the city's home builders and accounted for almost 40 percent of the market. Jews did enter several related fields, including household appliances and plumbing fixtures. When he was in construction with his wife's father's firm, Sy Bram worked effectively with Waste King, a Jewish firm, which provided him with such popular new items as dishwashers and garbage disposal units. Since Waste King had an excellent reputation, "we would use their products exclusively so our brochures would read 'featuring Waste King dishwashers and garbage disposals.'" Other builders like the Alden brothers appealed to potential buyers through such amenities as central heating and air conditioning. They also popularized such items as breakfast nooks and showers. Leftgoff thought that "the reason they were so successful was that they put a lot more into a house than anyone else ever dreamt of." Although the relationship between Jewish settlement and Jewish builders was strong, Jewish participation in the construction industry quickly exceeded the potential offered by Jewish purchasers. Of the approximately twenty thousand houses Bram's firm built, some were sold to people other than Jews. Conversely, Jews sometimes purchased homes in developments built by companies that catered exclusively to veterans.[54]

An even stronger relationship between Jewish settlement and Jewish builders developed in Miami. "No American community has seen the same concentrated impress of Jewish entrepreneurship as has the municipality of Miami Beach," averred Irving Lehrman, dubbed "Miami's favorite rabbi" because of his ecumenical efforts. The Jews of America "took Miami Beach to its heart and built," Lehrman thought, "the jewel of resort cities." Not only did Jewish builders cater to Jewish clients—as the hotel owners did—but many of the former also followed the same migration path as the latter. Samuel Cohen and Moses Ginsberg, both known in Brooklyn for the houses they built in the interwar years, turned southward and drew upon their previous experience to construct, not just houses, but hotels and office buildings in Miami and Miami Beach. Ginsberg's elegant office building on Lincoln Road and Washington Avenue housed the Mercantile National

Bank, Miami Beach's first commercial bank, organized by Philip Lieberman.[55]

Other former New Yorkers, getting into the spirit of the postwar real estate boom, decided to try building on a grand scale. Shepard Broad, a New York lawyer, first glimpsed Miami Beach in 1938 during a vacation fishing trip with a client. Dissatisfied with his successful career and suburban life in Great Neck, Broad liked the prospect of a small community where everyone was known and where he could play an important role. Miami Beach struck him then as a likely place to advance as an individual, and in 1939 he moved down with his wife. Broad immediately entered a partnership with a Gentile lawyer, offering investment advice since he could not practice law in Florida without passing its bar exam. In the short space of three months, from March to June 1940, without a license for law practice, Broad took in six thousand dollars in fees. Occasionally he helped clients who had debts in New York to invest in Florida. He figured, correctly, that creditors would be unlikely to trace the matter to Florida. After gaining entry to the Florida bar in August 1940, he went into business for himself.

In March 1946 Broad started dredging a mangrove swamp area in Biscayne Bay, and by the fall of 1947 he had constructed five miles of sea wall, laid out thirteen miles of streets, and built nineteen miles of water mains as well as a bridge connecting the islands to Miami Beach. Taking advantage of Miami's easy incorporation laws, he incorporated the town as Bay Harbor Islands, became the mayor, and began building apartments, hotels, and single-family homes. Though Broad admitted that the profit motive was important—he invested close to four million dollars—he averred that his deeper desire was to do something creative, to start from scratch and build an entire community.[56] Bay Harbor Islands attracted a large percentage of Jewish residents to its apartment buildings and comfortable private houses, and Broad managed to get noticed.[57]

Construction in Miami soared during the immediate postwar years. Boosters bragged that since 1950 "a new house or apartment is completed somewhere in Metropolitan Miami every seven minutes of the working day." The Florida Homestead Law exempted homeowners from paying taxes on the first five thousand dollars of assessed valuation. Since houses were regularly assessed at half their value, the law encouraged construction of single-family homes priced at $9,999. By the 1960s thousands of homeowners in Miami were paying no real estate taxes. One observer described Dade County as one subdivision after another stretching from the ocean's edge to the Everglades. On Miami Beach, however, more apartment buildings were completed in 1947 than private single-family homes. This signaled an important shift to a higher density of population as well as the appeal of apartment living to the newcomers who were familiar with it. As a result, although Miami Beach made up only 7 percent of Dade County's population, it paid 20 percent of the taxes by 1960. Then a new boom in high-density living occurred: In 1959 Nathan Guminick, a prominent Virginia builder of apartment houses headquartered in Richmond and, with his wife, Sophia, a longtime winter resident of Miami Beach, built Southgate Towers, the first of the high-rise apartment buildings. Others soon followed—Emil Morton with Morton Towers, Sam Halperin with Imperial House—enticed by the prospect of a year-round apartment for the price of a ninety-day vacation. As Jews shifted their residential preferences after 1960 to high-rise apartments, often cooperatives or condominiums that maintained the hotels' flamboyant style of lush lobbies, chandeliers, Olympic-size pools, sun decks, card rooms, and auditoriums, their settlement concentrated. Together they marked another dramatic change in Miami Beach's skyline and character.[58]

The widespread popularity of high-rise apartment living in Miami Beach contributed to the high density of Jewish population. In Miami, unlike L.A., fewer than two thirds of the Jewish residents owned their own house by the mid-1960s. Beach Jews preferred to rent an apartment, though they could afford a house in the country. "They want all the excitement of city living with none of its problems—no slums, no smog," noted an observer. A surveyor enumerated the attractions of apartments to Jews: First and foremost, Jews had lived in apartments all their lives; second, they formed their closest social relations with their immediate neighbors; third, the apartment building provided them with a large enough pool of people to find good friends; and finally, these Jewish apartment dwellers gained a sense of security from having so many people living in one building.[59]

The newcomers so transformed Jewish settlement patterns by creating many different residential areas that later arrivals discovered that they could actually choose where to live based upon a Jewish calculus. When Herbert Abrams first moved in 1950 to Los Angeles, his wife's childhood home, he didn't like "the hick town." He missed the culture of New York City and disdained the casual lifestyle. "If I went out on a date I expected to get dressed up, wear a shirt and a tie," he recalled. After two years he and his wife moved back to Long Island. Ten years later Abrams returned to Los Angeles. This time he found the city more cosmopolitan and more Jewish. An observant Jew, Abrams looked first for a good Hebrew school for his daughters and then for a house nearby. Arriving in the City of Angels two years earlier, Shimon Orenstein responded in a similar way. A committed Zionist, Orenstein came from Milwaukee "where most Jews were affiliated." He had lived in Israel for several years and chose Los Angeles because he wanted something resembling the promised land. Instead of finding a place near his in-laws, he asked friends who had arrived earlier where Jews lived. They told him City Terrace, West L.A., the Valley, Reseda—an area that was new, distant, and, less than ten years earlier, without Jews. Orenstein decided to live in the center of the Valley; so he folded a map in half, looked for synagogues, and drew a circle. He found a new house not far from several synagogues, albeit on a block with just a few Jewish families. Orenstein valued where he lived so much that when the company he worked for relocated in Downey, over thirty miles away in south Los Angeles, he quit his job rather than move.[60]

Less consciously committed Jews arriving in the late 1950s or early 1960s could also choose to live in areas with other Jews. Alex Bratman bought a house in Van Nuys in the only Jewish area he found near a school for his children with a large Jewish enrollment, Milliken Junior High School. Mike Wiener and his wife "decided we wanted a Jewish community. I'm not a religious Jew, but I'm a secular Jew," he explained. "I like to be around Jewish people." So, like the Orensteins, they "took the map of the San Fernando Valley, and we blocked it off, and every Sunday we walked up and down the streets." Finally, they found a neighborhood, and "we said this is great, it's near a park, it has sidewalks, you can walk, it has trees, the home prices are right, we can afford it, and it's right in Encino."[61] The Wieners' list of features of a desirable neighborhood derives directly from a big-city upbringing. Parks, sidewalks, trees, and opportunities to stroll, these were the components of comfortable urban living. Not to mention the presence of other Jews. Moving to Los Angeles for the Wieners did not necessarily mean giving up the good aspects of life in the northeastern metropolis.

The desire to live near other Jews was part choice and part necessity. Antisemitism persisted in the postwar era, and it limited Jewish housing choices. Restrictive covenants, declared unenforceable by the Supreme Court in 1948, continued to be written and honored. In Miami, for example, Bal Harbour and Coral Gables explicitly restricted Jewish residents. Sonia Klein Robins remembers that when her parents purchased a house in Coral Gables right after the war, they were the first Jews to do so. Two hours after the signing, when the seller discovered that they were Jews, he returned and tried to buy back the house. He warned the Kleins that no one would speak to them or befriend their daughters, but Sonia's parents replied that they would worry about such matters themselves. In 1945 as before the war, Jewish visitors to Miami Beach had to contend with signs advertising "Gentiles Only" or "Restricted." Despite Miami Beach's heavily Jewish tourist clientele who managed to find accommodations, residential restrictions greeted the early pioneers to Miami.[62]

There was less overt antisemitism in Los Angeles, which sprawled over a larger geographic area. Only a handful of housing developments refused to admit Jews. Realtors steered Jews away from Rolling Hills and the Portuguese Bend area; several Park La Brea buildings of the Metropolitan Life Insurance Project didn't accept Jews. But most Los Angelenos welcomed Jewish settlement in their desire to populate open spaces. In certain sections—for example, San Marino and parts of Long Beach, as well as Orange County and the San Gabriel Valley—Jewish newcomers encountered such forms of prejudice as restrictions on sales of property and refusal to admit Jews to civic memberships. Jewish merchants in Rosemead had to deal with incidents of open hostility that included defacing their property. However, relatively few Jews chose to settle in the San Gabriel Valley's less hospitable environment.[63]

In moving to Los Angeles, Jews anticipated that their migration would free them to change themselves, unlike relatives who settled in the suburbs of large northern cities. Choosing to live in a vacation paradise like Miami or L.A. set Jews on a different course from those who picked the suburbs in the postwar period. Both cities and suburbs provided affordable single-family houses and other amenities that Jews in those days associated with the good life. But suburbanization represented a postwar continuation and extension of the movement out of older and poorer city neighborhoods into new and more affluent ones, a movement that had started as early as World War I. In the interwar years the large parks and tree-lined sidewalks of Brooklyn and the Bronx offered urban amenities and civic culture to pedestrians. After World War II the suburbs of Long Island and New Jersey, the North Shore of Chicago and the Northside of Philadelphia, promised the privacy of backyards on tree-lined streets, distant from the bustle of commerce. These bedroom communities, so dubbed because of their exclusively residential character and absence of industry or commerce, relied upon automobiles, but they also linked their residents to the central city via commuter trains and public transportation.[64]

Visiting Los Angeles in 1959, Nathan Glazer located the difference between the sprawling city of private homes and the suburbs of New York and Chicago in the centrality of individual choice that shaped L.A. An astute observer, he understood the City of Angels as a frontier leisure town, whose values were embodied in its glorification of the single-family private house, utterly different from the suburbs despite the superficial similarity. "[F]inally you get off the freeway to descend into an endless Brooklyn or Queens: single-family houses, stretching for mile upon mile, with occasional streets devoted to business," he wrote, trying to explain L.A. to New York Jews. "But with this difference from Brooklyn or Queens: that here everyone has chosen his way of life, while Brooklyn and Queens have not been chosen, but taken out of necessity." Jewish suburbanization represented a collective migration; Jews moved together from one urban neighborhood to another until they reached the suburbs. Moving to Los Angeles was different. "We should not be deceived by the surface resemblance to the endless 'bedroom boroughs' of New York and

Chicago," Glazer cautioned. "Here the bedroom and living room are mixed. The streets with little houses are as busy with traffic as great thoroughfares in the east. This may offend our sense of the proper organization of a city," he admitted, "but in any case the curse of the bedroom is removed when it is not separated from the city by a long ride, at the same hour each day, by subway, trains, or bus."[65]

Unlike Jews who moved to L.A., suburban Jews did not lose touch with the city, its institutions and culture.[66] Many returned daily to work, and most visited on occasion. Suburbanization did not disrupt the family network, as migration did by cutting individuals off from their roots. Rather, it extended the reach of the intergenerational family. Similarly, although suburban Jews organized Jewish life anew as did the newcomers to Miami and Los Angeles, they also imported Jewish institutions. Frequently synagogues followed their more wealthy congregants to the suburbs. Such decisions provided suburban Jews with a significant measure of continuity and reaffirmed deference to established leaders. No true changing of the guard took place.[67]

By contrast, migration to Los Angeles or Miami transformed a Jew's relationship to his or her hometown. Patterns of deference to established leadership could not be imported across the continent. A movement of individuals, albeit on a mass scale, the migration to Miami and Los Angeles severed structures of collective continuity. Jews thought about themselves and their Jewish institutions differently after they settled in Miami or L.A. The decision of the Shapiro brothers to leave Milwaukee illustrates this. Harold Shapiro settled in Miami Beach after serving as a naval officer during the war. He rapidly became involved in local politics, winning election as mayor of Miami Beach in 1953. His brother, Albert Shapiro, became a physician and moved to Los Angeles. Albert changed his name to Sims, a less Jewish-sounding name than Shapiro, and made his home in Encino. The migration of the Shapiro brothers and others like them allowed Jews not only to change their residence but to change their identity.[68]

For Jews eager to break with persistent communities and traditions, Miami and Los Angeles represented alternatives to suburbanization. Both cities promised a life of ease more often associated with the tourist experience than with the mundane world of work. Although some, like Mike Wiener, who grew up in Brighton Beach, settled initially in the New Jersey suburbs, he grew disgusted with the commuting life and with "living for the weekends," and decided to give Los Angeles a try. When an aunt in L.A. said she had a room waiting for him, Mike left his parents, cousins, "the boys" he had grown up with and didn't look back. He decided to stay in Los Angeles despite difficulty finding work. After working as a camp counselor in the summer, he took a part-time job as assistant camp director with the Jewish Centers Association. That job facilitated his adjustment to Los Angeles. Eventually he enrolled in UCLA to get certification as a teacher and went to work for the Los Angeles Unified School District.[69] The ready availability of recreation and the appeal of the outdoor life induced many to choose Miami and L.A. over the countrified domesticity of the northern and midwestern suburbs.

The minority of roughly half a million Jews who sought to live under palm trees and sunny skies in Miami and Los Angeles pursued a vision of the golden land as powerful as the American dream that lured their immigrant parents and grandparents to cross the Atlantic Ocean. In a poignant Yom Kippur sermon, Jacob Sonderling, rabbi of Fairfax Temple in Los Angeles, reflected upon their new beginning. Sonderling challenged his listeners in the crowded Embassy Auditorium, rented for the occasion, to emulate their immigrant forbears. Newcomers to Los Angeles should build a great Jewish community as the immigrants had done after crossing the Atlantic. "In Brooklyn and in the Bronx you need no sermon for Jewishness," he mused. "Try to escape it in the Bronx or in Brooklyn! But here you need it— badly. Twenty years hence," he prophesied, "it might be different. Today you need it." Affirming his faith in the newcomers, the rabbi asserted: "I refuse to believe that you have lost 'excess baggage' from [the] Bronx and Brooklyn in coming here to California. By excess baggage, I mean Jewishness." Yet the situation in Los Angeles was different, as Sonderling tried to explain. "We find in this soil, in this climate, a future life. Many, many of you will understand." Was the rabbi assuring himself, or his temporarily assembled congregants? Perhaps both. "We have little to offer. You see, in ten years one considers himself a native in California! We are just ten years, twelve years, twenty years old."[70]

Herein lay the youthful magic of both Los Angeles and Miami. In these cities where everyone was a newcomer, one could start anew, make oneself over in one's own image. Jews came to Miami and Los Angeles to seek that opportunity no less than to fulfill each cities' alluring promise. That promise included an almost rural innocence, the intimacy of a small town, coupled with the glamour of movies and tourism, the enormous potential of a boom city. Neither Miami nor Los Angeles resembled cities Jews knew well; both lacked the density of population, the visible ethnic concentrations, the soaring high-rise buildings downtown with their crowded streets. Instead Miami and Los Angeles offered a leisurely paced life, bubbling with a heady optimism about the future's potential, a world filled with such icons of popular culture as movie stars and drive-in restaurants, glittering hotels and sportswear fashions. As Shepard Broad sensed when he glimpsed Miami Beach from the deck of his fishing boat, here was a city where he could count, where he wouldn't have to wait his turn behind others, where he had a good chance to get to the head of the line.[71] Miami and Los Angeles offered Jews a taste of individual freedom as permanent tourists in a community of strangers.

3
Permanent Tourists

There is no way of telling it is Sunday in Los Angeles unless
one looks at the calendar.

—Nathan Glazer
"Notes on Southern California," *Commentary*, July 1959

Migration from old familiar enclaves in aging metropolitan centers
to exotic cities noted for their leisure lifestyle changed Jews from
natives standing on the threshold of security and status into strangers
seeking to establish networks to sustain themselves. Choosing to settle down as permanent tourists in unfamiliar territory far from home
and family, they gradually discovered that where they lived bred in
them a diffuse, individualistic identity. Yet the changes occurred
slowly; what Jews first tasted was an uninhibited freedom, product
of the physical beauty of these sunny cities and of Jewish ignorance
of their cultural character. As newcomers, Jews wore their identity
on their sleeves. Unattuned to the mores of their new milieu, they
imported the cultural styles of their big city pasts. A brashness and
exuberance bred in the metropolis heightened the heady optimism of
those who chose Miami and Los Angeles. These zealous migrants
inundated the placid old-timers, who nonetheless responded eagerly

to the diverse possibilities the newcomers created. Coming to Los Angeles from Chicago, Bram Goldsmith recalled his initial reaction to his new home. "This community was loaded with dead wood, self-protected and self-preserved," he thought, at best "very sterile" and dull.[1] As a bold and more open Jewishness permeated the entire community, Jews embraced their rootlessness and forged an eclectic identity for themselves out of their encounter with the strange worlds of Miami and L.A.

"Jews are now free to be Jewish in a new way as an act of personal choice rather than imposition," Neil Sandberg concluded after surveying Los Angeles Jewry in the 1980s. The self-selection behind migration reinforced the principle of individual choice of identity. As early as 1959 Nathan Glazer found that "the sense of a chosen city, a desired way of life, a realized wish, is strong." Visiting Los Angeles, he marveled at how "freer styles of work prevail, operating in an urban environment which is more successful in obscuring the sharp division between work and non-work than any other." In the City of Angels, free choice permeated even the mundane aspects of life. "There are the backyard swimming pools and the beaches, which can be used three-quarters of the year," he observed, "there is the huge array of service jobs which can be worked at part-time and at odd hours and on odd days, there are all the non-working people who have come with a little money and invested in real estate, and those who have come with nothing but live on pensions." Glazer concluded that "more people act as if they were on vacation (and must feel it, too) than anywhere in the world." Except, perhaps, in Miami.[2]

But Jews not only discovered freedom and a feeling of vacationing in their new homes, they also met very different neighbors from the ethnic Catholics they had previously known. For Jewish newcomers accustomed to large Catholic immigrant populations in the northeastern and midwestern cities of their childhood, Miami and Los Angeles presented startling differences. Without the mediating influence of heterogeneous Catholic ethnic groups, Jews confronted directly the Protestant majority for their social cues. This majority lacked a visible common denominator of either a shared ethnicity or a church hierarchy, presenting Jews with an individualistic and fragmented society. "People had no identities except their personal identities, no obvious group affiliations to make possible any reference to them by collective nouns." Even some Jews growing up in Los Angeles lacked any sense of a collective identity. "I didn't know what a Jew was until I went east to the University of Chicago," Susan Sontag once told her son. Yet, as David Rieff notes, "she had lived in L. A., at the edge of the Valley, graduating from North Hollywood High School in the late forties," a characteristically middle-class Jewish milieu. Jews encountered as well the pervasive influence of fundamentalist churches, whose individualist ethos permeated even the ostensibly secular city of Los Angeles. As the newcomers found their social niche in Miami and Los Angeles, they became white or Anglo, meaningless categories in New York or Chicago.[3]

Jews adjusted to these burgeoning cities first by drawing upon their previous metropolitan experience. "Immigration and resettlement are as much a leaving behind as a going toward," noted one observer. "Seeking new beginnings, people reveal old dispositions. They dream in old frames, they think in learned categories, they act from habits confirmed over time, in other surroundings." New and old worlds exist in an uneasy tension. "To cast off a city in which one has grown up is like casting off one's own father and mother," mused the editor of the *California Jewish Voice*. "Perhaps it is even stronger than that. It is like casting off one's childhood, those memories which constitute the sweetest part of our lives, and which, with the years, acquire an added sweetness." As they settled in their new homes, Jews explored the implications of their freedom. What did it mean to be an American Jew in Miami or Los Angeles? "[W]hen you grow up in New York City—all the world is Jewish. When all the world is Jewish, nobody is Jewish, really," explained Nathan Perlmutter. "You've got to leave major metropolitan areas to fully understand what I mean about a sense of a Jewish community—of a 'we' and a 'they'— in New York, it's all 'we.'" As the director of the Anti-Defamation League's Miami office, Perlmutter was sensitive to this issue, returning to the question from another angle. "So it is that in New York one's Jewishness is often an unexercised muscle while one's secularity, for being in free use, grows."[4]

Newcomers to Los Angeles and Miami rarely met old-timers because they created different Jewish residential patterns from established ones. When Jews settled in freshly built subdivisions in the San Fernando Valley or moved into recently constructed apartment buildings in North Miami Beach, they entered a world without defined boundaries. Isidore Rosenthal recalled that when he bought a house in 1954 in Reseda in the San Fernando Valley, it was "the other end of the world at the time." People would come into the community and ask, "'Are there any Jews living in this area?'—which you didn't have to ask in other areas" where a Jewish presence was already visible.[5]

Although few newcomers realized it, L.A. did possess a small established Jewish community, one that reflected the city's frontier conditions. The largest, most visible, and concentrated Jewish area in the City of Angels was the Boyle Heights district in east Los Angeles, one of the few sections where newcomers and old-timers mixed during the 1940s. When Marty Rosenbaum arrived at age eleven with his parents, they chose Boyle Heights, and Marty spent his teenage years there. By the time he entered the service during the Korean War, his parents were ready to leave the area for the west side. The child of Holocaust survivors, Gloria Shulman Blumenthal grew up in Boyle Heights. Her parents found an apartment there "a few months after their arrival from Europe, ten days after my birth. The apartment faced Breed Street. From our balcony we could see the Breed Street Shul and a neon sign in the distance which read 'The Hebrew Christian Synagogue.'" For Gloria and her family, "Boyle Heights offered temporary shelter until we could save enough money to move elsewhere. It was, however, comfortable and comforting shelter," she recalled. Although Boyle Heights acquired a local reputation as the Jewish immigrant section, its open spaces, small houses, absence of overcrowding, and modest signs of public Jewish life distinguished it from the dense immigrant and second-generation Jewish neighborhoods in the large eastern cities and even from the adjoining Little Toyko section of Los Angeles. Yet Boyle Heights was a "walking" neighborhood; families lived nearby and children could visit easily.[6]

Boyle Heights was also Los Angeles's most heterogeneous and ethnically mixed area between 1930 and 1950. Before the war approximately twenty-five thousand Jews lived there, along with fifteen thousand Mexicans and five thousand Japanese. Home to roughly 40 percent of the city's Mexican population and 25 percent of its Jews, Boyle Heights housed several Orthodox synagogues and Jewish community centers and was the center for the city's vibrant Yiddish cultural life, union activity, and radical politics. Growing up in Boyle Heights, Marvin Zeidler recalled the popular social and athletic clubs, like the Cardinals at the Soto-Michigan Jewish Community Center and the Saxons who hung out at the Wabash Avenue playground. Although the SACs devoted most of their energies to playing baseball and meeting girls, occasionally they clashed with local Mexican clubs.[7]

Recollecting his childhood in Boyle Heights, Robert Gerstein noted that the "neighborhood was by no means exclusively Jewish, but the small business district on Wabash Avenue that gave it its flavor was entirely Jewish." Rarely crowded, the street was alive with people shopping and chatting. "There was the small fruit and vegetable market overflowing onto the street, with its huge pickle barrel, and fresh horseradish at Pesach. Then there was Block the Baker, a mild quiet man who was especially nice to children." Gerstein remembered "the small picture of Roosevelt on his wall. Then the fish store, owned by that huge woman, whom I found so frightening with her great cleaver and chopping block. There was a small delicatessen," he continued. "Finally, there was the poultry store, fascinating and frightening, with sawdust on the floor, feathers in the air, and the constant din of live chickens."[8]

Boyle Heights evoked little nostalgia upon its demise, a process hastened by the arrival of Jewish newcomers who sought homes in new neighborhoods. Gerstein admitted that "as I grew up, I became increasingly alienated from the neighborhood and its life. It all seemed shabby, ugly, disorderly, compared to the life I lived vicariously at the movies every week. I was happy to leave," he concluded. The construction of five freeways between 1943 and 1960 consumed 10 percent of the land in Boyle Heights, displaced over ten thousand residents, and speeded the neighborhood's decline. After her family left, Gloria Shulman Blumenthal recalled weekly visits to "other families waiting their turn to get out. The Sunday evening treat was to go to Cantor's in Boyle Heights for dinner." Eventually even Cantor's moved westward and relocated on the site of the Esquire, a former art movie theater on Fairfax Avenue, in the heart of a new, more middle-class Jewish section that attracted both newcomers and old-timers.[9]

Cantor's lingered longer than most of the Jews who patronized it. By 1951 an astute aspiring politician putting together a slate for the

Democratic county committee recognized that the new Beverly-Fairfax section was heavily Jewish. "We figured they voted and if we could get them to vote for us, we'd win, and we did!" Levels of Jewish concentration in the district approached eastern patterns where Jews made up a majority of a neighborhood's residents, yet the landscape of Beverly-Fairfax was uniquely Los Angeles. "On the little streets that make up the Fairfax residential community, the panorama is one of buildings out of the 1920s and '30s: pastel stucco apartments and cute little houses with gingerbread and tile roofs, miniature castles and haciendas." This area of mixed single- and multifamily dwellings also contained a number of large Jewish institutional buildings that reflected the perception that Beverly-Fairfax was the new "psychological center" of Jewish Los Angeles. The many Jewish stores along Fairfax Avenue led locals to dub it "kosher canyon."[10]

Arriving with an eagerness to enjoy L.A.'s pleasant rhythm of life, newcomers quickly adjusted to the city's dispersed settlement patterns. Rather than seeking out other Jews and rootedness in a common residential experience, they scattered into various sections and produced a cluster pattern of concentrated dispersal. During World War II Jews in Los Angeles lived in at least ten different parts of the city. The 1940 census data indicated a highly stratified Jewish population. Significant concentrations in both the poorest and wealthiest areas—with 25 percent and 22 percent, respectively—suggested that for Jews, unlike other minorities in the city, affluence did not produce residential assimilation. By 1960 Jews lived in an even wider range of areas, but most were far more prosperous than the prewar sections. Over two-thirds of Los Angeles Jews, largely married couples and families, owned their own house. The number of Jews in the San Fernando Valley doubled during the 1950s, keeping pace with general population growth. Jews averaged 10 percent of the total residents, although these estimates disguised Jewish concentrations within the Valley that contained double and occasionally triple the average. Over the course of the decade, the popular move to the Valley brought its share of the total Jewish population up from 10 percent to 19 percent, while the visible decline of Boyle Heights reduced its portion from 7 percent to 4 percent. The more densely populated Wilshire-Fairfax and Beverly-Fairfax districts continued to house 15 percent of Los Angeles Jewry, while 21 percent lived in the affluent Beverly Hills, Brentwood, Westwood, and Beverlywood sections.[11]

Yet even such low degrees of concentrated dispersal produced a distinctive Jewish pattern, albeit one that highlighted the salience of individual choice. Over two-thirds of Los Angeles Jews lived in sections that contained greater concentrations of Jews than their proportion in the county. For those who remembered growing up in New York or Chicago, what stood out in the residential pattern was the dispersion. "The sprawling atmosphere," Philadelphia-born Rabbi Jacob Pressman observed, "militates against the creation of a Jewish climate . . . in a given street or group of streets where people could come together informally and still be with like-minded persons." Yet the concentrated dispersal of migrant choices represented a compromise between Jewish ethnic concentration characteristic of eastern and midwestern immigrant cities and the absence of distinct clustering typical of white Angelenos. Jewish residential experience ultimately would shape their cultural encounter with L.A. as geographical distances translated into psychological ones, diluting bonds of collective consciousness.[12]

Jews developed a distinctive socioeconomic profile in Los Angeles. Prior to World War II almost 40 percent of the Jewish work force found employment in white-collar clerical and sales jobs. Relatively few, compared with Jews in eastern cities, earned a living as skilled workers. Nor did Los Angeles possess many Jewish professionals. Jews worked in the city's garment industry and its jewelry trade; they established businesses in wholesaling and retailing of furniture, produce, liquor, and clothing; they made money in real estate and insurance; but most important, they built the motion picture industry.[13]

Hollywood—the industry—influenced the economy of Los Angeles and dominated through its wealth the ethnic economy of the city's Jews; but in addition, its internal operations made it a Jewish industry, much like the garment industry in New York City. That's how Clancy Sigal saw it when he arrived in Los Angeles in 1951. " 'Jewish' was the show-biz idiom in the offices, on the set, in *The Daily Variety*," he observed from his position as a production assistant for a "cheapo studio." "This wasn't only because many Jews worked in the industry," he noted; "the lingua franca, the daily business language, was Jewish in vocabulary and intonation. A peculiar form of Yiddishkeit, matey and vernacular, drew many Gentiles into its warm embrace." Hollywood's *yidishkeyt* included both Yiddish street slang and "a Levantine style of bargaining" that even made some Jews become "more Jewish" to survive in the business. Ted Thomas, who started in Hollywood before the war as a dialogue writer, agreed that Jewishness was "the epoxy" of the industry. Comparing Hollywood to the Lower East Side of his youth with its bitter ethnic rivalries, the screenwriter Julius Epstein remarked that the motion picture industry provided a Jewish model for Jewish-Gentile cooperation. "Common hatreds" held Jew and non-Jew together: writers hated directors, directors hated producers, and so on up the ladder.[14]

The movie industry possessed enormous resources, generated great wealth and prestige, and exerted a powerful cultural influence upon the city's Jewish community. Max Nussbaum, the energetic and popular rabbi of Temple Israel who arrived during the war, contended that "basically, the Hollywood community is neither better nor worse than the balance of the country. And this goes for politics and morals, for social responsibility and religious affiliation." His informal survey of Jewish producers, executives, directors, and writers uncovered a surprising 44 percent belonging to a synagogue while half were members of secular Jewish organizations. In 1940 the $490,000 contribution of Hollywood to the annual United Jewish Welfare Fund campaign made up over 50 percent of the total moneys raised in Los Angeles.[15]

The arrival of the newcomers changed the occupational profile of Los Angeles Jews. Self-employment and trade, both retail and wholesale, gradually declined during the 1950s as the number of professionals and those working in service businesses increased. Although Hollywood suffered, the rise of television production offered opportunities for another generation of Jews willing to take risks in a new entertainment medium. The growing affluence of Los Angeles Jews registered in the continuing shrinkage of those employed as workers in manufacturing. In other areas—finance, real estate, insurance, and construction—there was little change. Most women who worked, a minority of those married, found employment in clerical and sales jobs.[16]

But the newcomers had their greatest impact on the organized Jewish community of Los Angeles. Their numbers, energies, ideas, and previous experiences overwhelmed this "backwater from the mainstream of Jewish life."[17] The city contained the gamut of institutions associated with an established American Jewish community: schools, synagogues, community centers, hospitals, social welfare and aid societies, Zionist groups, political organizations, women's and men's groups, country clubs and *landsmanshaftn*, a federation that centralized fund-raising, as well as a central coordinating body supported by most Jewish organizations, the Jewish Community Council. Yet easterners invited to survey the communal scene regularly reported their dismay at the modest size and scope of conventional Jewish institutions.

In 1942 Samuel Kohs, a leading figure in the field of Jewish social work, traveled from New York City to Los Angeles to survey the recreational and cultural needs of Jewish Angelenos. Examining a major community of over 100,000 Jews, Kohs considered that "in many respects Jewish forces in Los Angeles are still in the chrysalis stage. The form they will take in the future is more or less unpredictable." He recognized that few Jewish organizations possessed roots or vigor or imagination; they reached a mere handful of members and appeared a pale shadow of their eastern counterparts. Nonetheless, he was upbeat because of the city's wealth and potential for growth. "There is every reason to hope that as the community comes into its own, it will assume its proper place of leadership beside the older eastern communities, and will fructify the intellectual, cultural and spiritual life of the American Jewish community as a whole."[18]

Other outsiders were less generous, less inclined to look toward future possibilities. Coming from New York for a visit in 1943, Frank Weil, the head of the National Jewish Welfare Board, chided Los Angeles Jews for "living in the middle ages" so far as Jewish centers were concerned. Weil was appalled at the centers' primitive character, lack of professional staffing, meager facilities, and dull programming. Six years later Bertram Gold arrived in the City of Angels to recommend a course of action for the city's Jewish community centers. Gold had difficulty summoning any enthusiasm for what he saw. He described the West Adams Center as "a few grimy rooms in an unprepossessing building." The Beverly-Fairfax center, initially designed to be a showcase of what centers could do, reminded Gold "of a little doll's house—despite the additions that have recently been made." Financial allocations to Los Angeles's Jewish community centers confirmed the outsiders' assessment. Whereas eastern and midwestern Jews spent an average of ten dollars per capita on their centers, Los Angelenos mustered a mere seventy-five cents. Without any financial resources, centers of necessity existed as marginal institutions in L.A. rather than as the central meeting places—as suggested in the name Jewish community *centers*—for diverse Jewish organizations. If the centers stood on the fringes of the community, then the organizations were even more peripheral since they lacked any common framework.[19]

Aware of the weaknesses of Jewish organizational life, communal leaders in Los Angeles enthused at prospects they anticipated would flow from the population increase. "As an old-timer in Los Angeles I have been able to watch many changes as our city and our community moved into new prominence in the eyes of the world," Peter Kahn explained in 1947. "I have watched California grow to its present stature as third state in the Union and Los Angeles, third city." Kahn, a respected communal leader, looked at the newcomers and saw the future. "Today, California's position parallels New York's at the end of the last century. Even as that community grew by leaps and bounds with the great influx of European immigrants to the East Coast, creating what might be called the 'Atlantic Era,'" he prophesied, "so Los Angeles has grown and is still growing, and we who are here can watch the beginnings of a 'Pacific Era.'"[20]

Kahn drew an apt analogy with New York City despite a crucial difference between the old immigrants and the new migrants. "The growth of the Jewish population in Los Angeles is not a product of the old type European immigration," noted journalist William Zuckerman. He pointed out that "it is a result of an internal American transmigration process which is typical of the American Continent and of the American people. The 'Old Home' of these West Coast Jews is not Warsaw, Lodz, Kowno or Lemberg, but New York, Chicago, Philadelphia, Pittsburgh and other American cities." As a result, Zuckerman concluded, "they are Americans by birth and instinct, not by nationality and gratitude."[21]

Despite the newcomers' sturdy American identity, their displacement could not be ignored. It pervaded their self-perception and influenced their self-definition. "I am a refugee from Chicago to Los

Angeles of several years standing," Leonard Sperry announced after nearly a decade of living in Los Angeles. Sperry, "a charming and quiet, almost European kind of intellectual man" in the eyes of one old-timer, was related by marriage to the wealthy Rosenwald family of Sears, Roebuck. Yet his sentiments could be heard among all classes of Jews.[22]

Many migrants experienced a profound sense of dislocation accompanying their discovery of this new world. Reading the death notices in the Miami papers, one observer remarked how few people seemed to have roots in the city. After eighteen to twenty-five years of living in Miami, they were buried in Rochester, Detroit, Chicago. The pervasive snowbird presence in Miami accentuated the rootlessness of even permanent settlers. "In those days people came down to Miami but not for any length of time," Marty Peppercorn recalled. "Those who were wealthy may have bought a home or kept some little set up down there to which they came down for a month or two months. They never had a concept that this was a community or that it was their community—they still had loyalties to their own community." Rabbis and Jewish professionals chafed at the attitudes implicit in snowbird status. They especially resented the "irresponsibility" and "lack of commitment" that accompanied the sense of being tourists and the apparent desire "to get away from it all."[23] Yet they also did their best to reach the snowbirds; for example, by offering them special prorated synagogue memberships.[24]

Special synagogue memberships for transients were not the only difference between Miami and L.A. Miami's residential pattern diverged from that of Los Angeles: No one district dominated L.A. as Miami Beach dominated Miami. The Beach contained half of Dade County's Jewish population. The high level of concentration associated with Jewish urban life in New York and other large eastern and midwestern cities reappeared in Miami Beach and its neighboring towns, Surfside and Bay Harbor Islands. By 1960 observers estimated that roughly 80 percent of the Beach's population was Jewish. In Miami Beach, New Yorkers settled first in hotels and then in highrise apartment buildings. Later arrivals continued to cluster but in newer apartments and condominiums in North Miami Beach. Other sections of Miami, especially the southwest and northwest, drew a wider range of Jewish newcomers. In the Greater Miami area the old antagonism to New York Jews reemerged as a resentment by Town Jews of prosperous Beach residents. The Beach had become synonymous with its predominant Jewish population.[25]

Public perception linked the Beach's Jewish residents with the wealth and glitter of the new hotels and houses and the tourist way of life. The island's transformation captured the imagination of observers. "Wealthy, superoptimistic, pushy, sparkling Miami Beach has in less than one lifetime grown from a dense mangrove swamp inhabited by snakes and rats into one of the great resort and convention centers of the world," wrote one reporter. Thousands of hotel rooms and apartments amounted to a greater concentration of such accommodations per acre than on any other strip of "previously worthless real estate." Yet for those who lived across Biscayne Bay, what occurred on the Beach held little interest. "Most Miamians look upon the row of glistening hotels across the water as being no more a material part of their lives than a line of cumulus clouds on the horizon." Beach residents reciprocated the lack of interest. For many, "Miami had an image as a low-profile town, a banana-boat port, a courthouse where the local government was quartered, the home of people who worked in Miami Beach but could not afford to live there." Jews often described the difference between Town and Beach as the difference between making it and having made it.[26]

Reporting on Miami Beach for the *Jewish Frontier*, Toby Shafter marveled at the "restaurants whose varied national and hybrid origins exhibit an amazing phenomenon of self-zoning. From 1st to 7th Street there are several Italian restaurants specializing in spaghetti and pizza, a number of cheap beer joints," including "one at 7th Street advertised as 'Casey's Bar in the Heart of the Irish District' . . . some nondescript 'American' restaurants, and an occasional small and unpretentious night club." Shafter pointed out that "within these self-imposed limits lived the Gentile section of the lower economic strata." In short, this area housed the hotel service workers.[27]

The Jewish section started around sixth Street, where "one begins to see an occasional 'Hungarian' restaurant with a *mogen dovid* painted over the door or advertising 'kosher-style' food." Shafter observed along this stretch of Miami Beach through 14th Street "numerous vegetarian and kosher restaurants, delicatessens, and cafeterias where a bagel with a spot of cream cheese is 30 cents (the charge is 45 cents with lox) and herring and chopped liver are daily items on the menu." Shafter describes this zone as "inhabited by the older, Yiddish-speaking group who are the mainstay of most of the Jewish organizations in the 'Beach.'" When I. B. Singer arrived in Miami Beach, he visited the cafeterias and hotel lobbies and marveled at the vitality of Jewish life. "It was remarkable," he wrote. "Jewishness had survived every atrocity of Hitler and his Nazis against Jews. Here the sound of the Old World was as alive as ever." Jews transported to Miami Beach an exuberant, palpable public presence. Unlike those in Los Angeles, Jews here lounged on street corners to chat, they gathered in Flamingo Park to debate, they played cards on hotel porches, they strolled along Collins Avenue and Ocean Drive, they danced at Ocean Front auditorium, and they visited in the cafeterias, those "nostalgic places" that reminded Singer of the Yiddish Writers Club in Warsaw.[28]

Although many of these immigrant Jews were far from poor, the "self-styled Jewish upper-crust consider it more fashionable to live in hotels bordering the ocean beginning at 15th Street." These hotels, unlike the ones south of 15th Street, maintained private beaches. Miami Beach residents patronized "bagel beach," the public facility bordering Ocean Drive, also known as the 14th Street beach, South Beach, and Lummus Park. Concluding the culinary tour, Shafter observed that "from 15th Street to Millionaire's Row at 30th Street . . . the eateries are 'American,' expensive and well-appointed." These catered to more affluent, second-generation Jews. North of 30th Street stretched a rich Gentile oasis, isolated and insulated from wealthy Jews living in the hotels. Shafter's culinary survey neglected those Jews living north of 41st Street. One observer estimated that a quarter of the Beach's Jewish residents lived in the northern section between 41st street and Surfside. Many of them were second generation, middle-class Jews, permanent residents with businesses or professional offices in Miami.[29]

In the 1960s, as the migration of elderly Jews to Miami accelerated, class differences among Beach Jews became more pronounced. Poor immigrant Jews increasingly made their home in South Beach, the area below 14th Street with the older hotels, houses, and apartments. On Washington Avenue, south of Tenth Street, a commercial strip flourished with delis, kosher meat markets, fish stores, fruit and vegetable shops, bakeries, drugstores, and newsstands with Yiddish papers. Well-to-do immigrant and second-generation Jews, similarly retired, lived north of 17th Street. The fashionable shopping street, Lincoln Road, divided the classes from the masses. Both groups of Jews, however, preferred to live in apartments and hotels, which accentuated their concentration. As the hotels marched inexorably northward, Millionaire's Row gradually succumbed to the profits to be made in real estate. Towering hotels and palatial condominium apartment buildings replaced the private mansions. Young couples with children usually purchased single-family houses away from the ocean resort area. Beach Jews made up 46 percent of the total Jewish population of Dade County in 1950 and over 50 percent by 1960.[30]

Another Jewish settlement developed in North Miami Beach. Like the San Fernando Valley, North Miami Beach had few residents before the war; its total population was 871! The rapid rate of building of single-family houses, apartments, and, by 1960, condominiums caused the population to skyrocket, climbing from two thousand in 1950 to over twenty-five thousand in just a decade. But contrary to what occurred in the Valley, Jews, many of them from New York, here made up a majority of the new residents, a visible presence in the area. Scattered Jewish populations with relatively low densities that resembled the general Los Angeles pattern lived in southwestern Miami, especially Westchester and the unincorporated areas. One mid-sixties' survey of affiliated Jews found that 39 percent reported living in areas that were predominantly Jewish, while another 16 percent estimated that half of their neighbors were Jews. Only 24 percent thought that Jews were a minority where they lived, while 14 percent reported no Jewish neighbors. Such figures suggested the strong appeal of Jewish neighborhoods to the newcomers, who sought to replicate familiar residential patterns of the northeast under Miami's sunny skies.[31]

Miami's distinctiveness as a tourist center appeared in the occupational distribution of its Jewish residents. The tourist industry employed the largest number of Jews, followed by building and real estate. Others worked in service and retail industries catering either to tourism or real estate. As in Los Angeles, relatively small numbers found employment as professionals or worked in manufacturing, although Miami possessed garment, furniture, and scrap metal industries. By the mid-1960s the number of professionals increased substantially; together with managers, proprietors, and salesmen, they accounted for roughly two thirds of the occupations of Miami Jews.[32]

Given the newcomers' mobility, the home left behind served as an important reference point; Jews knew who they were because they remembered their origins. Like their immigrant parents—and their American Gentile peers—Jews looked to hometown associations for a source of support in their new, rapidly changing city of choice. Despite ambivalence, many newcomers could not erase memories and ties with the homes they had abandoned. Migrant organizations took the characteristic form of *landsmanshaftn* that reflected this ambivalence. These groups based upon town of origin existed in Los Angeles prior to the war, but mass internal migration greatly increased their numbers and diversity. By 1950 several dozen social clubs organized around city of origin flourished in Los Angeles, as did a smaller number in Miami. Newcomers occasionally joined an older established group; more often they formed an additional organization of their peers. Detroit Jews in Los Angeles had established the Detroit Aid Society in 1936 with all of the features of a traditional *landsmanshaft*, including a sick fund and burial society. Although it began a drive for new members after the war, it could not prevent the creation of the Detroiters Club, which appealed to young, unmarried men and women.[33]

Recognizing the need for peer group sociability, some of the *landsmanshaftn* established separate junior or youth groups. Three years after its organization, the Minneapolis and St. Paul Benevolent Social Club started a youth group. The Cleveland Junior Social Club also held its own events. The Senior and Junior groups of New Yorkers of California usually met separately but occasionally sponsored a joint activity. One mother who moved to Los Angeles with her family wrote to the local paper on behalf of her sixteen-year-old daughter. The teenager wanted to join a club but could not find a group for Jewish girls in Inglewood. "We are from Detroit and I wonder would there be any Detroiter Club for young people," she inquired. Both mother and daughter accepted the logic of peer group, hometown association.[34]

Unlike synagogues, chapters of national Jewish organizations, or even Jewish community centers, the *landsmanshaftn*'s Jewishness remained largely assumed and only occasionally articulated. Most of

the Los Angeles clubs met monthly, sometimes in a building under
Jewish auspices, such as the hall of the Jewish War Veterans. More often they held meetings at popular Jewish restaurants like the Park
View Manor opposite Westlake Park or the Park Manor, a new establishment on Western Avenue near Wilshire Boulevard that installed a
kosher kitchen in 1948. Almost all hosted annual picnics that usually
drew hundreds of participants to Hollywood, Westlake, or Griffith
Park. Many engaged in charitable activity. In 1947 the five hundred
members of the Omaha Friendship Club of Los Angeles decided to
raise money for a memorial to Henry Monsky, the recently deceased
head of B'nai B'rith, who had lived in Omaha. Others tied their social
events to a Jewish philanthropic endeavor. A typical example was the
decision of the Westchester County Social Club of former New Yorkers to hold a Purim and Package party to benefit the Jewish welfare
fund drive.[35]

But the clubs' main purpose was social; their appeal depended
upon the uprooted sensibilities of members who relaxed when they
were with fellow migrants from home.[36] The Chicago-Detroit Club
of Los Angeles announced that these former midwesterners had
"banded together for social and mutual assistance to each other."
Their activities included "dancing, music, art classes, golfing and
bowling parties." In L.A., *landsmanshaftn* often limited membership
to adults aged twenty-one to thirty-five. Those who didn't join could
use the services of the numerous introduction clubs that sprang up,
but many preferred to seek friends among fellow *landslayt*. For New
Yorkers, whose identity with home was linked to the neighborhood of
their youth, high school alumni associations often formed the basis for
landsmanshaftn. In Miami and Los Angeles, former classmates from
Thomas Jefferson or Abraham Lincoln high school in Brooklyn or
from DeWitt Clinton or Morris high school in the Bronx created associations that enabled members to keep in touch.[37] Even graduates of
New York's City College met under California's sunny skies. Their
dinners occasionally included a cultural presentation that reminded
them of home and encouraged them to hold on to their identity as
New York Jews. In 1951 Arthur Felig (Weegee), the author of *Naked
City* and a famed photographer, presented films on New York City
after dinner at the Ciro-ette Room on Sunset Boulevard.[38]

Despite differences in age and motivation for leaving the familiar, migrants turned to peer group organization. Like their immigrant parents, they broke bonds of intergenerational family ties to reconstitute a voluntary society of peers. Newcomers relied upon common experiences, memories of the past, and shared values to unite them. Rarely did newcomers to Los Angeles and Miami convert their impulse to peer group solidarity into social welfare and mutual aid. In 1948 former residents of Buffalo, New York, chartered a credit union through the Los Angeles Buffalo Club; a similar decision was made two years later by the Boston Club. More typical were the parties, dinners, dances, and picnics often linked to some holiday in the Jewish or secular calendar.[39]

Unlike immigrant *landsmanshaftn*, the new clubs did not sponsor regular religious activities. They did use the Jewish festivals as occasions for social events, but these often bore little relation to the specific holiday. The New York Friendship Club regularly celebrated Simhat Torah with a party that included dinner, a show, and a dance. In comparable fashion the New Brunswick, New Jersey, Social and Welfare Club sponsored a "post 'Matzo Ball' Dance." Neither event reflected the religious meanings inherent in either Simhat Torah or Pesach. Although the clubs' popular Purim balls and parties suggested a connection with Jewish festivities of the past, they actually had more in common with the new Yom Kippur dances than with traditional forms of Jewish celebration. One distressed observer deplored the veritable epidemic of Yom Kippur dances. "To label a dance with the name of the most sacred day of the High Holidays is indeed an ignoble sacrilege," he protested. A veteran journalist agreed that "Yom Kippur Dances have become something of a tradition for us. We know of five places, where lively dances came at the end of the hard fast." Yom Kippur dances also were popular in Miami. The Miami Beach Jewish Center regularly scheduled theirs in one of the newest and most elegant hotels.[40]

Some newcomers argued that an emptiness lay behind the multiplicity of the Jewish social scene. One rabbi noted that newspaper listings suggested such a myriad of social and educational activities that one might get the false impression that every Los Angeles Jew was steeped in Jewish knowledge. In fact, a poll of the "Jew-on-the-street" would dispel such mistaken views and reveal that the flurry of events reflected Jewish entertainments, a type of activity that might attract permanent tourists, not committed Jews. "Judaism wasn't sold like a commodity in my native Liverpool or Palestine in my six years there," he complained. The average Jew was so steeped in Jewishness that "he knew an inner peace born of a high invincible faith" that was sorely lacking among Los Angeles Jews today. Another observer offered a less blanket criticism. Thomas Novak praised the charitable activities of Los Angeles Jews but found Halloween and Valentine's Day parties distressing. "It is bad enough when un-informed Jewish youngsters hold parties on those days, but . . . altogether uncalled for . . . [for] Jewish adults to," he averred. "I have yet to see the Knights of Columbus hold a Chanukah or Purim party."[41]

The new *landsmanshaftn* remained essentially centers of secular sociability, anchoring their members in unfamiliar urban territory through nostalgic evocations of the well-known world left behind. Although snowbirds continued to return north each spring, the environment of their old homes changed, as did the socioeconomic structure of the large northern cities. It became increasingly difficult even for snowbirds to go home when changes transformed familiar neighborhoods beyond recognition.

As the world they left behind gradually disappeared, many migrants, especially in Miami, sought to replicate aspects of their old homes in their new one. Observers noted "a tendency on the part of Miami to think of itself almost as an extension of New York City." Especially on the Beach, Jews soon turned each of the apartment towers into a self-contained minicommunity, complete with its own clubs, entertainments, and philanthropies. One observer remarked laconically that "even before a new apartment building is fully occupied, there is already formed (with officers) a Men's Club, B'nai B'rith Lodge, Hadassah Chapter, etc." Newcomers swelled the membership rolls of Jewish organizations: The one B'nai B'rith lodge in 1945 grew to seven lodges and nine chapters, with a membership of over two thousand in less than a decade. Though they took a Jewish organizational form, these groups were created less for Jews to identify with the Miami Jewish community than "for the social needs, the drive to know people in a town that may be strange." The increased Jewish presence similarly fueled diverse forms of cultural endeavor reminiscent of the northeastern cities. "The New York-Boston-Philadelphia crowd that had apartments here were delighted to go to the finest concerts in the world," a synagogue cultural director affirmed. "So we never had to advertise or print a brochure. We were sold out immediately." After health reasons impelled him to move to Los Angeles, Louis Shub joined the local American Jewish Committee chapter. The chapter became very important "because I was really rootless, and without any feeling of any future at all."[42]

Seymour Philips followed an alternative path. He first rented a garden apartment when he came to Los Angeles with his family in 1948. The twelve couples who lived in the apartment complex decided to move together to the Valley. Most chose Woodland Hills; four families even bought houses on the same block. After settling down, Philips and his new friends used their friendship circle as a nucleus for communal activities that required a residential focus, ranging from synagogue membership to Little League to the creation of a local Democratic party club, Club 22. So powerful was the common transient experience of rootlessness that friendships born out of this experience endured even when individuals acquired widely varying levels of wealth.[43]

Others set out to create organizations to serve specific needs as they arose, initiating a process of communal innovation. Newcomers felt free to experiment. Mark Itelson wanted a day camp for his young children, so shortly after he moved to the San Fernando Valley, he joined other Jews to organize one. Camp Akiba met during the summer of 1950 in North Hollywood Park. "No one belonged to synagogues," Itelson recalled, so the camp provided a focus for Jewish identification. With forty families it proved a successful activity. Soon it attracted 150 families. The enthusiasm generated a second, family camp on weekends, Camp Fress-und-Shpiel (Camp Eat and Play). The following year, with help from the Los Angeles Jewish Centers Association, the impetus behind the day camp spurred the establishment of year-round activities for children and adults, including clubs, theater, folk dancing, and holiday celebrations. Thus, the Chaim Weizmann Jewish Community Center was born. The name chosen, honoring the first president of the State of Israel, indicates the center's role as a visible symbol of Jewish identity. Eventually a building was constructed on Burbank Boulevard, and the center expanded, changing its name to the geographically descriptive, but Jewishly neutral, Valley Cities Jewish Community Center.[44]

Not only were newcomers constrained by few restrictions, but they also discovered that it was remarkably easy to get involved in Jewish life. Itelson soon found himself president of the Chaim Weizmann JCC. From president it was a short step to membership on the board of the citywide coordinating body, the Jewish Centers Association. In 1947 Joseph Shane arrived in Los Angeles from his native Chicago, where he had been president of the Young Men's Jewish Council. "As soon as I came here," the lawyer recalled, "I became involved in the Jewish community." Without being solicited, Shane called the Jewish Federation and announced "that I was a contributor to the United Jewish Appeal in Chicago, and that I wanted to make my contribution here." By 1954 he was general chairman of the United Jewish Welfare Fund, a position of extraordinary responsibility and importance for a newcomer. Later arrivals similarly found a warm welcome. Herbert Abrams threw his energies into a Hebrew school for his children; from there he became vice-president for education of the United Synagogue's southwest Pacific region. He then served as a representative to L.A.'s Bureau of Jewish Education; that took him to the presidency of the Los Angeles Hebrew High School. Finally he returned as chair of the bureau.[45]

Even old-timers, Jews who settled in L.A. before World War II, found themselves energized by the arrival of so many Jews and the opportunities created by their presence. Walter Hilborn, a prominent lawyer in the old Los Angeles Jewish firm Loeb and Loeb, was convinced that the openness of the City of Angels to new talent led to his social rise. "I did not associate with the elite of New York. My association with the elite came after I came to California," he explained. "Then I became a very active man in the American Jewish Committee," an elite New York Jewish organization. When large numbers of Jews migrated to L.A. after the war, Hilborn, welcomed as a hard and committed worker, helped to establish a branch of the Committee in Los Angeles. He then headed the chapter for a few years and rose from that position to national vice-chairman. "If I had stayed in New York I never would have amounted to anything, I am sure," he concluded, recognizing L.A.'s easy acceptance of new leaders. Myrtle Karp, an activist in Hadassah and then chair of the Women's Division of the United Jewish Appeal, also thought that her migration to Los Angeles made a difference. "I wonder too," she mused, "if I were still living in the East, if I were living in New York, or in Brooklyn, whether it would have been the same thing." Karp came to L.A. in 1932, but she did not get involved as a Jewish leader until after the war when newcomers arrived. "I had never done any public speaking and suddenly I was catapaulted into this," she recalled. The clean slate that L.A. provided and its openness to talent encouraged many Jews to step forward and assert their Jewish interest and identity.[46]

Both outsiders and insiders, newcomers and old-timers, saw the opportunities. For outsiders there was the possibility to exercise leadership, to create a community in one's own image, to start anew without having to conform to any preexisting rules. For insiders there was the chance to recruit members, to build up their organizations, to tap the enormous wealth being made in these cities to support their programs. Because the situation was so fluid, distinctions between outsiders and insiders didn't last very long. Newcomers arrived, settled down, and within a couple of years these former outsiders transformed themselves into insiders. Writing to a friend who was contemplating moving to Los Angeles, Rabbi Paul Dubin described a typical situation: "There is a real need in the city for creative Jewish music but it might be the type of position where you have to pave the way yourself. Nevertheless," he encouraged her, "if you really want to come out West I am sure that things would work out O.K."[47] The need and the opportunity existed, but it was up to the newcomer to grasp the opportunity and create the position and agenda to fill them.

The chance to get involved and to create organizations existed despite the fact that Los Angeles had an established Jewish community of some complexity prior to the war. Old-timers divided into at least four major segments. At the top was an older German Jewish professional and business elite, dubbed the "charity barons" by their less wealthy coreligionists.[48] This elite supported a federation of Jewish philanthropies in addition to nonsectarian charities. An east European business class provided the mainstay of the B'nai B'rith and general Zionist organizations. The relatively small immigrant working class concentrated in the Boyle Heights neighborhood sustained both the handful of Orthodox congregations in the city and several vigorous Yiddish-speaking radical and labor Zionist organizations.

Finally, a diverse group of men and women in the movie industry contributed a major share of the United Jewish Welfare Fund's budget. All of these groups competed for influence in the centralized yet democratic coordinating Los Angeles Jewish Community Council.[49]

A contemporary observer thought that the establishment of the council, a "democratic body as the spokesman of the Jewish community of Los Angeles," was due, "in part, to the comparative youth of this community, and in part to the fact that, as late as the 1930s, Los Angeles still lacked those fixed patterns of local Jewish life which prevented the full development of similar bodies in most of the older Jewish communities in the United States." The very weaknesses criticized by eastern visitors—the ineffectual Jewish organizations, meager Jewish community centers, dispersed residential pattern, and tourist mentality—allowed innovation. Without "fixed patterns" of Jewish organizational activity, with each firmly entrenched organization defending its own turf, opportunities existed in L.A. for individuals and organizations to cooperate. As a membership body the council united hundreds of Jewish organizations and included the city's major fund-raising arm, the United Jewish Welfare Fund. The council established a Bureau of Arbitration to keep Jewish differences out of the courts, a Bureau of Education to support Jewish schools, a Community Relations Committee to fight antisemitism and defend Jewish interests, a Bureau of Kashruth to supervise the butchers, and a Youth Council for leadership training, as well as a number of administrative, planning, and charitable bureaus. The council indicated the possibility for creating potentially strong centralized coordinating bodies in a society where the constituent organizations themselves lacked much strength.[50]

In 1951, invigorated by the arrival of thousands of newcomers, the council built its own "giant" community building on the site of the former Pantages estate on the west side of Los Angeles. Five-ninety North Vermont became the central address of the organized Jewish community. The large, modern facility (albeit without air conditioning) proclaimed the Jews' communal coming-of-age in Los Angeles and symbolized the community's growing assertiveness and visibility. The decision to install a dairy kitchen in the building's cafeteria similarly represented an effort to implement the solidarity implied in the council's motto of unity (*achdut*). Not all of those involved appreciated the "commendable" effort to cater to the religiously observant minority. Some of the workers protested the decision and petitioned for meat, claiming to need protein at lunch.[51]

Though eastern observers might think that the council resembled the Americanized form of the *Kehillah*, the traditional European Jewish communal structure, Los Angeles leaders adamantly insisted that it "is not now and never will be a Kehillah organization." In their eyes a Kehillah implied control by an elite, a rigid communal structure that tolerated no deviance but followed Orthodox religious strictures rather than an open, democratic body. One participant-observer who grew up in Boston, Charles Zibbell, saw the council as a rallying point designed to dramatize the oneness of Los Angeles Jews. Zibbell simultaneously characterized the council as young, virile, flexible, experimental, but also unstable, undisciplined, lacking in tradition, and sometimes without law and order—in short, possessing all the virtues and vices of the frontier. Annual meetings in the postwar years were "a thrilling experience in Jewish communal democracy; with the milling of the crowds that turn out for the meeting, the electioneering that goes on, the 'slates' that have been prepared by Labor Zionists or Hadassah or B'nai B'rith, one gets a feeling of the genuineness of the participation of mass Jewish membership organizations in the life of this body." William Bruck recalled that "in the early days we had guys like Chaim Shapiro, who used to get up in front of the L.A. Jewish Community Council and harangue and speak in Yiddish. It may be that a considerable number of people did not understand," Bruck admitted, "but those who did loved it." The Los Angeles Jewish Community Council provided a substantial counterweight to the German Jewish elite entrenched in several established philanthropies.[52]

Miami's Jewish reality diverged from the communal world of Los Angeles. Miami lacked entrenched interests and contained just the bare bones of organized Jewish communal life: a handful of Reform, Conservative, and Orthodox synagogues, a few local sections of national Jewish organizations, a YMHA split into Beach and Town branches, several charitable enterprises, and a modest central federation.[53] Efforts to establish centralized and coordinating institutions faltered despite the small number of organizations. The Jewish community of Miami suffered from conditions of newness, competition among its leadership, and the boomtown mentality. "Fortunes are made (and lost) quickly. Graft and corruption are common. 'Deals' are a constant topic of conversation, with promotions and investments being considered by everybody," observed one visitor in 1954. The newcomers' presence aggravated the situation. As late as 1960 the newly arrived executive for the Greater Miami Jewish Federation, the central coordinating organization, could barely contain his dismay at the meager level of services and support offered by the organized Jewish community. Arthur Rosichan, who had thirty-four years of experience in social welfare work, dismissed the extenuating circumstances of Miami's newness. "If Miami is a pioneer community, then this community does not compare with the pioneer communities' tradition of venturesomeness and of open-handed generosity," he exclaimed.[54]

The Jewish community presented a picture of extraordinary fragmentation. "When one speaks of 'the Jewish community' in this area, the question that remains is 'which community?'" queried one frustrated analyst. "Are we speaking of the transient and unrooted community of visitors and the semiretired or retired?" he asked. Or "are we speaking of the frequently absentee owners who spend part of their year engaged in resort businesses in Miami and the rest of the year in other parts of the country?" Perhaps one should ignore the snowbirds and retired. If so, "are we speaking of those who have come to Miami to make it their permanent homes but who may leave quickly if a business opportunity opens elsewhere or if they accumulate sufficient capital to be able to leave?" Manheim Shapiro continued: "Are we speaking of those professionals who have established offices and clientele in this area and who will probably remain for the rest of their lives? Or are we speaking of 'an organized Jewish community?'" The numerous possibilities provoked enormous frustration. "This community does not think in terms of ideology," wrote another northeastern observer. "The community is still new, varied and anxious to get ahead. It has no tradition of long standing so that the basic elements of ideological quarrels are missing or shelved in favor of a constructive job." Nothing seemed to hold the Miami Jewish community together.[55]

Such a fractured community with its permanent tourist mentality opened up generous leadership possibilities for all who desired them. It did not guarantee, however, that these leaders could produce followers, let alone impose discipline. "In a community where 'old timers' are people who have lived here for more than five years," Seymour Samet remarked, "new leaders spring up every day. Many of these are frauds, bigots, reactionaries, communists, or just plain fools. Others," the area director of the American Jewish Committee admitted, "are people of unusual intelligence." While it was "comparatively easy" to rise to a "high position of nominal leadership within a year or two after arrival," there were no traditional channels of leadership. Newcomers found few precedents impeding their efforts to introduce a wide array of communal activities and organizations. Observers coming from highly organized Jewish communities found Miami's chaotic openness disturbing. "Any group is free to organize or to express itself within the already organized community organizations," complained Shapiro. "This manifests itself in such phenomena as the sudden springing up of new congregations which are likely to dissolve equally quickly with a public conflict between an unpaid rabbi and the congregation or with a summary dismissal of a rabbi."[56]

Both Miami and L.A. encouraged individual and collective entrepreneurship in communal endeavors. Just as many migrants moved in search of opportunity, a handful of ambitious Jewish communal professionals made the same move in pursuit of congregants and members. An elite of ideologically committed easterners came to Los Angeles after the war. Some wanted to establish branches of their institutions and solicit support among Hollywood's wealthy producers. Others desired to take over the leadership of Los Angeles's innovative centralized communal institutions. Moshe Davis, the young dean of the Teachers' Institute of the Jewish Theological Seminary (JTS) in New York, recalled the atmosphere of a typical parlor meeting in the home of Julius and Mollie Fligelman. The Fligelmans actively supported an array of Jewish causes. "Their home was extraordinary," Davis remarked. "It was like a Hassidic wedding, where they take a hall and put people on the first floor, the second floor, the third floor and the fourth." On this occasion, "as people walked in, they were assigned to the room where their particular case was going to be presented. Julius was on one side of the entrance and Molly on the other, hugging everybody. When I walked in," Davis continued, "there was Teddy Kollek sitting on the floor of the living room making his speech. It was the pre-'48 period; the State was being formed." Kollek, later mayor of Jerusalem, was raising funds for the Haganah, the Jewish defense forces in Palestine, at the same time that Davis was seeking support to establish a branch of the seminary in Los Angeles.[57]

Among the first of the professionals to settle in Los Angeles, Samuel Dinin left his position as professor of education at the Teachers' Institute of JTS in 1945 to head the Bureau of Jewish Education. Dinin already possessed many years of experience in Jewish education in New York City. A graduate of City College, Columbia University, and the seminary, he joined the staff of New York's pioneering Bureau of Jewish Education. There he worked with some of the most influential figures dedicated to creating a totally new type of American Jewish education. He subsequently served as principal of Marshaliah Hebrew High School, as director of the labor Zionist youth movement, Habonim, and as executive secretary of the Reconstructionist Society for the Advancement of Judaism. Dinin's substantial background revealed his ideological commitments to Zionism, Reconstructionism, Conservative Judaism, and new forms of Jewish education designed to produce a genuine American Jewish leadership. Yet after more than twenty-five years in Jewish education in New York City, Dinin decided to go west, to seek greener pastures and new opportunities.[58]

Abraham Gannes made a similar trek down to Miami in 1944. Unlike Dinin, Gannes was just beginning his career in Jewish education, and Miami provided a challenge to the ambitious young educator. Gannes saw an opportunity to implement the latest theories in Jewish education. Since Miami had so few Jewish schools, he could develop an intellectual framework for Jewish learning, establish standards, and give Jewish education the centrality he thought it deserved within the American Jewish community. Gannes created an integrative umbrella Bureau of Jewish Education in Miami and encouraged the rapidly growing community to organize a Hebrew high school to nourish an elite of knowledgeable Jewish leaders.[59]

A process of self-selection drew Jewish communal professionals to Miami and Los Angeles. Most were eager to build an institution according to their own vision. They wanted to create new forms of American Judaism, to use a rapidly growing community as a laboratory for innovation. The notion of starting from scratch excited them. They saw in the absence of well-established institutions the opportunity to rise to a leadership position by redefining their organizations as central and constitutive of Jewish identity. Like their fellow migrants, they did not come to prestigious jobs; rather, they came to positions with potential, albeit often with substantial salaries.[60] Most confidently assumed that they could produce the prestige and influence. A few wanted to implement ideas that had germinated in the northeast but needed an expanding, open society in which to flourish. Occasionally some came merely to transplant institutions or as a means of leaving work that had become unsatisfactory. When Bertram Gold, five years after he completed his study of Jewish community centers, moved out to Los Angeles in 1954 to direct the Jewish Centers Association, he transferred his previous experience in Newark and Essex counties. He took the metropolitan model of "centralized decentralization" that he had developed to cope with the impact of suburbanization in New Jersey and applied it successfully to the sprawling residential patterns of Los Angeles. Such people as Gold often stayed only long enough to accomplish their goals before they returned to the Northeast.[61]

During the war leaders of the Los Angeles Jewish Community Council, anxious to insure the continuity of generations through Jewish education, invited one of the most distinguished Jewish educators, Alexander Dushkin, to come west to survey Jewish education in Los Angeles. Dushkin incisively depicted the current inadequate situation, including the small fraction of students enrolled in Jewish schools, the few years most continued their studies, the poor level of preparation of teachers, and the outdated curriculum. Aware of the unfolding European holocaust, he stressed the need to build for the future and closed his report with an appeal to Los Angeles's Jews. "Upon this generation of American Jews has been imposed an historic task," he wrote, "that of creating new cultural and new communal institutions, new social tools, which will make possible the development of the great new center of Jewish life in America. An effective democratic Jewish educational system is an essential instrument for creating that American Judaism," he explained. "Our Jewish schools in the new American home must be worthy of our spiritual and cultural heritage, and worthy too of the warm heart and democratic dream of America."[62]

The destruction of European Jewry prompted Los Angeles Jews to confront in stark terms the hopelessly inadequate education offered to their children. Unable to rely upon the vast reservoirs of European Jewish learning and culture, Jewish leaders in L.A. turned to New York as an alternative for help and guidance. Aware of the need to foster a Jewish identity in their children, especially in a milieu that did not encourage collective consciousness, the council was prepared to hand the chairmanship of the bureau to Peter Kahn, a socialist radical who nonetheless knew Hebrew well and was committed to Jewish education. The man who saw the dawning of a new Pacific era accepted the challenge and the position with the understanding that the council was dropping its historic opposition to supporting Jewish education. As Kahn pointedly observed, "Certain Council members used to think that Jewish education was 'unAmerican' and led to socialism."[63] Such opinions, in light of the Holocaust, now became untenable.

Ambitious leaders like Kahn recruited Dinin from the Jewish Theological Seminary. Dushkin had called for a bureau that set forth common educational principles and recognized the right of Jews to differ among themselves. Possessing a mandate for change, Dinin fashioned an integrative bureau that facilitated the cooperation of Orthodox and Yiddishist, Zionist and Reform, under one communal roof. "If, in the world as a whole, we are beginning to emphasize the need for thinking in terms of one world and one community, certainly in the affairs of any one Jewish community it is important to begin thinking in terms of one community and one school system," affirmed the bureau.[64]

Dinin expanded the bureau's network of schools, which had consisted largely of congregational afternoon Hebrew and Sunday schools, as well as a few *yidishe shule*, Orthodox talmud torahs, and Zionist Hebrew schools. He promulgated standards for teacher certification, established a salary scale for teachers with regular increments, started a pension fund, developed two programs of teacher training—one for weekday Hebrew schools and one for Sunday schools—and created a flexible curriculum for each category of schools under bureau auspices. He also introduced selected innovations in leadership training and in more intensive Jewish education. These included several weekday high schools, each one catering to a particular segment of Los Angeles Jewry: Orthodox, Conservative, Reform, and Yiddishist. Even the Jewish day school under Orthodox auspices was supported by the eclectic bureau and acquired a foothold in Los Angeles. Some disliked the new tolerance for diversity, be it conservative or liberal. Rabbi Maxwell Dubin of the prestigious Wilshire Boulevard Temple did not welcome changes brought by newcomers to his own Reform Judaism. "I do not like the influence that is being exerted on the Temple by Jews who recently came from the Eastern cities. I am not happy with the trend in modern Reform towards more ritualism," he complained. Others saw signs of progress in changes that came with the newcomers.[65]

Within a decade, the number of schools enrolled under the bureau's auspices grew from 12 to 123, and they accounted for approximately 80 percent of the students attending Jewish schools in Los Angeles. The bureau's budget increased, from $40,000 in 1944 to $290,000 ten years later. The funding marked a shift in communal attitudes in favor of Jewish education. "With the outbreak of World War II," recalled the president of the Hebrew Teachers Federation, "suddenly the walls of indifference of Los Angeles Jews toward Jewish education were breached and they awoke to the roaring voice of the thousands of new Jewish migrants that streamed to this city from the four corners of the country." Despite the newcomers' impact, two thirds of the children in Jewish schools in Los Angeles attended only Sunday school compared to one third in other large cities. A mere handful of teenagers took advantage of the more advanced Jewish education offered in the four new secondary schools. Nonetheless, Dinin struck an upbeat chord. In 1956 he saw "a hopeful sign" in "the remarkable growth" of secondary and postsecondary education in Los Angeles. The city "is fast becoming an important center of Jewish learning which will soon rival in significance the accomplishments of other Jewish communities in the United States," he predicted. Los Angeles Jews were ready to assume the mantle of diaspora leadership that fell upon them in the wake of the Holocaust and to accept the imperative to create a new Jewish learning keyed to America's democratic ethos.[66]

Miami's tiny wartime Jewish population lacked visionaries like Kahn; it was too small an outpost of Jewish settlement to provide them with sustenance. Yet because its local leaders also turned to New York for assistance, they adopted an almost identical Jewish education program. Desiring to help the handful of congregational schools and establish some coordination among them, Miami's Jewish federation leaders invited a leading educator, Israel Chipkin, down from New York to evaluate the education offered Jewish children. Chipkin proposed a model of coordination and supervision that respected congregational differences and accepted congregational schools as the primary educational unit. Synagogues sponsored these schools under their auspices usually as a service to their members. He recommended Gannes to implement the proposals, and Gannes succeeded in setting Miami's Bureau of Jewish Education on a constructive path.[67]

His successor, Louis Schwartzman, continued efforts to set standards and then to raise them, to provide some secondary education in a Hebrew high school, to offer adult Jewish studies, to license teachers, and to introduce Hebrew language study into the University of Miami. Although no institutions of higher Jewish education were established in Miami, its Hebrew high school actually enrolled only fifty fewer students than did the several L.A. high schools combined. Miami, unlike Los Angeles, saw student registration at the primary level split almost evenly between afternoon Hebrew schools and Sunday schools, indicating that Miami Jewish children were receiving more intensive Jewish education. In 1958 Schwartzman introduced a novel program on television that offered weekly Hebrew language lessons every Thursday evening. The popular series soon became a permanent fixture and enjoyed a wide audience.[68]

The remarkably similar programs of the Bureau of Jewish Education in Miami and in Los Angeles reveal how national leaders like Dushkin and Chipkin responded to local initiative not only by preparing a critique of the present and a blueprint for the future but also by encouraging the recruitment of ambitious and committed professionals. Gannes and Dinin welcomed the chance to shape communal policy on the frontiers of Jewish life and to put into practice values and ideals nurtured in New York City. They both championed communally supported, eclectic, and tolerant educational bureaus that encouraged cooperation and respect for Jewish diversity. Both valued intensive Jewish learning and tried to create venues where the gifted few might be inspired to pursue advanced study. Each saw the field of Jewish education as appropriate for pioneering, yet their actions reflected a tourist mentality. Both men abandoned the bureaus for greener pastures once they had implemented the initial recommendations, leaving the more routine administration in the hands of competent but less visionary professionals. Dinin, however, stayed in Los Angeles because that booming city promised more mobility and influence than he could hope to achieve in New York. Gannes didn't wait for Miami to keep growing but returned to Philadelphia, ready to face the challenge of a large, established Jewish community.

Even as its numbers soared, local Miami leaders looked less to challenge New York for leadership of American Jewry and more to achieve prominence as the best place to campaign among American Jews. Such ambitions befit its realities. Miami Beach regularly tripled its population during the peak winter season. Increasingly, national Jewish organizations booked their annual conventions in Miami Beach, and the United Jewish Appeal (UJA) held important, star-studded events to launch its yearly fundraising drives. As wealthy Jews from throughout the nation vacationed on the Beach, fund-raisers discovered that they could reach many of the most influential givers from such diverse cities as Chicago, Cleveland, New York, Philadelphia, Boston, and Detroit in addition to affluent Jews from smaller cities like Hartford, Baltimore, and Pittsburgh. Relaxed, enjoying the sunshine, and spending money, Jews visiting the Beach were more likely to give generously than when they were busy and harried at work. But like the ostentatious style of vacationing popular on Miami Beach, Jewish fund-raising drives eschewed subtlety. One observer likened the aggressive, high-profile campaigns of the national agencies to the descent of "beasts in a jungle." A United Jewish Appeal professional agreed: "Miami was a battleground." Marty Peppercorn recalled that "we used to campaign to a point where chances of Miami being anything as a Federation were very limited." Local federation leaders representing Miami's organized Jewish community could hardly compete with such intensely pressured fund-raising.[69]

The fund-raisers spent their time trying to locate the vacationing Jews. Recalling his efforts on behalf of the UJA, William Weinberg noted that "we worked during the day . . . and at night we also went to the various hotel lobbies after dinner to see who was sitting around smoking a cigar." Describing the lengths of ingenuity he regularly used, Weinberg continued, "We even went to race tracks and one of the greatest race performances of all time took place. We were there,

but we didn't see it because when everybody stood up we were looking for people in the audience and the horses were running behind
us!" The best way to locate Jews was to learn who was coming to town
for a vacation. Weinberg regularly would ask to see a hotel's advance
registration list. "I used to shmear the clerk and he used to bring
cardex files into the men's rooms and I would copy the list right there."

Once he located a wealthy prospect, Weinberg pursued him assiduously. One day Weinberg accompanied William Rosenwald of Sears,
Roebuck to meet Nathan Cummings of Consolidated Foods. "In the
morning when we got there, Mr. Cummings was not in. 'What do you
mean he's not in?'" Weinberg queried. "'We have an appointment.'
'Well, he's not here.' 'Where is he?' 'Sorry, we don't know.' So I said
to Bill, 'Let's go down to the Beach Club.'" After they broke through
the cabana of the private club, they were rewarded. "Standing there
in all his glory on the sand was Nate Cummings, wearing a white
bathing suit with a gold stripe on the side of it. When he saw us,"
Weinberg recalled, "he went into the ocean. Bill Rosenwald, wearing
a three-button suit and a vest and a tie and pants took off his shoes
and walked right into the ocean after him."[70]

In both cities Jews faced the challenge of creating a Jewish home
for the next generation who would be native Angelenos and Miamians. Children growing up in Miami and Los Angeles might take these
newfound paradises for granted and forget earlier struggles to survive. Those who found their roots among the subdivisions of the San
Fernando Valley, in the mountains of Beverly Hills, North Hollywood, and Santa Monica, along the broad streets of Beverly-Fairfax
and West Los Angeles, and in the winding roads of Miami Beach or
the subdivisions of Westchester, Coral Gables, and Northeast Miami
might forget the terrors of the cold world and harshness of the new.
Under the bright sunshine of Miami and Los Angeles, a sense of Jewishness might seem less necessary. The question of identity appeared
to be a matter of personal choice, not a compelling issue.

Yet an awareness of difference lingered. Sometimes Jews associated it with religious identification: Many children knew that they were
not Christian; hence, they were a minority. Other times the difference appeared to be an ethnic matter of culture, food, or politics,
though few children inherited their parents' brash exuberance bred
in the intensely Jewish neighborhoods of the cold northeastern cities.

Especially on Miami Beach with its predominant Jewish population, Jewish ethnicity persisted.

Growing up on Miami Beach, Ronald Kronish had "no concept of such a thing as a non-Jew." As a rabbi's son, he lived in a totally Jewish society; all of his friends were Jewish, and he felt completely comfortable as a Jew. Although he was vaguely aware of antisemitism at some country clubs, this knowledge did not impinge significantly on his outlook. For Kronish, Miami Beach was an insular Jewish world, a golden ghetto, an island shtetl. He rarely bothered to cross the bay, visiting Miami only for occasional basketball games or to go to the coffeehouse at the University of Miami that featured folk singers. Across Biscayne Bay in the Shenandoah section of Miami, Harriet Sadoff Kasow also could recall no antisemitism. Two of her mother's brothers and sisters lived around the corner, and Uncle Max came down regularly each winter with his large family and stayed in a Beach hotel. They had a cousins club, and Harriet remembered feeling that New York was not far away. "I thought I was a New York Jew," she admitted. Growing up in Miami, she recalled its freedom, the freedom of a small town. She rode her bike to school, played tennis in the park two blocks from her house, and used the "good bus service" to go to her evening job at Jordan Marsh.[71]

Los Angeles lacked the concentration of Jews that existed in Miami Beach, so Jewish ethnic sensitivity was more muted. Growing up in Beverly Hills, one knew it wasn't 100 percent Jewish, "but it felt like it was," a resident recalled. For some, like Dena Kaye, this sense of ethnic distinctiveness appeared to be mainly culinary. "All of my Jewish friends ate rye bread with mustard and there was one non-Jewish boy in the group that I went around with and he . . . used mayonnaise on white bread, and we used to call him 'mayo,'" she remembered. "Jewish foods, I think, are the most important part of growing up," Judith Nelson Drucker affirmed. She moved down as a teenager to Miami from New York in 1941 when her father decided to retire early from the garment business. "In those days, you couldn't get delicatessen in Miami. . . . So whenever my father would go up to New York, he'd come back with a big box of salamis." She concluded that they were important: "We identified with the salami." On Sundays, she recalled, it was a tradition that "the whole family came to our house . . . and there was huge whitefish and noodle puddings and lox and bagels." For Judith and her three brothers, the food and the family fellowship around the table defined their Jewishness in Miami and linked them to Jews in New York.[72]

Politics kindled an ethnic sensibility in other Jews. Fay Kanin lived on Westwood's Loring Avenue with her family. Built by her father-in-law, her home was a replica of Cary Grant and Katherine Hepburn's dream house in the movie "Bringing Up Baby." She remembered Westwood as "the neighborhood for the young liberal writers." Maurice Rapf had a house around the corner, and there were the Panamas, the Franks, Betty and Milton Sperling, and Oliver Schwab and Johanna, in addition to two doctors, David Marcus and Harold Bernstein. When the children were young, the parents formed a cooperative nursery school in Marcus's backyard, hired a teacher from nearby UCLA, and took turns as volunteers. Kanin recalled that they all shared the same liberal politics, a common enjoyment of their work as Hollywood writers, and the sense that they could really make a difference in the world.[73]

Schools helped to bridge the physical and psychological distances separating Jews in L.A. They provided some continuity for children, who often picked up cues regarding their identity in school. Although Jewish students rarely constituted the majority in any Los Angeles public school, they did make up an increasingly visible plurality in certain high schools. In 1953 Fairfax High School, known for its large Jewish student body and high academic standards, introduced a course in modern Hebrew language. Ronnie Tofield, principal of the Hebrew school in the Beverly-Fairfax Jewish Community Center, taught the class. Within a decade Beverly Hills and Grant high schools joined Fairfax in offering modern Hebrew classes. Grant drew students from the San Fernando Valley. Its tracking program placed many college-bound Jewish students in the same classrooms, making their presence more visible than numbers alone would warrant. Robin Rheingold recalled liking the Hebrew class at Grant, taught by Miriam Wise, wife of the rabbi of the Valley Jewish Community Center. "She was teaching Hebrew, yes, but it was a lot of history, too." These courses signaled a positive assertion of Jewish culture and represented an active desire on the part of parents and children to regain their roots and strengthen their Jewishness in their new surroundings. The introduction of Hebrew was an extraordinary

After they had moved to Miami or L.A., Jews would remember street scenes of their childhood as typical of the "old home." Pitkin Avenue in Brooklyn, Brownsville's Main Street, is busy with crowds in front of Hoffman's cafeteria, a favorite gathering place in 1937. (*Courtesy Collections of the Municipal Archives of the City of New York*)

In 1940, Miami Beach's modest South Beach section was a world away from Pitkin Avenue, yet vacationing Jews inadvertently brought their Brooklyn mores to the sun and sand. Christian residents frowned on picnicking and wearing street clothes on the beach and on bringing baby carriages there. Sensitive to criticism, the Anti-Defamation League tried to guide Jewish tourists regarding proper beach attire and behavior. (*Courtesy Acme, UPI/Bettmann Archives*)

When the Army Air Corps turned Miami Beach into a training ground during World War II, it introduced many servicemen, including Jews, to the pleasures of this vacation paradise. (*Courtesy Mosaic, Jewish Museum of Florida*)

Coming down to visit family in the military, Jews got "sand in their shoes" and decided to stay awhile. Miami's bright, modern hotels along Ocean Drive in 1940 captivated them. The sunlight, space, and palm trees suggested heaven on earth compared with the cold, gray cities of the northeast. (*Courtesy Acme, UPI/Bettmann Archives*)

The post–World War II revelations of Nazi genocide profoundly changed the self-perceptions of American Jews. When they returned home from wartime service, many who had seen the horror were determined to build a new Jewish world. American military personnel with former prisoners and victims at the Buchenwald concentration camp soon after liberation in 1945. (*Courtesy YIVO Institute for Jewish Research*)

Newcomers to Miami responded to the plight of Holocaust survivors and efforts to rescue them. Understanding the will to start a new life, they were especially receptive to the struggle to establish a Jewish state. Golda Meir (*neé* Meyerson) with (*l to r*) Stanley Myers of Miami, president of the Council of Jewish Federations; Henry Morgenthau, Jr., national chairman of the United Jewish Appeal; and New York Governor Herbert Lehman, at the first UJA phon-a-thon in 1948. (*Courtesy Mosaic, Jewish Museum of Florida*)

Jews of all types migrated to Miami Beach after the war. Jewish gangsters found lucrative gambling opportunities in the burgeoning tourist industry. A few, like underworld leader Meyer Lansky, gave money to the Jewish community and received recognition for public-spirited endeavors. A stained glass window in the sanctuary of Beth Jacob synagogue, one of the oldest in Miami Beach. (*Courtesy Mosaic, Jewish Museum of Florida*)

Migration brought young and old. Here, two generations of the Weiss family sit outside their home in the Royal Apartments in the 1950s. Most of the migrants came from northeastern and midwestern cities; approximately 40 percent were New Yorkers. Some settled down while others became "snowbirds," spending the winter months in Miami. (*Courtesy Mosaic, Jewish Museum of Florida*)

Jewish newcomers generated business opportunities, and entrepreneurs sought to develop a market among them. Advertising "Florida" in Yiddish and English, an enterprising grower, W. G. Roe, used this label on citrus crates in the 1940s to capture Jewish customers for his oranges and grapefruits. (*Courtesy Mosaic, Jewish Museum of Florida*)

פלאריד'א

FLORIDA GRAPEFRUIT & ORANGES

W.G. ROE & CO INC. SHIPPERS

WINTER HAVEN, FLORIDA.

Jewish entrepreneurs with experience running resorts in the Catskills came down to Miami Beach to expand its tourist industry. The hotels lured Jewish visitors to the golden city and a life of leisure. Perhaps the epitome of extravagance, the Fontainebleau Hotel capped a decade of frenzied building that made Miami Beach an icon of American popular culture. (*Courtesy Lake County [IL] Museum/Curt Teich Postcard Archives*)

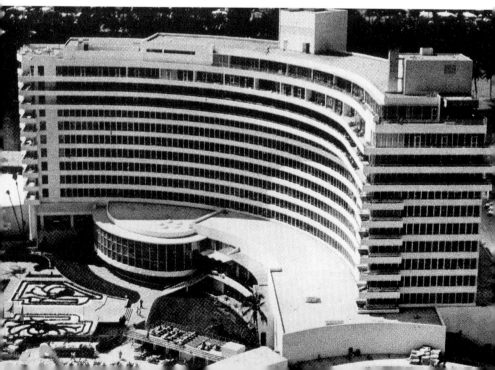

Tens of thousands of Jewish newcomers transformed Miami Beach in the decade after the war. With money in their pockets from postwar prosperity, they sought a taste of paradise on earth and helped to make a vacation in Miami Beach part of the American dream. This aerial view looking north up Collins Avenue, lined with one luxury hotel after another, shows the advanced development of Miami Beach's Gold Coast by 1957. (*Courtesy UPI/Bettmann Archives*)

In the 1950s when few married Jewish women worked outside the home, young Hadassah women volunteered to recruit members in the organization's annual door-to-door campaign to help build the Jewish community at home and in Israel. The rootlessness of new arrivals in Miami Beach made Hadassah membership rolls balloon. (*Courtesy Mosaic, Jewish Museum of Florida*)

Rabbi Irving Lehrman of the Miami Beach Jewish Center on Washington Avenue and 17th Street wanted the synagogue's gold dome to outshine the hotels' glitter. Lehrman tried to make a place for Judaism within a leisure vacation world by fashioning religious observance into a form of spiritual recreation. (*Courtesy Library of the Jewish Theological Seminary of America*)

Rabbi Leon Kronish hoped that Temple Beth Sholom's modern architecture would dramatize its contemporary and liberal form of Judaism to those seeking religious roots. Kronish blended commitment to Israel and social justice with innovative ritual in an effort to appeal to diverse Jewish newcomers to Miami Beach. (*Courtesy Lake County [IL] Museum/Curt Teich Postcard Archives*)

Despite the strenuous efforts of Rabbi Lehrman to convince Jewish parents to give their daughters the same level of education as their sons, boys predominated in afternoon Hebrew school classes in the 1950s. Transmitting a Jewish heritage and identity to children growing up in a vacation paradise challenged Jewish spiritual leaders. (*Courtesy Temple Emanu-El of Greater Miami*)

event in this western outpost; only a handful of eastern school systems included it among their modern languages.[74]

Schools gradually acquired reputations linked to the character of their student body. Because it drew upon the heavily Jewish neighborhood surrounding the school, Fairfax became known as a Jewish high school. Those parents uncomfortable with the tone set by Jewish students occasionally transferred their children into schools with fewer Jews. Jewish students similarly dominated Miami Beach Senior High School by the 1950s, a dramatic shift from the previous decade when wealthy Christian students set the tone. "The important kids there were the Gentiles who belonged to the Surf Club and the Bath Club," Judith Nelson Drucker recalled. "We found out before long, in those days, that you really couldn't get into the social world, because it was barred to Jewish people." When Jewish students became a majority, Gentile parents regularly took their children out of Miami Beach Senior High School.[75]

Across the bay Jewish parents responded in an analogous fashion. They usually sought out a high school with more, rather than fewer, Jewish students. Throughout the 1950s parents avoided Coral Gables High School, using pupil transfer to send their sons, and especially their daughters, to Miami Senior High School. The refusal of the high-status girls' service clubs to admit Jews as members made Jewish teenagers feel uncomfortable. Their parents recognized that college-bound youngsters needed to accumulate extracurricular credits. Being blackballed from a service club could hardly be entered on a high school transcript. Jews made up a sizable minority of Miami Senior High School; in the advanced classes they sometimes formed a majority. Many of them socialized together in "LJ" (Little Jerusalem), a small patio of the Spanish-style school building.[76]

More significant than social discrimination practiced by service clubs and high school sororities and fraternities were Christian religious practices in the schools. In Miami daily Bible reading, usually from the New Testament, and daily recitation of the Lord's Prayer, as well as annual elaborate celebrations of Christ's birth at Christmas and the Crucifixion and Resurrection at Easter, reminded Jews of their differences from their Christian fellow students. In 1953 first graders in a special demonstration school in Miami came home singing "Jesus Loves Me" and "Onward Christian Soldiers" to their parents' distress. But parents hesitated to complain; many were intimidated and looked to Jewish leadership for help. Occasionally, enterprising Jewish students found their own solutions. Forced to attend daily Christian chapel services in a private school, David Hudson started wearing a mezuzah around his neck in seventh grade. Another Jewish student, elected president of his senior class at North Hollywood High School and required in that capacity to give the invocation at the vespers service before graduation, brazenly chose to recite the *Sh'ma*, the Jewish affirmation of faith in God and God's oneness—in Hebrew and English.[77]

Jewish holidays also created an awareness of difference. "I never knew about the High Holidays until I got to public school," David Hudson admitted. "I had always gone to private school," he recalled. "When in ninth grade I got to public school suddenly someone said, 'Are you coming to school tomorrow?'" David didn't know why he wouldn't be coming, but "they said it was the High Holidays and suddenly I thought that was a big deal." When he asked his parents, "Do I have to go to school tomorrow?" they said no. Another student at Grant High School remembered that on the High Holidays "the Jewish kids would empty out of school and a lot of the non-Jewish kids would not come."[78]

The principal and teachers at Grant took a laissez-faire attitude to the Jewish sacred calendar, but the Los Angeles school board deliberately ignored it. In 1947 and again in 1958 and 1961, the Los Angeles school system scheduled the opening day of school and student registration on Rosh Hashanah. In a blistering editorial, "Hit 'Em When They're Little," Samuel Gach attacked the school registration policy of the Board of Education as bordering "on the type of negligence that needlessly opens the board to a charge of malice." With overcrowded kindergartens the board decided to register students strictly on a first-come, first-served basis until all the places were filled, despite Jewish protests. The Community Relations Committee of the Los Angeles Jewish Community Council regularly distributed free calendars with the dates of Jewish and Christian holidays to the L.A. city and county school boards, as well as to principals and teachers. Such efforts to educate the educators generally failed to sensitize them to accord respect to Jewish holidays.[79] One evangelist in Miami attacked a similar distribution of Jewish calendars over the radio. He condemned the calendars with their list of Jewish and other holidays as a "nefarious attempt to impose Jewish customs on a Christian world."[80]

Jewish parents in Miami also encountered difficulties when they requested permission for their children to be absent on Jewish holy days. Even when the principal of a school was Jewish—as was the case with Miami Beach Senior High School—Jewish students were pressured to provide proof that they had spent the holy day in synagogue and not on the beach. Alan Weisbard remembers the principal of the local junior high school, who also served as principal of a synagogue religious school, regularly patrolling the beach in the afternoon of Sukkot, to see if any of his students were enjoying the sun and sand. At such moments Weisbard didn't know which hat the man was wearing. Keenly aware of Protestant norms of religious observance, these Jewish educators were uncomfortable with secularized Jewish practices and embarrassed when their students were seen taking the holy day as a holiday.[81]

Israel's existence and the crises that periodically afflicted the Middle East impinged on the consciousness of Jewish students. The Suez crisis of 1956, the Eichmann trial in 1961, and the Six-Day War of 1967 often touched the lives of Jewish teenagers. Though she was only ten years old at the time, Harriet Sadoff Kasow remembers sitting in the backyard under the orange trees and listening to the radio. In that peaceful setting, while her mother cranked the laundry through a ringer, they heard Israel declared a state. But her early images of the Jewish state came from watching Zionist films, shown as part of the High Holiday program for young people, at the Syrian and Lebanese social club located across the street from Beth David synagogue. Although many did no more than debate the issues, a few were stirred to action or deeper reflection. "The thing that I remember" about the Six-Day War, David Hudson recalled, was "a real sense of pride among the students, the Jews, even the kids who weren't particularly religious. . . . As it progressed I remember that people began to listen [to the radio] with great interest, much more than high school kids would normally follow current events." Israel's presence stimulated an awareness of a larger Jewish world, even as occasional trips back to the Northeast or Midwest to visit relatives made young Jewish Angelenos and Miamians realize the distinctiveness of their childhood world.[82]

A survey of the predominantly Jewish student body at Miami Beach Senior High School offers a glimpse into the experience of growing up Jewish on Miami Beach in the 1960s.[83] Only 70 percent of the students lived at home with both their parents. The survey uncovered a high Jewish divorce rate of 20 percent. Half of the students lived in single-family homes, and the other half lived in apartments, testimony to the continuing attraction of high-density living among Beach Jews. Despite their relative rootedness—only 25 percent had moved within the past five years—over half regularly left Miami Beach during the summer months. Some attended summer camps in New York and Maine; others visited relatives in the Northeast or went to the Catskills. This pattern may have contributed to the expressed desire by a full quarter of the students to seek work and a home in the Northeast after finishing their education. Perhaps some of these students, like Kronish, came to object to the Miami Beach Jewish identity of their childhood. Kronish especially rejected its crass materialism and flashiness, the eager pursuit of wealth along with all of the symbols of having made it.[84] The affluence of the students' families registered in the fact that 70 percent of the students did not work after school and 25 percent owned cars exclusively for their own use. The students also came from highly literate homes—80 percent reported that their parents subscribed to at least one magazine, and over 20 percent noted over eight magazines in the house (the median was five). Their parents were well-educated: 44 percent of the fathers and 25 percent of the mothers had graduated from college. Despite their education, literacy, and affluence, fewer than 40 percent reported family membership in a synagogue.

A plurality of students, 30 percent, were born in Florida; the second largest contingent, 25 percent, came from the mid-Atlantic states, and another 16 percent were born in New England. Most of the students were third generation with native-born, albeit not Florida-born, parents; only 12 percent reported that their father was born in Europe. The students were very bright and motivated. They ranked well above the national norms in standardized tests. A tiny fraction, 3 percent, dropped out of school, while 75 percent went on to college and university. Over half of the student body—girls as well as boys—expressed ambitions to become professionals. The majority of their mothers did not work outside the house; unlike them, only a small minority of girls intended to be housewives.[85] Despite these impressive percentages, one student recalls that an anti-intellectualism dominated Miami Beach High School. The honors students weren't "cool," to excel academically was not an "in" thing to do. The rich kids set the tone, and what counted for them was clothes and cars and planning the next party. The popularity of teenage "house parties" during the 1950s suggests the significance of socializing and the impact of Miami's tourist culture. Zionist and B'nai B'rith youth groups rented hotel facilities for a period ranging from a day to a week at the end of the school year so that their members could spend their time and money partying away from home.[86]

The rhythm of life in the setting of a leisure world retained its peculiar magic for parents who settled in Miami and Los Angeles. After all, memories of the old country—the cold and intense cities that they had left behind—endured, and occasional visits home kept them vivid. What these Jews discovered and rediscovered in Miami and Los Angeles was intoxicating. Here was the opportunity to develop a life, a Jewish life, in the tranquil "context of complete freedom."[87] Where some saw a world without limits, others saw rampant anarchy, but no one denied the opportunity. But uninhibited freedom rarely meant roots. Most migrants remained permanent tourists, finding in the home of their childhood the source of their identity. They left the burden of developing roots in the foreign soil of Miami and Los Angeles to their children, who grew up with a freedom to choose—and to innovate—that their parents had scarcely imagined.

Looking back, a few regretted the loss of constraints. "Los Angeles is a culture in disrepair in many ways," the lawyer Howard Friedman reflected. "And I think it needs, if you want to really transmit values, it needs a steady, a structured way of doing it." Friedman didn't provide that structure for his children because, at the time, neither he nor his wife "were sufficiently sensitive to the importance of it," he concluded. "In the past, Jewishness was absorbed by young people as they grew up in Jewish community and family environments," argues Sandberg. "No parental decision was involved in the creation of a sense of Jewish identification in the young person's growing identity and self-image. They were immersed in a culture where Jewish language, behavior, and symbolism developed as automatic responses. . . . Today," he concludes, referring specifically to Los Angeles, "most Jews have grown up without the support of such a community." Under the bright sunshine of Miami and Los Angeles, Jewishness ceased to be "a matter of natural inheritance." It became, instead, a matter of choice.[88]

Jewish migrants chose Miami and Los Angeles in order to bask in balmy weather, take advantage of economic opportunities, and escape from constraining intergenerational intimacies of parents and kinfolk. The principle of self-selection that initially had guided them continued to influence them when they settled down. Jews transformed themselves into individuals acting out of free choice, and they made their new cities into open communities without clear boundaries, hierarchies, deference, structures. Jews continued to act and think as newcomers, assuming that they were starting from nothing. But in a post-Holocaust world individual redemption was not enough. However, in groping for something more—an ethnic persona—the old ways would not do. Thus, they created new patterns of Jewish communal life that upheld the centrality of the consenting individual. Long before converts to Judaism adopted the label "Jews by choice," newcomers to Miami and L.A. had transformed Jewishness into a matter of one's choosing. They posited a Jewishness rooted in the future, in peer group sociability, in shared values, and in personal choice, all linked to powerful but distant surrogates—the old neighborhood that was disappearing and the Jewish state of Israel that rose like a phoenix on the ashes of the Holocaust.[89] Only their children took this permeable community and its understanding of Jews as permanent tourists for granted.

4
Seeking Religious Roots

Here there are no vested interests, here there are no sacred
cows, here there is no cold hand of the past. There is an
opportunity to develop new forms of Jewish communal
living geared in a realistic fashion to the actual needs of the
Jewish community.

—CHARLES BROWN
Head of the Los Angeles Jewish Community Council, 1952
(quoted in Max Vorspan and Lloyd P. Gartner,
A History of the Jews of Los Angeles)

As Jews pulled up their roots and turned their backs on the old home
and neighborhood to migrate across the continent, many left their
parents' religious traditions behind, those familial religious and ethnic practices that seemed an integral part of the northern urban life
and territory. Some, growing up in secular Jewish households, had
only known religious tradition from their neighbors and the synagogue down the street. Others remembered sabbaths and seders
from childhood in another time and place. Upon arrival in the open
golden spaces of Miami and L.A., these childhood religious traditions
seemed less appropriate, more of an anachronism. As one self-styled

upper-middle-class San Fernando Valley Jewish mother explained, "Our children know and appreciate their heritage, but the realities of university academic competition, part-time jobs and family and household obligations cannot be ignored. Nor can my husband and I set aside the rigorous full-time effort we must put forward to provide the home, education and general lifestyle we've chosen for ourselves" in order to "return to the kind of practicing Judaism we knew as youngsters. Anyway," she cheerfully confessed, "let's be really honest and admit that those practices were forcibly imposed upon us by our parents, and this was the case for most of our peers."[1]

Jews in Miami and L.A. embraced a kind of rootlessness that proved even more pervasive than the upbeat confession of one San Fernando mother would suggest. Their apparently casual abandonment of religious tradition left them more open to an innovative personalism and eclecticism than would be countenanced by their more rooted relatives in the Northeast and Midwest, many of whom also discarded parental religious traditions. The permanent tourist mentality bred insecurity as well as the sense that every day was a holiday; it undermined the significance of religious traditions by changing their social and cultural context. In the diffuse and loosely structured Jewish communities of Miami and L.A., communities that lacked any real authority, those seeking religious roots necessarily engaged in an individual, personal quest, not a collective endeavor.

Without familiar institutional guides or fixed patterns of living derived from close-knit Jewish families and neighborhoods, newcomers turned to new and ambitious leaders eager to teach and inspire them. A handful of religious entrepreneurs felt the magnetic pull of Los Angeles to be irresistible. Like their fellow Jewish migrants, they liked the atmosphere—often discovered during a stint as chaplain in the armed services—and sought to escape stifling family ties. Many of these young rabbis were more liberal than their peers and possessed a flair for showmanship, a skill vital to those who wish to attract widely dispersed people with no institutional loyalties to join a congregation. They saw in the City of Angels a market economy in religious culture that encouraged inventiveness and salesmanship and placed few restraints upon them. Self-reliant, flexible, and self-confident, they knew how to mobilize people to build a congregation around themselves. Seeking new lives for themselves and dissatisfied with established rabbinical patterns of behavior and belief, they were eager to break out of the rabbinic mold that had been established in the Northeast. Many also were willing to take risks, to experiment with new forms of Judaism, to start with the individual and his or her desires, to craft religious practices in response to the needs of their rootless fellow newcomers.[2]

In the freewheeling atmosphere of Los Angeles, Jews invented new religious traditions and rediscovered old ones. Denominational distinctions common between Orthodoxy and Conservatism, and Conservatism and Reform lacked clarity in L.A. In the Northeast and Midwest, Orthodoxy's emphasis upon the immutability of sacred law, the divine character of the oral and written Torah, and the necessity of upholding ritual observance—especially separate seating of men and women in the synagogue—set it apart from Conservatism, which stressed the changing character of Jewish law, evidenced a willingness to modify ritual observance through mixed seating, and staunchly supported Zionism. Reform championed modernity, rejected most rituals and laws as outdated, argued for a form of Judaism without an ethnic dimension, and took a non-Zionist posture.[3] But in L.A., where Jews were unconstrained by the past, an easy eclecticism took hold, based in more congenial peer group structures than in traditional hierarchies. Rabbis mixed old and new, invented and restored, to see what would work, what would attract other Jews, what would bring people into the fold.

As a new generation of pioneer rabbis settled in this outpost of American Jewry, they transformed the prevalent rabbinic image by their flexibility and adaptiveness to the new climate. The older view considered L.A. a desolate place where only desperate circumstances would force a rabbi to settle. Jews used to joke that the only rabbis who were attracted to such a city as Los Angeles—known for its clean air, offbeat society, meager numbers of Jews, and lackluster Jewish religious life—were those with either one lung or two wives. Nevertheless, the arrival of thousands of newcomers every month created enormous opportunities for empire building and changed L.A.'s reputation into an attractive one. Most rabbis who came, however, departed from patterns of rabbinic leadership established in the Northeast. Los Angeles was still a town for the rebellious and outrageous.

Los Angeles's preeminent rabbi, whose unbroken tenure at the city's most prestigious Reform temple gave him enormous prominence within the community, viewed many of the changes brought by newcomers with alarm. He disdained the innovations and eclecticism, the mixture of ethnicity and religion that characterized the newcomers' search for religious roots. A blunt, outspoken man, who personified a type of rabbi rarely found in the northeastern and midwestern centers of Jewish life, Edgar Magnin of the Wilshire Boulevard Temple looked back at the changes since the end of World War II. "This is a different ballgame today," he told reporters; "you've got another Brooklyn here. When I came here, it was Los Angeles." Magnin had more than the Dodgers' franchise in mind. Were the Jewish mores of Brooklyn infesting the palm trees of Los Angeles? The newcomers' persistent and public search for a Jewish identity in the era of ethnic revival irked Magnin. "I see these guys with their yarmulkes eating bacon on their salads at the [Hillcrest Country] club. They want to become more Jewish, whatever that means. It's not religious, it's an ethnic thing. What virtue is there in ethnic emphasis?" he asked. "You know," he concluded, "it's insecurity, the whole thing is insecurity. Roots, roots, roots—baloney!"[4]

Magnin's outrageous and improbable juxtaposition of yarmulkes and bacon spoke to potential contradictions in the newcomers' experimental and eclectic approach. Associating yarmulkes with visibly orthodox, ethnic, east European, and, for Magnin, Brooklyn Jews, he scoffed at the inappropriateness of eating any food in a tref (unkosher) country club.[5] But in Los Angeles who possessed the authority to say that such contradictions mattered?

Rabbis with a vision welcomed the challenge of an unformed Jewish community and its religious contradictions. They saw an opportunity to unify Jews and develop a community around a synagogue. Their vision usually included distinctive traditions, which they designed and nurtured. Once they glimpsed the possibilities of shaping their own congregation, they found it hard to leave; they were "built into the bricks," as one rabbi put it. Under these circumstances, the identity of rabbi and congregation gradually merged. "[I have] become too involved with too many people in the life of Temple Isaiah," Rabbi Albert Lewis wrote, trying to explain to Maurice Eisendrath, the head of the Reform Union of American Hebrew Congregations

(UAHC) in New York City, why he was turning down a much more prestigious position with a Detroit congregation. "Essentially it is a close-knit group and many of us have been working together for more than five years. We are just now at the fruition of a part of our program as our Temple nears completion. We have laid plans for the future and these people are looking to me to carry them out." The intimacy and commitment, the opportunity to lead people who really cared and who depended upon a spiritual leader, and the potential to shape a meaningful Jewish religious community from scratch tempted young, imaginative, and aggressive men more than did traditional paths of professional mobility in the established communities left behind.[6]

Miami too had the attraction of being practically virgin territory for eager young rabbis. Its promise enticed in particular three who left their strong imprints on the community's religious life. Irving Lehrman, Joseph Narot, and Leon Kronish successfully built distinctive synagogues and crafted a Jewish tradition that spoke to their congregants' rootlessness. Despite their allegiance to different religious ideologies—Narot to Reform, Kronish to a version of Reform that he called Liberal Judaism, and Lehrman to Conservatism—the synagogues they created exhibited surprising similarities. Kronish and Lehrman arrived during the war, a few years after the founding of the congregations they came to lead. They began, as it were, from scratch. Narot came after the war to the oldest, and for many years the only, Reform congregation in Miami. All initiated and oversaw the physical, spiritual, and educational institutions in which to shelter and sustain their congregations.

These three rabbis presided over substantial construction programs, determining thereby the physical appearance of the synagogues and their attached schools and community buildings. All three assiduously pursued members. Kronish organized his temple into "congregational commandos" to enlist unaffiliated Jews. Lehrman regularly carried membership blanks in his pocket, prepared, for example, to sign up new members at a *simha* (a festivity). As membership grew, so did the programs offered by the congregations. That the rabbis were remarkably effective preachers was attested to by the crowds that regularly came to hear them. Each used his pulpit as a base to participate in the wider world of city and national affairs. All three expected to become leaders of American Jewry as had their mentor, Stephen Wise, yet their individual stories reveal widely different values, styles, and outlooks.[7]

Lehrman arrived in Miami in 1943, thirty-two years old and fresh out of rabbinical school. The son of Abraham Lehrman, an Orthodox rabbi, Irving graduated from the high school program of the Orthodox Rabbi Isaac Elchanan Theological Seminary (RIETS) and studied at City College.[8] He married Bella Goldfarb, daughter of a prominent Brooklyn rabbi. Despite the presence of ten generations of rabbis in his family, Lehrman initially decided to go to law school. However, drawn by his father's friendship with the Talmudic scholar Chaim Tchernowitz, Lehrman entered the Jewish Institute of Religion (JIR), the rabbinical school established by the liberal Zionist rabbi Stephen Wise. Wise had designed the Jewish Institute of Religion to train rabbis for all Jews, across the denominational spectrum, but few fully observant Jews studied there. The institute emphasized Zionism and Jewish peoplehood, especially the common ethnic bonds uniting Jews despite their religious and ideological differences, and encouraged in its students an openness to religious innovation and a disregard for denominational labels. Students tended to model themselves on Wise, and like him, they imagined the rabbinate as committed to Zionism, the Jewish people, and social justice. The school's flexibility provided ideal training for pioneering among Jews without religious roots.[9]

Wise's close connections to the Miami Beach Jewish Center brought young Lehrman to the attention of leading men in the congregation who wanted a Conservative rather than an Orthodox synagogue (at least they wanted men and women to sit together). Invited to apply for the position—but only on the condition that he pay his own way down to Miami Beach for the interview—Lehrman agreed to take the gamble. He arrived in August with his wife and two children and never left.[10]

Lehrman rapidly began to shape the congregation. Most of the men came from immigrant Orthodox backgrounds familiar to him. Financial success in business encouraged them to embrace a more modern traditionalism. As observant Jews and accomplished businessmen, they wanted their synagogue to blend Jewish traditionalism and American success. Lehrman decided to steer toward Conservatism, a middle path between his father's Orthodoxy and his liberal rabbinical training, a choice that would be especially acceptable to his congregants. He started the late Friday evening service that had become a hallmark of Conservatism. Earlier the congregation had only held a traditional Friday eve service before the festive Sabbath meal. Now they enjoyed Lehrman's persuasive sermons and a musical service that occurred after dinner, extending the joyful Sabbath spirit. On Shabbat Shuva, the sabbath of return that falls between the High Holidays of Rosh Hashanah and Yom Kippur, he introduced the Conservative prayer book in place of the Orthodox *siddur*. Its more contemporary English translation of the standard prayer service signaled the congregation's new modern posture.[11]

Lehrman's engaging good looks and effective oratory drew one hundred additional members to the center within a few months of his arrival. One early congregant, who grew up in Brooklyn, remembered how she fell in love with him as a young woman. "Pearls came out of his mouth!"[12] Lehrman initiated popular breakfast services for teenagers on Sunday morning in an attempt to foster a peer group community within the synagogue's orbit and to inspire adolescents to become committed Jews. An enthusiastic congregation raised his four thousand dollar salary after two months in appreciation of his unanticipated success.

By the end of the year, Lehrman elicited a commitment from his congregants to build a synagogue north of 14th Street, in the affluent part of Miami Beach where the synagogue's dome would stand out as a religious symbol among the glitter of the hotels.[13] The men of the synagogue, threatened with Lehrman's departure if he did not get his way, pledged $200,000 toward the million dollars needed.

When the war ended and the center unveiled its plans to build a new synagogue, Lehrman came under attack for misguided priorities. How could a synagogue launch a major fund-raising drive at a time when Jewish survivors in the DP camps desperately needed help? Although shaken by the attacks, Lehrman defended the drive. Those who give to build a synagogue would be the same to give to rescue survivors, he argued. One gift did not preclude the other. The sermon was effective, but the controversy reflected the sometimes conflicting pulls of past and future, Europe and Miami Beach, on these pioneering communities. Trying to build anew, they were often seen as self-absorbed and indifferent to the past. The epic struggle for nationhood, by contrast, galvanized Jews in Miami Beach; Zionist rhetoric inspired thousands as well as politicizing and secularizing their faith. Beside such an heroic battle to rescue survivors of the Holocaust languishing in DP camps and bring them to the newborn State of Israel, a drive to build a bigger synagogue paled in comparison. The Miami Beach Jewish Center moved into its impressive new synagogue on Washington Avenue and 17th Street in 1948. Further construction and fund-raising occupied the leadership throughout the 1950s due to the ever-expanding Jewish population and the synagogue's increased membership.

Lehrman's influence could be measured by the constant construction of elegant facilities for worship as well as for festive events and even meetings, or by the crowds that snaked around the block waiting with their tickets to get in to hear him preach on Friday evenings, or by the steadily increasing numbers who joined the synagogue, or by the life tenure awarded him by a deeply grateful congregation—all signs of Lehrman's success in building a Jewish religious community within the brief span of the postwar period.[14] Seeking to establish Judaism in America's popular playground, Lehrman made synagogue life an acceptable leisure activity for Jews in Miami Beach, both residents and regular visitors. After an elegant meal at one of the many restaurants on the Beach, well-dressed congregants strolled over to the synagogue to hear Lehrman preach on topics of the day. Others joined many of the clubs sponsored by the Miami Beach Jewish Center, including a popular little theater group that "included people from all walks of life, rich and poor."[15] Its entertainments extended the synagogue's reach, bringing both secular and religious leisure activity under congregational auspices.

One of Lehrman's most significant innovations concerned the position and education of women within his synagogue. Here Lehrman worked with Bella, his wife, who helped to pioneer a distinctive role for the rabbi's wife beyond her traditional supportive position. Prewar Conservative congregations had taken tentative steps toward expanding the religious participation of women and enhancing the education of girls. Lehrman went further and encouraged his congregants to treat the supplementary Jewish education of their daughters with the same seriousness as that of their sons. If he was going to build anew, he would incorporate the postwar appreciation of women as active workers in all causes and missions. Man's work, even in such a domain as the synagogue, which traditionally excluded women from active participation, was no longer for men alone. Lehrman reminded members that "the Jewish girl of today is the Jewish mother of tomorrow and it is most important that she receive an intensive education." At the beginning of the school year, which corresponded to the start of the Jewish year, Lehrman regularly urged: "Give your children a Jewish education! Do not disinherit them from the wealth of knowledge and tradition that is rightfully theirs!" Education, he noted, offered children "stability by giving them roots!"[16]

Educating girls and boys together implicitly diminished traditional distinctions between the roles of men and women in Judaism. Women played a secondary role in Jewish public religious observance; the home was their religious realm. But intensive education without participation in synagogue ritual suggested empty promises. Though boys continued to outnumber girls in the afternoon Hebrew school, Lehrman moved toward equality of women within the synagogue.[17] In 1952 he instituted a custom of asking the entire congregation to rise on *Simhat Torah* during the Torah reading, in contrast to the usual practice of calling individuals to receive that honor of an *aliyah* (literally, "going up"; that is to read from the Torah). The entire congregation then repeated the blessings said by one given an *aliyah*, and as Lehrman explained, each member should consider himself or herself personally called to the Torah in the Jewish tradition. To his surprise he received a letter of thanks from Bess Gersten for the "thrill" of having been called to the Torah for the first time in her life. Gersten also enclosed a check for fifty dollars, the usual practice upon receiving such an honor.[18]

Later that year the congregation celebrated its first bat mitzvah, a new religious ceremony for girls modeled on the bar mitzvah ritual for boys who reach the age of thirteen. A bat mitzvah recognized the accomplishments of girls in mastering a more intensive educational program by honoring them within the synagogue and inviting them to accept their religious responsibilities as Jewish adults. Among the first to become bat mitzvah was Marjorie Friedland, daughter of the synagogue's president, a major supporter of Lehrman and the center. Despite the encouragement, only a devoted few gave their daughters a bat mitzvah though all parents wanted their sons to become bar mitzvah.[19] The introduction of so radical an innovation occurred as the men leading the congregation debated whether to continue the venerable practice of *shnoddering*, or bidding competitively for the honor of an *aliyah*.[20] Thus, old and new, tradition and innovation, coexisted at the center.

Lehrman wanted his congregants to pray, to *daven*, to become intoxicated with Judaism. He wanted them to embrace a personal spirituality. He started a junior congregation run by children at the school, in which "the girls, too, have an opportunity to participate." He admitted that he was "envious" of the thirty thousand young Christians who turned out for a Miami revival meeting of Billy Graham's Youth for Christ movement "to participate in a most moving demonstration of prayer." Lehrman compared Graham's movement to "our synagogue youth organizations . . . our young people who are given all sorts of lectures and forums and discussion groups—everything except good old-fashioned prayer." Despite the attraction of Protestant evangelicalism, Lehrman stopped short of transforming his congregation into a center of fundamentalist fervor. Crowds of four thousand on the High Holidays was his limit. Yet his recognition of a deep need for Jews to find meaning in a Judaism that spoke to them as individuals, comparable to the personal spirituality of Protestant evangelicalism, suggests how attuned he was to what might motivate his fellow permanent tourists in Miami Beach.[21]

If he eschewed a crusading pietism, he and Bella did try to teach congregants the art of Jewish living. They sought, that is, to instruct women in the kind of experiential spirituality associated in the past with the woman's role in Judaism. Through women they hoped to spiritualize the entire family. By the 1950s it was apparent that mothers, previously responsible for home ritual, no longer knew what to do. Somehow—perhaps through neglect or disinterest, perhaps as a result of migration—women had lost the skills to celebrate home rituals. The pious home had all but vanished in this city by the sea. Prodded by the rabbi and his wife, the religious school PTA and synagogue sisterhood sponsored workshops explaining how to observe holidays at home. The workshops demonstrated how to set the table, what food to cook, what blessings to say. Women learned by actually doing. The workshops began with the Hanukkah holiday with its focus on children, but soon expanded to include Pesach (Passover), with its elaborate home seder ritual, and Rosh Hashanah.[22]

Bella Lehrman introduced into the center a novel and entrepreneurial institution: the sisterhood gift shop. The gift shop addressed simultaneously several congregational needs: It provided a steady source of income for the synagogue; it made available ritual objects not easily purchased in Miami; and it helped to link the congregation's younger and older married women. It encouraged as well the development of the women's business skills because running the gift shop required knowledge of purchasing, bookkeeping, and merchandising. Since very few married women worked in an era that promoted women's domestic nature and role and many had maids to help take care of housework, the gift shop provided a rare workplace outside the home for their entrepreneurial energies and skills. Many Jewish women actively sought such volunteer work.[23]

The women running the gift shop sold merchandise that they thought would appeal to other women, their target audience, as the chief purchaser for the household, but they also tried to expand their customers' repertoire of ritual objects. Jews do not actually need all of the ceremonial objects that they possess, although many reflect a desire to beautify ritual activity. Most of the required items—like *tallit*, the prayer shawl, and *tefillin*, the small leather boxes holding scriptural inscriptions that are strapped with thongs to the forehead and arm—belong in the almost exclusive domain of men. The gift shop encouraged Jewish women to change their attitude toward ritual objects, to see them as decorative, functional, and experiential. Women were invited to explore a world of possibilities opened up by postwar affluence, to beautify their homes with Jewish symbols. A pair of silver candlesticks, for example, might decorate a mantlepiece during the week, hold a pair of candles, and even stimulate a woman to kindle and bless the sabbath lights. The shop enhanced the art of living Jewishly even as it contributed to the buying and selling of Jewish culture.[24]

The shop highlighted the commonality of Jews, a people with its own crafts and decorative arts. It became a means to showcase Israeli ceremonial and art objects, linking Israel to American Jews by encouraging women to consume these products of the new Jewish state.

Like a miniature museum, the shop displayed artifacts of Jewish culture. Visitors to the shop implicitly learned that Judaism concerned itself with aesthetic issues. The shop's location within the synagogue symbolically placed a religious seal of approval upon its contents. For some a gift shop visit became part of a ritual associated with the synagogue or with shepherding children to religious school. A purchase satisfied both the customer and individual who received the present, creating a Jewish network linking them with the synagogue. The profit from sales contributed to a worthwhile congregational endeavor, such as the synagogue library.

The shop began, as did the workshops, with Hanukkah and bar mitzvah, offering gifts of toys, books, and records for children, jewelry from Israel, and items to decorate the house.[25] It soon expanded to include bride's Bibles and kiddush cups for weddings, tie clips and ID bracelets for bar mitzvahs, Israeli menorahs and art objects, and cookbooks for the housewife. By the late 1950s the gift shop contained such elegant items for the home as sterling silver trays, candy dishes, and Israeli coffee spoons that had merely tangential Jewish symbolic significance. In addition, it included specialized ritual objects used only by more observant Jews, like silver spice boxes for the *havdala* ceremony marking the end of the sabbath and matzo covers for Pesach. With an eye on the ornamental, women also bought mezuzot, small cases holding scriptural inscriptions that are placed on door lintels to fulfill a religious commandment, and spice boxes to decorate their home. But the shop never became exclusive in its merchandise and continued to carry such American inventions as Jewish New Year's greeting cards and personalized Bar Mitzvah napkins. The wide range of items available for purchase, in terms of cost, quality, and religious culture, suggested the diversity of commercial Jewish symbols and the eclecticism of popular piety. Although not an exclusive feature of the Miami Beach Jewish Center, the sisterhood gift shop found a broad audience in this innovative and adaptable community because it offered types of portable, symbolic insignia of roots that newcomers welcomed.[26]

A year after Lehrman found his place in the sun, Leon Kronish and his wife, Lillian, arrived in the "spiritual wilderness" of Miami Beach. A New York native like Lehrman, Kronish also graduated from JIR. Unlike Lehrman, neither he nor his wife came from a rabbinical family, although like Bella, Lillian was a college graduate. Without the pull of parental orthodoxy, Kronish moved easily toward liberalism, not conservatism. When he came to the Beth Sholom Center, it had perhaps forty members in good standing. The fledgling synagogue had been established only three years earlier, and despite its name, which meant "house of peace," it was weakened by internal conflict. The handful of founding members, like those of the Miami Beach Jewish Center, thought, but could not agree, to have an Orthodox-Conservative congregation. They hired Kronish in the summer of 1944, and by the fall he was telling the first general congregational meeting of the new year that they were "a Modern Conservative Jewish organization."[27]

Like Lehrman, Kronish immediately made an impact upon the congregation. A tall, handsome man and a persuasive speaker with a good sense of humor—he often began his sermons with a joke—Kronish rapidly attracted followers. He regularly greeted each congregant after services and quickly learned the names of all. Within a few months one hundred new members joined—the new rabbi actively solicited them—and by the spring Kronish was encouraging the board to give the center a more specifically religious name.[28] With the change from Beth Sholom Center to Temple Beth Sholom came a commitment to become a "liberal congregation" that would guarantee freedom of the pulpit.[29] The congregation minutes suggest that Kronish desired to follow his mentor Stephen Wise's path to Reform Judaism, accompanied by a strong commitment to Zionism, Jewish peoplehood, and social justice. During the summer Kronish returned to New York City, charged by the temple's religious committee with purchasing prayer books published by the Reform UAHC. Despite the decision to become a liberal congregation, members continued to quarrel over whether that actually meant what the label *Reform* implied. Many associated *Reform* not with liberalism, social justice, and openness but with elitism, non-Zionism, and a religious service devoid of Hebrew that resembled high-church Protestantism with its organ music, strict rules of decorum, and formal quality of worship.[30]

The issue of denominational labels irritated Temple Beth Sholom throughout the 1940s. Although Kronish urged the board to affiliate with the UAHC, several men resisted the stigma associated with *Reform*.[31] They preferred *liberal* because it lacked the ideological freight associated with *Reform*, especially Reform's long opposition to Zionism and the establishment of a Jewish state, a position that had changed only under the pressures of World War II. Kronish, however, carried his congregation into the Reform Union.[32] When issues arose that might have aligned Temple Beth Sholom with more Conservative practices—such as how many days of a Jewish holiday to observe—Kronish persuaded the board to follow Reform custom, though he rarely justified his argument by referring to Reform authority.[33] By the 1950s, once the hurdle of affiliation was overcome, Kronish pointedly referred to Temple Beth Sholom as a liberal congregation, not a Reform one, since he, too, disliked Reform's lukewarm support of Israel.

Kronish gradually began to give both form and substance to *liberal* through the Friday night and Sabbath services and an extensive educational program. The late Friday eve services were largely in English, accompanied by an organ and dominated by the sermon. After the crowds departed, Kronish and his family, often with a few of his devoted followers, would go to Juniors Restaurant, located on Collins Avenue not far from the Temple, to discuss the sermon, an indication of the vigorous debate and enthusiasm generated by the young rabbi. Saturday mornings Kronish reserved for a more traditional service that included the weekly reading of several chapters of the Torah as well as a sermon, or *d'var Torah*, designed to explain some aspect of sacred scriptures; he also used more Hebrew prayers in that service. The congregation left the decision regarding the wearing of prayer shawls up to individuals but insisted that anyone ascending the pulpit for the honor of an *aliyah* don one.[34]

Kronish started to experiment with the religious content of such holiday services as Shavuot, which celebrates the time when the Israelites received the Torah from God at Mount Sinai, and Purim, which commemorates the Jews' rescue from an antisemitic pogrom. For Shavuot, he wrote a cantata on the theme of Israel Reborn; for Purim he crafted a new megillah, that is, he retold the story found in the biblical Book of Esther in a modern idiom. Kronish also experimented with the popular holiday of Hanukkah, writing a poetic dramalogue. Touched by the positive response to his innovations, he thanked his congregants for their "understanding spirit which makes possible these creative experiments in religious worship." Many of the men leading Temple Beth Sholom were second-generation Jews, familiar with religious changes introduced by Conservatism during the interwar years. Thus they accepted the young rabbi's innovations and supported his efforts to develop "a dynamic ritual that is traditional in spirit, rich in Jewish warmth, and liberal in form." Kronish wanted to create a new *minhag*, or rites, for American Jews, that would be the substance of a religious ritual "that would win the hearts of the masses." Miami Beach, with its cross section of Jews drawn from all corners of the United States, provided an ideal setting for such an ambitious national endeavor. Kronish rapidly filled the temple to capacity, supervised a successful building expansion program, and received recognition from the Miami Jewish community.[35]

Given his articulate and self-conscious religious liberalism, Kronish moved openly and rapidly to enhance the status of women within the congregation. He instituted some innovations even a few years before Lehrman did. Although an early proposal that women be guaranteed places on the board of directors did not change the congregation's governance, Kronish announced in 1948 a special bat mitzvah class. "Mothers are the cornerstone of the Jewish family," he explained. "Women, too, are becoming more prominent in Jewish community life. To provide intelligent leadership and to equip our girls for these responsibilities, we are instituting this year a special BAS MITZVAH program" with a newly designed ceremony. The following year, when members complained about the presence of women on the pulpit during the High Holidays, he recommended that they enroll in his adult education classes to learn the reasons behind Beth Sholom's practices.[36]

Lillian Kronish, like Bella Lehrman, introduced a sisterhood gift shop and holiday workshops. The gift shop started in 1947 with presents appropriate for bar mitzvahs, weddings, holidays, and, of course, Hanukkah. "Gracious Living Means Giving," the sisterhood advertised. "Make it a habit to choose your gifts at the Sisterhood Gift Shop." The shop was open daily from nine to five and on Sunday mornings when children came to school. Holiday workshops began the same year. The rabbi helped guide families in planning their own home seder for the second night of Pesach, following the congregational seder on the first night. He urged members to "make Passover an unforgettable experience, a joyous experience, a family get-together. Children will subconsciously know that God and Israel, freedom and family joy are all one." Herein lay the true art of Jewish living, an experience that was joyous, spiritual, homey, and aesthetically appealing.[37]

Kronish practiced what he preached. "Undoubtedly, the most lasting legacy that I have from my father, the educator, is that Jewish education begins in the home," recalled his daughter. In describing her childhood home, Maxine Kronish Snyder portrayed the art of Jewish living that the rabbi and his wife tried to inspire in their congregants. "The walls, with the Jewish art and books, convey Jewish learning and Jewish feeling; the music on the stereo is Jewish, and it has helped link us to our roots in Europe and Israel," she wrote; "the conversations at the Shabbat and holiday meals are experientially Jewish, and they helped us keep Judaism, Israel, and especially Jerusalem, uppermost in our minds; the kitchen"—not a kosher one but Jewish nonetheless, "where my mother has always been in charge—is intensely Jewish, not just in its delicious foods and smells, but also in its human atmosphere, brimming with caring, concern and sensitivity." This vision of the Jewish home as the source of Jewish spirituality animated efforts to educate Jewish women. Maxine considered herself "fortunate" to have been able "to learn and experience" as she grew up "the power and value of a Jewish education that is centered in an intensely Jewish home."[38]

Given the similarities of the synagogues that Lehrman and Kronish built—of Temple Emanu-El (the more religious name adopted by the Miami Beach Jewish Center in 1954) and Temple Beth Sholom— wherein lay the differences? Jews living on Miami Beach during the 1950s used to point to the fact that worshipers needed a ticket to attend Friday night services at Temple Emanu-El whereas they could just walk in to the services at Temple Beth Sholom. Indeed, Beth Sholom made a commitment to such democratic practices part of its creed. An early membership brochure affirmed: "We demand that [the synagogue] be Democratic. That means an equitable dues system."[39] It also meant no financial barriers to membership, no assigned pews, and no tuition fees. Temple Beth Sholom's modern low-profile brick buildings, recessed from the street, physically expressed similar liberal democratic sentiments and presented a contrast with the tall, elegantly appointed buildings of Temple Emanu-El, especially its multistoried, domed synagogue that sat diagonally at the corner intersection.

The Jewish religious ideals of the congregations also differed, reflecting their rabbis' perspective. In 1948 Temple Beth Sholom published in its bulletin a definition of a good Jew. Such a person was impatient with the sociopolitical ills plaguing society and eagerly sought remedies for them. The definition assumed both marriage and family because it listed educating one's children Jewishly as part of being a good Jew. The good Jew was seen to respond to the needs of his people, read Jewish books, and not be demoralized by antisemitism. Such a Jew is intelligently Jewish, affiliates with a synagogue, and has self-knowledge. Compare this to the Miami Beach Jewish Center's checklist for Jewish adults published in 1951. Its minimum rating scale of Jewish practice included a "fair knowledge" of synagogue ritual, familiarity with the background of Jewish observances, knowledge of general Jewish history, a "working knowledge" of Hebrew, and familiarity with Jewish music. A Jewish adult with this background ideally attends every sabbath service he can, enrolls his children in a Jewish school, reads at least five books of Jewish content each year, and fluently expresses ideas about Judaism. Finally, a Jew should both know and recite the kiddush and blessing for his children each sabbath eve. The concern with specific Jewish knowledge and ritual behavior versus liberal values and general Jewish commitment in part distinguished Conservatism from liberalism in postwar Miami.[40]

Despite these differences, not to mention those of style and temperament, Lehrman and Kronish had more in common with each other, especially their strong Zionist commitment to Israel, than they did with the third influential Miami rabbi, Joseph Narot. Ironically, Kronish and Narot joined the Reform rabbinical association, and both led congregations affiliated with the UAHC. Yet the two stood poles apart on many of the most important issues facing American Jews.

Narot came to Miami in 1950 at the age of thirty-seven with ten years of experience as a rabbi of a Reform congregation in Atlantic City. Born in a small town near Vilna, Lithuania, Narot grew up in poverty in Warren, Ohio. He received a traditional Jewish education from his Orthodox parents. In 1969 Narot looked back upon his life in an extraordinary sermon, a personal confession rarely made by rabbis before their congregants. The sermon revealed some of the motives driving these pioneering rabbis. Surveying the rows upon rows of over four thousand congregants gathered in the Miami Beach Convention Center on the eve of Rosh Hashanah, Narot began to preach.[41] "Where shall I begin?" he asked, addressing the thousands sitting before him. What have I learned from my life? "My parents never left the old world—spiritually speaking. They always referred to Europe as 'home'—'in der haym.' For that reason I thought that the gap between them and me was due to culture and language," he admitted. "Years later, when I confronted my own children, I learned how mistaken I had been." Narot rebelled against his father and his father's Orthodoxy. When he was eighteen, he discovered Reform Judaism and "took to it with the zeal of the convert." This zeal never abated. "Reform's fervor for social justice, its loyalty to all knowledge and experience, its readiness to innovate and modify, its faith in reason, filled my imagination."

But Narot confessed to more than a fervent devotion to Reform. He acknowledged as well that the Reform rabbinate promised a poor boy a way out of Warren and a chance to earn a decent livelihood. Narot characterized himself as "a self-made man," a vision that drew upon American frontier imagery but discarded any notion of tradition handed down through the generations, a notion that was critical to Jewish continuity and that Jews usually assumed animated their rabbis. Yet in Miami, a city without traditions and roots, Narot's vision of self-creation hardly outraged his congregants. Perhaps more shocking, he admitted learning "that a man can never get enough money. There is no end to the wanting of things." He confessed, too, "in my secret depths I have yearned to be the world-renowned rabbi and have even envied the acclaim which other colleagues seem to get." Such ambitions, appropriate to secular newcomers, rarely came from a rabbi. Narot's decision to confess his eagerness for fame and fortune, measured by conventional standards, set him apart from his northeastern and midwestern peers, who often championed learning, piety, communal service, and spiritual sacrifice as their motivation for serving in the rabbinate.

As the oldest and most prestigious Reform congregation in Miami, Temple Israel did not suffer from the chaotic conditions of newness faced by Lehrman and Kronish. When Narot arrived to take the pulpit there, he could build upon a solid base, and build he did. Like Lehrman and Kronish, Narot was a handsome man. (Good looks appeared to be a requisite for the Miami rabbinate; it certainly helped attract congregants). Narot expanded the Temple's membership, constructed new school buildings, and attracted increased attendance at Friday evening services—the main sabbath services for Reform congregations. He also strengthened Temple Israel's position as the representative Jewish institution to Miami's Christian religious world. Though in perhaps less dramatic fashion than the congregations on the Beach, Temple Israel grew rapidly under Narot despite heavy membership turnover typical of established synagogues. Measured by the same criteria of numbers, buildings, attendance, congregational support, and communal recognition used to gauge Lehrman's and Kronish's achievement, Narot's success was considerable.[42]

But Narot did not change the position of women or the education of girls. Temple Israel fixed minimal educational requirements of several hours once a week for both boys and girls that Narot considered appropriate. He steadfastly opposed using Jews' desire to see their sons become bar mitzvah as a means of encouraging them to give their children more Jewish education, and he attacked this process sharply, ridiculing such synagogue schools as bar mitzvah "factories." Similarly, the radically reduced home rituals of Reform, consisting of a festive meal on the High Holidays and, occasionally, Hanukkah celebrations, sufficed. There were no workshops in the art of Jewish living. Narot urged, instead, making attendance at Friday night services a "fashionable" weekly activity.[43]

Narot managed to leave his stamp upon the synagogue, a more formidable task than that faced by his Miami Beach peers since Temple Israel had a number of local traditions from its previous quarter century.[44] He adamantly adhered to the radical teachings of classic Reform Judaism, especially its rejection of religious ritual and Jewish law, its emphasis upon ethics and the primacy of belief in monotheism, its non-Zionism and lukewarm acceptance of Israel, and its opposition to Jewish ethnicity associated with the idea of Jewish peoplehood. He resisted congregants' efforts to give centrality to bar mitzvah, relegating Hebrew instruction to voluntary weekday classes. He also insisted that such religious symbols as prayer shawls and head covering for men be eliminated as they were in classic Reform temples. Finally, Narot championed the right of Reform Jews not to observe more than one day of each Jewish holiday, since classic Reform had eliminated the traditional second day. In sermons and in printed "letters to my congregation," Narot explained the modern vision of Reform Judaism, its rational religious message, its aesthetic and ethical ideals. Some members thought he apologized for Reform Judaism too much and that he was forever rejecting his own non-Reform origins. But perhaps this psychological spur gave his personal charisma its attractive edge.[45]

This hint of insecurity suggested the drive of the self-selected pioneer to carve out his own domain. Narot's passion for radical Reform was integral to his leadership. He could not take his faith for granted but abrasively and defensively wore it on his sleeve. When he went to the racetrack on Saturday—an unusual Shabbat activity for a Reform rabbi—he defended his sport as legitimate: "Relaxation and recreation must . . . be part of our Sabbath regimen, along with study, prayer, and synagogue attendance."[46] Indeed, his demand that congregants choose Reform as he had chosen it identified him as akin to Lehrman or Kronish in his desire to found a distinctive congregation in his own image.

In the mid-1960s Narot invited a well-known sociologist to survey Temple Israel's Sunday School, Miami's largest.[47] The survey delineated the Jewish values held by the students. Most essential, they said, was a belief in God, in order to be "a good Jew." This emphasis upon belief in God contrasted with the values encouraged by Kronish, who stressed the pursuit of social justice as critical, or by Lehrman, who focused on observing Jewish religious ritual. Neither Kronish's nor Lehrman's congregation bothered to include belief in God as part of their definition of a good Jew. Narot's students, however, learned effectively his interpretation of Judaism, for following their faith statement was an affirmation of identity, that is, accepting oneself as a Jew and not trying to hide one's Jewishness. The students ranked worshiping God, knowing the fundamentals of Judaism, attending services on the High Holidays, and leading an ethical life after these two fundamentals of being a good Jew. Over half thought it essential to gain the respect of their Christian neighbors, thus exhibiting Jews' traditional concern with their Christian neighbors' attitudes toward them. Other issues so central to the congregations of

Kronish and Lehrman, including support for Israel, synagogue membership, contributions to Jewish philanthropies, efforts in behalf of equality for all minority groups, and marriage "within the Jewish faith" received recognition as desirable but not essential.

Like the programmatic statements of the two Miami Beach congregations, this list faithfully reflects Narot's concerns and the values of radical Reform. Its focus on belief in God and one's social identity as a Jew, coupled with concern for basic Jewish beliefs and how Jews appeared before their Christian neighbors, indicates Temple Israel's distinctiveness in Miami.

Narot's dedication to Reform, Kronish's commitment to liberal Judaism, and Lehrman's attachment to Conservatism set these three rabbis apart, but their extraordinary ambition, drive, and success in the business of the rabbinate united them. They understood implicitly that in a town of rootless Jews, a rabbi had to be a showman to draw crowds into his synagogue. He had to offer Jews a social as well as a religious identity, political values as well as moral ones. They shared a similar vision of the place of the synagogue in Jewish life: It was a broad, all-encompassing, representative Jewish institution. And despite their different interpretations of Judaism, they imagined religion as spiritual recreation, an opportunity to enjoy learning and working together, men and women, boys and girls, the ideal complement to Miami's leisure lifestyle. These values distinguished them from many of their fellow rabbis but linked them with the characteristic rabbinic figures of Los Angeles.

Edgar Magnin, Los Angeles's leading rabbi for over half a century, was perhaps prototypical of the pioneer American rabbi. Born and raised in San Francisco, Magnin attended the University of Cincinnati and Hebrew Union College (HUC). Like Narot, he saw the rabbinate as a vehicle for social mobility; he wanted to be a Reform rabbi because "the class of people were more refined." Unlike Narot, Magnin inclined toward tradition and away from classic Reform. When Magnin came to Los Angeles in 1920 as rabbi of the city's leading Reform congregation, he opposed changing the Jewish sabbath to Sunday, an action that had been championed by several leading classical Reform rabbis. He consistently leaned toward Conservatism in the context of Reform and thus reintroduced abandoned traditions. Magnin restored the bar mitzvah ritual that classic

Reform had rejected in favor of a new ceremony of confirmation and reinstituted blowing the shofar rather than a trumpet on the High Holidays.[48]

Magnin built an impressive sphere of influence for himself. He oversaw the construction of an imposing new synagogue building with "proportions like a theater" on a prestigious site on Wilshire Boulevard, and he urged his congregation to change its name to the Wilshire Boulevard Temple. "I wanted people to know the location," he remarked. He socialized with his wealthy congregants, joining the Hillcrest Country Club at a time when no other rabbis were members in pursuit of the power and influence he needed to build his synagogue and its importance. A large, gregarious man who spoke colloquially, Magnin symbolized the rabbinate in Los Angeles for many years; most non-Jews knew of no other. Neal Gabler dubbed him "rabbi to the stars."[49]

Magnin spoke bluntly about his own singular accomplishment: over fifty years in one pulpit at a prestigious synagogue. His self-assessment and perspective offer insight into the values of pioneer rabbis and their contrast to prevalent American rabbinic norms. Magnin castigated the misplaced rabbinic agenda of the eastern establishment. At annual national meetings, he felt, rabbis discussed silly things like theology or Jewish survival rather than talking about the purpose of the rabbinate or how to succeed in religion, which was, to Magnin's way of thinking, a business like lawyering. When Jews go to a synagogue service, he explained, "they must come out touched. If they don't come out laughing or crying, then there's something wrong." He elaborated: "You should go *away* with some *feeling* of lift and some feeling of 'I'm glad I'm a Jew. There *is* something to life, some meaning.'" The rabbi produced this effect through his preaching. Magnin, who taught homiletics, saw the rabbinate as "a leadership job." It was his duty to inspire his congregants and give them pride in their Judaism, not to make pronouncements. He disdained those eastern "rabbis who compare themselves to prophets" as "idiots and phonies" and much preferred his own pioneering type of rabbi, who enjoyed the good life. Prophets, after all, "never received a salary, they never had a pension, they never lived in nice homes, they never ate at Perinos or the Bistro out in Beverly Hills."[50] Nor, one might add, did they ever go to racetracks.

Magnin's pragmatic and personal approach to the rabbinate did not preclude a commitment to more intensive and advanced Jewish education or to a more experiential form of Judaism than had traditionally been available in Reform. In 1954 he criticized Reform's tendency to become static and its failure to make demands upon its adherents. Under his guidance Wilshire Boulevard Temple continued to grow and to make new demands upon its members, especially its youth.[51] In the two most significant developments—the College of Jewish Studies and Camp Hess Kramer—Magnin recognized and encouraged the vision of another Reform rabbi eager to draw uprooted Jews into a community around the congregation, Alfred Wolf.

Wolf had come to Los Angeles in 1946 to organize the West Coast Region of the UAHC and collaborated with Magnin and other Reform rabbis in establishing the College of Jewish Studies, which was aimed at Reform Sunday School teachers and interested adults. In 1949 Magnin encouraged Wolf to initiate a camping program under Wilshire Boulevard Temple auspices. Wolf first discovered camping as a teenager in Nazi Germany. "Called upon to organize Jewish youth groups in Heidelberg," he reflected, "I realized how much of Jewish values I could get across to young people as we were hiking or camping together under the open sky." Exposure to American Protestant church groups' use of camp meetings confirmed Wolf's convictions that Jews could learn from them. That fall Wolf presented his idea for "camping in the spirit of Reform Judaism" to the temple's men's club. The men agreed to sponsor the program.[52]

While well established prior to World War II as a Jewish summer activity, camping under specifically religious auspices—especially sponsored by a synagogue—was a new, postwar innovation. Wolf recalled that "there was no tradition then of any temple activity after Confirmation."[53] Even a temple leader like J. Robert Arkush, head of the men's club and a supporter of the camp project, had difficulty convincing his daughter to go. Once the teenagers got to the primitive campsite in the Pacific Palisades, however, they discovered the friendship and closeness camp could engender. Their enthusiasm for camping convinced several temple members to provide their children with a decent campsite.

The decision to purchase property for a camp revealed a serious rift between those who saw religious school as ideal for Jewish youth and camp as a commercial gimmick and those who considered Sunday School ineffective and camp as an inspiring Jewish communal alternative. Wolf tried to mediate by suggesting that camp and school could complement each other. School provided "periodic religious reminders in an otherwise secular week" while camp represented the integration of Jewish "religious principles and practices with daily living."[54] It also allowed teenagers to remain connected with the temple after confirmation and it strengthened loyalty to Reform institutions. Despite lack of enthusiasm among some members, an absence of qualified camp directors, and the problem of time for supervision by the rabbis, the men's club directors in 1951 voted to purchase a campsite. The following year Camp Hess Kramer opened on 110 acres in Ventura County.

Magnin never spent a night at camp—he was a "Waldorf Astoria camper"—but he supported the venture. He thought that the camp provided an ideal setting to cultivate religious feelings. Several hundred campers and their counselors experienced Judaism within a surrogate home. "You can give the kids all the tools in the Religious School that you want," an early camping convert argued. "But until they actually have an opportunity to live what they've learned, they just don't get the relationship, they don't get the values. At Camp the kids *live* the Sabbath and they find out it works."[55] Some were inspired to participate more actively in temple educational activities and to exercise youth leadership after their camp experience. Occasionally individuals recruited for positions in camp moved over to full-time employment at the temple as youth directors, teachers, and even cantors. Camp also offered a venue for year-round conferences. Its separate incorporation as a temple subsidiary allowed it to initiate community projects that asserted Reform Judaism's importance in Los Angeles. In 1953 the camp started its annual interracial and interreligious weekend conference on human relations for university students and faculty. Camp Hess Kramer brought influence, personnel, leadership, and, of course, members to Wilshire Boulevard Temple.[56] Its creation expanded the synagogue's orbit as it taught youth how to be Jewish. Like gift shops and holiday workshops, summer camping under synagogue auspices sought to fill space left by absent religious traditions in Miami and L.A.

Facing the disruptive effects of migration, admitting the absence of a "natural" public Jewish environment in Los Angeles, and unable to depend upon transmission of a pattern of Jewish living by newcomers to their children, ambitious and pragmatic rabbis, eager to experiment, initiated novel programs to fit needs of potential members. On the way they built their own distinctive congregations, establishing their sphere of influence. They borrowed the idea of summer camps from youth leaders in Y's, community centers, and settlement houses, from innovative Jewish educators, from Zionists, Socialists, and Communists in order to nurture and incorporate their own youthful elite.[57] Camping under synagogue sponsorship would show Jews how to live as religious Jews by giving them at least a minimum ritual competence and allowing them to enjoy a Jewish spirituality. It would imbue youngsters with loyalty toward their brand of Judaism, a loyalty that might even extend beyond devotion to "their" rabbi. Though a rabbi like Magnin preferred Judaism without any Jewish ethnicity, camping inevitably introduced elements of shared sociability associated with a sense of family, belonging, and peoplehood.

Wolf's success in carving out his own domain under the institutional umbrella of Temple Wilshire was unusual—a tribute both to his and Magnin's abilities. Magnin's willingness to share his power was exceptional. More often, an ambitious rabbi coming to Los Angeles built his own synagogue and imprinted his personality on the institution. As did their peers in Miami, most Los Angeles rabbis yoked their congregations to a national denominational movement. A few tried to promote what they considered to be a unique Los Angeles vision.[58] "Since its inception the Valley Jewish Community Center has refused to adopt any label other than that of 'Jewish,'" proclaimed its rabbi, Sidney Goldstein. A graduate of the Jewish Institute of Religion, Goldstein championed an inclusive vision for the center. "Its services are traditional yet liberal and its program is many faceted. It seeks to serve all the Jews in the Valley." But most rabbis did not follow his lead. Goldstein himself left the center less than six months later after fighting with members who disputed the substance of his sermons and disagreed with his interpretation of the rabbi's prophetic role.[59]

Deciding to throw "its lot in with the Conservative Movement" and to reject a nondenominational vision, the center board recognized that "naturally, there are many in our midst who do not know what Conservatism represents. . . . This confusion exists in many parts of the country but reaches its acme here on the West Coast." The board solved its dilemma by employing a new rabbi, Aaron Wise. In those years "they accepted whatever I recommended and whatever I did because I was their spiritual leader," Wise recalled.[60] Not only did Wise oversee all of the details of building a congregation, but he also linked his efforts and the resources of the Valley Jewish Community Center (VJCC) to the growth of Conservative institutions in Los Angeles, specifically the fledgling University of Judaism. Less than three months after he arrived, Wise praised plans announced by the Conservative Jewish Theological Seminary (JTS) to establish a branch in Los Angeles. "We who have faith that the Jewry of Southern California has a great future are reassured by the Seminary's program," he told his congregants. "Not only will we become a great physical center for Jewish life but also a spiritual and cultural center." Even before his formal installation, the board voted unanimously to support the seminary. As Kronish had affiliated with the Reform UAHC in Miami, so Wise supported the University of Judaism in Los Angeles. He grabbed hold of the national movement to clarify the center's identity as a Conservative synagogue.[61]

Wise discovered California in 1945 when he spent a summer in Santa Barbara as a civilian chaplain. He came to the Valley Jewish Community Center with his wife, Miriam, and children in the summer of 1947 at the age of thirty-four because he wanted to work with his own peers, congregants who "were my age, and not the age of my parents and grandparents."[62] The center had almost ten years of history when Wise arrived. As the first congregation in the San Fernando Valley, it was ideally situated to benefit from the large numbers of Jews finding new homes there. The center also attracted Jews who worked in the motion picture industry. Their impact registered most visibly in the center's music program. However, despite a membership of approximately three hundred, the center was located on a dead-end street in a modest building. Like the Miami Beach Jewish Center, the Valley Jewish Community Center possessed unrealized potential.

Wise quickly began to shape the center into a Conservative synagogue, koshering the kitchen and insisting that men cover their heads during worship. He started regular Sabbath morning services and required all bar mitzvah and confirmation candidates to attend. After the short (one hour), largely English service, Wise told stories drawn from Jewish folklore. Soon membership began to grow. Like his Miami peers, Wise rapidly achieved success. By 1958 the center had the reputation of being *the* synagogue in the Valley; so many had joined that, with a surplus of funds, it temporarily closed membership. Wise used the center's bulletin to reach out to and educate members, supplementing its schedule of events and personal notices with didactic messages. "A cardinal tenet of our faith is Zionism, and its hope for the rebirth of the Jewish people on its own soil, for the renascence of Hebrew culture and art," he wrote on one occasion. Conservatism, he explained, respects Reform for its innovation and is drawn to the tradition of Orthodoxy, but it loves America. "In this, of all nations on earth, we are native-born: for American democracy is in a profound sense the child of the Judaic tradition."[63]

Yet Wise recognized that the Judaic tradition had "faded from the lives of most" of his congregants. "You would expect that an individual Jew, a father, a grandfather, would belong to a synagogue and have so much to communicate to his children, his own family in the home. But most of that is lost now," he reflected. Wise suggested compensating for the absence of a male Judaic heritage by expanding women's religious education. These innovations resembled those introduced by Lehrman and Kronish in Miami. Like them, Wise relied on his wife to develop new roles for women. Before the first Hanukkah, Aaron and Miriam Wise started a "novel book and gift shop service" under sisterhood supervision. Among the initial items offered for sale were mezuzahs and Magen Davids—six-pointed Jewish stars— as well as Hanukkah gifts and books for children and adults. A year later the merchandise included a larger array of ceremonial objects, such as yarmulkes, *tallithim* (prayer shawls), candlesticks, menorahs, and *yarzeit* (annual memorial) bulbs to honor the dead, along with games, Bible coloring books and statuettes. A poster promoting the shop proclaimed "Make your Jewish home beautiful."[64]

The sisterhood continued to expand the possibilities of making a Jewish home beautiful. Upon completion of construction of a new synagogue building with its stained glass windows by Mischa Kallis, an artist working for Universal Pictures, the sisterhood transferred the design of the stained glass windows to plates. These they offered for sale, inviting members to decorate their homes with the beauty—and, implicitly, the spirituality—of the synagogue by purchasing the dishes. In 1948 the sisterhood introduced a competitive note by sponsoring a contest for the most beautiful Hanukkah home decorations. Over sixty families participated. By 1949 it was clear that these measures were insufficient. Recognizing "a definite need in our Jewish homes to know how to celebrate Hanukkah," the sisterhood initiated a workshop. Over ninety women came to learn how to cook *latkes*, sing songs and blessings, and decorate their homes while they heard the story of the Maccabees and discovered the holiday's contemporary meaning. One workshop's success led to another one for Rosh Hashanah so that members wouldn't feel lost on the "Days of Awe." This workshop, a joint venture of PTA and the sisterhood, included model table settings, explanations of prayers, the design and creation of New Year's greeting cards, and even a skit on High Holiday etiquette. These activities bespoke a determined effort by Aaron and Miriam Wise to create among their congregants a distinctive Jewish lifestyle in a place where such natural rhythms of Jewish living were not part of the landscape.[65]

Wise encountered more difficulty convincing members to give their daughters an intensive religious education. The year he arrived, only one girl out of forty-five students attended Hebrew school. The following year saw little improvement: four out of sixty-two students were female. In 1950 Wise introduced a bat mitzvah program for the four girls. That June, on a Friday night, Connie Chais became the center's first bat mitzvah. The daughter of Zionist activists George and Ruth Chais, Connie read some prayers and spoke on the founder of Hadassah, Henrietta Szold. Although the bulletin noted that "the equality of women in Jewish religious life has been emphasized," the Friday night bat mitzvah ritual hardly approached equality with a sabbath morning bar mitzvah. Wise soon closed the gap by calling women to the Torah during sabbath morning services—as is done for a bar mitzvah—giving them the honor of an *aliyah* in recognition of their learning how to read from the Torah scrolls.[66]

Miriam Wise took bolder and more innovative steps to encourage women's equality within the synagogue. Like her Miami peers, she had received an advanced Jewish and secular education. Like them, she consciously positioned herself as an authoritative model for women congregants, opening possibilities for voluntary synagogue leadership while raising her children. She regularly reviewed books of Jewish interest, and she fostered an appreciation of Jewish learning. Most significant, however, she recruited five women to study Hebrew and Torah together. The four years of study culminated in an adult bat mitzvah in which the group of women were called up to the *bimah*, the raised platform where the Torah scroll was read, in order to read from the Torah. They were not the first women to receive such an honor of an *aliyah*, however. That occurred in the mid-1950's during High Holiday services in the El Portal Theater, rented for the occasion. "I was standing in the lobby," remembered Irma Lee Ettinger, the center's administrator, "when all of a sudden the doors opened and several hundred people streamed out. I stopped one of them," she recounted, "and asked him what was happening. He said, 'There's a woman on the bimah and she has an aliyah.' I said, 'Who is the woman?' and he said, 'Miriam Wise.' The crowd gathered in front of the theater, discussed the major change in religious policy and after they calmed down, they returned to the services," she recalled. "That was the rabbi's rather unique way of advising VJCC that women were going to be given equal rights," she observed.[67] In Los Angeles, a rabbi like Wise could pursue equal rights for women without waiting for congregants to confer.

In Miami as in Los Angeles, rabbis and their wives did their best to whet an appetite for things Jewish, to awaken a desire to experience Judaism, to develop an experiential spirituality, to encourage Jews to choose the art of Jewish living. The cities' Jewish frontier setting drew rabbis seeking fame and influence, men willing to take risks and to innovate in order to pull newcomers to the cities into their synagogues. Seeking to further Judaism, rabbis hitched their personal ambition to the migrants' inchoate desires and needs. They intuitively grasped the mentality of permanent tourists and offered a form of Judaism that fit a leisure lifestyle. Entertaining, uplifting, enriching, such a Judaism appealed to uprooted men and women. Rabbis like Lehrman, Kronish, and Narot in Miami, Wise and Wolf in Los Angeles, along with Albert Lewis and Jacob Pressman and later Isaiah Zeldin and Harold Schulweis, joined earlier figures like Magnin and Max Nussbaum in pioneering new types of congregations. In a world with few constraints, traditions, or established patterns of deference, the eclectic possibilities depended largely upon the imaginations of ambitious pioneer rabbis. Eager to build synagogues of their own, they experimented to create new liturgies, to give Judaism an aesthetic dimension, to fashion novel educational programs. They brought the American Jewish culture of the East, of their upbringing and education, to the South and West where they adapted it to new circumstances.

These men and their wives seized the opportunity to experiment with new ways to be Jewish and to pioneer self-consciously in a world where "the very meaning of Jewishness is changing."[68] The entrepreneurial spirit moved rabbis as much as other Jews. They saw the promise of a frontier society—its openness, venturesomeness, and willingness to tolerate innovation. Rabbis grasped this promise, each in his own way, and offered a personalized path to Jewish fulfillment to the engaged minority seeking religious roots.

5
Spiritual Recreation

To understand Judaism, you must experience it.
—Jacob I. Hurvitz
Report on Brandeis Camp Institute

In their efforts to build congregations of newcomers, pioneering rabbis introduced changes within the synagogue's sacred sphere, initiating a process to adapt Judaism to the leisure culture of Miami and L.A. Perhaps their most significant and far-reaching innovations came in the education of women and the expansion of their role in the synagogue. But rabbis working within the framework of the synagogue, an old and established Jewish institution, were constrained by its structure. They could not, for example, eliminate worship, although they could, and did, change the character of Jewish prayer services. Possibilities for innovation increased, however, once another institutional structure was adopted. Camps and schools offered particularly appealing contexts for experimentation with new ways to be Jewish. They also provided opportunities for other types of Jewish leaders, who were not trained as rabbis, to implement their vision of Jewish living, their personal path to Jewish roots.

Because of its size, wealth, and openness, Los Angeles attracted several ambitious easterners who saw a chance to translate their personal visions into specific institutions. These eastern Jews tried to shape the Jewish character of the emerging second city, to put their distinctive stamp upon it, and to export their particular brand of Judaism. But the free wheeling milieu of Los Angeles transformed their efforts. Although three institutions of higher Jewish learning were established in L.A. within two years of the end of World War II—the University of Judaism, Brandeis Camp Institute, and College of Jewish Studies—initial differences among them gradually became muted. Instead, several common denominators emerged that marked these institutions as typical L.A. products. The men guiding each institution soon accepted the reality that the newcomers had lost whatever Jewish memories they had once possessed and took up the challenge of providing new memories derived from emotionally rewarding experiences. As these leaders reckoned with L.A.'s reality, especially its permanent tourist mentality, they came to recognize that Judaism can only be known through experience and that the only way to entice Jews to taste the pleasures of Judaism was through recreation. This notion of spiritual recreation soon animated these institutions.

Building institutions of higher Jewish learning in Los Angeles involved old-timers as well as newcomers. An old-timer like Peter Kahn recognized the dire need of L.A. Jews for a better and more comprehensive system of Jewish education to secure the Jewish future. Kahn was considered "one of the most erudite members of the Jewish community and an intellectual with a life-long record in behalf of Jewish education." A former political radical who read Hebrew, an influential businessman, and a confirmed secularist—one rabbi doubted if he had ever set foot in a synagogue—Kahn threw his considerable energies into recasting Jewish education in Los Angeles. By September 1947 when he penned his annual report on Jewish education in Los Angeles, he could look with some satisfaction not only on the revitalization of the Bureau of Jewish Education but also on the establishment of the University of Judaism, Brandeis Camp Institute, and College of Jewish Studies.[1]

In order to improve L.A.'s meager educational offerings, Kahn trekked east to New York City in 1944 to recruit experts, aid, and advice to help him establish a new institution of higher Jewish learning in L.A. He impressed two former Brownsville boys: Louis Finkelstein,

the new president of the Jewish Theological Seminary, and his energetic young assistant, Rabbi Moshe Davis. Coming to the seminary to
recruit Samuel Dinin to head the Bureau of Jewish Education, Kahn
spoke to Finkelstein about the need for an institution of advanced
Jewish learning in Los Angeles. Davis remembered Kahn as "that Lit-
vak with the broad-rimmed California ranch style hat. He walked in,
and already at the door stated, in an accented English, 'Dr. Finkelstein, we need you to come out. We need the Seminary—otherwise
nothing will happen.'" Davis was impressed by this big westerner.[2]

Kahn's turn to the East awakened Jewish leaders there to L.A.'s
potential as a western center of Jewish learning and as an aid in the
expansion of their Jewish religious movement. Oriented toward
Europe and its richly cultured Jewish community, eastern leaders had
ignored the western outpost. By 1944, however, it was clear that
European Jewry was being systematically annihilated and that resources to strengthen American Jews would have to come from new
sources. L.A. appeared virgin territory; it lacked any representative
institution of the Reform, Conservative, or Orthodox movements
other than synagogues. But L.A. was not poor. The fabled wealth of
Hollywood beckoned easterners, who thought that they could combine western money with eastern initiative to build both their movement and an institution of higher Jewish learning.[3]

Kahn initiated a partnership to export Jewish learning to the City of
Angels. Because of his visit, institutions of higher Jewish education
were established in L.A. after the war that were sustained and nourished by committed easterners in collaboration with a growing network of westerners. These veterans of eastern institutions dedicated
their energies to cultivating Jewish youth in L.A. for leadership roles in
the community of tomorrow. The partnership served the interests of
both communities. Earlier ventures in American Jewish higher education had produced a network of Hebrew teachers colleges, rabbinical
seminaries, and yeshivas throughout the Northeast and Midwest as a
response of indigenous ethnic leaders to local needs. In contrast, the
Los Angeles institutions developed out of an interaction between western initiatives and eastern colonizing impulses, both of which were
required to shape a still young and amorphous Jewish community.

Yet the western institutions deviated from eastern models even as
they attempted to emulate them. In the East institutions of Jewish

learning had emphasized Judaic studies as preparation for training rabbis and teachers. The curriculum included knowledge of Hebrew, mastery of such sacred texts as Torah with its commentaries and the Talmud, and study of Jewish philosophy and history—ancient, medieval, and modern. In addition, certain contemporary fields like modern Jewish literature, sociology, and education were offered. In L.A. the goal was not professional training but a form of Jewish liberal arts learning. The elite, intellectual Jewish tradition of shared beliefs was transformed into a popular, experiential culture of common feelings. Rather than study a language, philosophy, or sacred texts, students shared an encounter with these in order to elicit an identification with the Jews who had produced this culture, not to master the learning. Personality and showmanship, the style associated with charismatic rabbis, replaced sacred text and scholarship as vehicles of an education whose starting point was the individual Jew.

Students sought not to uncover the past or even to reinterpret a received tradition but to connect themselves with other Jews through the activities of studying and thus to claim their Jewish heritage. "When I arrived at the Institute, I felt no particular attachment to the Jewish people," one University of Southern California student admitted. "On leaving, however, I took much away with me. Pride in Jewishness; a desire to preserve the continuity of a brave people; a sense of belonging in a well-defined group."[4] The L.A. institutions of higher Jewish learning focused upon cultivating such personal feelings as pride, belonging, and commitment to Judaism; they responded especially to the inchoate desires of Jews to affirm their identity as a people with distinct values and attitudes.[5]

A year after Kahn's visit, Mordecai Kaplan set forth a rationale for Jewish liberal arts learning at a special meeting to honor him upon his retirement as Dean of the Teachers' Institute of the Jewish Theological Seminary. Conservatism's influential theological radical, Rabbi Kaplan was the founder of Reconstructionism, a small religious movement that developed around Kaplan and whose principles derived from his magnum opus, *Judaism as a Civilization*. In this book Kaplan argued that Judaism was more than a religion, it was an evolving religious civilization created by the Jewish people. Judaism embraced art, music, politics, social organization, as well as religious beliefs and practices.[6] Not one to focus upon the past, Kaplan proposed a new type of school of higher Jewish learning to reflect the reality of Judaism as a civilization. He called his institution a University of Judaism and described it as a model of Jewish liberal arts learning.

Kaplan argued that with democratic principles of freedom of thought "differences in religious belief and practice are inevitable." One could not expect synagogues, or even an umbrella group like the Synagogue Council of America, to bridge Jewish diversity. Rabbis, focused on strengthening their synagogues, would not be able to nurture a new generation of Jewish secular leaders. American Jews, he urged, required another kind of leadership, one that would transform Jewish institutions into "instruments of Jewish consciousness and peoplehood" and respond to the challenge of modern nationalism posed by the nation-state. Because Kaplan understood Judaism as a civilization that included what American Christians usually considered secular aspects of culture, he imagined a leadership that would be a blend of religious and secular, just as Judaism merged the two.[7]

In a bold vision Kaplan demanded that Jews forge bonds of peoplehood to transcend both religious denominationalism and the constrictions of citizenship. Imagining Jews as a model international people possessing a pluralist religious civilization, that is, one that included varieties of religious expression from Reform to Conservatism to Orthodoxy, Kaplan wanted to go beyond Zionism and its inclusive national ideology to an ideology of international Jewish peoplehood that would link Jews dispersed around the globe. He admitted that "no one can question the inherent merit of the Zionist solution—for those who will or can go to Palestine. But," he argued, "it is no solution for the five million American Jews—the only strong surviving remnant of our people." His alternative to Zionism and the experience of being a people in Zion was a school, a University of Judaism to train a new leadership. Kaplan recognized that American Jews lived in two civilizations, the American and the Jewish. Though he admired American civilization greatly, he thought that Judaism could offer something beyond the boundaries of citizenship of American political culture. Leaders trained in the University of Judaism would show American Jews how "to supplement American civilization" with an inclusive Jewish "religious civilization that transcends America."[8]

Kaplan did not propose a parochial college or a liberal arts school under Jewish auspices, nor, despite the extraordinarily ambitious

concept, did he merely build castles in the air. His university blueprint contained five schools providing leadership training in religion,
education, social service, art, and democracy, that is, learning to live
with one's non-Jewish neighbors. In addition, he suggested a
research institute at the university's pinnacle and a junior college to
recruit young people at an impressionable age to orient them toward
Jewish leadership. He wanted to educate Jews to live their civilization and to experience their communal bonds not only in the synagogue but in all aspects of modern life.

The concept evoked sympathetic interest among New York Jewish
intellectuals. After a press conference to promote the proposal,
Kaplan noted that he was "touched by the genuine yearnings which
all who spoke expressed for a spiritual home." Among those devoted
to Kaplan and his philosophy of Reconstructionism was Moshe
Davis, Kaplan's successor as dean. Davis understood the appeal of
Kaplan's proposal. It promised a Jewish intellectual institution that
would rise above religion and ideology while providing spiritual sustenance. Davis saw the university as the "first institutionalization of
the concept of Judaism as a civilization," the fundamental idea of
Reconstructionism. Unlike a Jewish-sponsored university, a university of Judaism would deal with "the whole evolving civilization of the
Jewish people."[9]

Kaplan had hoped that the seminary in New York could be restruc-
tured according to his proposal. But as internal opposition to such
changes mounted, Finkelstein promoted Kaplan's concept as the basis for a West Coast branch of the seminary. He sent Davis west to
find supporters who would turn the vision of a University of Judaism
into a reality.[10]

When Davis reached Los Angeles, he had an interview with the
well-known film producer Walter Wanger in the hope that Wanger,
who was active in the United Jewish Welfare Fund campaigns, might
chair the lay committee for the university in Los Angeles.[11] The widely held belief was that a Hollywood personality could ensure success.
But Wanger rejected Davis's proposal. So Davis turned to the
younger producer Dore Schary, a member of Rabbi Jacob Pressman's
Conservative congregation and an active supporter of the Hebrew
University. Pressman accompanied Davis to their meeting at the
RKO studios. "When we walked into the office of Dore Schary, I

knew I would succeed," Davis confessed, "because there on the left wall was a picture of his mother—a matriarchal, beautiful face. He had set up a synagogue for her. As he sat in his chair, he also had somebody massaging his back." The scene was vintage Hollywood. "Between my attraction to the portrait and observing the masseur, I tried to tell Dore Schary—with Rabbi Pressman's help—why we ought to have a University of Judaism in Los Angeles." Davis succeeded in persuading Schary to chair the board.[12]

The plans for building the University of Judaism brought tensions between Reform and Conservative rabbis in Los Angeles to the surface. Reform leaders like Alfred Wolf and Edgar Magnin feared that the Conservative movement was about to preempt higher Jewish education in Los Angeles, especially teacher training. Magnin wanted one nondenominational school in Los Angeles. After all, he observed, "Hebrew is the same; Jewish history is the same; the Talmud is the same. The only difference is whether you want this ritual or that ritual." On the other hand, when Kaplan came west in the winter of 1947 to further plans for his brainchild, he was accompanied by Simon Greenberg, the recently appointed seminary provost. A well-known religious conservative, Greenberg disagreed with Kaplan's theology and did not share his vision of the future of Conservative Judaism in America. Max Nussbaum, the charismatic rabbi of the Reform Temple Israel of Hollywood, found himself torn between his loyalties to the Reform movement and his friendship with Kaplan. In an effort to mediate the incipient conflict, he arranged a conference between Kaplan and Wolf to discuss the proposed university.[13]

But the meeting did not go smoothly. Wolf recalled that "when I arrived for my appointment, I found that Dr. Greenberg was not only present but insisted on answering any question that I put to Dr. Kaplan. Dr. Greenberg's thesis was that the Jewish Theological Seminary was the logical organization to handle post–high school education in the Los Angeles Jewish community." Wolf demurred. "My suggestions that such an endeavor could best be handled cooperatively by the Jewish community in cooperation with the Conservative, Reform, and possibly the Orthodox institutions were dogmatically negated," he reported. Greenberg wrote home after the meeting that "they want joint sponsorship of the school, but that is out of the question."[14]

Denominational politics constrained Kaplan's inclusive vision of a University of Judaism that would be a spiritual home for all types of Jews. The New York Jewish Theological Seminary's impulse to strengthen Conservative Judaism proved stronger than local desires to create a nonsectarian communal institution. The one effort to turn the prospective University of Judaism into an interdenominational institution failed. The authority of the eastern establishment thwarted the initiative of the province.

Dinin's support for the University of Judaism as a center for teacher training in Los Angeles proved crucial. Like most of the Los Angeles leaders Greenberg and Kaplan met, he expressed concern for local autonomy and he worried about stimulating denominational competition. Although he was a newcomer, Dinin recognized that most of the denominational differences existing in Los Angeles were *siddur* (prayerbook) differences of liturgical niceties between rabbis, not laymen. Rabbis were more loyal to their respective rabbinical associations than they were to any philosophy of Jewish life. He also thought that the general approach of Reconstructionism "has come to be widely accepted and practiced in the community, and everybody, in a sense, has become a Reconstructionist." Since few Jews subscribed to a notion of norms of Jewish conduct, the Reconstructionist emphasis upon customs and its idea that the past had a vote, not a veto, fit the Los Angeles situation. Reconstructionist views of Judaism as a civilization included the creative arts and encouraged imaginative use of music, drama, and dance; its exuberant embrace of Israel and Zionism as central to American Judaism meshed with attitudes of many L.A. Jews. As Dinin observed, "The concept of peoplehood, the Reconstructionist views on Zionism and Israel and relation of Israel to the American Jewish community," even, he noted, "the Reconstructionist views on the role of the arts . . . are no longer matters of controversy in the community." From this perspective Los Angeles offered the ideal setting for a nondenominational University of Judaism. Nonetheless, despite the denominational reality Dinin agreed to transfer the Bureau of Jewish Education's fledgling teacher-training program to the new institution and to accept a tentative offer of "a leading position on the Faculty."[15]

Greenberg grasped the school's potential to educate and strengthen Judaism and the Jewish community, and he wanted it to promote

Conservative Judaism, as did the JTS back home. "We feel that we would be missing an extraordinary opportunity," he wrote to Finkelstein, "not only to broaden the scope of the influence of our movement, but also to vitalize the religious and spiritual life of a large and growing Jewish community which is bound to serve as the pivotal center of Jewish life on the West Coast." To local leaders reluctant to enter the fray of denominational politics, Greenberg kept "hammering away that there wasn't a single person of distinction in Jewish scholarly matters on the coast."[16] Nor were there any university-trained Jewish leaders possessing the type of Jewish knowledge comparable to the secular learning of the average college graduate.[17] These blunt arguments helped to convince men who were sending their children to college that they needed to produce a new type of Jewish lay leadership.

Greenberg's deep loyalty to Conservative Judaism and his assumption of the self-evident impossibility of bridging differences among Orthodox, Conservative, and Reform made little sense to Los Angeles Jews. In their Jewish world, these were distinctions without meaning. Recognizing the dilemma, Greenberg admitted the usefulness of the school's name because it "indicated that it was a *Klal Yisrael* program, even though everybody recognized that the institution was being backed by the Seminary."[18] *Klal Yisrael* meant the entire community of Israel, and suggested that the University of Judaism existed to serve all Jews as an inclusive Jewish institution despite the denominational reality.

When the school opened in a couple of Sinai Temple classrooms in the fall of 1947, it was a far cry from Kaplan's original proposal. It was not a university—that is, an institution of advanced learning—nor did it do justice to Judaism as an evolving religious civilization. The heart of the university curriculum consisted of extension courses designed to give adult Jews a taste of Judaism. Its most academically serious program, the teacher-training courses, attracted only a handful of students. The seminary in New York retained financial and academic control of its branch, with Greenberg overseeing the enterprise. Dinin, officially dean of the school of education, accepted responsibility for running the university and implementing decisions made in New York.[19]

The faculty consisted of local rabbis, including Jacob Kohn and Pressman, who served as registrar. Kohn had been leading classes for area rabbis for years; these now became the university's graduate program. Greenberg did fulfill his pledge to bring prominent scholars to the West Coast. The seminary used the university to introduce European scholars to Los Angeles Jews. In 1948 Martin Buber traveled to L.A. to inaugurate a lecture series. Subsequently the philosopher Abraham Joshua Heschel and Kaplan came to speak. In response to requests from Yiddishists in L.A. for teacher training, Greenberg recruited the scholar Shalom Spiegel and the east European scholar Abraham Menes to teach two courses each during the 1948 academic year. The following year the young anthropologist Shlomo Noble taught.[20]

The presence of these scholars did not disguise the fact that, like synagogue workshops and sisterhood gift shops, the university appealed largely to women. They filled its extension classes held in locations scattered around Los Angeles. The university also offered separate courses designed for women and tailored some classes to Hadassah's needs. It created a special Women's Institute that complemented the University Institute of Adult Jewish Studies. In 1948 a wealthy New York supporter of the seminary visited Los Angeles and, seeing the university's meager resources, arranged to purchase a small two-story house on Ardmore Street for fifty thousand dollars. The Ardmore Street house highlighted the incongruity of the University of Judaism's grand vision and its humble reality. Davis came to lecture and was struck by the large sign outside of the building. "It reminded me of the *hazzanim* (cantorial) signs they used to put in front of the synagogues in Brownsville, Brooklyn, where I grew up—a big sign with bright paint, not even elegant." Nevertheless, for the women who attended classes, the university, however humble, offered them an opportunity for Jewish self-knowledge.[21]

In 1952 the extension division students participated for the first time in graduation ceremonies. "What is the meaning of a graduation that confers no new degree and is not the prelude to a profession or career?" asked one graduate. Her answer suggests how much Kaplan's ideas continued to animate the university despite the abandonment of his original vision. "Even as he proposed the creation of a University of Judaism to help overcome the abysmal Jewish ignorance of the average contemporary Jew," she wrote, "so also has Dr. Kaplan proposed that upon reaching the age of maturity, the

American Jew participate in a religious ceremony." Estaire Koplin correctly observed that "Kaplan maintains that being born a Jew no longer in itself conveys the feeling of belonging to the Jewish people, and, therefore, the modern Jew needs an opportunity to make a conscious and voluntary affirmation of his identification with the Jewish people and its destiny." She concluded that graduation from the University Institute of Adult Jewish Studies and the Women's Institute of the University of Judaism was just such a ceremony of affirmation and identification.[22] Her assessment revealed the university's strengths as a school designed to cultivate an educated lay female leadership and its limitations as an institution of advanced learning.

In 1949 the university began a program in dance and drama under the direction of Benjamin Zemach, a former member of Habima, the Russian Hebrew theater, and Artef, the Yiddish theater of the American International Workers Order, the left-wing fraternal organization. The innovative arts program represented local initiative and sparked genuine interest and support for the new school. Zemach attracted talented artists and eager students. His efforts to encourage Jewish cultural creativity flourished when the university acquired larger quarters on Sunset Boulevard. The course in Jewish creative arts spoke directly to the imaginative, eclectic interests of Los Angeles Jews and appealed to the city's many young talented individuals. In 1960 Zemach directed a theatrical trilogy, "Jewish Life As Mirrored in the Arts," that suggested how the university implemented some of Kaplan's ideas.[23]

In addition to Zemach, the University recruited Max Helfman, an inspiring musician who came to Los Angeles to work at the Brandeis Camp Institute. Before settling in L.A., Helfman led the New York People's Philharmonic Choral Society, directed the Park Avenue Synagogue's Sabbath Eve Service (which introduced the work of contemporary Jewish composers), and served as music director of Temple B'nai Abraham of Newark. Zemach and Helfman were not the only Brandeis staff members to join the university faculty. The orbit of musicians around Helfman at Brandeis soon overlapped with the university when he began to teach there. Max Vorspan, its first full-time staff member, left his position as associate director of Brandeis when asked to be the university's registrar in 1953.[24] Vorspan switched jobs because, as a seminary graduate, he could not resist the appeal to his loyalty, but Helfman came to the university because he dreamed of creating a Jewish school of the arts.[25]

In 1961, on Vorspan's suggestion, Greenberg went to Helfman's hospital bed to invite him to initiate a school for the arts under university auspices. Kaplan was ecstatic. "I am confident [that Helfman] . . . will succeed in integrating the activities of the school into the main function of the University of Judaism." Helfman recruited a distinguished faculty and encouraged an imaginative eclecticism.[26] One performance program combined the "mystique" of Hasidism with jazz. Although Helfman died in 1963, the lay board of directors established for the arts school proved to be so successful at raising funds that the university leadership invited its members to become the university's governing body when, for financial reasons, the seminary decided to give its branch independence.[27]

Despite such local initiatives the University of Judaism continued under the close control of eastern leaders well into its second decade. The local board's failure to raise sufficient funds to support the university guaranteed that it would remain a ward of the seminary. But the marketplace milieu of Los Angeles transformed its intellectual agenda from the pursuit of advanced liberal learning and the creation of a new generation of leaders into an eclectic offering of introductory courses, teacher training, and creative arts geared mainly to women. Its publicity soon promoted it as a "people's university." It catered largely to the Jewishly unlettered on the frontier of Jewish life through weekly classes that uplifted as they educated. Even its modest graduate school provided "refreshment" and "inspiration" to local rabbis and teachers attending class.[28] Without intending to depart from eastern models of higher Jewish education, the university adapted to the realities of Los Angeles Jewish life and purveyed forms of learning that enhanced its students' Jewish identity. Ironically it created this entirely new course of adult Jewish study while staying nominally under the supervision of its parent institution.

The establishment of the University of Judaism provoked the founding of yet another Jewish educational institution, the College of Jewish Studies. If Conservatism established a university in Los Angeles, then Reform could at least start a college. Fearing that teacher-training classes under auspices of the Bureau of Jewish Education would preempt training in Los Angeles to the detriment of

Reform schools and teachers, Magnin convinced his congregation to sponsor once-a-week classes for Sunday school teachers. Dinin then agreed to have the bureau supervise them. When Kaplan and Greenberg arrived to mobilize support for the University of Judaism, Magnin and Wolf were growing increasingly concerned about what appeared to be a denominational effort to dominate higher Jewish education in the city. Like Wolf's interview with Kaplan and Greenberg, conversations Magnin had in New York with Finkelstein and Maurice Eisendrath, head of the Reform Union of American Hebrew Congregations (UAHC), confirmed their suspicions.[29]

The educational situation in Reform Sunday schools in Los Angeles was serious. "Bear in mind the fact that there is not a single religious-school here in Los Angeles with a faculty of teachers worthy to be found teaching in a religious institution. They are 'am ha-artzim' [ignoramuses] in the truest meaning of that term," Albert Lewis wrote Eisendrath. Subsequent statistics confirmed his impression: 40 percent of Reform teachers had one year or less of Jewish education. They were certainly ignorant, the *am ha-artzim* Lewis described. Reform rabbis "cannot afford the terrible stigma of having these people being considered adequate for the tasks of teaching in our schools. The level of Jewish content in their backgrounds and knowledge has got to be raised," Lewis insisted. "As it stands now," he concluded, "we would be better off to close most of our schools and let the children stay home than have them spend any time at all with these teachers." Lewis assured Eisendrath that he would be "thoroughly abashed and ashamed" at the quality of instruction. "You would find it hard to defend the Reform movement as a fountain of living waters."[30]

Magnin and Wolf determined to pool their resources—the UAHC providing the funds and Wilshire Temple the facilities—to establish a College of Jewish Studies. Unable to convince Nelson Glueck, the new president of the Cincinnati-based Hebrew Union College (HUC), to engage in competitive sectarian building with the seminary in Los Angeles, Magnin enlisted the support of Eisendrath and the UAHC. When the College of Jewish Studies opened in the fall of 1947, it, too, offered adult education and teacher-training classes. Its first brochure advertised "popular courses in subjects of Jewish interest and Religious School teacher training as a service to its affiliated congregations and the Jewish community of Southern California."[31]

Local rabbis and Dinin agreed to teach. The city's two leading Reform rabbis, Magnin and Nussbaum, served as president and vice-president, respectively. Unlike the university, the new college represented largely local initiative. Since the rabbis did not wait for HUC recognition but accepted UAHC sponsorship, they aligned the new school with the Reform movement's congregational wing, not its rabbinical or academic arm. Faced with a denominational challenge from outside the city, local Reform rabbis preferred action to potentially damaging delay. Undoubtedly they hoped that Glueck would be more likely to accept the school as a reality than as an idea.

The energy displayed by local rabbis and their handful of supporters as well as internal Reform political considerations produced the desired cosponsorship by the end of 1948. As early as December Wolf received letters from Cincinnati expressing the hope that "perhaps the College of Jewish Studies can serve as the spear-head of a recruitment program" for "a large number of rabbinic students." Glueck visited Los Angeles in April and agreed to have HUC supervise the academic content of the College and to let the school use HUC's name, provided this involved no financial commitment. He left the support and direction of the college in UAHC and local hands. Glueck's pointed lack of interest consigned the new school to modest growth until the arrival of Rabbi Isaiah Zeldin in 1953.[32]

Zeldin, like the other pioneer rabbis, possessed entrepreneurial instincts and ambitions. Born and raised in an Orthodox home in New York City, Zeldin attended Hebrew Union College. He did not rebel against his father's Orthodoxy as had Narot. Zeldin acknowledged that he inherited his renowned speaking ability from his father. He chose Reform because of its concern for the individual: "Judaism became personally and immediately relevant" irrespective of its form. His position as head of the Southern California Council of the UAHC, Wolf's old job, included promoting the growth of Reform Judaism in the Los Angeles area and serving as dean of the college. Within a year of his arrival, Zeldin had doubled enrollment in the college, and he was arguing persuasively that he could recruit ten students for HUC each year. "A Rabbinical Department can be accomplished on the West Coast if it is wanted by the Board of the College," Zeldin averred. With one eye on the University of Judaism, he pointed out that though its budget was $100,000 and most of its large contributors were board members of Reform temples, it lacked a rabbinical department. The college, by contrast, on its modest budget trained twice as many teachers. Zeldin recognized that if the college started a rabbinic program, it would be a step ahead of its rival and potentially able to tap university supporters.[33]

In 1954 Jack Skirball, a rabbi turned successful movie producer, convinced Glueck and the board of governors to authorize a western branch of HUC with an initial grant of ten thousand dollars from the HUC budget. A state charter was secured for a "California School" because Glueck refused to countenance the name "College of Jewish Studies." The title "college" could easily be confused with Hebrew Union College and did not accurately describe the lectures and courses that the school gave to laymen and sabbath school teachers. Zeldin became dean of the combined school. That year he introduced formal prerabbinic classes in elementary Hebrew and hired Dov Bin-Nun, the first full-time faculty appointment, to teach them. Zeldin also incorporated the program to train cantors initiated by Helfman and encouraged William Sharlin to transform it into a regular department of sacred music.[34]

Steady growth under Zeldin's guidance precipitated a crisis. Zeldin discovered that the newly-created California School, established as a branch of HUC and designed to offer degrees, could not give credit for its classes because it lacked its own building. The University of Judaism received accreditation and was capitalizing on it, he observed to Glueck. Zeldin received his first setback when Magnin vetoed a proposal to have Wilshire Temple's classrooms legally considered the school's property. Magnin's decision prompted a search for a suitable building. In 1956 the school purchased a former home for Jewish asthmatic girls high in the Hollywood Hills overlooking the San Fernando Valley for the modest sum of thirty thousand dollars. The steep, winding road up from Laurel Canyon assured the school's isolation. Zeldin transferred to the Appian Way building only prerabbinic classes and graduate classes inaugurated by Samuel Cohon when he retired from Cincinnati to Los Angeles. College classes remained accessible at Wilshire Temple. The music classes also continued at the temple, barred from the new building because of protests by "unfriendly" neighbors. In 1957 Glueck visited Los Angeles to meet with an accreditation team that was favorably impressed with Zeldin's program.[35]

But by raising the stature of the school, the numbers it enrolled, and the stakes involved in its control, his very success drew the attention of the two feuding wings of Reform Judaism that shared in the school's administration and support: Eisendrath's union and Glueck's college, now amalgamated with the Jewish Institute of Religion (HUC-JIR). The specific battle in Los Angeles revolved around the issue of degree-granting power and appointments to the school's local governing board. Eager to build an influential institution, Zeldin wanted to recruit board members from among a broad segment of Los Angeles Jewish leaders. His opponents, most notably Skirball, preferred to keep the school the preserve of the Reform movement and to select board members almost exclusively from the leaders of the two most prominent Reform congregations. Zeldin and Skirball also clashed over the issue of Zionism, especially when Skirball enlisted the support of outspoken anti-Zionists.[36]

Having secured degree-granting power, Zeldin ambitiously planned to expand the school to offer a Bachelor of Arts degree. In fact, he had started to implement this idea when Glueck discovered the plans on his 1957 visit. Furious that the plans had been made without his permission, Glueck "scotched that fast. It is not the purpose of our HUC-JIR, nor any part of our Reform movement," he scolded, "to enter the field of general education and to compete with Brandeis University or the Yeshivah College or any other Liberal Arts College." Despite its origins as a Reform alternative to the University of Judaism, the California School and College of Jewish Studies was not to compete with its rival. Faced with Glueck's insistence on running the California School from Cincinnati, Zeldin retreated. He urged that the College of Jewish Studies be separated de jure as it was de facto from the California School of HUC-JIR. As he explained to Eisendrath, the two schools required different types of faculty and needed to handle their students differently. In addition, the college was oriented toward the congregations: They supported it, used its educational materials, and relied upon it for a more intense adult "educational experience" than they could supply. Zeldin's recommendation to split the schools received support from almost all of the local Reform rabbinate. The proposal was implemented in January 1958 after the UAHC executive committee agreed.[37]

The situation of Jews in Los Angeles undermined Glueck's emphasis on maintaining clear denominational distinctions between Reform and other wings of Judaism. Glueck insisted on the Reform vision that Judaism was a religion and therefore engaged primarily in offering supplemental religious education. Zeldin recognized that L.A. Jews did not define themselves according to rigorous religious criteria and ignored denominational norms. To be successful in L.A., Zeldin understood, meant starting with one's potential students, those women who were uprooted from their old homes and possessed both the leisure time and desire to explore their Jewish identity. From the perspective of Cincinnati, Reform Judaism in Los Angeles seemed to be running wild and out of control, forgetting even first principles—like its differences from Conservatism. The possibility of offering a B.A. seemed utterly outrageous to Glueck. But Zeldin did not transform the College of Jewish Studies into an expression of his own vision of the Jewish educational experience. Despite his success in increasing the College's enrollment fivefold to over one thousand in just four years, he was forced to resign when his contract ended in the spring of 1958. The UAHC resented the time he was devoting to the college. Zeldin, however, had taken the pulse of Los Angeles. In less than a decade, he started to build his own "Kingdom on the Hill," the nickname given his impressive and extraordinarily popular Stephen S. Wise Temple. By the end of the 1960s, Zeldin's Stephen S. Wise Temple and the University of Judaism occupied adjoining sites atop Mulholland Drive.[38]

The story of the California School and the College of Jewish Studies can be profitably counterpoised against the early history of the University of Judaism. Elements of local initiative and colonizing impulses, of entrepreneurial endeavor and denominational rivalry, worked largely to the disadvantage of the California School and college. The earnest efforts of local Reform rabbis were overwhelmed by the intrigue of two feuding branches of the Reform movement. Zeldin, the one genuine entrepreneur, lost his balance between contending groups. As an outsider from New York City who was more observant than most Reform rabbis and was also a committed Zionist, Zeldin demonstrated the school's potential. But he failed to transform it into either a communal enterprise serving Los Angeles Jews or a vehicle for his own ambition. The college and school remained constrained by the denominational politics of its birth, although Zeldin's successor, Alfred Gottschalk, did eventually make the branch of HUC-JIR into a reputable competitor to the University of Judaism. What began as an independent venture of Reform rabbis became a subordinate branch institution, reversing the path followed by the University of Judaism.[39]

Only the Brandeis Camp Institute, started in the East and transplanted to the West, eluded denominational and ideological definition. Under the charismatic leadership of Shlomo Bardin, the Institute synthesized all of its innovations into an eclectic package: summer camping, adult education, holiday workshops, programs in Jewish creative arts, even experimental religious ritual. Bardin deliberately set out to arouse emotions: to awaken interest in the Jewish people, to stimulate a desire to pursue Jewish knowledge, to instill a sense of responsibility for the Jewish future. "Above all," he explained, the institute "attempts to create an atmosphere which enables the young Jew to gain new insight into himself."[40] More than the university and college or any of the synagogues, the institute tapped the talents of Jews working in the motion picture industry. Bardin enlisted them to create the "atmosphere," to write scripts and stage pageants, to compose music and design rituals, to inspire the art of Jewish living in their own lives and in the lives of others. Bardin grasped the manifold possibilities of Jewish spiritual recreation.

The future Brandeis Camp Institute began as an experimental summer leadership training program initiated by the recently established American Zionist Youth Commission and run by its energetic director, Shlomo Bardin. The camp institute intended to demonstrate to campers the compatibility of their Jewish and American identities. It intentionally catered to young adults, aged eighteen to twenty-five, whose Jewish ties were most vulnerable. This vision owed something to Louis Brandeis's version of Zionism. The goal was "to give the young a feeling of belonging; . . . to make him feel at ease as a Jew in an American environment." Bardin later credited Brandeis with an enduring concern for American Jewish youth and insisted that Bardin's own involvement with the youth commission and the camp institute resulted from Brandeis's efforts on his behalf. In the early years every camper received a copy of Brandeis's essay "True Americanism." So when Brandeis died after the successful first summer institute, held in Amherst, New Hampshire, in 1941, Bardin asked for the use of the Justice's name. Renamed the Brandeis Camp Institute, the one-month summer program carefully blended aspects of Bardin's own education: his memories of growing up in Zhitomir; his adult years in Eretz Yisrael (the land of Israel), marked by the values of the kibbutz; his doctoral studies at Columbia University's Teachers College, where he wrote on the experiential educational methods of the Danish folk high schools (especially the importance of music); and his admiration for the informal give-and-take of American discourse.[41]

Born and raised in Zhitomir, Bardin left Russia after World War I for Palestine. He briefly attended and taught at the Reali School in Haifa before leaving Palestine for Berlin. After several years of study in Berlin, Bardin went to London for further education. Eventually he landed in New York at Columbia University's Teachers College. Accepted as a graduate student, Bardin studied under an impressive group of educators gathered at Columbia in the early 1930s, especially George Counts, who encouraged him to examine the Danish folk high school. While in New York Bardin married Ruth Jonas, daughter of a wealthy Brooklyn lawyer. He returned to Haifa with a wife, an advanced degree, a book called *Pioneer Youth in Palestine*, and the determination to start a school modeled on Brooklyn Technical High School. A meeting with Frieda Warburg, who had read his book, prompted her to provide funds. Bardin established Haifa Technical High School in 1936 and a special nautical school two years later. In 1939 he returned to the United States to earn money and remained when the war began. Bardin's manner and accomplishments impressed American Zionist leaders, who considered him a model of the new Jew created in Palestine. He can also be seen as the prototypical *yored*, the Palestinian (and later Israeli) who leaves the homeland to seek his fortune in the diaspora. Bardin's credentials as a pedagogue made him the perfect choice to direct the new American Zionist Youth Commission.[42]

By the middle of the second summer, Bardin knew that he had the formula guaranteeing success. In a letter to Judith Epstein, vice-chair of the commission and president of Hadassah, Bardin wrote that the group was typical of the rank-and-file members of Junior

Hadassah as well as the leadership. "Without hesitation we may say that whatever has been achieved with this group could be achieved with any similar group," he assured her. Bardin reiterated his conviction that now "we have a very effective instrument for our Zionist youth education." His success was recognized by Abraham Goodman, a wealthy New York businessman, a Zionist, Reconstructionist, and supporter of Jewish creative arts. Goodman arranged to purchase a camp in the Poconos for Brandeis. In 1943 Bardin transferred his entire program to the new site, even renaming the lake, Kinneret, the Sea of Galilee in the Poconos.[43]

Each session, meticulously planned no less as an emotional than as an educational experience, was designated an *aliyah*, clearly an unorthodox use of the Zionist term. Bardin subscribed to Zionist doctrine that "there is only one homeland for the Jew, and that is the ancient homeland in Palestine." He also admitted that although "we don't expect our young people to return to Palestine, . . . there should be a tie with the homeland." He fostered this connection through an extensive reading list on Zionism, study of Hebrew, and cultivation of elements of Palestinian Jewish culture, "because of the normalizing character of [its] Jewish community." As one contemporary put it, Bardin was a small-*z* Zionist.[44]

Bardin's approach turned Brandeis into a surrogate homeland and Jewish home rolled into one, letting campers taste previously unfamiliar experiences. His program made campers responsible for the camp's physical needs (except its food) and included a healthy dose of gardening. Bardin thought doing menial work acted "like a tonic" inside campers' souls by giving them the feeling that Judaism was rooted in real life. It counteracted the tendency of young Jews "to associate Judaism with wealth." It also linked camp life to the kibbutz's notion of physical work as a creative and redeeming enterprise. The daily program ran on a rigorous schedule. Before breakfast there was a dual flag-raising ceremony honoring the American and Zionist symbols. Then came lectures, study, work, and singing in the morning, followed by rest, recreation, and workshops in the afternoon. The evenings, except for Shabbat and Thursday nights, which were reserved for a campers' campfire program, consisted of informal but structured gab sessions, Hebrew lessons, discussions with lecturers, and singing and dancing.[45]

The sabbath was the focal point of the week. Bardin used his considerable dramatic skills to evoke a sense of reverence, spirituality, and beauty among the campers. During the week they learned Shabbat melodies so that the Friday night and Saturday morning rituals could be participatory. But Bardin particularly redesigned the traditional brief *Havdala* ritual to close the sabbath. He developed a *Havdala* ceremony whose emotional stagecraft regularly brought campers to tears. Standing in a circle, with arms on each other's shoulders, campers sang farewell to the sabbath as candles flickered. Bardin's *Havdala* became "a symbol of a great camaraderie." He even orchestrated the lighting to produce the desired emotional effect: a sense of loss at the beauty that had been Shabbat. Irma Lee Ettinger, girls' head counselor from 1948 to 1955, recalled how exacting Bardin was in regard to raising and lowering lights and how upset he would get if she missed a cue.[46]

Bardin wanted a national constituency. He expanded his recruitment efforts to reach local Zionist Youth Commissions scattered in over one hundred cities throughout the United States and Canada. In 1943 only 20 percent of the 150 campers came from the New York metropolitan area. Among the first campers recruited from Los Angeles was the daughter of Julius and Mollie Fligelman, active Zionists and members of the L.A. commission. The Fligelmans were so impressed with the program's impact on their daughter that they sponsored scholarships for other young people to attend.[47] Julius Fligelman also began to correspond with Bardin. Buoyed by success, Bardin envisioned a network of half a dozen camps around the United States. By 1946 he was ready to bring the Brandeis Camp Institute to the West Coast. Moshe Davis, a member of the youth commission, recalled that at the meeting "the vote was even—on the line, an absolutely neutral vote. As a matter of fact, a neutral vote meant a negative vote, and Bardin was not going to get his camp on the west coast. At that point," he continued, "I said to them rather formally, 'Ladies and Gentlemen, before you reach a final decision I want you to know that the Seminary has just decided to establish the West Coast branch. . . . We believe that Los Angeles is going to be the second largest city of Jews in the United States." Davis's persuasion worked. A second vote was called and this time the meeting lined up in favor of the West Coast camp.[48]

Bardin arrived in November for a series of parlor meetings with potential supporters organized by the indefatigable Mollie Fligelman. He told all who would listen about his plan to establish an all-year-round camp, the "largest Jewish camp of its kind in the United States and the first of its kind in the West," on the outskirts of Los Angeles. At Sinai Temple, at Hadassah and Zionist meetings, in the Fligelman's home, to Max Laemmle and other Jews in Hollywood, Bardin brought his message of youth redemption and education for leadership. By February he had generated enough support for a gala "Stars for Youth" dinner in the Ambassador Hotel, hosted by the comedian Phil Silvers, with such well-known stars as Danny Thomas and Chico Marx and a rare appearance by Al Jolson. The goal was to raise $250,000 to purchase a campsite.[49]

The enthusiasm of local leaders and the enormous untapped wealth of Los Angeles Jews soon turned Bardin's vision into reality. After many weekends of driving around hunting for a site, the local committee purchased Oak Park Ranch, a two thousand-acre estate in the Simi Valley that included tennis courts, riding stables, and the hunting lodge of a former beer baron. The land was rapidly readied for the first session in the summer of 1947. The local Ventura County paper, its interest piqued by the arrival of a Jewish camp, interviewed Uri Ariav, a twenty-six-year-old Sabra and agriculture student hired as the gardener. The reporter discovered that Ariav hoped to "bring some American boys and girls to Palestine" because they were desperately needed. "Now, when we need men to perform some act of sabotage in the city," Ariav explained, "we have to get them from the farms and that leaves them short-handed there." Young American Jews could help facilitate plans for sabotage!

The newspaper story threatened the entire enterprise. Bardin worked furiously to repair the damage, firing Ariav, giving a talk before the local Rotary club, cultivating area churches, and even inviting an area folk dance group to use the camp facilities. Eventually he quieted the outcry, and the first *aliyah* received good press.[50]

Bardin transported not only his program but most of his staff from the Poconos to the Simi Valley. Max Helfman, appointed music director of the Hebrew Arts Commission of the Zionist Youth Commission in 1944, brought his considerable talents to the West Coast. He shared Bardin's assessment that young Jews "are atrophied emotionally. They have lost their will for passionate living as Jews." Helfman brought this passion, combined with a love of music, Palestine, and philosophy to the campers. One camper from Winnipeg called him the soul of the camp. Even onlookers, watching him rehearse a choral group, sensed the enormous enthusiasm he evoked. "If the Brandeis Institute would have done nothing more than present Helfman to the West Coast, it would have been 'dayenu'!" exclaimed an excited local fund-raiser citing the refrain of a popular Passover song that praised each action of God with "dayenu"—it would have been enough. But Bardin did more. He brought dancer Katya Delakova and well-known philosopher Horace Kallen. In addition, he started to nurture his own staff from among the most promising campers, sending a select handful— among them, Irma Lee Ettinger—to Palestine for a year to soak up its culture.[51]

Yet even while he looked to Palestine for its rich Jewish culture, Bardin started to reinterpret Zionist categories. Chava Scheltzer, whom Bardin recruited as a representative of the Yishuv in 1945, struggled to introduce *halutziut*, or preparation for pioneering in Palestine, into the camp. Bardin opposed such efforts, although he "claims that he is for *halutziut*. In truth, he is not for it," she observed, but sees the pioneer as standing for a *halutziut* that exists in all areas of life.[52] The potential of the California camp excited Bardin; he wanted to develop it into a year-round institute. But members of the Zionist Youth Commission balked at the prospect. So Bardin talked several major supporters, including Abe Goodman and Judith Epstein, into establishing a separate Brandeis Youth Foundation to run the camps and related programs. By the summer of 1948, as the State of Israel fought its war of independence, Bardin severed the remaining Zionist connections. Even the camp's rhetoric changed, as did its reading lists. "The orientation of the camp is definitely towards Israel, but it is not a Zionist camp," wrote a camper, David Sokolov. "The accent is on Hebrew culture, not because Yiddish is inferior, but because [of] an unfortunate and almost unshakable association . . . with the call of the ghetto, with persecution, and shame."[53]

Bardin evidenced a remarkable ability to respond to the needs, styles, and tastes of American Jews. His starting point was his audience, his potential campers and supporters. Zionism, in its classical European and even American form, served Bardin as a resource to be winnowed and transformed, much as the pioneer rabbis treated Judaism. Thus, Bardin took the language of Zionism—of *halutziut*, of *aliyah*—and used it to promote individual growth and self-knowledge with a Jewish flavor. Bruce Powell, a former camper and counselor at Brandeis, wrote that Bardin "interpreted Zion as the spiritual center of one's mind; Zionism was simply a return to that center." Powell thought that "Bardin created a 'Jewish Zionism,' a yearning to return to one's own personal center of Judaism and Jewish vitality."[54]

Aware of the institute's transformative impact on youth, Bardin solicited testimonials. These letters spoke in moving terms of a profound change in Jewish identity produced by the institute, akin to a conversion experience. One woman even used religious language in an article she wrote on the institute when she returned to college. "I was born again," she affirmed. An articulate young man, Sokolov, wrote: "We lived like . . . Sabras . . . to whom the meaning of anti-Semitism has to be explained. Although our atmosphere is completely Jewish, paradoxically, we do not think as Jews here the way we do in the 'outside world.' We think as human beings, not colored by particular pressures." Bardin used to say to campers, "Let's strike a contract. You give me twenty-eight days and I'll give you an experience that will last a lifetime." Indeed, one woman later reported that "Brandeis was the turning point of my life." Her message confirmed Bardin's bargain and the power of an institute experience. "Brandeis charted the way for me," she explained. "Because of it I still attend school, I feel relatively secure as a Jew, and my family has enjoyed a Brandeis 'feeling' about religion, Shabbat, and festivals. They have learned a positive Judaism," she concluded. "I believe your scholarship to me paid off in producing four positive Jewish children and our home has provided an example for many of our friends."[55]

Like the other innovative programs, Brandeis attracted a majority of women, partly a result of the draft (both for World War II and the Korean War), partly due to recruitment through Junior Hadassah and alumni, and partly stemming from the character of its program.[56] In many respects, Bardin's experientially based and emotionally structured education consciously articulated the unarticulated mode of traditional learning for Jewish women. For a month the camp became a home to campers who learned largely by doing and living. Bardin and his staff turned themselves into ideal Jewish parents, aunts, uncles, cousins, and grandparents who transmitted a love for Jewishness in all its rich variety as much through example as through specific didactic instruction. "It would not be an exaggeration to say," wrote one observer, that Bardin "induces his young people to surrender themselves to him for one month and during this period he and his staff replaces feelings of estrangement with a love for Judaism." Brandeis nurtured as it taught, inspired as it educated. "Charisma and seduction are hard to resist and most of those who experience this combination at Brandeis succumb," the eastern observer concluded. Bardin wanted to reach the hearts of his American-born campers even more than their minds, one reason why he chose to work with youth at what he called "the plastic age," the "age when the young person makes his great decisions." As the pioneering rabbis and their wives tried to recapture the family for Judaism by directing their innovations to women, so Bardin sought to grab the children, especially the daughters.[57]

Graenum Berger, an eastern executive in Jewish communal recreation, visited Brandeis in the 1960s and astutely observed how Bardin linked the centrality of the Sabbath with traditional women's learning. "One prepares for it all week, but officially it begins on Friday morning just like it used to in the traditional home," he noted. "Brandeis changes its bed sheets and laundry on Friday. Not on Tuesday or Thursday or any other day. Along with clean sheets, clean clothes, the buildings and grounds are all cleaned up in preparation for the Sabbath." Berger understood the importance of such a routine. "These are so-called mundane things which most of the youngsters never did," he wrote. "It wasn't done in their own homes, unless a traditional grandmother lived with them. It is something which they had to experience as part of the Jewish Sabbath." The result was a sense of the sabbath's sacredness, its santification of time. "No vehicles scurry within the campgrounds on that day. There is a festive air and there is a Sabbath quiet. Food is different too." Berger concluded that this spiritual recreation "is religious in the traditional sense, despite all disclaimers." Bardin also extended the traditional education for women. With girls making up over half of the campers, he quickly discovered that they had nothing to do during Friday night and Saturday morning services. So he included them in sabbath services. Female campers read Torah and *Maftir* (the prophetic portion accompanying the weekly Torah reading) in English and joined in singing Hebrew prayers.[58]

By 1951, Bardin was eager to move to Los Angeles from New York. Only the L.A. camp had the year-round potential he sought to exploit and a circle of men and women dedicated to him. At the fall meeting of the board of governors, Goodman recommended accepting Bardin's proposal to move himself and the national office to Los Angeles and to introduce a year-round program in 1952. As Goodman reiterated, Bardin intended not to create a local institution for Southern California and the West, but a national one. Without Bardin's presence, eastern supporters found it difficult to raise funds, though Goodman remained enthusiastic. He was particularly impressed with what he considered the unusual cooperation of different types of Jews united in one enterprise and under one roof. In 1953 he recommended selling the eastern camp and suggested, in a compliment to Bardin's accomplishment, that a site be found an hour from New York City to duplicate the Los Angeles program.[59]

Bardin, however, was concentrating on developing and extending his Los Angeles program. Hollywood provided a congenial milieu for his own showmanship. He diligently recruited supporters who could contribute creative talents as well as finances and particularly courted Jews working in the movie industry. These wealthy men would drive out to the Simi Valley in their limousines and Bardin would make them send their chauffeurs home. Then he would have them dig in the garden. "They loved it!" Wolfe Kelman recalled. Los Angeles offered opportunities for individual entrepreneurship that Bardin, a natural entrepreneur, could hardly resist. In 1952 he introduced a tree-planting ceremony for families that combined *Tu B'Shevat* with *Lag B'omer*, the holiday of trees with the scholars' holiday. Michael Blankfort, a left-wing screenwriter, came to camp, fell under Bardin's spell, and started to contribute scripts for various pageants, including one on Maimonides. "The first five hours I spent with Shlomo Bardin were apocalyptic," Blankfort recalled. He responded by spreading the message, recruiting Dore Schary and writer Norman Corwin, as well as screen writers Fay and Michael Kanin. Schary and Corwin developed a ceremony for the tree-planting ritual; Blankfort also wrote programs for Purim and Hanukkah and other holidays and contributed his services to camp over the summer.[60]

With weekend institutes for couples inaugurated in 1952, Bardin could reach effectively into the Hollywood community. To cultivate supporters, he worked with lawyer Joseph Rifkind and especially his wife, Betty, a wealthy Beverly Hills couple, whose son Robert attended Brandeis in 1948 and served as a staff member in 1949. The Rifkinds would recruit a prospect to a weekend institute. Then on Sunday, after the institute had ended, Bardin, who loved to cook, would invite the selected couple up to his private apartment for conversation over a nonkosher dinner (in contrast to the institute's meals). If the couple were moved by the Shabbat experience and Bardin's charisma, he would ask them for just one favor—to introduce one friend to Brandeis. Bardin could "inspire people. He was a Pied Piper," Fay Kanin recalled. The camp "really celebrated all the cultural richness of being Jewish, and that kind of appealed to us. Through it we were exposed to some of the ritual that I had had a little of in my home—the Friday night candle-lighting and all that," she remembered. "We enjoyed them again, and we brought them home and did them for a while with our children."[61]

Fligelman, an ardent supporter, recruited the old-timer Max Bay. "I went most reluctantly," the physician recalled. "I was not particularly dedicated." Then in 1954 "a stag weekend at Brandeis turned me around completely." The stag weekends melded Shabbat celebration and learning with male camaraderie; it introduced Jewish men to the warm fellowship of a Jewish world their fathers might have known in the synagogue. Max Bay dated his Jewish education from his first weekend at Brandeis. Bay then brought his wife to a couples weekend at Brandeis, and that transformed her and she became involved in the Jewish community. "Experiencing a Shabbat at Brandeis is what it is—it also gave you a sense of pride in your heritage," he explained. "One of the feelings I had from my weekend was a sense of remorse for the lack of education that we had given our son. As a result, when I came home, and told the family about it, I sounded like a holy roller, because I suddenly had gotten religion, born again, born again before Carter!" Not everyone was touched by Bardin's charisma and showmanship. Ted Thomas, a writer and director and friend of the Kanins, visited camp but left unimpressed. Thomas remembered Bardin as "an arrogant son-of-a-bitch Israeli." Son of the famous Yiddish theater couple, Boris and Bessie Thomashevsky, Thomas had his own vibrant memories and didn't care for Bardin's spiritual recreation of the sabbath.[62]

By the mid-fifties, a decade after moving to Los Angeles, Bardin completed the transplantation. Brandeis contained all of the year-round components he originally had envisioned: weekend institutes for adults—couples, stag weekends, and sorority weekends; a summer camp for children; special holiday-related events and workshops for families; and the original leadership program for youth. Financial support came from individuals loyal to Bardin; the leadership consisted largely of West Coast figures.[63]

Despite the remarkable continuity of program and personnel, the Brandeis Camp Institute in its migration westward lost its Zionist ideological thrust, though it retained a Zionist reputation. In the mid-sixties the non-Zionist lawyer and communal leader Walter Hilborn went to a weekend institute "with my tongue in my cheek, because I thought that he [Bardin] was going to try to make me a Zionist." But Hilborn discovered that Bardin "didn't try to do that. What he did was to make me feel much more interested in why I was a Jew, and what it meant to be a Jew, and he got me reading history about it." Not only did Hilborn read, but he also was inspired to study regularly for several years with Max Nussbaum on the sabbath.[64]

In Los Angeles Brandeis became a vehicle for Bardin's individual entrepreneurship. Its eclectic, inspirational programs led by a charismatic figure made Jews with minimal Jewish knowledge feel good about being Jews, offered a heterogeneous clientele a wide range of ways to be Jewish, and affirmed through drama, dance, and especially music the spiritual values of Judaism. One reporter recognized that the institute fostered "an appetite for things Jewish—music, literature, traditions." A supporter considered the transformation wrought by Brandeis to be "a miracle." Participants became "real Jews, many of them for the first time in their lives." As one old-timer observed, "You come, you get the inspiration and the thrill of real total Jewish living, without interruption and without influences being brought to bear." Bardin's status as a secular lay leader—he was not a rabbi—enhanced the power of his spiritual message.[65]

Eventually, easterners interested in programmatic efforts to foster Jewish identity and revitalize American Jewish life found their way to Brandeis. Berger's visit was not unusual. In the 1960s several other eastern Jewish leaders came to analyze and learn from the Brandeis camp experience. One astute observer examined the institute for the American Jewish Committee. He summarized succinctly the assumptions of its educational program: "1. To understand Judaism, you must experience it. 2. Judaism is not primarily a creed or theology; it is concerned, mainly, with the art of living with one's fellow men." He went on to point out that Brandeis tried to restore two lost Jewish traditions: a lay leadership and a Jewish home culture revolving around Shabbat and the festivals. To revitalize the home, and thus all of Jewish life in America, one had to start with the sabbath. "I definitely feel that we should make a very serious effort to introduce the Sabbath into our own lives," Bardin affirmed, "and, maybe, through us, it will spread to the whole of America, for it is not merely the Jews who need it." This meant, of course, that women and their home domain now occupied a crucial, central place in American Judaism. At the heart of Bardin's program lay the conviction that women held the key to the Jewish future. Only women really possessed sufficient leisure time to be Jewish now that Judaism had become a form of spiritual recreation.[66]

If Los Angeles did not have "the privilege of becoming one of the major centers of Jewish learning in the United States," as early boosters had predicted it would, it did lead the way in creating institutions for adult Jewish education, especially for women.[67] In order to educate a population illiterate in Jewish knowledge, these institutions experimented in nurturing a cadre of lay leaders in a far from hospitable environment. Los Angeles did not contain many schools of adult education, nor was the idea of attending classes once a week particularly popular among the general population. Yet the University of Judaism, Brandeis Camp Institute, and College of Jewish Studies regularly enrolled hundreds of students in the early years, and these numbers grew substantially in the 1960s. During the decades when married women refrained from working outside of the home, ambitious Jewish leaders recruited them to learn how to be Jewish within their own sphere.

In Los Angeles the delicate balance that usually animated American Judaism—between claims of tradition to transform the Jew and demands of the individual Jew to modify tradition—shifted decisively in favor of the latter. As Bruce Powell noted enthusiastically, Bardin enjoyed "the freedom to 'select' from the best in Jewish culture instead of having to take it all."[68] And what guided Bardin's choices, indeed, what served as the starting point of all of the successful pioneering rabbis, was the audience—those uprooted Jews living in a Jewish desert on the edge of paradise. Rabbis devised programs that would reach them, move them, inspire them, transform them. If the process also transformed Judaism—or in Bardin's case, Zionism—this was one of the unexpected outcomes. Both Judaism and Zionism were resources to be exploited; neither were constraints.

An American Jewish folk religion developed in Los Angeles. Popular, eclectic, and experiential, this new Judaism drew upon spiritual modes traditionally associated with women. Such modes emphasized the centrality of experience to knowing. Without experiencing Judaism—be it the joy of the sabbath or the thrill of hearing an inspiring lecture or the pleasure of singing Jewish songs—it would be impossible to be Jewish. Since such experiences with their attendant emotions of solidarity and feeling good about being Jewish did not fill the homes of L.A. Jews, institutions of higher learning sought to convey them. In Los Angeles Judaism gradually lost much of its elite, male, theological, and halakhic form and substance. At the time, the difference between Judaism in the City of Angels and Judaism back home appeared to be a difference between east and west, center and periphery—even, perhaps, between parent and child. Only later would observers realize that as permanent tourists pursued their spiritual recreation, they were changing the character of Judaism.[69]

If there was a measure of chutzpah in these experimental endeavors, it fit comfortably into the L.A. milieu where anything appeared possible, even the reimagination of such an ancient religion as Judaism. Unencumbered by tradition, Los Angeles Jews proved receptive to an innovative eclecticism that crossed denominational and ideological boundaries. The institutions of learning established after the war, even more than the synagogues, offered spiritual recreation tailored to L.A.'s pace and lifestyle. Through them, East met West; the Brandeis Camp Institute, College of Jewish Studies, and University of Judaism refracted eastern visions through western realities.

6
Politics in Paradise

I think it would be a sad commentary to admit that Jews
may not fight for what they believe is not only right but
constitutional because of the fear that to do so would expose
them to anti-Semitism.

—Haskell L. Lazere
Memo to American Jewish Congress staff, 23 December 1960

On a spring night in 1951, a blast shattered the sleep of residents living in the vicinity of 6500 North Miami Avenue. Dynamite exploded
a substantial section of the still unfinished Tifereth Israel Northside
Jewish Center. Rumors pointed to the Ku Klux Klan, whose revival
throughout the south troubled Miami Jews. Indeed, since 1946 Ku
Klux Klan Welcomes You signs had greeted visitors to Miami's
Northwest section. The Anti-Defamation League of B'nai B'rith
(ADL), the only national Jewish defense organization with a professionally staffed office in the state of Florida, issued a statement calling for calm. In the recent session of the state legislature, ADL had
secured passage of legislation prohibiting activities associated with
the Klan. The bill outlawed wearing masks, burning crosses, and similar Klan practices. Some suggested the bombing was an act of retali-
ation against the successful Jewish lobbying effort. However, as long

as the incident appeared to be an isolated one, Miami Jews did not panic. Then in the fall dynamite was discovered at Temple Israel of Miami, and in December, during the tourist season, a bomb inflicted substantial damage on the Miami Hebrew School and Congregation on Southwest 12th Avenue. A week later an attempt to blow up the Coral Gables Jewish Center failed when the dynamite did not ignite. Clearly Jews were being targeted: all was not well in paradise.[1]

This was not Jews' first encounter with antisemitism in their vacation paradise. Returning from wartime service in 1945, they had seen the familiar signs—No Jews Wanted, Christians Only, Restricted Clientele—dotting the Beach of the predominantly Christian community. However, they had assumed that these were vestiges of an earlier era. Had a whole war been fought to defeat Hitler and Nazism only to return to living with American bigotry? Some soldiers determined to do something about such blatant advertising of antisemitic prejudice. As soon as the Army returned the Miami hotels they had requisitioned to their civilian owners, Burnett Roth and sixteen ex-servicemen made the rounds to persuade hotel and rooming house owners to remove the offensive signs. Their quiet persuasion achieved moderate change, but enough signs remained to remind Jews of their unwelcoming neighbors.[2]

When their growing numbers had sufficiently escalated, these Jews turned to politics to seek redress. A Miami Beach resident since 1935 and an active B'nai B'rith member, Roth ran for a position on the Miami Beach City Council and won. In 1947 the council passed an ordinance forbidding discriminatory advertising on the Beach. Harry Adams, head of the Beach Jewish War Veterans' post, immediately tried to put the law into practice. He obtained a warrant for the arrest of a woman who had posted a sign reading Restricted Clientele in front of an apartment on Harding Avenue. When the case came to court, the judge ruled against Adams and nullified the ordinance on the grounds that the council lacked adequate charter powers to enforce such a law. Undeterred by the setback, Jews convinced the Dade County delegation to the Florida legislature to introduce enabling legislation to allow cities to enforce such ordinances. After the bill passed in 1949, the Miami Beach City Council then forbade "any advertisement, notice or sign which is discriminatory against persons of any religion, sect, creed, race or denomination in the enjoyment of privileges and facilities of places of public accommodation, amusement or resort."[3]

Given the otherwise widespread acceptance of segregation in Florida, as in the rest of the South, the modest action of the Miami Beach City Council reverberated as a resolute rejection of discrimination. By passing the ordinance, the council hung out a welcome sign for Jews, at least on Miami Beach. The law did not eliminate antisemitic discrimination nor did it affect the many resorts outside of the council's jurisdiction, but it made Miami Beach's public milieu more accommodating to Jews and set an important precedent. The unusual character of such legislation in the segregated South attracted national attention. In 1950 Jews noted with satisfaction that the United States envoy to the United Nations cited the law as an example of American progress in the field of human rights. Beach Jews also recognized the effectiveness of the new assertive Jewish politics that used the fragmented local political machinery of Dade County, especially the jurisdictions of its many separately incorporated cities, to achieve larger group goals.[4]

As they became insiders to the political process, Jews began to change Miami's civic culture to reflect their values. In 1951 another active B'nai B'rith member, David Pollack, won election to the city council of the neighboring town of Surfside. Pollack recapitulated Roth's accomplishment and convinced the council to adopt an ordinance similar to that of Miami Beach. Two years later the Anti-Defamation League's survey of discrimination against Jews in Florida tourist hotels recorded the effectiveness of the legislation, especially when coupled with an expanding Jewish presence in the tourist industry. Not only had the offensive advertising largely disappeared, helped immensely by the widespread purchases and construction of hotels by Jews, but actual discrimination had also declined. Patterns of discrimination statewide contrasted sharply with Miami Beach and Surfside. There only 20 percent of the hotels barred Jews, compared to 55 percent in the rest of Florida.[5]

Although Roth and Pollack were responding to Miami Beach's unique resort character in their legislative efforts to remove signs of antisemitism from the landscape, they also were expressing postwar political concerns shared with American Jews in the Northeast and Midwest. The legislation represented an attempt to change Miami's visible public culture much as Jews across the nation were trying to make public spaces nonsectarian. Anti-sign ordinances did more than ban advertising discrimination; they allowed Jews to enjoy the pleasures of their vacation paradise without unpleasant reminders of the presence of antisemitism. Roth's and Pollack's activities reflected a local variation on the Jewish domestic political agenda. That postwar communal agenda included fighting discrimination in public accommodations, housing, education, and employment through legislation, litigation, and public pressure.[6] Miami Jews were pursuing these very goals, albeit in a particularly inhospitable environment. As a result, their efforts to achieve comparable aims took some curious turns and produced an unexpected outcome.

Established politics in Dade County hardly encouraged an ethnic political agenda to delegitimate discrimination. In Miami as in the rest of the South, the premier political distinction was derived from race, despite the relatively small percentage of African-American residents.[7] Once the basic lines between black and white had been drawn, differences between Christian and Jew—that is, between Protestant and Jew—loomed large. "Remember," Seymour Samet cautioned, "Florida, although one thinks of it as being a kind of adjunct for New York City, was and is part of the Bible Belt."[8] The bifurcated politics of religion and race outweighed any ethnic group politics and limited possibilities of building coalitions. The consequences of Jews pursuing an antidiscrimination agenda would be substantially different in Miami than they had been in New York and other multiethnic cities of the Northeast and Midwest.

A one-party system dominated Miami politics and gave Jews little room to maneuver and negotiate their agenda. The Democratic party governed Miami as it did the rest of South; Republicans made up only one seventh of the registered voters in Dade County. Choice existed essentially on the primary level, and these contests emphasized individuals, not issues. Florida politics also suffered from amorphous factions that coalesced around individual politicians before elections and then dissolved once the contest was over. Every election possessed the potential to become a nonpartisan free-for-all.[9] The one-party system contributed to the nonpartisan character of Dade County politics as did the middle-class virtues associated with its suburban subdivisions and the lack of rootedness of its residents. The county contained twenty-seven incorporated cities that were united in 1957, together with the unincorporated areas, into a countywide metropolitan government known as Metro. Political struggles over jurisdictional rights and responsibilities between the city of Miami and Metro, as well as between the city of Miami Beach and Metro, did not abate until the mid-1960s. In Metro's early years, Miami Beach only cooperated in traffic engineering.[10]

Politics centered largely upon individuals, frustrating Jewish efforts to build stable political blocs. Most leaders developed personal followings that regrouped for each election. Endorsements from the media, especially the *Miami Herald*, often provided the margin of victory. Large numbers of newcomers and one-party politics delayed the development of patterns of local action by voters, except on Miami Beach. There the first signs of the new Jewish politics appeared among the Jewish migrants.[11] However, in Miami's fractured political milieu a Jew could run for mayor of the city of Miami—and win—without that fact carrying any religious or ethnic significance because a Jewish politician, like his white Protestant peers, lacked any stable political bloc. He was an individual among other individuals, doing his best to put together a faction to win an election.

Abe Aronovitz became the first Jewish mayor of Miami in 1953. An old-timer, Aronovitz avoided appeals to Jews as an ethnic group and he did little during his two years as mayor to advance their collective agenda.[12] His success derived from his reputation for honesty in a period known for its graft and corruption, dramatically revealed in the Senate hearings on organized crime led by Estes Kefauver.[13] Despite the fact that many of the Miami gangsters were Jews, no Jewish communal leaders apparently saw such Jewish criminality as their particular responsibility.[14] Aronovitz's election did not change such perceptions.

Jewish local politics and agendas depended to a large extent on national politics. Jews came to Miami steeped in Franklin D. Roosevelt's New Deal politics. Most had grown up in the urban heartland of the New Deal; few were critical of Roosevelt and his policies. During the war American Jews increased their steadfast commitment to FDR. Twelve years of New Deal policies had gradually erased many of the more bitter political divisions among Jews, particularly class politics. "When Roosevelt died no group in the nation felt more homeless politically than the Jews," the political scientist Samuel Lubell observed. "The synagogues were more crowded after Franklin Roosevelt's death than they had been for a long time," noted another analyst. "None felt a greater sense of loss and grief than America's Jews." Their extraordinary loyalty to Roosevelt and reluctance to challenge his wartime priorities provided the political context for their interpretation of postwar politics. Jews could not afford to be myopic in their goals. They had to look far beyond their local needs to secure their future.[15]

Foremost among the postwar problems confronting American Jews was rescuing the displaced persons. How could they assist survivors of the Nazi concentration and death camps? As word of the extent of Nazi atrocities spread after the war, Jews throughout the United States mobilized to pressure the American government to ameliorate conditions of the Jewish DPs and facilitate their permanent resettlement. Although President Harry Truman allowed a steady stream of refugees, many of them Jews, to enter the United States, most Jewish DPs expressed a preference for Palestine.[16] Jews in Miami, especially on the Beach, became convinced that the only way to rescue and rehabilitate these survivors was to establish a Jewish state.

The vital need for independent Jewish political power to achieve international goals first gained wide currency among American Jews following the May 1942 Biltmore Conference. At this meeting in New York City, Zionist leaders called for the creation of a Jewish commonwealth in Palestine as the best means to rescue Jews from the Nazi holocaust. The resolution generated controversy even within the Zionist movement, but the American Jewish Conference, which represented a broad spectrum of Jewish organizations in the United States, adopted it in 1943. Although its adoption spurred a counter movement, the establishment of the American Council for Judaism, which opposed the creation of a Jewish state, ever-widening circles of American Jews came to agree with the Biltmore platform's logic. The alternatives—repatriation of the refugees to the countries that had expelled them or resettlement in the United States, which wasn't too eager to have them—posed seemingly insolvable problems. "The idea of exploring other possibilities for Jewish settlement," an editorial in the *Jewish Floridian* urged, "can be regarded only as a base betrayal of the Jews. We know that these Jews are not welcomed in any other countries. Our own country will not take them. How can it ask other countries to admit them?" The only answer was a Jewish commonwealth. When the war ended, the need to act assumed enormous urgency. Graphic press accounts, horrifying newsreels, and disturbing reports of returning servicemen kept the survivors' fate in the public's eye. The only obstacles to liberating the DPs appeared to be British refusal to permit Jewish immigration to Palestine, codified in the 1939 White Paper, and Arab hostility to Zionist efforts to absorb new immigrants.[17]

Zionism's revival in Miami Beach began during the war. In 1940, after he moved to Miami, Shepard Broad met Edmund Kaufmann, a native-born son of German Jewish background who owned the Kay chain of jewelry stores and the Hollywood Beach Hotel. Ed Kaufmann was "an elegant chap and he had all the earmarks of the type of person who would be far-removed from Jewish causes." But Kaufmann was an active Zionist with a reputation for militance; in 1940 he was elected to the executive committee of the Zionist Organization of America. He urged Broad to organize a Zionist district in Miami Beach. Kaufmann made Broad realize that Zionism was not a movement just of immigrants "who brought their Zionism with them to America." Impressed by the Washingtonian businessman, Broad led a group of wealthy Beach Jews, many of them recent arrivals like himself, into the Zionist organization, and the new district "grew by leaps and bounds." In typical newcomer fashion he acted without telling his plans to established residents organized in the Miami City Zionist district. They had offered little leadership in response to the refugee crisis and had not protested energetically the British White Paper of 1939 that restricted Jewish immigration to Palestine.[18]

Broad ignored the advice of established communal figures when they told him that the path to leadership led through the Greater Miami Jewish Federation, the charitable fund-raising body that tried to unify Miami Jewish organizations. Several Federation leaders thought Zionism was too controversial because it raised the specter of dual loyalties. They feared that a Jewish state would force American Jews to choose between their American and Jewish identities, to avow only one citizenship and thereby disavow their concern for Jewish suffering in Europe. Comfortable without political power, these Jews hesitated to enter the international political arena, preferring to rely upon Gentile goodwill. Broad demurred. "You remain where you are, do the nice thing of fund-raising and raise as much money as you can," he told them. "But let me roll in the gutter with those that oppose me on the idea that the Jews ought to have a state of their own." Broad kept on enrolling newcomers, and by 1945 the Beach district had over one thousand members and figured prominently in the national Zionist Organization of America. He also took his Zionism seriously and read such classic texts as Theodore Herzl's *Jewish State*, Leo Pinsker's *Autoemancipation*, and Moses Hess's *Rome and Jerusalem*.[19]

Local white Christians responded positively to new aggressive expressions of Jewish support for Zionism and its political goals of achieving a Jewish commonwealth in Palestine. Many were moved by the terrible Jewish suffering under the Nazis to express their solidarity with militant Jewish Zionists. Establishing a Jewish state was an act, albeit belated, of international justice. In April 1945 the three hundred members of the Miami chapter of the American Christian Palestine Committee endorsed a resolution to President Truman calling for "the immediate opening of Palestine to unrestricted Jewish immigration and colonization and the establishment there of a free and democratic Jewish Commonwealth." The Christian resolution coincided with a Warsaw Ghetto memorial meeting at Temple Israel that similarly demanded the abrogation of the White Paper and the establishment of a Jewish commonwealth in Palestine. As the tempo of Zionist activity increased, Beach Zionists joined City Zionists in the formation of a branch of the American Zionist Emergency Committee. Political energies were being channeled into intense lobbying on behalf of a Jewish state.[20]

In July 1946 the committee coordinated its first mass rally in Flamingo Park. The rally capped a day of organized picketing of the British consulate in Miami. In the July heat and humidity two hundred men and women marched in front of the Pan American building to protest British refusal to accept the conclusions of the Anglo-American Committee of Inquiry. Its report recommended that Britain immediately admit 100,000 Jewish refugees into Palestine. Continuing his activist style, Roth took to the streets of Miami and joined young and old protesters. Their signs expressed their outrage over British policies in Palestine and tried to stimulate sympathy among Miamians. "British tyranny—America 1776, Palestine 1946" read one sign; another asked, "Britain, aren't 6,000,000 Jewish dead enough?" This was the first such public political demonstration by Jews in the city. In it Miami Jews joined groups of Jews across the nation. Despite their small numbers the pickets generated sympathetic attention and positive publicity. Later that day the Flamingo Park rally drew over three thousand people and attracted prominent Christians and local politicos. Congressman-elect George Smathers vehemently castigated the British, using appropriately Christian imagery. "The Jews of Europe are dying on a cross of British stubbornness and ignorance," he proclaimed.[21]

While Zionists worked to mobilize public opinion to support a Jewish state, a handful quietly raised funds and covertly purchased supplies to arm the Haganah, the underground Jewish defense forces in Palestine. Broad attended the secret July 1 emergency meeting with David Ben Gurion in 1945 at the home of Rudolf Sonneborn, the wealthy Baltimore industrialist.[22] Ben Gurion came to America on a special mission to plumb the depths of Zionist militance among American Jews to determine if they would support the Yishuv's decision to fight the British and the White Paper. "The meeting resolved into a commitment on the part of most of us who were there to respond to any and every reasonable need that Ben Gurion might have in terms of furthering the establishment of the State," Broad recalled. Broad served as the Miami address of the "Sonneborn Institute," and soon he was responsible for obtaining and outfitting two ships, a Greek tub and a Canadian corvette, that left the Miami harbor for Marseilles to carry illegal Jewish immigrants to Palestine.[23]

Understood as support for the establishment of a Jewish state to redeem survivors, Zionism touched many Miami Jews who were shaken by the revelations of the Holocaust and emboldened by their years in the American armed services. They seized the political moment and planned additional demonstrations to keep the twin issues of rescue and a Jewish state in the public eye. In May 1947 a parade of all Jewish organizations in Miami Beach, except the socialist Workmen's Circle, wound its way through the streets to demand Jewish rights in Palestine. Like its predecessor, it culminated in another mass rally in Flamingo Park.[24] The following year Zionists rejoiced in their victory. Over six thousand turned out to celebrate the announcement of the establishment of the new State of Israel. The shofar, blown in the synagogue only on the High Holidays, was now sounded to proclaim "freedom throughout the land," as Miami Jews greeted "the rebirth of a nation."[25] "We must not forget," editorialized the *Jewish Floridian*, "that we, too, though not citizens of the new state, are part of 'Am Israel,' the People of Israel."[26]

As the editorial suggested, Miami Jews quickly identified with Israel and brushed off fears of accusations of dual loyalty.[27] On the first anniversary of Israel's independence, the mayor of Miami requested Israel's foreign office to establish a consulate for Miami "in view of the large element of Jewish people in Greater Miami." The mayor anticipated heavy travel between Miami and the new nation because of keen interest in Israel. Smathers picked up the issue and seconded the request for a consulate. In addition, he introduced a bill in Congress amending the 1940 Nationality Act. Smathers's bill to restore citizenship to all Americans who participated in the Israel-Arab war confirmed Miami Jews' assumption that they need not worry about charges of dual loyalty.[28]

The aggressive political style of Miami Beach Zionists, coupled with their ability to attract some of the wealthiest Jews in the city, overshadowed the activities of the recently established South Florida branch of the American Council for Judaism. The Council attracted supporters largely from among those earlier settlers in Miami who had tread softly so as not to arouse their neighbors' antagonism to Jews. Many were members of the Reform Temple Israel of Miami. A February 1946 meeting in Temple Israel featured Lessing Rosenwald and Rabbi Morris Lazaron, two of the national leaders and founding members of the anti-Zionist organization. But Miami's staid anti-Zionism could not compete with the newcomers' noisy support of a Jewish state. Nor could the council draw upon the emotional resources of the Zionists. When Israel became a reality in May 1948, the vice-president of the council's Florida chapter announced his resignation and disavowed his anti-Zionism. He urged the Council for Judaism to dissolve itself in a public letter to Abraham Goodman, chair of the Greater Miami Zionist Emergency Committee. In the interest of unity, former Council for Judaism members should "offer every resource at our command to the new state of Israel as American citizens of the Jewish faith." Increasing numbers of Miami Jews followed his lead.[29]

Miami Jews rapidly established both emotional and pragmatic connections with Israel, going beyond the achievement of political goals. Recent pioneers themselves to a sun-soaked land, Miami Beach Jews agreed to help Israelis settle their new land and construct hotels to foster a tourist industry. Using their Miami expertise, several hotel men raised funds and sailed to Israel to plan and build hotels in Tel Aviv and Haifa connected with the Dan chain. Not yet an article of faith, Israel's presence animated Jewish public activity and permeated its communal culture. Although the annual celebration of Israeli Independence Day remained a public political event for the first decade, Israel gradually entered the Jewish sacred calendar as congregations started to observe its founding with special synagogue services. Support for the Jewish state linked Miami Jews with their brethren throughout the United States as well as in Israel. "Our position today is not unlike that at the time when the Jews were permitted to leave Persia and to rebuild Israel," proclaimed one local leader, comparing the return to rebuild the Second Temple with contemporary events. "The pioneers who left for Palestine then could not have succeeded without the financial help and also—and I want to emphasize it—the political help of the Jews who remained behind," he concluded. The message for today was clear: "the continued existence of Israel depends upon the continued existence of us as full-fledged citizens in our democracy." Even Israel's needs empowered Miami Jews.[30]

Then the bombs exploded. The coincidence of attacks on Jews and blacks forced Jews to recognize their vulnerability at a time when they thought they were making progress. All segments of the Jewish community joined the unsuccessful effort to find the culprits. Frustrated with the slow pace of FBI investigations, Jewish war veterans requested that they be deputized. Horrified, Miami rabbis hastened to oppose the idea, arguing that the problem was not specifically a Jewish one but a general community matter. The local Workmen's Circle and the more left-wing radical Jewish Cultural Center agreed. Establishment of a nonsectarian, interracial Dade County Council on Community Relations the following spring seemed to confirm the approach of those rejecting a specifically Jewish response. It promised as well the possibility of building political coalitions. Most Jewish leaders expressed satisfaction with the grand jury's interim report condemning the Ku Klux Klan as a "cancerous growth." One ADL leader urged that the report's conclusions argued for the inclusion of the Klan on the Attorney General's list of subversive organizations.[31]

The bombings attracted national attention. The local liberal Los Angeles Jewish weekly prophesied that the bombings—and a subsequent explosion that murdered the Florida head of the NAACP— were "ugly symptoms of uglier times ahead. *I fear the apathy of a federal administration that permits these fascist crimes to go unpunished because of political reasons.*" The labor Zionist editor emphasized that the Florida crimes were political crimes "aimed at weakening the United States" and should be prosecuted as such. This would be a more profitable use of congressional committee energies than hunting communists. "The bigotry which flowers in criminality is nourished where civil rights are lacking, where fair employment is . . . non-existent, where racism is encouraged and upheld," he editorialized. There were many ways of reading the Florida violence; Jews looked at Miami and saw the frontlines of the Jewish future.[32]

The bombings hastened the growth of the Jewish communal infrastructure. Suddenly Miami was drawn into the vortex of national communal politics. After all, Miami was where the action was. The bombs revealed deep tensions between thousands of northern newcomers and their hostile neighbors. Miami was not a suburb of New York, where antisemitism was expressed discreetly. The bombs in Miami directly challenged Jewish security, opportunity, and freedom, and the Jewish defense organizations wanted to offer their solutions to such intergroup conflict. In 1952 John Slawson, the executive director of the American Jewish Committee, attended a meeting in the Delano hotel to encourage a handful of local Jews to form a chapter. Slawson's efforts succeeded in establishing an AJCommittee chapter in Miami. Since ADL had arrived before the war and was well entrenched in Miami, AJCommittee's national office took pains to convince Baron de Hirsch Meyer, the prominent old-time Miami Beach resident who agreed to chair the new chapter, that there was indeed a need. Even national ADL agreed "that it is in the best interests of both our organizations for chapters of both groups to be formed in all communities."[33]

This sentiment contravened the opinion of the National Community Relations Advisory Committee, a group established in 1944 to coordinate Jewish efforts to fight antisemitism, commonly called defense activities. Trying to rationalize mushrooming postwar efforts to combat antisemitism, it commissioned a study by the sociologist, Robert MacIver. The recently published MacIver Report, whose recommendations were subsequently endorsed by the Greater Miami Jewish Federation, heartily condemned the type of duplication of effort represented by the arrival of the American Jewish Committee in Miami. The ADL and AJCommittee responded that since each organization had its own following, together they enrolled more people in the "total cause of combating antisemitism and strengthening Christian-Jewish relationships." In fact, a substantial overlap existed in the initial memberships of the ADL and AJCommittee.[34] B'nai B'rith—ADL's parent organization—had greatly expanded by 1952 and included many newcomers and leading communal activists.[35]

Throughout the 1950s AJCommittee justified itself as nonideological, including as members "Republicans and Democrats, liberals and conservatives, Zionists and non-Zionists." Nathan Perlmutter, who came down in 1956 to head ADL and later worked for AJCommittee, considered AJCommittee to be "the long shadow of the social workers" while ADL was "the long shadow of an attorney mentality." AJCommittee emphasized process and interaction; its members helped to set their own agenda, which they reached through study and discussion. ADL took a more combative posture: It developed legislation, pressured politicians to speak out against antisemitism, kept a close watch on antisemitic rabble-rousers, and publicized antisemitic incidents. In Miami, however, AJCommittee stressed that its quiet, behind-the-scenes approach distinguished it from other defense agencies engaged in combating antisemitism rather than its ideology.[36]

Paul Jacobs, a socialist and labor organizer who worked for AJCommittee after the war, tells a fanciful story that has since become legendary of the differences between the major defense agencies, each of which claimed that it was the true defender of American Jewry. Suppose, Jacobs writes, "that some guy walks into the toilet of a gin mill on Third Avenue, New York, and while he's standing at the urinal, he notices that someone has written 'Screw the Jews' on the toilet wall. He goes outside and immediately calls up" the Jewish defense organizations. Jacobs describes the response: "An ADL man rushes down to the bar, carefully dusts the wall with fingerprint powder, photographs the prints, and goes back to the ADL office to check them against the two million prints of known anti-Semites." Then ADL features in its bulletin a photo of the slogan to prove increasing antisemitism in the United States and to justify why everybody should join B'nai B'rith.

AJCommittee takes a different tack. "When the man from the American Jewish Committee arrives at the bar, he purses his lips, studies the slogan from all angles, and leaves quietly. Shortly thereafter," Jacobs continues, "the Committee announces that it is making a large grant to a social-science research center at Columbia University to do a survey of anti-Semitic wall writing since the burial of Pompeii." While this research is being conducted, AJCommittee staff writes a pamphlet to prove that a Jew invented the martini. Mocking AJCommittee cautiousness, Jacobs explains that "this pamphlet is then exhaustively pretested and tested for its effect by the AJC's research department." Finally, "after all the bugs in the pamphlet are taken out and all possible 'boomerang' effects eliminated, it is distributed by all the liquor dealers in the country, to be put in bars where drinkers can pick it up to read while they are getting stoned."

Jacob's third representative from the American Jewish Congress, "shows up at the bar, and while he is inside the toilet looking at the writing, two dozen pickets from the organization are already marching up and down outside, carrying signs that say 'Tear Down the Wall!' and 'We Demand Action by the UN!'" Then, Jacobs concludes, the Congress's legal staff readies a brief, "to be taken to the Supreme Court the next morning requesting the Court to issue an order forbidding the sale of liquor in the United States to anyone making an anti-Semitic remark."[37] Jacobs's tale humorously captures differences in style and approach of the three major Jewish defense agencies during the postwar era.

Unlike AJCommittee and ADL, which were largely restricted to men, American Jewish Congress had a strong mass base of support in Miami concentrated in its women's division.[38] It did not have, however, a permanent, professionally run office until 1956, when a number of male activists moved to Miami and pressured national headquarters to establish a branch. The preceding year the American Civil Liberties Union (ACLU) had opened its first office south of the Mason-Dixon line in Miami. The joint presence of AJCongress and ACLU, with their skills and penchant for litigation, would prove to be important for Miami Jews. Even the Jewish Labor Committee, the national defense organization of Jewish socialists and unionists, moved to Miami, but it did not became an influential participant in local politics in the 1950s. For at least a decade after the first bombing attack, Miami's local problems remained in the national spotlight because of its prominence as a premier resort and convention center and because of its public efforts to eliminate discrimination against Jews and to support and identify with the young and energetic state of Israel.[39]

The city possessed as rich an array of community relations problems as any southern town. One analyst chronicled them as ranging "all the way from bigoted or biased intergroup attitudes to religious practices in the schools, from restricted hotels and communities to the existence of a strong Freedom Club, from reactionary radio and TV commentators to segregation in schools."[40] Given the diversity of problems, it is not surprising that Jews encountered difficulties trying to pursue their antidiscrimination agenda in Miami. Because of the centrality of the resort industry, the struggle throughout the decade focused on the hotels.

Eager to eliminate discriminatory advertising against Jews and open public accommodations to them, Jewish hotel owners soon faced comparable requests by African-American leaders. Miami's black minority lived largely in segregated, substandard houses in the central city and in scattered subdivisions in the unincorporated sections. Miami Beach didn't even have a black ghetto; a local ordinance required African Americans to leave the Beach by nine o'clock each night. Most Jews accepted such pervasive racial discrimination and segregated their hotels and restaurants according to local custom. A few Beach hotels cautiously moved to offer limited integrated facilities. In 1952 Brandeis University's football team came down to play the University of Miami. The African-American players stayed in a Beach hotel with their teammates and enjoyed the use of all the facilities, including the swimming pool. Guests complained the next day, but these complaints did not deter some of the hotels from pursuing liberal policies.[41]

That year Beach hotel owners, many of them now Jewish, agreed to host an integrated National Education Association (NEA) convention when Miami hotels refused to modify their policy of segregation. This time "severe criticism" came from leaders in the hotel industry; it unnerved Jewish owners. Even more frightening were angry protests of a jeering crowd in front of the oceanfront Betsy Ross hotel. After receiving a threatening phone call, the jittery hotel owner summarily canceled a scheduled convention of African-American ministers of the Church of God in Christ without even notifying them. Despite the hotel's outrageous behavior, the ministers decided not to pursue the matter.[42]

Faced with pressure from the top and the bottom, Jewish hotel owners retreated. Although they did not back out of the NEA convention, they did cancel an earlier commitment to provide rooms for an anticipated overflow of African Americans to a Baptist convention that had been invited by the city of Miami on a segregated basis. The backlash frightened Beach hotel owners enough so that they made their offer of rooms for the Baptists contingent upon at least a gesture by some Miami hotels to provide integrated facilities. Obviously it was controversial to follow even a cautious policy, although the NEA convention subsequently convened without incident. Steps required to undo segregation on a piecemeal, convention-by-convention basis, were extraordinary and complex. Taxi companies had to be convinced to carry black passengers, restaurants had to be persuaded to feed integrated groups, any of the local facilities that conventioners might use had to be contacted and urged to reverse, temporarily, their established policies.[43]

Beach Jews found themselves in a most uncomfortable position. When they moved cautiously toward integration—or even agreed to make facilities used by whites temporarily available on a segregated basis to blacks, as in the case of the Betsy Ross hotel—they suffered the sting of criticism by the Christian white community of which they wanted to be a part. Although new to the city, Samet recognized the dilemma. "If the Beach facilities are not made available for Negro use, there is a likelihood that Negro and white liberals and radicals will accuse the Jews of being un-American," he wrote. The issue involved not just morality, acting toward others as you wanted them to treat you, but American values. Liberals and radicals agreed that true Americanism demanded equality of all, blacks and whites. However, as Samet knew, such sentiments were not widely shared among southern whites, who defined Americanism quite differently. "If facilities are made available, substantial segments of the white community will accuse the Jews of being Communists and revolutionists in their social thinking. In either case," he concluded, "Jews will be accused of being more concerned with profit-making than community welfare." The last comment reflected the fact that hotel owners usually doubled their rates to African American conventions to take advantage of their lack of choice of accommodations. The pursuit of social justice rarely accompanied the pursuit of profits.[44]

But Jewish hotel owners could not dodge the issue. In 1956, two years after the Supreme Court ruling overturned segregation in the nation's public schools, a convention of fifteen thousand members of the African Methodist Episcopal Church found accommodations in both city and Beach hotels, the latter "as a result of a special campaign by some [Jewish] hotel men in the area." Despite the Supreme Court ruling putting desegregation on the nation's political agenda and no violent incidents or threats, a fearful Miami Beach Hotel Owners Association, most of whose members were Jews, tried to have the convention canceled. Afterward a respected representative of several large insurance companies told the City Commissioners of Miami Beach that it would be almost impossible to obtain mortgage loans for the hotels in the future because they were depressed in value due to their use by African-American clientele.[45]

The timing of the church convention—just before primary elections—led to calls for Governor Leroy Collins to close all hotels which admitted African Americans. Collins's opponent capitalized on the convention to link Jews with desegregation. Though Beach hotels housed a minority of the delegates, he broadcast films on television of black conventioners "using beach hotels and restaurants. Considerable footage was given those restaurants that had kosher signs or the Star of David prominently displayed on their fronts." Despite the provocation Collins did not yield to the segregationists' demands. Considered a moderate on integration, he openly opposed "the mixing of the races." Collins won the primary and the support of most Miami Jews. But the kosher restaurant featured on television did not fare as well. It suffered a boycott by many of its regular Jewish patrons, "not on the basis, they said, of opposition to integration but because the restaurant's eating utensils were now defiled by persons who never practiced kashruth," caustically reported Leo Mindlin. "Who is kidding whom?" he queried. Jack Orr, the liberal state legislator from Dade County, thought that the campaign "did more to set back race relations than anything" in his lifetime.[46]

It is not hard to understand a tentativeness that emerged in Jewish responses to the obstacles they faced. Changing the civic culture to accommodate Jews, something Jews passionately desired and were ready to fight for, inexorably involved changing it for African Americans, something that raised feelings of ambivalence in many Jews. On the one hand, Jews empathized with the injustices and suffering of blacks in a segregated society; on the other hand, many did not identify the struggle to end racist discrimination in the United States as their particular Jewish concern, partly due to racist assumptions they had absorbed growing up as Americans. Only the politically liberal Zionists and left-wing radicals clearly saw the connection between American antisemitism and racism and the necessity to fight both simultaneously. Like the defense organizations, these Jews recognized that their postwar agenda to end discrimination in housing, public accommodations, employment, and education could only be accomplished by vigorously opposing all forms of discrimination based on race, religion, or national origin. Several were willing to take personal risks in the struggle for a just society in Miami.[47]

Although desegregation increasingly captured national attention, the issue of restricted public accommodations and discriminatory advertising against Jews remained a political one for Miami Jews throughout the 1950s. Jewish groups, especially B'nai B'rith and its ADL, repeatedly protested when such public figures as Vice President Richard Nixon or Eleanor Roosevelt announced plans to register as guests at hotels that excluded Jews. As the national attack on segregation gathered force, the number of hotels discriminating against Jews declined. In 1955 Governor Collins, known as "the voice of the New South," signed into law an act to prohibit discriminatory advertising by places of public accommodation. The state law reserved an owner's right to select clientele while forbidding him the prerogative of advertising his prejudices. Such a cynical compromise preserved the freedom to discriminate dear to the hearts of the majority of Florida's white voters while it eliminated public expressions of bias so disturbing to Jews.[48]

Changing the public atmosphere made Jews more comfortable in Miami because it brought the city closer to familiar northern customs. Jews willingly avoided the country clubs and hotels that discriminated against them as long as they didn't advertise their bias. They wanted, and got, public tolerance. By 1957 only 24 percent of Florida's hotels and motels restricted their clientele to white Gentiles. Two years later the number had dropped by half. Florida's hotels, once among the nation's most biased, had shown over the course of a decade a "healthy and substantial decline" in antisemitic practices. The persistent political efforts of Miami Jews and their communal organizations produced a public consensus condemning such discrimination.[49]

Jews were pleased when buses or golf courses or the drive-in movie theater were integrated without incident. They also tried to use quiet persuasion to get Jewish owners of such large Miami department stores as Burdine's to end policies of segregation in lunchrooms and dressing rooms.[50] Occasionally they took the initiative to be the first to desegregate. In 1952 the first Jewish hospital in Dade County, Mt. Sinai, appointed an African-American doctor to its staff. When it opened in 1949, the hospital pledged to treat all, irrespective of race, color, or creed. The appointment of a black physician to the medical staff represented a first for Miami and prompted the NAACP to praise the hospital's "demonstration of vision and courage."[51]

But Jews were also accused of not taking the lead among whites, and when they did, they often got caught in the crossfire. When Shirley Zoloth and Thalia Stern, "a couple of fireballs," took the initiative to contact the Congress on Racial Equality (CORE) for help in desegregating Dade County's public schools, they quickly found themselves in an untenable position as activist leaders. National CORE leadership recognized that pervasive antisemitism in Miami handicapped the effectiveness of biracial direct action when the whites involved were Jews.[52] In fact, when CORE, with the support of Jewish radicals, targeted the relatively small, Jewish-owned Jackson-Byron Department Store for desegregation in 1959, the "employees working behind the luncheon counter" responded to the interracial sit-in demonstration with antisemitic remarks. "Which nigger is the Jew?" they taunted. The irony in this "crazy situation" was that both management and ownership of the store were Jewish, yet no one wanted to desegregate by taking advantage of a 1957 state law that permitted places of public accommodation or eating establishments to determine whom they would serve.[53]

Most Jews avoided taking the lead in urging compliance with the Supreme Court's ruling desegregating the public schools for fear that it would compromise their newly earned acceptability. They were ready to help create a liberal climate of opinion in Miami, but they were at a loss how to do it without appearing to white Christians to be fomenters of an aggressive drive by African Americans for equality. In the late 1950s Jews organized grassroots committees of parents through the auspices of the nonsectarian Dade County Council on Community Relations to Save Our Schools—i.e., keep the schools open in the face of court-ordered desegregation rather than close them to resist integration.[54] Uprooted from their familiar cities, Miami Jews looked to their northern brethren for advice, assistance, and approval, but they also resented the apparent ease with which northern Jews embraced the cause of integration in their more open communities. "You must be aware of the feeling of isolation which most liberals appear to have in the South," Samet explained. "They are reluctant to make sound statements or to initiate positive action because many of them believe that once they have gotten into the situation outside liberal forces such as ours will then 'go back to New York,'" he observed. "This would then leave them alone to face the wrath of their friends and neighbors." Their very connectedness with other Jews forced upon Miami Jews a split perception. This multifocal political vision kept Jews uncomfortable as they groped cautiously for a solution acceptable to their neighbors, to their relatives back home, and to themselves.[55]

Not all Jews took refuge in silence or partial measures. Jews on the left, ranging from communists to socialists to outspoken liberals, condemned segregation and did their best to change southern mores. They supported integrated organizations, condemned attacks upon African Americans, and urged Jews to act as leaders of the white community. The Jewish Culture Club on Miami Beach served as a center for such radical organizations as the Jewish Peoples Fraternal Organization and its women's group, the Emma Lazarus clubs. The socialist Workmen's Circle also had several branches. But this vocal minority also had to defend itself from anticommunist investigations that threatened to silence it. Indeed, the anticommunism of the cold war era severely hampered the effectiveness of Jewish radicals and communists in Miami. Southern whites often interpreted opposition to segregation as communist-inspired efforts to overthrow a democratically elected government that supported segregation. Many considered Jews to be communists and were especially willing to prosecute them when they began agitating for integration. When called before congressional committees or local grand juries, these left-wing Jews looked to the Jewish community for support. To their dismay they often discovered ambivalence rather than solidarity. Yet the confrontation with governmental witch-hunts chastened Miami Jews and ultimately led them to oppose such assaults on civil liberties.[56]

Miami Jews encountered anticommunist investigations as McCarthy's power was waning. Before the execution of Julius and Ethel Rosenberg in 1953, concern for antisemitic vandalism in Miami eclipsed worry over Jews being targeted by anticommunist forces. Only during the last months of the congressional Army-McCarthy hearings did the state attorney empower a grand jury to investigate communist activity in Florida. He quickly turned the grand jury's focus on Miami and subpoenaed 138 witnesses, 135 of them with Jewish names. Those individuals who pleaded the Fifth Amendment on grounds of self-incrimination—it was illegal to be a member of the Communist party in Florida—were arrested for contempt and jailed without bail, even if they decided to appeal. Although the state supreme court ruled that bail could not be denied during appeal, individuals still received jail sentences without bail and were told to appeal to the supreme court. Given the large number of Jews investigated, many Miami Jews feared that protection of civil liberties would become a Jewish issue. More than any other matter, it made them "confused, uncertain, and afraid." A Sunday morning breakfast meeting in July to consider the problem of civil liberties drew forty-five concerned and interested individuals.[57] The meeting produced a fifteen-member ad-hoc joint committee of representatives of Jewish defense organizations to protect civil liberties. "The violation of civil liberties has just begun," Roth warned. His warning was not heeded.[58]

By September two Jewish professionals working for Jewish agencies avoided a subpoena by going directly to the FBI and voluntarily giving information on communists and their activities. But other

subpoenaed members of Jewish agency boards refused to name individuals, invoked the Fifth Amendment, and were cited for contempt.
A Senate subcommittee questioned Leo Sheiner, a lawyer active in
Jewish communal affairs and a member of the board of the Greater
Miami Jewish Federation. The committee asked about his affiliation
with the Southern Conference Education Fund and whether he was a
member of the Communist party. Sheiner invoked the Fifth Amendment, and many of his friends considered him "something of a hero."
They wanted to give him a standing ovation at a Jewish Community
Center board meeting, but Sheiner demurred. Such support was
hardly typical, nor did it spell the end of Sheiner's difficulties. The
circuit court disbarred him for his resort to the Fifth Amendment, and
he began in 1955 a three-year process appealing the ruling. The Jewish Cultural Center closed and put the building up for sale. Many of
its members, especially the officers, moved back to the North to avoid
subpoenas.[59]

A frightened Jewish Federation drafted a statement to deal with
board members and professionals of Jewish organizations who were
subpoenaed to testify. The proposed policy guidelines recommended
that board members voluntarily resign their position if they were
called upon to testify. Such a disavowal of solidarity with a fellow Jew
questioned about his political opinions and affiliations indicated how
much federation feared the public taint of communism. If a board
member took the Fifth Amendment, federation recognized "his
inalienable right as an American citizen to do this" and that his action
did not "constitute an indication of guilt. Nevertheless," the guidelines continued, "a situation of public embarrassment is thereby
erected to the agency and, until the final significance of the person's
reliance upon the Fifth Amendment had been determined, both as to
community attitude and as to the validity of the charges, it is expected
that the board member will" resign. If not, the board member could
be removed. Professionals would be suspended, although they would
continue to receive their salary for ninety days.[60] The federation's
strong stand in refusing to employ professionals who were subpoenaed reflected not only its staunch anticommunist politics but also its
assumption that Jewish communal organizations should not knowingly employ communists. It accepted responsibility for purging communists from its member organizations.

Subsequently, the joint committee on civil liberties considered the advisability of instituting a "loyalty oath" for all board members and new employees of Jewish agencies. Two questions were proposed: "Are you or have you ever been a Communist?" and "If subpoenaed to appear in any investigations on Communist activities, would you invoke the Fifth Amendment?" Although they recognized that the oath had good public relations value, most committee members rejected the oath, finding it too distasteful a way to indicate that the Jewish community was "cleaning its own house."[61] Nonetheless, the discussion reflects Jewish willingness to comply with anticommunist assumptions of disloyalty even at the expense of civil liberties.

When the state legislature established its own version of HUAC, the Johns Committee, to investigate communists, its willingness to brand all supporters of integration as communists emboldened several Jewish communal organizations to take a stand in favor of civil liberties. Haskell Lazere, who had recently arrived in Miami to take the position of southeast regional director of AJCongress, immediately made his influence felt. Targeting the NAACP and Urban League for investigation as communist-front organizations in 1958 also prompted more Jews to recognize that the threat to their security came from the radical right and that they as Jews needed to support civil liberties. Not a party to the Greater Miami Jewish Federation agency guidelines penalizing board members and professionals, which were developed under pressure of the grand jury investigation, Lazere called a meeting in the Town Restaurant to reexamine communal policy. The discussion produced a modified version of the guidelines. Both the AJCommittee and ADL accepted the new policy guidelines, which argued that "the mere fact that a person is subpoenaed or investigated, in and of itself, should be given no consideration either favorable or unfavorable." If an employee invokes a constitutional guarantee that "causes embarrassment to the Agency," then the agency could ask for an explanation, and if it were unsatisfactory, the person "should be suspended or removed if, and only if, the retention of that person, in the mind of the Committee or Board, would be destructive to the Agency or its work."[62]

Despite Lazere's initiative AJCongress rejected the guidelines in favor of more severe ones coupled with a strong statement condemning investigative committees like the Johns Committee.[63] Congress attacked investigative committees as "a danger to our civil liberties" because they "do not have clearly defined purposes or procedure designed to protect the rights of the individual." Privately Lazere argued that the Jewish community was "mature enough" to realize that "the mere presence of a number of 'Jewish names' in a hearing" doesn't necessarily create antisemitism. "Surveys taken at the time of the trial of Ethel and Julius Rosenberg established no appreciable rise in anti-Semitism because of them. To maintain otherwise," he urged, "is either to ignore fact or seek to arouse unnecessary fears." Subsequently AJCongress issued a second press release opposing "the investigation of the lawful activities of any private association. The Johns Committee cannot erase its public criticism of the NAACP by an investigation of the White Citizens Councils' activities, nor can it equate the NAACP with the White Citizens Councils."[64]

Ironically, the Johns Committee's revised mandate—to investigate communists (albeit in the NAACP) and racists (in the White Citizens Councils)—came very close to ADL's 1950 legislative policy guidelines designed to link antiracism and anticommunism.[65] Only by 1958 the political climate had changed. The middle way that looked so promising at the start of the decade had dissolved into a murky muddle. Jews increasingly recognized that in Miami anticommunist investigations were designed to thwart desegregation. Thus, it behooved them to oppose any investigations that potentially violated individual civil liberties.

Irrespective of their politics, Jews repeatedly found themselves singled out. White supremacists would not let Jews quietly contribute to changing Miami's civic culture. On a spring night in 1958, a dynamite blast heard throughout the city tore a hole in the school of the Orthodox Temple Beth El, one of Miami's oldest synagogues. The explosion shook houses in the 500 block of Southwest 17th Avenue and carried debris over 150 yards. The next day an ADL official announced that there was no "emergency," and the following day the FBI rejected requests for help from Dade County police. Others were less sanguine. Jewish war veterans told the press that a conspiracy lay behind the bombings because other southern synagogues had been dynamited. Those who remembered the bombings of 1951 protested that nothing was being done and that the new crime would similarly remain unsolved.[66]

Perlmutter interpreted the bombing as a warning to those who were part of the moderate, but silent, South. There had been over forty bombings of African-American homes and institutions in the previous eighteen months, but it took the dynamiting of a "Jewish church" to prompt some expression of outrage by moderates. "Hopefully," he wrote, "the bombings of Jewish institutions have served to rouse the silent South to the danger posed by the enemies in its midst—if so, it is ironical that the Southern Jew, whose own silence had been so pronounced and emphatic, should serve as the alarm bell." Jewish observers attending Klan rallies noted that really large rounds of applause came when speakers lambasted the Jews. Jews were seen as the brains—and the money—behind black attacks on segregation. Even when Jews remained silent—as many did, fearful of speaking out on the issue of integration—they suffered vilification by antisemites. Lazere found that "the problems which confront us are not understood by the Jewish community or by the general community. There is," he concluded, "an apathy rooted in fear," and a lack of leadership in Miami comparable to, but worse than, the situation in Los Angeles.[67]

Perlmutter's and Lazere's interpretations of the 1958 bombing point to their conviction that Miami Jews could no longer stake out a middle road because, in fact, no such choice existed. Jews could not find a way between white extremists and the silent South, between the Scylla of Christian antisemitism and the Charybidis of Christian anticommunism. They had, perforce, to reject both: extremism and silence, antisemitism and anticommunism. Jews had to find the courage to articulate their full aspirations and to implement their antidiscrimination program, even in Miami. Caught in the middle, Jews had to recognize that the time for halfway measures had ended. These changing perceptions reflected not only the glimmer of a new era but also an understanding of how local anticommunist investigations had sparked Jewish fears and paralyzed many segments of the Jewish community.

Miami Jews ultimately made their independent stand not in defense of civil liberties, nor in support of integration, nor even in pursuit of an antidiscrimination program. Instead, they audaciously brought a case contesting the widespread religious practices in the public schools. Here they stood as Jews, insisting upon the significance of their religious differences from white and black Christians. Here they took up directly the political challenge of Miami that legitimated religious politics while ignoring ethnic ones. Yet, as in their efforts to secure a more hospitable civic culture, which entangled them in charges of being "nigger lovers" and "commies," Jews failed to anticipate the ramifications of their actions. Many who supported the case undoubtedly assumed that they were struggling to remove an obstacle to fuller integration into the Miami community. Instead, the case emphasized Jewish distinctiveness and articulated just what set Jews apart from their Christian neighbors. It contributed to forging an ethnic political identity for Miami Jews.

The issue of religion in the public schools confronted Jews as soon as they settled in Miami. The Dade County public school system, among the nation's largest, required five minutes of Bible reading each day. Teachers chose verses from either the Old or New Testament. No less distressing was the state law that defined teachers' duties to include the inculcating of "Christian virtues." Jewish parents had long suffered Christmas and Easter celebrations that included explicit school plays depicting the birth and death of Christ, displays of Nativity scenes, and singing of religious hymns. The 1960 Easter assembly program of Miami Senior High School included tableaus of The Last Supper, Bearing the Cross, and Lo, He Is Risen. One of the Y-Teens contributed a prayer whose final stanza affirmed: "Because He lives, His Cross transmutes/Death into Life, for me;/And failure, fear, disease, and death,/Love crowns with victory."[68]

Teaching Christian virtues began in primary school. Fairlawn Elementary School sent home invitations on school stationery to its students to watch three films, Crucifixion, Resurrection, and Thirty Pieces of Silver, all for a modest ten cents. When parents complained, the school attorney didn't see the problem, but he agreed to speak to the principal so that such films would not be shown again. Even Christmas greetings often expressed explicit Christian sentiments, as did the one sent by Miami Shores Elementary School: "May you come to know . . . what Christ means." The school system reflected southern Christian values associated with the Bible Belt rather than those norms (or the lack of norms) identified with a boomtown.[69]

Jews responded by opposing efforts to introduce additional expressions of Christian piety into the schools. In 1955 Jews rallied to fight off a proposal to bring the Dallas plan of after-school religious instruction under sectarian auspices to Miami. The one Jewish member of the school board, the old-timer attorney Anna Brenner Meyers, effectively led the struggle against this innovation. Jews also opposed the request of the Dade County Baptist Ministers Association to introduce formal Bible study in the schools. In 1956 Jews threatened a law suit to discourage the Gideon Society from distributing New Testaments to seventh graders when Brenner Meyers failed to get the school board to withdraw its permission to the Gideon Society. However, Jews reluctantly cooperated with the plan of Thomas Bailey, state superintendent of public instruction, to develop materials to teach the understanding of moral and spiritual values needed for a child's development. These Christian initiatives, far from being unique to Miami, represented local expressions of national campaigns. In response to such challenges, Miami Jewish leaders agreed to cooperate in discussions. In 1956 they established a joint advisory committee on religion in the public schools to present a Jewish point of view and to coordinate activities of rabbis, communal leaders, and defense agencies.[70]

But no real consensus existed on what position Jews should take on the issue of religion in the public schools, especially given the strong Protestant commitment to Bible reading—even among Southern Baptists—and other forms of religious expression. Traditional adherents of a strong state/church separation, Jews encountered a new situation in Miami's southern milieu. The extent of their lack of consensus and even confusion appeared in a request from the Greater Miami Rabbinical Association to the Jewish defense organizations for a workshop on religion in the public schools. Among the items to be covered were: Should rabbis accept invitations to participate in public school programs? Should rabbis act alone? Should they be bound by decisions of the defense agencies? And what should the Jewish position be on Bible reading, released time, prayer, baccalaureate, religious symbols, joint observances of Jewish and Christian holidays (usually Christmas and Hanukkah), Christmas cards, exams on Jewish holidays, proof of attendance at services if students were absent from school on Jewish holidays?[71] The range of issues that Miami Jews had not resolved regarding religion in the public schools suggests the extent to which they were preoccupied with civil rights concerns and reluctant to antagonize their pious neighbors.

In 1959 Harlow Chamberlin, an agnostic with three children in the public schools, approached ACLU about bringing a case protesting religious practices in the schools. As ACLU attorneys began to develop the case, several Jewish parents volunteered to participate in a similar case. Unlike Chamberlin, Philip and Thalia Stern were religiously identified Jews, members of Temple Beth Sholom. Their commitment, and that of two additional codefendants, Edward Resnick and Elsie Thorner, strengthened the prospective case. The Jewish plaintiffs and Thorner, a Unitarian, agreed to bring a suit to challenge extensive religious practices in the Dade County public schools. In 1960 the court consolidated the two cases as one, with Leo Pfeffer serving as counsel to the plaintiffs in both cases. *Chamberlin v. Dade County*, as it came to be called, challenged the outspoken expressions of Christian piety in the Dade County public schools. The case promised to have national repercussions.[72]

Pfeffer, director of AJCongress's Commission on Law and Social Action, acquired a well-deserved reputation as a forceful advocate of strict separation between church and state. He decided to take the initiative in Miami to pursue congress's vision of the proper separation of church and state in the public schools. It was an ideal situation because of the widespread religious practices within Miami schools and the absence of a centralized Jewish community-relations committee that might have opposed congress's choice of Miami as the site for a test case. Pfeffer came down to Miami in the spring of 1959 to speak to local leaders at the federation and at meetings of the rabbinical association and joint advisory committee on religion in the public schools. Although the competing defense organizations opposed congress's bringing a suit, their position by itself carried little influence since they usually preferred not to litigate. Efforts over the summer to negotiate a compromise with the school board before congress filed the case proved futile. The board was not interested in modifying what it considered to be perfectly acceptable practices.[73]

The episode illustrated the chaotic quality of organized Jewish communal life in Miami. A handful of leaders seized the issue of religion in the public schools and prosecuted the case. Dade County provided an ideal forum for national intervention: It was new, fractured, guided by a boomtown mentality, open to all types of leadership, and it had a growing population. Sizable numbers of Jews in Miami encountered southern mores in the public schools. Jews formed a visible minority within the school system, and in some schools, such as those on Miami Beach, they were actually a majority. Their irritation and distress over the schools' Protestant piety allowed AJCongress to offer a solution. As Miami Jews were a new community, there were few precedents for Jewish behavior or established channels of influence and communication. The autonomous positions of the defense agencies, especially ADL and AJCommittee, made possible by the fractured and upstart character of the Miami Jewish community, precluded Miami Jews from establishing a community-relations committee under Jewish Federation auspices to coordinate competing programs. Since both ADL and AJCommittee opposed establishing a central community-relations committee, they could not curb congress's initiative. Without an authoritative leadership Leo Pfeffer and AJCongress were free to provide guidance.[74]

Once congress filed the case in September, de facto Jewish collaboration followed. Jews began to gather information for the suit that would seek to answer their own questions about the proper role of religion in the public schools by proposing a strong separation of church and state. Despite the refusal of AJCommittee and ADL to support the case financially, two local lawyers who were leaders of the respective defense agencies, Stuart Simon and Burnett Roth, volunteered to help prepare material. Attorneys for AJCommittee and ADL coordinated with AJCongress a survey of religious practices in the schools. They appealed particularly to rabbis for help in gathering reliable data by questioning children enrolled in synagogue schools. At a meeting to organize the survey, the men and women expressed concern at "the coercion inherent in religious services over the loud speaker, attendance in classrooms which have religious symbols, participation in nativity plays, pressures not to be absent for holidays." The suit's substance clearly spoke to real distress Jews felt regarding religious practices enshrined in the public schools.[75]

The Resnick and Chamberlin cases highlighted the extent of Christian piety in the Miami public schools and revealed what most Jewish parents and children had come to accept as part of their American education. The school day began with an American and Christian ritual. The devotional aspect started with daily Bible reading, which was often accompanied by prayer and, for older children, short sermonettes. Then came reading the Lord's Prayer, in the Protestant version, either over the public-address system or in individual rooms. At Christmas and Easter elaborate schoolwide assemblies celebrated these Christian holidays. At Edison High School "the nailing of Christ to the cross was enacted, with one of the students stretched out on a cross." In the words of one witness: "The lights were focussed on the boy, and then at Christ's death there was heavy breathing from the boy, and then finally collapse, and that was the end of the program, I mean then they told everyone to go back to their rooms." The case also documented joint holiday observances as another intrusion of religious practices in the public schools. At Miami Beach High School, Hanukkah was celebrated along with Christmas, including telling the story of the Maccabees. Although parents were unaware of the practice, Dade County teachers were ranked on their religious attitudes for promotion. The highest grade of 4 was given to a teacher "who takes part in his own religious organizations and respects other religious beliefs."[76]

As the evidence suggested, Miami public schools reflected the Protestant piety of the white majority. Nine Protestant defendants organized by the Greater Miami Council of Churches—a coalition of all Protestant churches except the fundamentalists—intervened in behalf of the school board. Their parallel briefs emphasized the extent to which Christians viewed the case as an attack upon religion and God's holy word. Yet Jews seemed taken aback by the virulence of the Christian mobilization, perhaps forgetting in their initial enthusiasm for the case that Miami was also part of the Bible Belt. "People live in a Christian world here and by that they mean that it is a Protestant world and to have Bible reading, to have references to Christ, especially during holidays, is every bit as ingrained and natural a state of things as segregated social facilities would be," Perlmutter wrote. His analogy to segregation was incisive. "Consequently, the tremendous reaction of surprise, confusion, indignation on even the part of persons who are in no wise consciously anti-Semitic within our working frame of reference," he concluded.[77] When the Dade County Metropolitan Commission and the Junior Chamber of Commerce passed resolutions supporting Bible reading in the schools, Jewish convictions wavered.

At the trial itself, "supporters of Bible reading were first in line every day before the trial commenced, and so a phalanx of white-shirted, blue-trousered, [red-tied], Bible-toting young men occupied the front two rows of the spectators' sections." Spectators lined up waiting to enter the courtroom. A Presbyterian youth group held a round-the-clock prayer vigil outside. The six-day trial attracted front-page attention in the *Miami Herald* and generated anxiety and conflict within the Jewish community. Coming in the summer of 1960 at the end of a school year preoccupied with tensions over desegregation, the case appeared to isolate Jews further from their Christian neighbors. Newspapers treated the trial more often as a conflict between the Jewish and Christian communities than as a constitutional test. Numerous civic groups, including women's clubs, city commissioners, and chambers of commerce, publicly supported the school board. The Miami Council of Churches even collected thirty thousand signatures on a pro-Bible petition.[78]

The strong position taken by Christian religious organizations contrasted sharply with the ambivalence of the local rabbinical association. Before the case came to trial, rank-and-file members of the association "seemed quite eager to accept the idea that where it is convenient to take a strong position against religious practices in the public schools they should do so," Lazere wrote Pfeffer, "but where taking such a position would precipitate an uncomfortable situation . . . that the issue had better not be raised." Concerned lest they antagonize their fellow clergymen and fearful of speaking out in public, the association refused to issue statements endorsing the case. Lazere observed two months after the case recessed that "if a vote on the propriety of filing the litigation were taken of the Miami Rabbinical Association tomorrow we would find ourselves losing by at least two to one majority." Leon Kronish, a strong AJCongress supporter and one of the witnesses in the trial, wanted to get the national leaders of the respective rabbinical associations to urge local rabbis to uphold national policies favoring separation of church and state.[79]

The Resnick and Chamberlin cases, because they emphasized Jewish differences from their Christian neighbors, made many Miami Jews profoundly uncomfortable. Writing to Kenneth Oka, a member of the Miami Beach City Council and one-term mayor of Miami Beach, Sidney Aronovitz frankly stated the issue: "I do not question the principle or principles which the litigation seeks to establish, but . . . I seriously question the propriety of the litigation, and particularly object to the fact that it has the effect of identifying me as a Jew in support of something that I do not condone, namely, this litigation." Aronovitz, an old-timer, wanted the problems resolved quietly. He opposed teaching religion in the public schools, but like many Miami Jews, he feared antagonizing his Christian neighbors more. Aronovitz wanted to negotiate with the school board and hoped to get them to agree to eliminate all religious practices except Bible reading and the Lord's Prayer. Supporters of AJCongress, like Oka, were less attuned to southern sensibilities. They pursued a form of politics that would win them few Christian friends in Miami. "I tell you unequivocably," Aronovitz warned, "that the efforts of fifty years of promoting Good Will and better understanding in Dade County will go out the backdoor window if that suit proceeds." But Aronovitz was wrong; the situation in 1960 did not differ from the previous year. Although AJCongress lawyers agreed to meet to negotiate a settlement, the school board rejected any compromise.[80]

In retrospect Samet thought it was "the wrong case in the wrong place at the wrong time," but he did not think it "set back Christian-Jewish relations by several years," as did some ADL leaders. "However, one must also remember that this is Miami," Samet noted. "It is essentially a leaderless area. People are motivated by self-interest more than intellectual conviction." Samet blamed Miami's individualistic character and its absence of shared norms for the decision made by several highly committed Jews to press the case. He did not see the case as an important test of principles. Lazere, understandably, disagreed. "We feel that with many thousands of Jewish children in our public schools that the problem of religion in public education is one of the most important and meaningful ones to pursue," he affirmed. "We believe it is far more important than a creche in front of the Coral Gables City Hall or in front of the Miami Public Library. We believe," he concluded, "that what we have done is to tackle one of the most fundamental problems which confronts the Jewish community not only in Miami but all through the country."[81]

By the time the trial court judge ruled in April 1961, nine months after the trial itself, tensions had eased. Judge Gordon ruled against the plaintiffs on most matters, upholding Bible reading, the Lord's prayer, religious tests for teachers, holiday celebrations, baccalaureate, and religious symbols in the classroom. He did enjoin sectarian holiday observances depicting the nativity and crucifixion of Jesus, screening religious movies, and use of public school facilities for after-school religious classes. Jews expressed some satisfaction with the outcome, as did Christians who praised the judge for preserving Bible reading in the schools. Newspapers remarked on his evenhandedness. Even before the decision, Jack Gordon, president of the local AJCongress chapter and a member of ACLU and CORE, managed to win a seat on the school board despite a tough campaign against a conservative Republican running on a Bible-reading platform. Gordon had won the Democratic primary, tantamount to election, before the case came to trial. His subsequent bitter electoral struggle reflected anger aroused by the trial. But his close victory suggested that Jews could pursue their vision of a more democratic civic culture even in Miami.[82]

Chamberlin reached the Supreme Court in 1964, too late to be of the historic significance of the *Schempp* and *Murray* cases that produced decisions banning Bible reading and the Lord's Prayer in the public schools. The Supreme Court vacated *Chamberlin* and remanded the case to the Florida Supreme Court. However, in the wake of *Schempp* and *Murray*, the Florida Supreme Court refused to knuckle under and reaffirmed its original opinion upholding the trial court. The court expressed its "conviction that the establishment clause of the Constitution was never designed to prohibit the practices complained of" and rejected the invitation "to speculate the extent to which the Supreme Court of the United States intended to expand its philosophy." The Supreme Court responded in turn by summarily reversing the Florida courts without addressing any of the other religious practices contested in the case. As a result, only Bible reading and the Lord's Prayer were forbidden in Dade County public schools as in schools across the nation. This was a disappointing conclusion for a most promising case. Unlike *Schempp* and *Murray*, *Chamberlin* challenged a diverse array of religious practices in the public schools, including baccalaureate services, holiday observances, Bible distribution, display of religious symbols, singing of religious hymns, instruction in the dogma of the Nativity and Resurrection, religious tests for teachers, and religious census of pupils, in addition to prayer—both the Lord's Prayer and other prayers—and Bible reading. Many of these practices subsequently would be litigated in other cases because of the Court's refusal to hear *Chamberlin v. Dade County.* Leo Pfeffer considered it "the most interesting of all the church-state cases in which he was involved." Certainly it was the most comprehensive.[83]

The case marked a turning point for Miami Jews. Alhough it revealed the contingent character of Jewish support for separation of church and state, it nonetheless defined Jews vis-a-vis their Christian neighbors. Had *Chamberlin v. Dade County* not aroused such virulent Christian opposition, it would have been possible to conclude that Miami Jews were staunch supporters of church/state separation. Instead, the case revealed how equivocal Jewish convictions were, how concerned Jews remained with being good neighbors, how reluctant they were to man the barricades. Yet the outcome gave Jews both more and less than they anticipated. The court decision did curb some Christian practices, and the Supreme Court removed additional observances that made Jews uncomfortable. And despite their doubts Jews were identified with opposition to religion in the public schools. Jews discovered, as well, that the politics of religion could serve as a vehicle of Jewish identity. Out of the struggle over religion in the public schools emerged a popular Jewish political profile that included newcomers and old-timers, those who subscribed to its values as well as those who demurred. Although the decision to bring the case reflected the disorganization of Miami's Jewish community, the final outcome pleased Jews since it made the public schools less sectarian. Even those who had questioned the wisdom of bringing a case, like Aronovitz, desired the diminution of religious practices in the schools.

Miami Jews were identified with opposition to religion in the public schools as they were identified with support of desegregation despite the reluctance of many to speak out in favor of the 1954 Supreme Court decision. Ironically, these political positions in favor of integration, so tenuously arrived at, also defined Miami Jews as a separate white ethnic group. Their very efforts to create an integrated society and to change Miami's civic culture to accommodate Jews— unlike comparable efforts by Jews in the Northeast and Midwest—set them apart from their fellow white Christian migrants to Miami. By contrast, Jewish support for the rescue of survivors and creation of the state of Israel, as well as concern for its political and economic viability, attracted outspoken sympathy from their neighbors. Thus, Jewish political efforts in behalf of Israel, a separate and distinctively Jewish issue, actually served to integrate Jews into Miami politics rather than set them apart. Paradoxically, Miami Jews inadvertently discovered that the path to integration lay in their assertion of their own particular Jewish political concerns, not in efforts to shape a civic culture that did not distinguish between Jews and Gentiles.

Jewish political activity ultimately transformed not only Miami Jews but the political character of Dade County. When new immigrants from Cuba entered Miami politics a decade later, they found a political milieu more accustomed to the practice of ethnic politics than it had been before Jews settled in Miami. Jewish willingness, no matter how hesitant, to adhere to the tenets of political liberalism even on Miami's inhospitable soil hastened the process by which Miami politics came to resemble those of other large American cities.

Jews also learned from their Protestant neighbors that religious faith found legitimate expression in political values. If an interest-group politics of ethnicity alienated their Christian neighbors, a sentimental politics of religion excited Christian sympathies and respect. Israel, as homeland and holy land, gradually acquired centrality in the politics of Miami Jews. Their support for the establishment of the state and their subsequent identification with Israel as an expression of Jewish idealism helped to make sentimental Zionism into a collective glue unifying Jewish politics. It also allowed politics to define what it meant to be a Jew in Miami and to proclaim that identity.

7

Choosing Sides

It was somehow arranged that we did not face the common
enemy with a united front. In the end, many of us were
persuaded to place the knife in others' backs.

—CLANCY SIGAL
"Hollywood During the Great Fear," *Present Tense* (Spring 1982)

Miami Jews transplanted their political faith into an environment
shaped and defined by conflict between blacks and whites. Although
the process transformed them, their politics, and their city of choice,
Jews could find many common grounds for unity. In Los Angeles the
situation was different. There the newcomers engaged in bitter intramural struggles to achieve the unity that emerged. However, unlike
Miami Jews, whose sense of entitlement was often tempered by the
segregationist sentiment of their city, Los Angeles Jews shared a sense
of commonality of purpose at the end of World War II that drew them
together irrespective of their political beliefs. From Republican stal-
warts on the right to devoted Democrats in the center to zealous communists on the left, Los Angeles Jews adopted a common political
agenda. Together with other American Jews in the Northeast and
Midwest, they embraced the ideal of one world at peace, and they
imagined a unique role for Jews in world affairs as a freedom-loving

people, staunchly opposed to fascism. They accepted as well the Zionist solution of an independent Jewish commonwealth as the answer to the problem of the displaced persons. At home, Los Angeles Jews championed a broad antidiscrimination program to eliminate American antisemitism and racism. They pushed for legislation to outlaw discrimination in employment, supported fair housing, and opposed segregated schools and quotas in education. This was, they thought, the political agenda of true Americanism; as the feisty editorialist, labor Zionist Samuel Gach, put it: "Certainly what's good for the Jew can never conflict with what's good for the nation!"[1]

The cold war, however, severely tested their definitions of Americanism and their assumption that the inclusiveness that was good for the Jews was good for the nation. Congressional and state un-American activities committees plunged Los Angeles Jews into a bitter internal struggle that not only upset their political agenda and chastened the Jewish community but also challenged their definition of an American Jew.

The early postwar unanimity of Los Angeles Jews was apparent in activities ranging from voting patterns to sponsorship of rallies on behalf of DPs to resolutions passed by the central Los Angeles Jewish Community Council, an organization which included virtually the entire spectrum of Los Angeles's Jewish groups. The council provided L.A. Jews with a democratic body in which communal policy could be debated, political positions voted upon, and leadership openly contested. Theorists and ideologues had argued for years that American Jews deserved democratic institutions for their communal self-government rather than the elitist organizations that dominated the communal scene.[2] Despite the theory and occasional nod toward democratic practice, the Los Angeles Jewish Community Council remained a relatively rare egalitarian phenomenon in American Jewish life. In December 1944 the council had set the stage for its future political role when it voted to democratize representation. With the cooperation of its mass-membership organizations—Jewish War Veterans, labor Zionists, Hadassah, and American Jewish Congress—the council decided to list candidates alphabetically and to limit terms of office to no more than three consecutive ones. Those council members who missed six meetings a year would be suspended. The following month sixteen incumbent and five new members won election to the council's board, including one man who ran as an independent.[3]

The momentary sense of common commitments at the close of the war was all the more remarkable given the extraordinary diversity of Los Angeles Jews and the fact that they had been at political cross-purposes for several decades. Despite its low profile the established prewar Jewish community possessed a developed political network and a diverse politics. The visible, immigrant, Yiddish-speaking community centered in Boyle Heights ardently supported FDR and the New Deal. A minority leaned further left toward radicalism, both socialist and communist. Liberal and radical Zionist organizations also recruited members among Boyle Heights Jews. German-speaking refugees who arrived in the 1930s usually supported Roosevelt and the Democratic party, which they perceived as having saved them from Nazism.[4]

Among the substantial numbers of acculturated east European immigrants and second-generation Jews in the motion picture industry could be found all political stripes, from communist to left-wing liberal to Democrat to Republican. Unlike Boyle Heights radicals, Hollywood communists joined fellow travelers in nonsectarian front organizations to pursue their politics. Few of these Jews participated directly in Jewish politics. Jewish political concerns interested them only to the extent that Jews were victims of discrimination and prejudice, a condition Jews shared with other minorities. There was no ethnic dimension to their communism. For many, communism undoubtedly represented a path out of the Jewish community into an alternative international fraternity. Michael Blankfort, a close friend of the communist writer Albert Maltz until he and Maltz parted ways over anticommunist politics, penned a description of a Hollywood communist in his 1956 novel *The Strong Hand.* "He wanted to be three things all at once, a writer, a rich man and a hero. He found a way of satisfying all three by working as a scenarist in Hollywood and joining the Communist Party," Blankfort wrote.[5]

Finally, a small, almost extended family of native Los Angelenos, many of them descendants of nineteenth-century German Jewish immigrants, supported the Republican party and politicians "not noted for liberalism," in return, it was alleged, for favorable treatment in the press. These old-timers headed most of the established communal philanthropies, including the federation, and controlled the Los Angeles Jewish Community Council. In fact, old-timers were as likely to be Democrats as Republicans.[6] For both, ethnic politics was anathema. As Rabbi Edgar Magnin expressed it, "We are a people, but I'm not an ethnic Jew. I think it's the religion that counts." The Jewish religion did not prescribe any particular politics.[7]

Los Angeles politics discouraged the growth of ethnic coalitions. Although the city contained sizable minorities of Mexicans, Japanese, and African Americans, prejudice and discrimination constrained their pursuit of ethnic politics. Fringe groups of the left and the right flourished instead.[8] Politics meant expressing one's individual preferences; group preferences were unheard of and unthinkable. During the war even the moderate Republican attorney general, Earl Warren, sanctioned the internment of first- and second-generation Japanese Americans, as did communists and most liberals. Warren's stand did not hurt his political prospects after the war when he ran for governor and was mentioned as a possible presidential candidate. As governor, he blithely rejected a request of the Christian Council on Palestine to issue a proclamation supporting a Jewish commonwealth despite the endorsement of thirty-five other states. His dismissal of such an ethnic political gesture did not diminish his subsequent attractiveness to Jewish voters.[9]

California's nonpartisan political orientation similarly mitigated against the growth of ethnic politics. The cross-filing system allowed candidates to register in both parties' primaries without disclosing their own party affiliation, thus inhibiting a strong party system. Primary elections were open to any candidate able to garner sixty signatures and deposit a filing fee of $250, and most politicians competed for the nominations of both parties. Often as many as seven candidates ran for one position in the primaries. Republicans won Democratic nominations and vice versa, so that campaigns usually focused on personalities. California nurtured a politics of individual personalities to a far greater extent than the machine politics of the East. The absence of ethnic group identities "and of neighborhoods associated with those identities may be one reason for the enormous emphasis on 'personality,'" observed the political scientist James Q. Wilson. Warren, well-known nationally as a Republican, ran three successful campaigns for governor on a nonpartisan platform. He won with the votes of many Democrats. The popularity of referendums and initiatives on the state level suggested the relative weakness of the legislature.[10]

Newcomers discovered that party labels just did not carry the same meaning they had in the Northeast and Midwest. The Democratic party, the party of most Jewish migrants to Los Angeles, was exceptionally diverse. It contained former Ku Klux Klan members and erstwhile Republicans as well as communists, fellow travelers, and supporters of Upton Sinclair's EPIC program (End Poverty In California).[11]

As Jews responded to the refugee crisis and the struggle to secure the new State of Israel with increasing contributions to the United Jewish Welfare Fund, the prestige, power, and influence of the Los Angeles Jewish Community Council grew. Since the council allocated fund monies, it rapidly became the single most important arena for Jewish communal politics in Los Angeles. In 1945 the Council voted to expand its membership to include the city committee of the Jewish People's Fraternal Organization (JPFO) with its twelve lodges and three thousand members.[12]

The Jewish People's Fraternal Organization began life as the Jewish Section of the International Workers Order (IWO), a radical fraternal order founded in 1930 by dissident former members of the Jewish Socialist Workmen's Circle. The IWO rapidly grew into a multinational order, but Jews remained the largest single group; they dominated both the English-language and Yiddish-language, or Jewish, sections. In 1942 Jews reorganized into a single unit, and two years later a second reorganization produced the JPFO, making it the largest single unit in the IWO. Historian Arthur Liebman noted that "the promotion of Communism, the struggle of the working class, and the eradication of ethnic and racial prejudice figured prominently among the goals of the IWO." The council decision to admit the JPFO to membership occurred at a meeting in which the spokesman of the socialist Jewish Labor Committee failed to appear. In the past, strongly anticommunist labor representatives had vigorously opposed admitting the communist-linked JPFO. For Jewish socialists, long-standing opponents of communism, the Soviet Union was the real betrayer of the working class.[13]

But sentiment now favored an inclusive community council. JPFO had contributed energetically to the war effort by raising funds. In 1945 JPFO and its "progressive" politics belonged within the communal fold. Ironically, this policy of inclusion did not extend to intensive Jewish day schools. Despite support from radicals and a number of nonreligious men like Peter Kahn, the council rejected a recommended allocation to the Orthodox Hebrew Academy. The majority, including the leading Reform and Conservative rabbis of the community, Edgar Magnin and Jacob Kohn, condemned parochial education as "un-American."[14]

The Zionist program quickly dominated communal and local Jewish politics. The refugee crisis, revelations of the horrors of the death camps, and Jewish armed struggle against the British in Palestine generated enthusiasm for Zionism in Los Angeles and united Jews against the specter of the past and in support of the needs of the present. As early as August 1945 an observer noted that "the Zionist and Nationalist view in Los Angeles has wide organizational and mass support and much of the complexion of the community is reflected on this level." Zionists captured leadership of the council in 1946 when they elected clothing merchant Charles Brown, from a well-known old-time Zionist family, to its presidency. "Charlie was a real power," Magnin averred. Although he never received a formal Jewish education, Brown had memorized the psalms in English. Indeed, a rabbi recalled that one only had to speak to him for five or ten minutes for him to quote a psalm. "If it is possible to use the word 'saint,'" Henry Montor, the executive director of the United Jewish Appeal, remarked, "I would say that was the description which I would apply to him. He was a man of extraordinary idealism, and he felt Palestine has to be fought for."[15]

A Jewish consensus rapidly formed on Palestine; Zionist rallies drew supporters from all segments of Jewish Los Angeles. At the annual labor Zionist spring festival in 1946 a militant called for a Jewish Republican Army, like the Irish one, to fight against the British in Palestine. "Our fight is more than for ourselves. It is for mankind. Upon the world's treatment of the Jew hinges the world's own future," she proclaimed. Her sentiments echoed at a Call to Freedom meeting sponsored by Hollywood radicals.[16] Over twelve thousand people packed the American Legion Hall—actually a boxing arena—filling it to capacity. Gene Kelly stood at the mike on the raised boxing ring in the middle of the hall, coordinating the rally, as speaker followed speaker, Jew and Gentile, demanding "justice for Palestine." Hollywood director Jules Dassin spoke and appealed for funds. Charlotta Bass of the National Negro Congress declared her solidarity with the Jews. "I raise my voice to all colonial peoples, in India, Indonesia, Africa and China to ally themselves strongly and tightly with the Jewish people in this common war against imperialist slavery," proclaimed the publisher of Los Angeles's leading African-American paper. Charles Brown echoed her sentiments. "We are one world," he affirmed, "one people, with one common conscience."[17]

The fervor and unity rallied for Zionism could be channeled into domestic politics as well. When Los Angeles Jews went to the polls in November 1946, they voted overwhelmingly for a Fair Employment Practices Committee, although only 30 percent of the California electorate did. Whether they lived in Boyle Heights or Beverly Hills, Jews lined up in favor of the antidiscrimination proposal. Future Jewish voters for Henry Wallace's Progressive Party and Thomas Dewey's Republican Party supported FEPC despite the referendum's sponsorship by extreme leftist groups.[18] The same elections that defeated a California FEPC sent several liberal legislators from Los Angeles to Congress. Although an antisemitic and anticommunist rabble-rouser like Gerald L. K. Smith drew crowds of ten thousand when he visited the city, Jews believed that he represented a vocal minority and that they possessed the means to defeat him and his supporters.[19]

Yet between 1946 and 1947 this Jewish solidarity dissolved. In the spring of 1947, the House Un-American Activities Committee (HUAC) set up shop in a Biltmore Hotel room and unleashed its anticommunist investigation of Hollywood. When HUAC moved the hearings to Washington in the fall, Jews appeared among both friendly and unfriendly witnesses. "What the hell are Jews doing there, crawling with the rest of the mob?" Samuel Gach fumed. "Have they forgotten the sequel to the Reichstag Fire?" His query assumed that Jews had learned that attacks on communists served as prelude to persecution of Jews. Gach feared that the appearance of friendly witnesses "clearly points to the beginning of an era of vicious witch-hunting, thought-stifling, and persecution of anyone even expressing a truly liberal Americanism." His premonitions proved astoundingly accurate.[20]

In November, within weeks of the HUAC hearings' recess, a nervous group of Hollywood producers met at the Waldorf Astoria hotel in New York and hammered out an agreement not to "knowingly employ a Communist or a member of any party or group which advocates the overthrow of the Government of the United States by force." The producers acknowledged that "there is the danger of hurting innocent people. There is the risk of creating an atmosphere of fear." But they promised to "guard against this danger, this risk, this fear." Dore Schary accepted the responsibility of announcing the new discriminatory policy though he had voted against it. One of the most outspoken liberals among the producers, Schary testified to HUAC that he would continue to hire performers on the basis of merit alone until they were proven personally guilty of subversion. Yet Schary acquiesced in the decision to discriminate against communists. Creation of the blacklist pitted Jews against each other, echoing another fratricidal struggle occurring in Palestine.[21]

Fierce divisions among Jews in Palestine reverberated in Los Angeles. The militant Irgun, one of the Jewish underground organizations in Palestine, escalated its terrorist tactics against the British and shocked public opinion when it bombed the King David Hotel, killing ninety-one people. Charles Brown, in his new capacity as head of the council, announced that "we are unequivocally opposed to the assassinations and provocative acts of violence being perpetrated. . . . All funds expended in Palestine from the moneys raised in Los Angeles," he assured potential supporters, "are invested in land and equipment, in creation and support of agricultural colonies, in health and welfare agencies, and in the resettlement of the thousands of refugees from Nazi terror." Rabbi Jacob Sonderling, in a High Holiday sermon, blamed the British for turning Jews into terrorists. Distraught over the King David Hotel bombing, he praised Hadassah as an alternative "army of women" that opposed Arab intransigence by healing all, Arab and Jew. Raising funds in Los Angeles for the Haganah, Reuven Dafni "battled it out" with the Irgun's supporters. Director Fred Zinnemann invited Dafni to meet in his office with around twenty leading liberals in the movie industry, including Schary and screenwriters Michael Blankfort and Carl Foreman. Before the assembled group Dafni debated his opponent, a representative of the League for a Free Palestine. "Luckily, I convinced the people at that time," he recalled, that the Haganah and labor Zionists were the only ones "who were really doing something for the refugees."[22]

Despite these tensions within Zionist ranks, eighteen thousand turned out in October 1947 for a Hollywood Bowl rally for the freedom of Palestine. Henry Blankfort and a group of Hollywood communists and fellow travelers produced three playlets by writers Norman Corwin, Howard Fast, and Walter Bernstein, starring actors Edward G. Robinson, Larry Parks, and Alan Reed. Helen Gahagan Douglas spoke, and Frank Sinatra entertained the crowd.[23] Then, on November 29, 1947, the U.N. voted to partition Palestine into a Jewish and an Arab state. Both the United States and Soviet Union supported the measure in one of the last acts of the old wartime alliance. Public rejoicing of Jews in Los Angeles overshadowed any privately held misgivings of a small minority associated with the anti-Zionist American Council for Judaism.

At the height of the euphoria, as the United Nations voted the future Jewish state into being, Jews in Los Angeles felt the chill of anticommunism. The Zionists' success coincided with the first attacks upon left-wing Jewish radicals so recently admitted into the Jewish communal fold. The U.N. decision on partition came within a week of the Waldorf producers' conference initiating discriminatory hiring practices against communists in the motion picture industry. These parallel, albeit unrelated, events drastically changed the style and substance of Los Angeles Jewish politics. Spurred by the unrelenting pressures of cold war politics, Jews initiated their own investigations into beliefs of members of Jewish community organizations. Jewish leaders gradually insisted that all Jews take a stand on the issues of communism and Zionism, or more accurately, anticommunism and anti-Zionism. Los Angeles Jews chose the former and rejected the latter. Reluctantly and hesitantly at first and then with greater stridency, they branded communists and anti-Zionists as deceivers. As Los Angeles Jews determined who could remain within the community and who could not, the boundaries of their political discourse narrowed. Searching for safe ground, Jewish political energies increasingly focused upon the struggle for statehood in the Middle East. Israel became the uncontroversial core of communal concern.

Of the two politically charged issues confronting Los Angeles Jews, anti-Zionism generated the lesser passion. Walter Hilborn, a prominent lawyer active in the L.A. Jewish Community Council, concluded that the anti-Zionist American Council for Judaism never amounted to much in Los Angeles because "the leaders in the community were largely pro-Zion, you see, and the men who were in the Council were not very religious people." Since the Council for Judaism argued that Jews were a religious group with no ethnic or national ties to other Jews and certainly no loyalties to a Jewish state, the anti-Zionists' lack of religious commitment weakened their influence among Los Angeles Jews. Louis Boyar, an old-timer who moved to Los Angeles from Chicago during the Depression for his wife's health, fought anti-Zionists. "'I'm an American,' that was their answer," he recalled. "And they spoke of dual citizenship and dual loyalty—dual! Men that have only two loyalties aren't worth living," he scoffed. Hilborn described his law partner, native Angeleno Joseph Loeb, who headed the local chapter of the American Council for Judaism, as a man who "had no Judaism in his soul at all. Joe was a member of the [Wilshire Boulevard] Temple, but never went there. He felt he had to be a member, because he was practicing law in Los Angeles. We lost many clients because Joe Loeb was a member of the Council for Judaism."[24]

Even dedicated non-Zionists—those who viewed a Jewish Palestine as no more than an asylum for refugees—faced difficulties garnering support in Los Angeles. Maurice Karpf, a newcomer who arrived during the war to serve as executive director of Federation, wanted to turn the about-to-be-established local chapter of the American Jewish Committee into a non-Zionist stronghold. Writing to John Slawson, the committee's executive director, Karpf indicated his concerns: "I am rather dubious as to whether Zionists, particularly the more ardent kind, should be sought or invited to join. Nevertheless," he admitted, "it is difficult to draw a line." Karpf received an answer clearly rejecting his non-Zionist position. "The fact that a person is a Zionist (or an Anti-Zionist) need not necessarily exclude him from membership," Slawson wrote. Although the local chapter recruited few committed Zionists, it never became a bastion of ideologically principled non-Zionists. It couldn't; there were too few. Despite its appeal to several prominent natives, anti-Zionism never acquired more than a toehold in Los Angeles. Jews really did not have to struggle to enshrine support for the State of Israel as part of the Jewish political credo.[25]

The issue of anticommunism generated far more controversy, and its ramifications extended beyond merely ideological debate. The struggle in Los Angeles, because it involved Jews in the motion picture industry, echoed across the United States as did the issue of desegregation in Miami. The anticommunist blacklist revived "the age-old tragedy of the Jew-as-victim, Jew-as-scapegoat, Jew-as-betrayer."[26]

Los Angeles Jews addressed the anticommunist crusade from a number of perspectives: as a civil liberties issue involving the right of Jewish communists and fellow travelers to speak at open forums sponsored by Jewish community centers; as a civil rights question involving the rights of employees of Jewish institutions—especially social workers in Jewish social welfare agencies but also attending physicians at Jewish hospitals—to keep their jobs without taking loyalty oaths; as an ideological issue regarding political positions taken by the Jewish community on various anticommunist measures; and as a matter of collective conscience concerning whether Jewish communist organizations belonged within the Jewish community. The venues of anticommunist struggle included the L.A. Jewish Community Council and its Community Relations Committee (CRC); several local Jewish community centers and their recently established coordinating organization, the Jewish Centers Association; the public forums of rallies and the press; and the local chapter of the most liberal of the national defense organizations, the American Jewish Congress.

The Community Relations Committee provided a central arena for several important anticommunist debates. Its executive director called it "the public face of the Jewish community in Los Angeles." The council incorporated CRC as its agency and voice in the area of community relations in 1945 and expanded its size from fifty to seventy members.[27] The enlarged committee included representatives from national and local organizations involved in fighting antisemitism. Mendel Silberberg, a Republican lawyer for the film industry with "no small reputation as a politician," chaired the enlarged committee. At a time in Los Angeles when "law firms were virtually all segregated by religion and by race," Mitchell, Silberberg, and Knapp was one exception, "a law firm truly integrated by religion" due to Silberberg's "forceful personality and community leadership." Under Silberberg's guidance the committee rapidly became the authoritative body dealing with issues of discrimination, Jewish social and political status, and intergroup relations. Although officially subordinate to the Jewish Community Council, its recommendations were never overturned. Paul Jacobs, an active CRC member, considered it "a natural place" for contacts to be made "because you had the studios represented through Silberberg; you had the Jewish war veterans there, who were able to go to the Legionnaire types, and you had other people who were close to union people." Its early appearance on the Los Angeles scene, its adequate budget, and its leadership gave the Community Relations Committee authority within the Jewish community.[28]

HUAC's decision to investigate subversion in the motion picture industry and the subsequent subpoenas of those who became known as the Hollywood Ten forced Jews in Los Angeles to confront anti-communism even before McCarthy arose on the national scene. Not all of those investigated were Jews, but public perception, especially among political conservatives, fed upon the antisemitic stereotype linking Jew and communist. As Victor Navasky has argued, to look for communist subversion in an industry in which Jews were prominent seemed self-evident to such right-wing politicians. Recognizing this implicit (and occasionally explicit) bias, several of the Hollywood Ten charged HUAC with antisemitism.[29] "We knew that it wasn't as if Harry Cohn or L. B. Mayer was Himmler putting a gun to our heads," wrote Clancy Sigal, a blacklisted writer, in retrospect. "Yet, at times, it felt that way. We had survived Hitler's war, only to face the possibility of a kind of Hitlerism at home. Our fears," he concluded, "were not groundless."[30]

In fact, Jewish involvement in the motion picture industry and Hollywood's participation in the Jewish community were sufficiently prominent to raise the issue of a Jewish response to the investigations and charges. As attorney for the producers, Silberberg attended the Waldorf meeting and helped to craft the agreement barring communists from employment in the film industry. He brought his Hollywood experience to the Community Relations Committee, as did other entertainment lawyers like Martin Gang, a leader of the local AJCommittee chapter and an active CRC member. Though Gang stood a considerable political distance from Silberberg—Gang had joined the liberal National Lawyers Guild in the 1930s when he considered the American Bar Association to be a narrow, reactionary

organization—the two lawyers managed to get along.[31] Gang's perception of the political realities facing his Hollywood clients undoubtedly
influenced his interpretation of the dangers facing the Jewish community. He defended many of those subpoenaed by HUAC, tried to do
his best to help them, and gained a reputation as a "clearance" lawyer,
one who would get an individual cleared to work again in the motion
picture industry.[32] Despite the forceful presence of such men as Paul
Jacobs and Martin Gang, the Community Relations Committee ultimately declined to take a stand defending those who pleaded the Fifth
Amendment.[33]

The committee could refrain from responding to HUAC's investigation of Hollywood, but it could not ignore Los Angeles's home-
grown anticommunist, State Senator Jack Tenney. A right-wing
Republican and antisemite, Tenney chaired California's un-American
activities committee and directed its attention to Jewish communal
institutions. In 1948 he launched a bitter attack on the Soto-Michigan Jewish Community Center in Boyle Heights, charging that the
center's staff, member organizations, and programs contained communists. Tenney persistently equated Jews and communists and prof-
ited politically from his accusations.[34] Summoned to testify before
the Tenney Committee, Joseph Esquith, Soto-Michigan's director,
defended the center as a laboratory of democracy where free speech,
free association, and free assemblage flourished. Esquith's eloquence, however, did not undermine Tenney's accusations; his reiterated charges confronted the community committee and the Jewish
Centers Association. After the hearing the association and individual
centers held an acrimonious joint board meeting that nonetheless
staunchly reaffirmed established policies. Esquith subsequently
asked the community committee to expose Tenney's attack as an
"unwarranted canard" while his board demanded a public response
from the Jewish Community Council.[35]

When no vigorous public statement was made, Soto-Michigan ner-
vously surveyed its activities over the 1947–48 year. Most of the communist front groups singled out by Tenney sponsored relatively few
events and drew less than 5 percent of the center's annual participants. The center noted that it consistently rejected requests from political parties ranging from the Communists to the Republicans to use

its facilities. Despite its spirited response to the charges and support from several left-wing organizations, the center suffered a subsequent decline in membership. The stigma of Tenney's charges lingered.[36]

Tenney's investigation threatened the nonsectarian Los Angeles Welfare Federation as well. Frightened, the welfare federation issued an anticommunist directive to its agencies, Soto-Michigan among them, demanding that they deny their facilities to any organization on the attorney general's subversive list. Soto-Michigan's board vehemently rejected the welfare federation's right to make policy and challenged its directive as contrary to the Jewish centers' "concepts of freedom of assemblage and open forum." In a letter to Leslie Cramer, president of the Jewish Centers Association, the board noted that the radical Jewish People's Fraternal Order, "an integral part of the Jewish Community of Boyle Heights," regularly rented space at Soto-Michigan and cosponsored the Bureau of Jewish Education's Yiddish Mittelshule. Sam Bates, center president, summed up the matter succinctly: "Compliance with the Welfare Federation directive would remove what we feel is a very real segment of Jewish life from participation in Center activities." Jewish communists in the JPFO could not be excluded from the Boyle Heights community without substantially changing its character. But Soto-Michigan's forthright stand inspired few expressions of solidarity from other Jewish communal organizations, which feared being tainted as fellow travelers were they to support the rights of an organization on the attorney general's list.[37]

Immediately following the Tenney hearings, the local AJCommittee branch initiated its own purge and challenged the JPFO's membership within L.A.'s Jewish Community Council. The chapter requested an investigation to determine whether JPFO was a Communist organization. According to council rules political organizations could not be members. JPFO claimed that it was a Jewish fraternal organization, as indicated by its name and reflected in its Yiddish cultural and educational endeavors, its welfare and insurance programs, and its commitment to radical social action. JPFO identified itself as a "progressive" organization, a term that increasingly came to be seen by others as a pejorative code word for communist.[38]

Beginning in December 1948, the community committee held five hearings, listening to written and oral testimony from JPFO representatives. Jacobs, a socialist veteran of anticommunist union battles in the East, participated in the bitter debates. He quickly discovered, however, that "this campaign was far more difficult than in New York. Many of the people involved were so unsophisticated politically that it wasn't possible to make the kind of arguments with them that had been so effective in New York." In the East Jacobs could easily remind Jewish liberals of communist vacillation over opposition to Nazism during the years of the Soviet-Nazi pact and point out the twists and turns of Soviet policy. In Los Angeles there had been few bitter struggles between Jewish liberals and radicals during World War II. Jacobs also recognized that "the issue of Communists operating inside the Los Angeles Jewish community was even more difficult and traumatic to deal with because the case of the Hollywood Ten and the start of the movie industry's blacklisting of real and alleged Communists was beginning to have ugly repercussions." Men and women were losing their jobs because of past political associations as FBI investigators hounded families accused of being communists and even children suffered taunts by their peers. Searching for a middle ground, the committee concluded that JPFO qualified for membership. However, they declared its affiliation with the International Workers Order, an organization that had lost its tax-exempt status because it was on the attorney general's list, was "detrimental to the character" of the Jewish Community Council.[39]

In 1949 and 1950 JPFO carried its case to Los Angeles Jews. It staged rallies and ran ads in the local Jewish press. Its speakers attacked "international bankers" on the community committee for seeking to split the Jewish community. Its ads praised JPFO's progressive, philanthropic, and working-class activities and condemned "reactionary" elements within the council that wanted to expel the organization. JPFO also appealed to the Jewish community centers for their support and an open hearing of the charges. Soto-Michigan responded with a letter protesting the council's undemocratic efforts to oust JPFO, while the Beverly-Fairfax Center sent two representatives to monitor the hearings. Gach ruefully observed that "our own Jewish Community Council is tolerating a 'Little Dies Committee' within its body," comparing CRC hearings with those of HUAC. He scoffed at the notion of expelling JPFO on the grounds that it was political. "Is the American Jewish Committee not political?" he asked rhetorically.

"Is the Jewish Labor Committee not political when it supports the policies of the British Government?"[40]

In June 1950, upon the recommendation of the community committee, Joseph Solomonov of the Jewish War Veterans officially charged that JPFO was a political organization, part of and subordinate to the International Workers Order, a nonsectarian, not Jewish, political organization. As the council held sixteen hearings from June through November, debate continued in the press. A left-wing commentator argued that "a dangerous precedent" would be set that would transform the council into "a sort of un-Jewish activities committee." But a principled anti-Stalinist offered a stinging rejoinder: "Their [JPFO] crimes against the Jewish community are many. Shall we, in the name of unity, give our enemies a chance to destroy us?" he demanded. But many Jews now felt external pressure. The cold war conflict in Korea—and the convergence of Israeli and American positions—clarified the issue for Gach and he reversed his stand. When JPFO called for a peace march through Boyle Heights in August, he unceremoniously drummed them out of the community. All "legitimate Jewish" groups condemned the "red-inspired 'peace proclamation,'" he noted. Thus, he concluded, the Jewish People's Fraternal Organization was neither Jewish nor the people's, and if fraternal, its only fraternity was with Moscow.[41]

Not only did events in Korea influence Jewish perceptions of the need to choose sides, but the relentless anticommunist campaign at home also affected them. Public rage was such that liberal organizations hesitated to oppose the most flagrant breaches of civil rights. When the Los Angeles County Board of Supervisors required that all members of communist organizations register, "only the American Civil Liberties Union clearly spoke out against the whole principle of the ordinance," an outsider observed. Testimony of other groups "implied acquiesence in the principle of registering Communists." Finally, in December the L.A. Jewish Community Council's membership committee concluded that JPFO had political purposes and was subordinate to the International Workers Order. At the 1951 annual meeting in January, the council expelled fourteen JPFO lodges and one Emma Lazarus lodge from the official Jewish community. However, it held out the possibility of reinstatement if JPFO severed its ties with the International Workers Order. Jewish communists had enjoyed a brief five years within the Jewish communal fold.[42]

Jewish efforts to foster coalition politics in Los Angeles met a similar fate to their desire for unity. After two years in the city as director of the American Jewish Congress's Pacific Coast region, Mel Springer thought he saw the future in the cooperation of minorities to achieve a common political agenda. One out of three Angelenos belonged to a minority, either Jews, Mexicans, African Americans, or Japanese, he observed. Were these groups "to ally themselves in a fight against restrictive residential covenants and racial and religious discrimination," Springer argued, they could "wield a tremendous political power." AJCongress did try to pursue such politics. In 1948, for example, it collaborated with the NAACP in picketing a Sears, Roebuck store in Santa Monica to demand that the store hire African Americans.[43]

But Springer's vision did not reckon with political realities of Jewish Los Angeles. Relations between Jews and African Americans were not particularly good despite common political goals. The latter's leaders complained that "the Jews come to us only when there is a mutuality of interest." Many Jews felt uncomfortable with African Americans. Similarly, Jews did not have close ties with Mexican Americans despite the votes of Boyle Heights Jews that helped elect Edward Roybal to the Los Angeles City Council.[44] As for Japanese Americans, few Jews protested their internment in concentration camps during World War II. In the postwar era Jews had little contact with Japanese Los Angelenos. Instead of a unified ethnic coalition fighting for FEPC, the organized Jewish community looked to labor and the left for support. Rather than oppose restrictive covenants as Springer urged, the Community Relations Committee pragmatically accepted them. When queried by local Jewish lawyers for guidelines to follow if a client asked them to write a restrictive covenant on a property, the committee recommended drawing up the covenant but telling the client that the lawyer would not enforce it.[45]

AJCongress itself succumbed to struggles between communists and anticommunists, swinging for a time in favor of the former until finally being squelched by the latter.[46] At the first Pacific regional convention in 1949, five hundred delegates elected a left-wing Los

Angeles businessman, Myer Pransky, to the presidency instead of Rabbi Max Nussbaum, a national vice-president. Nussbaum admitted that he had "always considered the American Jewish Congress a movement 'left of center' and until recently, all of us seemed to have agreed on what that meant." Now Nussbaum had serious "ideological differences" with most of the new local leadership. The "tempestuous" meeting that prompted Nussbaum to refuse renomination to the presidency passed a host of resolutions indicating its radical, procommunist posture. These included an appeal for "an end to the cold war," world disarmament, outlawing the atom bomb, and destruction of all atomic stockpiles. AJCongress called for the dissolution of HUAC and the "abolition of loyalty oaths." Finally, the locals asked the national office to support a bail request for eleven convicted Communist officials and to file an amicus curiae brief to test the constitutionality of the Smith Act. The national AJCongress convention responded the following month (November 1949) by determining "to clean house of all Congressites who . . . manifest more loyalty to alien directives than to the needs of either this country or their own brethren." When the L.A. Jewish Community Council expelled JPFO, the national congress office took over the local Los Angeles branch and froze its bank accounts.[47]

Neither the vote expelling JPFO from the council nor the takeover of the local congress branch resolved the issue of communist and left-wing participation in Jewish community life. The controversy shifted to the centers' popular open forums. Historically, secular Jewish centers attracted liberal and often radical Jews. Centers now became the battleground for the struggle over the place of communists and "progressive" politics within the Jewish community. In March 1949 the Jewish Centers Association's board adopted a statement of principles and policies designed to guide member centers through troubled times. It affirmed that centers were "typically American institutions conceived and maintained by the Jewish community to fulfill its recreational, health, cultural, educational and social needs." It pointed out that "like the public schools," centers "do not inquire into the political affiliation of individuals who make use of their facilities, but they do not permit such individuals to use Centers as a means of promoting political ideologies." While affirming the centers' commitment to an open-forum principle of free speech and assembly, the statement elaborated that this justified excluding any organization deemed illegal by the United States government. As a result, the open forum fell under certain restrictions, and approval was required to rent facilities.[48]

But the new policy gave individual centers room for interpretation, thus bringing the issue of the extent of Jewish communist participation in communal affairs down to the neighborhood level. Despite the new rules the left wing, its freedom circumscribed, still had access to the centers' forums.[49] Their popular lecture series reflected liberal and radical politics of the day, with subjects ranging from the H-bomb in 1950 to the Smith Act in 1951, the Rosenberg case in 1952, and the McCarran Act in 1953. Individual centers also vigorously opposed such anticommunist legislation in Congress as the Mundt-Ferguson bill, which proposed to register all communists and deny them passports if they didn't comply, even as their boards tried to protect centers from investigation. Jewish opposition extended beyond statements by center boards to letter-writing campaigns to Congressmen, as well as a protest rally organized by the Community Relations Committee in concert with Hadassah.[50]

Committed to the concept that "Judaism is a way of life . . . that calls, without question, for the practice of the principles of social justice," Milton Malkin, director of the Beverly-Fairfax Center, navigated an increasingly narrow path between critics on the right and left. Soto-Michigan, its progressive staff supported by a board dominated by liberal and left-wing Jews, continued to sponsor its intercultural Festival of Friendship. This annual event involved groups from the Mexican-American, Japanese-American, and African-American communities. Center staff saw intercultural activities as quintessentially American, the "training ground for democracy." Soto-Michigan's emphasis on interculturalism also reflected its radical ideological commitment to welcome all "regardless of racial, religious or political differences."[51]

Not under direct attack by Tenney, the Beverly-Fairfax Center nonetheless faced similar dilemmas. Like Soto-Michigan, Beverly-Fairfax's board contained many liberals and "progressives," including Henry Blankfort, who had a reputation among more conservative Jews as a "notorious leftist," that is, they considered him a fellow traveler because of his support of radical politics.[52] Unlike Soto-Michigan,

Beverly-Fairfax was established as a model center to bring to Los Angeles the caliber of cultural programming associated with New York City's 92nd Street Y. In 1949 the center initiated the first Los Angeles exhibit of Israeli artists. The cooperative venture garnered praise from all segments of the Jewish community. Not so other aspects of center programming. When the center invited artist Rockwell Kent, known for his communist sympathies, to open another exhibit, the board found itself forced to discuss whether the guidelines required them to scrutinize a person's political background when the subject under discussion, like art, was "neutral." Soon after, the Community Relations Committee considered investigating center activities, implying that "programs were slanted so as to favor public appearances on platforms by leftist or progressive elements in the community." In fact, it was easier to secure speakers representing the progressive point of view because they were "always eager for a platform." Much more difficult was "securing speakers from the opposite point of view . . . since they refuse to participate in forum programs in which alleged radicals are also appearing." Threat of governmental scrutiny and fear of losing a job made it dangerous to share a platform with progressives, even when expressing the opposing viewpoint.[53]

Criticism escalated in the summer of 1950 when the Beverly-Fairfax Center's drama group presented a play at the New Globe Theater, *How I Wonder*, by the communist writer Donald Ogden Stewart. Henry Blankfort, chair of the center's drama committee, responded somewhat disingenuously to questions by board members regarding the play's theme. He had not known the content of the unwritten play when he convinced various center groups to sponsor performances, he explained. Active in Hollywood communist circles, Blankfort, of course, knew the playwright and his politics. The performance "provoked in the minds of some people queries as to whether a play having the theme of peace and of social justice should be presented by the center in these times." The cold war climate of the Korean War cast a pall on the theme of social justice and made the subject of peace subversive, an enemy ruse. But if the center, as Malkin explained, should not become "the dupe of leftists," neither "should it serve the equally unacceptable interests of the rightists." Even the alternative that the center only provide recreation for children still required that it have "some social principles for motivation to guide its young people, because we deal with our people," he remarked, "as thinking individuals and not as mere physical beings who come to use our swimming pool, inhabit our rooms and play volleyball."[54]

There was, in fact, a third alternative: Jewish programming and Jewish values. The popular success of Beverly-Fairfax's Israeli art exhibit suggested the Jewish public's response to such programs. Socialist and ex-radical anticommunists used Zionist arguments to attack the "progressive" bias of Jewish community centers. Jacobs recalled his embarrassment when he "got up at a CRC meeting to make a speech denouncing the way in which the community centers . . . were being used for the 'progressive' causes instead of having more Jewish content." He later admitted that "in truth I cared no more about giving a Jewish content, whatever that meant, to the community-center program than did the supposed Communists I was attacking. I just objected to the specific programs *they* were substituting for Jewish content," he explained, "since I thought their choices were heavily oriented toward a political line with which I did not agree."[55] More Jewish programming under the cold war's deepening shadow became a weapon to fight left-wing policies.

In March 1951 the Jewish Centers Association informed center boards that they would be held responsible "for deciding in each case whether a particular speaker or his treatment of a subject is fitting and desirable for presentation in the Center." The reason: "The Boards of Jewish Centers must recognize the change of public attitudes which has developed in our country with regard to the political activity of individuals and organizations publicly charged with being unfriendly to American democracy." Board members debated how to interpret the new ruling. At Beverly-Fairfax the chair of the adult education committee that supervised the controversial forums refused to "place himself in the position of being a censor as to who would or would not be considered controversial." Blankfort agreed. He protested that the letter implied "a weakening of the fundamental principles of democracy in the Center and . . . a capitulation to the current hysteria." Referring to a pile of recent newspaper clippings, he pointed out that "anti-Semitism is at present on the uprise." His message was clear: "Unless we guard our civil liberties, we are helping to destroy them." After extensive debate and despite misgivings, the boards accepted the prohibitive responsibility.[56]

Within the Los Angeles Jewish community by 1951, centers remained organizations most sympathetic to the left, led and staffed by Jews who supported liberal, "progressive," and occasionally communist programs. Excluded from the community council, local branches of JPFO continued to meet in center rooms. Center boards also resisted increasing pressure to subject staff members to loyalty oaths, yet left-wing control of centers weakened. Struggles for a union contract, ideological competition with Zionists, and recommendations of two eastern experts—Bertram Gold and Herbert Passameneck—invited to survey centers in relation to changing Jewish residential patterns combined to undermine centers as bastions of radicalism. These battles occurred while centers were facing attacks on their programming and staff.[57]

The displacement of Jewish radicals among the social workers stemmed from the refusal of the Los Angeles Jewish Federation board to renegotiate a union contract in 1949 and 1950 and paralleled a change in center board leadership. Liberal and left-wing supporters of radical Jewish social workers lost their positions on center boards less because of deliberate efforts to purge centers than because of implementation of professional recommendations made by Passameneck and Gold. As liberal outsiders both men ignored ideological issues and focused instead on pragmatic matters, especially the changing character of the Boyle Heights neighborhood and the fundamental inadequacy of the Beverly-Fairfax facilities. They urged Los Angeles Jews to build a large central community center in place of Beverly-Fairfax on the west side, where so many Jews were moving, and to consolidate facilities in an old neighborhood like Boyle Heights, with a declining Jewish population. Los Angeles Jews accepted the advice of these eastern professionals because they wanted to improve and strengthen their community centers in response to the large influx of newcomers. Vital, modern Jewish community centers would help mark the maturation of L.A. Jewry.[58] But the effects of such decisions on the local level were unanticipated.

Despite diminishing Jewish populations neither of the two centers serving the east side—Soto-Michigan and the Menorah center, located less than two miles away—had experienced a substantial drop in membership. (Beverly-Fairfax, on the west side, attracted many newcomers to its meager facilities.) Yet anticipating further decline, the consolidation plans ignored this evidence of continuity and were put into effect.[59]

Amalgamation of the two Jewish community centers serving the east side involved more than administrative efficiency. Board members recognized that there was a "fundamental difference in the ideology" between Soto-Michigan's intercultural emphasis, derived from left-wing political values, and Menorah's Zionist-based Jewish cultural approach. Non-Jewish participation in center activities reflected the different emphases: Menorah drew only a small minority of non-Jews, 3 percent, to its programs, while 15 percent of Soto-Michigan's participants were not Jewish. Furthermore, Soto-Michigan's radicalism remained an issue. Soto-Michigan's board learned of plans to consolidate the two east side centers in the midst of fending off yet another attack by Tenney. This time, in the middle of a Community Chest fund rally, Tenney "advised those present not to contribute to the Chest" because it supported "subversive" elements in the Jewish community centers. When faced with the decision to amalgamate Menorah's program, including its Hebrew school, with Soto-Michigan, the Menorah board revolted. "We here at Menorah are as much interested in the promulgation of Jewish culture and Jewish values as in intercultural activities, but our emphasis is on Jewish content, because a Jewish Center, which receives Jewish funds should emphasize what they were originally intended to do," they protested. The Menorah board even considered becoming an independent center. But ultimately its protests and threats were to no avail.[60]

On September 9, 1952, the Soto-Michigan Jewish Community Center, a favorite object of vilification by Jack Tenney as a Jewish communist stronghold, dissolved itself and transferred its assets to the amalgamated Eastside Jewish Community Center. The Jewish Centers Association transferred Joseph Esquith, Soto-Michigan's controversial director, and moved Milton Malkin, the head of Beverly-Fairfax, to the new, untainted center. The amalgamation not only responded to changing Jewish demographic patterns but, through a reorganization of staff and center board members, also eliminated many radicals and progressives.[61]

Closing the Beverly-Fairfax Center the following year, despite its good location near a new, popular area of Jewish settlement, reflected a different but related set of priorities shared by the federation and Jewish Centers Association. Beverly-Fairfax fell victim to the association's decision to build a large, modern center to serve the rapidly growing Jewish population on the west side. As in the amalgamation of the east side centers, the association used the opportunity of building a new center to change the character of its board, thus eliminating many radicals and progressives. The association chose members of the operating committee for the new Westside Jewish Community Center over the protests of Beverly-Fairfax board members, who wanted to serve as the leaders of the new center. Board members of the old center recognized correctly that they were losing the opportunity to determine the new center's membership and character, to shape its cultural and political activities, and to pick its staff. When the new center board was formed, a minority of thirteen members out of thirty came from Beverly-Fairfax; the other seventeen members represented Jewish constituencies on the west side with different concerns. The process eliminated several left-wing members from the new board.[62] The association's desire to include individuals from different city constituencies—especially the wealthy Beverly Hills crowd—led them to minimize the influence of the old Beverly-Fairfax board. As a result, the politics of the Westside Jewish Community Center focused less on radical issues than on Jewish cultural questions.[63]

Ideological debates within the L.A. Jewish Community Council paralleled changes in the Jewish community centers. In January 1953 Zionists swept elections for the council's executive board, displacing several well-known non-Zionist leaders, including Walter Hilborn and Martin Gang, up for reelection. Zionists marked their victory not only by voting in a precampaign budget formula that favored aid to Israel over local federation social service agencies but also by resolutions attacking, explicitly and implicitly, political positions of Jewish communists. The resolutions committee ignored the furor over the trial, conviction, and sentence of Julius and Ethel Rosenberg, two New York Jews convicted of spying for the Soviet Union and sentenced to death. Instead it attacked the purge trial of Rudolf Slansky, the Jewish Czechoslovak communist leader. The council resolution condemned the "deliberate use of anti-Semitism in order to justify the policies of a Communist government which must divert its enslaved people from realizing the depth of their degradation." The Prague trial was a "tragic reminder" of the "bitter cold war between communism and the United States, Israel," and other unnamed havens of freedom. Just before the Rosenbergs were executed, efforts to get the council to condemn the death sentence again failed, despite long picket lines around the Federal building and several mass meetings.[64]

Gach recognized the dilemma. Because communists rallied so fervently to support the Rosenbergs and protest their death sentence, the council avoided taking a stand. Gach took the risk. "I abhor the death sentence and despise the judge [Irving Kaufman] who proclaimed it," he wrote. Though he knew that "our enemies, the Communists, will take full advantage of the episode," Gach excoriated the "witches brew . . . stewed by the McCarthys and McCarrans" that tempted "the nostrils of the Kaufmans and other weaklings too scared to hold out for the enduring sustenance to be gotten only in a *pure democracy*." His editorial produced a spate of letters and prompted him to write another column in the *California Jewish Voice* explaining that the communists had mistakenly interpreted his stand on the Rosenbergs as support for the communist cause. In fact, Gach saw a "degrading fear" in Jewish willingness to jump in to attack anyone who was accused of being subversive, whether justified or not.[65]

Another case came before the council, one that involved three physicians dismissed from the Cedars of Lebanon Hospital after being subpoenaed to testify regarding their political activities. In trying to steer a middle path between the conservative hospital trustees and several left-wing organizations that wanted to censure Cedars of Lebanon, the council urged the hospital to reinstate the three doctors and to give them a fair hearing.[66] The hospital, whose trustees represented the old-time German Jewish elite in direct contrast to the centers' leadership, refused to accede to the council's demands and defiantly rejected its recommendation. In a provocative act the Cedars board dismissed four additional physicians for political reasons. Radicals urged the council to withhold funds from the hospital in response. Despite clear sympathies with the physicians and opposition to the conservatism of the non-Zionist Cedars board, Zionists refused to join forces with the left. They would not unequivocally condemn the hospital's discriminatory actions. Instead a majority supported a resolution censuring Cedars for its unwillingness to give the physicians a hearing and for placing its policies above the "overriding community interest in the entire situation." The council refused to withhold funds, however, because that would only penalize the sick, the innocent victims.[67] It would also by association have implicated organized Jewry with questionable political beliefs.

Council resolutions on the Prague trials and Cedars of Lebanon Hospital articulated political views that tried to distinguish the Jewish community's anticommunism from that of HUAC and the radical right. The L.A. Jewish Community Council walked a thin line in attempting to mediate between diverse political opinions held by Jews and the felt need to establish Jewish Americanism in the public eye during a period of fear of communist subversion. By taking no stand on the Rosenbergs' death sentence and limiting its position on civil rights and job discrimination—choosing to censure the Cedars of Lebanon board only for acting in an arbitrary manner—it sent a clear message. It indicated the extent to which communists were excluded from, and left-wing "progressives" consigned to the margins of, the organized Jewish community by 1953.

Zionists tried to define a middle ground that included aid to Israel as a "normal part of Jewish community responsibilities in America," as well as condemnation of the McCarran-Walter act, which imposed narrow immigration quotas and contained stiff anticommunist provisions. The council wanted the act revised to keep America a "haven of refuge" and to reaffirm the United States' traditional policy of respecting individual integrity by not restricting individuals' political beliefs. In 1954 Jews on the left and center joined forces to protest a 1952 Los Angeles ordinance requiring organizations to sign a loyalty oath to receive tax exemption. Despite vigorous debate and efforts by several Christian churches to challenge the law's constitutionality, Silberberg's Community Relations Committee ultimately recommended that all Jewish congregations sign the loyalty oath even if they also sent in letters of protest. Several protested, but all of them signed under pressure from the Jewish Community Council. The following year, despite nervous anticipation of a new HUAC investigation of Hollywood, Zionists set aside their fears of being tainted by support of left-wing groups and repulsed attempts by anticommunist

Jewish newcomers from northeastern and midwestern cities thought Los Angeles was a city without poverty because its broad streets, low buildings, and absence of overcrowding contrasted vividly with familiar Jewish neighborhoods in the urban northeast. Here is Wabash Avenue, a main Jewish shopping street in Boyle Heights, L.A.'s Jewish immigrant neighborhood in the 1930s. (*Courtesy YIVO Institute for Jewish Research*)

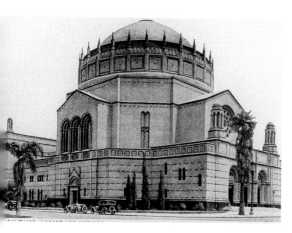

Newcomers observed the affluence of Los Angeles Jews, earned in the motion picture industry and visible in its premiere synagogue, the Wilshire Boulevard Temple (formerly B'nai B'rith). Rabbi Edgar Magnin built the temple into the preeminent Reform congregation in Los Angeles during his more than fifty years' tenure. (*Courtesy Lake County [IL] Museum/Curt Teich Postcard Archives*)

The elegant Moorish facade of Temple Sinai, the leading Conservative congregation in Los Angeles, captivated visitors from New York in the 1940s, as did its well-dressed, scholarly rabbi, Jacob Kohn, and the city's palm trees. Newcomers thought they glimpsed the possibility of living a Jewish life in heaven on earth. (*Courtesy YIVO Institute for Jewish Research*)

Los Angeles enticed thousands of young Jews seeking opportunity. They came west after the war, riding the train from the East Coast. Ben from Brooklyn and Marilyn from Chicago met and fell in love on a train heading west. They married and began a new life together in L.A. Here the Leftgoffs stand in front of their first Los Angeles house on 42nd Street in 1947. (*Courtesy Ben and Marilyn Leftgoff*)

Life in L.A. was relaxed, casual, and easy, a mixture of work and leisure that blurred boundaries between the two. Important rituals were often informal, like the wedding of Alexander Alpert and Frances Greenseid, held in the backyard of her parents' Los Angeles apartment building, 1949, with the dome of Wilshire Boulevard Temple in background. (*Courtesy Michael Alpert*)

Growing up in Los Angeles meant an opportunity to enjoy the private pleasures and personal freedom of a world devoted to leisure, far removed from the intense collective Jewish life of their parents' "old home" in midwestern and northeastern cities. Al and Frances Alpert's eight-year-old son Michael swings from the bar in their West Los Angeles backyard in 1962. (*Courtesy Michael Alpert*)

In the 1950s and 1960s young Jews from New York or Chicago, Boston or Philadelphia, increasingly discovered the spacious San Fernando Valley, where intensive construction of reasonably priced private single-family homes transformed acres of farmland into residential tracts. Brooklyn-born and bred, Bud Hudson came to the valley in 1949 with his wife Ellie, and posed with his son David and daughter Judith outside their home in Van Nuys, where the air was sparkling and wildflowers still bloomed in 1954. (*Courtesy Bud and Ellie Hudson*)

Because few married Jewish women worked outside the home, innovative rabbis and religious leaders recruited them to study and learn how to be Jewish. Here, the first women to become bat mitzvah as adults at the Valley Jewish Community Center study Torah with Miriam Wise, the rabbi's wife, in the 1950s. With Miriam Wise (*far left*) are (*l to r*) Shirley Whizin, Romola Jarett, Pauline Halote, Marian Wail, and Sarah Epstein. (*Courtesy Adat Ari El*)

Initiated by Miriam Wise, the Sisterhood's first Book and Gift Shop encouraged Jewish women to decorate their homes with ritual objects to express the beauty of Jewish religious culture. It was hoped that Jewish women would set the standard for religious observance in their families. Miriam Wise (*center*) flanked by Ruth Gribin (*left*) and Sarah Helfman (*right*) in 1948. (*Courtesy Adat Ari El*)

Rabbi Isaiah Zeldin and two girls stand with a scroll on a mountaintop by Mulholland Drive, future site of the Stephen S. Wise Temple, ca. 1967. The physical site expressed the spiritual hopes of many congregants for their "place in the sun"; its location, between the San Fernando Valley and western Los Angeles, reflected Zeldin's aim to build a congregation for all Jews seeking religious roots; the girls' presence indicated a new emphasis on educating women as critical to the Jewish future. (*Courtesy Stephen S. Wise Temple*)

Shlomo Bardin struck a bargain with his campers to the Brandeis Camp Institute at Santa Susana in the Simi Valley outside Los Angeles: In return for a month of their time, he would change their lives as Jews. Bardin in 1947 addressing the first camp *"aliyah"*—his unorthodox use of the Zionist term for immigration to Israel signaled his reinterpretation of Zionism as a return to one's Jewish self. (*Courtesy Brandeis-Bardin Institute*)

Shlomo Bardin hoped that, by experiencing Judaism, rootless American Jews would acquire a sense of their cultural identity. The arts—music, drama, painting, and dance—were important elements of the Brandeis Camp Institute's program. Modern Israeli folk dancers rehearsing outdoors at the Brandeis Camp Institute in California, 1948. (*Courtesy Brandeis-Bardin Institute*)

The drama and beauty of the Brandeis Camp Institute's carefully choreographed havdalah services at the sabbath's close evoked powerful emotions and an intense spirit of camaraderie in participants. These L.A. Jews discovered that they enjoyed Judaism as a form of spiritual recreation; many were inspired to incorporate some aspect of Jewish sabbath observance into their lives after leaving the institute. Musician and composer Max Helfman leading havdalah services in 1957. (*Sid Avery, courtesy Brandeis-Bardin Institute*)

Jews working in the motion picture industry, especially left-liberal independent Jewish producers, writers, and directors, were moved by the story of the establishment of Israel. Several tried to film the drama. Universal Pictures' fast-paced action movie *Sword in the Desert* (1949) presented the Zionists' heroic struggle against the British for a land and state of their own. Dana Andrews, Stephen McNally, Jeff Chandler, and Marta Toren in Robert Buckner and George Sherman's film. (*Courtesy Museum of Modern Art Film Stills Archive*)

Milly Vitale as the Israeli, Yael, restrains a desperate Kirk Douglas, who plays Holocaust survivor Hans Muller, in Stanley Kramer's *The Juggler* (1953). The first Hollywood feature shot on location in Israel, *The Juggler* explored the painful problem of homecoming in the Jewish homeland after the destruction of European Jewry and showed Americans how Israel was the only true home for survivors. (*Courtesy Museum of Modern Art Film Stills Archive*)

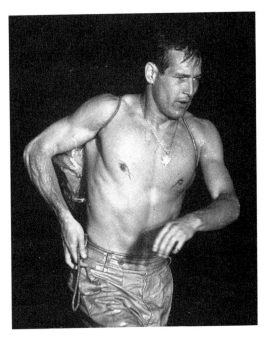

Leon Uris, a newcomer to Los Angeles, saw in Israelis a heroic vision of the new Jew that captured the imagination of Jewish and Gentile Americans. Both his novel *Exodus* and Otto Preminger's movie version (1960), with their portraits of fighting Jews, decisively shaped American perceptions of Israel, transforming the Jewish state into a Hollywood star. Paul Newman as Ari Ben Canaan, the new Jewish hero, braving British patrols in the Mediterranean to rescue illegal Jewish immigrants to Palestine. (*Courtesy Museum of Modern Art Film Stills Archive*)

In this central scene, the American (Eva Marie Saint) embraces the new Israeli Jew (Paul Newman) and his fight to win freedom and independence for his people in their ancient land. Because L.A. Jews translated Israel's history into Hollywood's language of romance and heroism, they helped make Israel a popular American cause. (*D. R. Guthrie, courtesy Steven Spielberg Jewish Film Archives of the Hebrew University*)

Jewish organizations to purge the council of additional groups.[68] By 1956 Zionists had developed a formula that reflected their understanding of a middle ground for Los Angeles Jews, exemplified in a resolution supporting civil rights and civil liberties while condemning the "twin totalitarian evils of Communism and Fascism."[69]

The council's annual resolutions concerning political issues of the day increasingly clarified a Jewish position linking support for Israel with anticommunism. A 1957 resolution typified this trend. It praised Eisenhower's condemnation of the Hungarian Communist government and urged the president similarly to attack Egypt's government for its oppression of Jews. Continuing the analogy, the resolution requested that Egyptian Jews be admitted to the United States as refugees like the Hungarian anticommunists. Here the council deftly equated Communist oppression with antisemitism and implicitly linked this to opposition to Israel.[70] The two parallel events that had occurred ten years earlier—the U.N. decision on partition and the Waldorf meeting ejecting communists from the film industry—converged by 1957. From the point of view of many Los Angeles Jews, communism and antisemitism went hand in hand—as they often did in Eastern Europe—and support for Israel logically accompanied anticommunism.

Israel's existence and cold war domestic politics dramatically altered the Jewish communal agenda. The search for a new common ground acceptable to the larger American community facilitated efforts of newcomers to transplant the ethnic politics they had known in the Northeast and Midwest into southland territory. Since the old politics did not seem able to produce a consensus, newcomers could introduce a new type of politics into Los Angeles. The migrants contributed to a realignment of Jewish political groups in Los Angeles by supporting those old-timers whose values and styles seemed most similar to their own. Their presence helped to wed an emerging Jewish political ideology centered on Israel to a cluster of domestic issues focused primarily on civil rights and secondarily on civil liberties. The resulting amalgam of domestic liberalism with strong support for Israel and opposition to communism had much in common with the politics of American Jews throughout the United States. However, as it had in Miami, the political culture of L.A. led to some unexpected results and produced a distinctive postwar brand of Jewish ethnic politics. Despite the victory of the American right, Los Angeles Jews did not completely disavow their faith, nor did they abandon their notion of politics as the pursuit of a better world. They refashioned their political culture and cautiously placed a new hero, Israel, at the center of their beliefs.

The newcomers' influence registered most quickly on the subject of religion in the public schools. This issue spoke directly to most American Jews, and pursuit of a more neutral, less Christian public sphere in education engaged the energies of ordinary people. Sensitivity to church-state issues contributed to a rapid reevaluation of the position previously held by Los Angeles Jews of the prewar era.

During the war the Protestant Church Federation had spearheaded efforts to introduce the plan for released time for religious instruction in California, receiving strong support from the Catholic Church. The released-time program allowed public school students to leave school to study for several hours each week at a religious school of their choice. After California adopted the released-time option, the Los Angeles Board of Education voted to implement released time in 1944.[71] The following year the program survived a court challenge to its constitutionality, the ruling being that it did not violate the separation of church and state since religious instruction was not given in public school facilities or by public school teachers (although it was given during regular school hours). Both the Southern California Board of Rabbis and Los Angeles Bureau of Jewish Education accepted released time and cooperated with the plan. In 1945 the bureau was conducting released-time classes in ten public schools and planned to add another five. The bureau saw the supplemental classes as fostering interfaith understanding. Two years later the Valley Jewish Community Center urged Jewish students in North Hollywood Junior High School to enroll in released-time classes, warning that if Jews did not support the program, they would be open to "suspicion and prejudice."[72]

Despite such encouragement probably only one tenth of the eligible number of Jewish students participated in the program. Many parents undoubtedly preferred not to give their children any religious instruction, since only a small percentage of Jewish students received a supplementary Jewish education in L.A. In 1949 released time enrolled 1,500 Jewish children, compared to 9,000 Roman Catholic,

4,500 Church Federation (liberal Protestant), 1,700 Evangelical, and 1,100 Christian Science.[73]

In 1948 released time became an issue for Los Angeles Jews. The challenge to the communal position favoring released time arose from two discrete sources: a Supreme Court case and a local initiative. The successful prosecution by the American Jewish Congress, together with ADL, AJCommittee, and the national coordinating committee of the Jewish defense agencies, of the McCullom case in Illinois attacked released time as bridging the separation of church and state. The dissatisfaction of several young Jewish mothers, recent arrivals to the city, led them to oppose the introduction of the plan into their children's school in Oxnard, an outlying district of Los Angeles. Despite the rabbis' reluctance to reverse themselves and condemn the program, the national Jewish defense agencies eagerly competed to raise the consciousness of Los Angeles Jews about church/state issues. AJCommittee even sent a lawyer to help the Oxnard women organize their fight.[74]

But Silberberg rejected the help proffered by the eastern establishment—in part because the local AJCongress lawyer was too well known for defending communists in his other capacity as chief counsel to the American Civil Liberties Union.[75] After spurning the AJCongress, AJCommittee, and ADL, Silberberg also bypassed the rabbis by arguing that the issue of separation of church and state involved an area outside of rabbinical competence. In 1949, citing the pragmatic rationale of saving an annual sum of ten thousand dollars, he moved to have the Jewish community officially withdraw from released time. At that time roughly half of the fourth through sixth graders in Los Angeles public schools were participating in the program. The departure of Jewish students from the program forced several schools to cancel their involvement because of a lack of pupil enrollment. Only after establishing a new Jewish position in opposition to released time did Silberberg consider developing a case against the Los Angeles program in cooperation with local branches of the national agencies.[76]

By 1955 the Jewish Community Council endorsed a resolution on public education that supported separation of church and state and opposed efforts to introduce religious teaching into the schools through released time. The left-wing Southland Jewish Organization and the mainstream Community Relations Committee proposed similar resolutions, reflecting how views had coalesced within a short period. Two years later the now-standard resolution reaffirmed a "tradition of separation of Church and State which allows public schools to teach children of varied religious backgrounds without sectarian indoctrination." In less than a decade support for separation of church and state in the public schools became a "tradition" among Los Angeles Jews. The council confidently condemned released time among the "sectarian religious encroachments" that "are divisive and violate the spirit of our Constitution and the purposes of public education."[77]

Other victories separating church and state in the public schools followed with relative ease. Unlike the Dade County school board, the Los Angeles public schools denied without any repercussions the Gideon Society's request to distribute Bibles to school children. In 1955 state attorney, Pat Brown, ruled that Bible reading was unconstitutional in California, as was the Gideon's effort to distribute Bibles. Los Angeles Jews also tried to influence the public schools from within by supporting school board candidates sympathetic to Jewish communal values. Until the late 1950s, however, they were singularly unsuccessful in defeating conservative candidates. Occasionally a Jewish attempt to separate church and state in the public schools angered their Christian neighbors. In 1957 the local school board in Sierra Madre decided to outlaw Nativity plays and New Testament Christmas readings upon the request of a Jewish parent. Cross burnings and wide dissemination of antisemitic literature followed the decision. Yet religion in the public schools rarely aroused powerful passions in the secular City of Angels, unlike the issue of communist participation in American society.[78]

The "tradition" established on released time and related issues involving expressions of Christian piety in the public schools did not extend to Christmas-Hanukkah celebrations. These appeared in increasing numbers of public schools with substantial Jewish student enrollments.[79] The Community Relations Committee could find neither common ground in support of these activities nor widespread agreement to oppose them. In the mid-fifties it commissioned a survey of Jewish attitudes on the topic in an effort to locate a popular Jewish position. None emerged. Although the survey was inconclusive, the committee gradually changed its posture on Christmas-

Hanukkah celebrations from opposition to neutrality to support but still failed to find a consensus. AJCongress rigorously opposed any form of religious expression in the schools, including intercultural or interreligious ones; AJCommittee considered public school Christmas celebrations to be forms of an American civic faith that Jews should not find offensive; while ADL recognized that holiday observances were embedded in the schools and agreed to provide material dealing with the Hanukkah part of the celebrations. As a result, opinions on Christmas-Hanukkah celebrations served as dividing lines articulating differences among Jews in contrast to their common outlook on released time, prayer, and Bible reading.[80]

As Los Angeles Jews developed a position on religion in the public schools that resembled the posture of Jews throughout the United States, they also began to coalesce on other political issues. The year 1953 proved to be a pivotal one. Not only did Zionists achieve a victory in the Jewish Community Council by winning a majority on its executive board, but Jews also returned to local electoral politics. The behavior of new migrants to L.A. was critical to both.

No one expected Jews to enter electoral politics because of their long absence from the political scene, the low-key posture adopted by old-timers, and the strength of conservative Republicans. There had not been a Jew on the Los Angeles City Council in over half a century.[81] In 1953 a generally conservative electorate responded to a campaign marked by racial and religious bigotry by voting Republican congressman Norris Poulson into the mayor's office because he outspokenly opposed public housing, which would benefit minorities. Such an environment hardly seemed conducive to Jewish electoral success. Yet in the same election voters in the newly redrawn Fifth District, which included heavily Jewish Beverly-Fairfax, elected a Jew to the city council. "It's a girl" ran the *Mirror* headline. "For the first time in nearly forty years a woman was elected"—Rosalind Wiener. At age twenty-two Wiener was also the youngest person ever to sit on the city council.[82]

A product of Jewish Los Angeles, Wiener grew up on Kenmore Avenue, went to the district's public schools, and knew the neighborhood's problems. For campaign contributions she turned to prominent Jews active in the Jewish community, such as Lou and Mark Boyar. Joel Moss, a builder like the Boyars, found Wiener fascinating and helped her raise money. He had never been involved before in politics and was intrigued that a "nice Jewish girl" would run for local office. Other men, like Oscar Pattiz and Ed Mitchell of Beneficial Life Insurance, saw nothing interesting in a young Jewish woman running for office. When Wiener asked for a campaign contribution, they told her to "go out and find a husband and get married and stay home."[83]

Wiener recruited college students to run a door-to-door campaign, handing out soap for a clean city. But she wisely concentrated on two overlapping areas: those that voted for liberal and intellectual Adlai Stevenson in 1952 and Jewish sections that supported her when she ran for the Democratic county committee. Her strategy reflected an awareness of the liberal inclinations of Jews and the fact that they did not necessarily vote as their Gentile neighbors did. Because she developed an ethnic political strategy that targeted Jewish voters in the Fifth District and appealed to Jewish liberal concerns, she could afford to run on unpopular issues for most Los Angelenos, including support for public housing. As the campaign progressed, Wiener began to receive an education in other specifically Jewish dimensions of ethnic politics. Campaigning at a meeting of the Hebrew Academy, Wiener discovered that the orthodox day school faced imminent fore-closure and sale of its building by a bank unless it immediately came up with eight thousand dollars. She stayed to contribute money and then alerted the local Jewish press to the school's plight. "My Jewish-ness really came later," she admitted. After winning the election, she "wanted to be active in the Jewish community." Wiener found the nascent Jewish community of the newcomers to be vibrant and engaged, quite different from the quiet L.A. Jewish world she had known as a child in the prewar era.[84]

Wiener's pragmatic discovery of ethnic politics occurred as Los Angeles Jews struggled to build anew a basis of political agreement. Her success derived not just from timing, however. She combined an ability to win in the primaries and runoff elections characteristic of local L.A. politics with a growing involvement with the Jewish orga-nized community that brought her into synagogues and Jewish cen-ters, where she spoke before Jewish groups. In the process she learned what issues concerned Jews and what political values they espoused. Wiener deviated from the emphasis on nonpartisanship characteristic of city council members, and she avoided the popular politics of personalities. She evinced instead a steadfast commitment to the Democratic party, as did most of her Jewish constituents, who brought their loyalty to the party of the New Deal with them to L.A. She possessed as well an independence not normally available to first-term councilmen. Living first at home with her parents and then with her husband, Eugene Wyman, a successful lawyer active in Democratic party politics, Wiener did not rely upon her position for a livelihood. She felt free to espouse a number of issues without worrying whether she would remain in the minority; in fact, she quickly developed a minority coalition similar to that advocated by Springer seven years earlier. As soon as she arrived on the council, she lined up with Ed Roybal, the Mexican-American Councilman from Boyle Heights, to oppose unsuccessfully the mayor's nomination to the Library Commission of a woman who advocated book burning. Within a month Wiener and Roybal had been headlined "left wing" by the *Los Angeles Times*.[85]

Rosalind Wiener Wyman pioneered a type of white ethnic politics in Los Angeles that identified Jewish concerns with a broad political agenda. Her politics brought her within the orbit of the Jewish community and made her very popular. In her first bid for reelection in 1957, she won 90 percent of the vote.[86]

Wyman contributed to the emerging Jewish ethnic profile by espousing those local issues that generated agreement across a spectrum of Jewish political commitments. Unlike Aronowitz's brief term as mayor of Miami, her twelve years on the city council helped shape the politics of Los Angeles Jews. She acknowledged Jewish political support by sponsoring legislation designed to benefit Jews. In 1957, an election year, she introduced both a resolution in favor of Israel and legislation to allow Jewish employees of the city to take a day off on Rosh Hashanah and Yom Kippur. The latter represented a symbolic step beyond the politics of the previous mayor's incumbency, a politics that had penalized Jews for observing the High Holidays. This brand of ethnic politics, however, still made some Jews in Los Angeles nervous. After "considerable study" the Community Relations Committee decided to try to dissuade her from supporting the second measure. The committee proposed an alternative that would not recognize Jewish distinctiveness but instead give all employees two additional personal absences per year.[87]

Unlike public recognition of the High Holidays, equal-opportunity legislation did not distinguish Jews from other minorities. Throughout the 1950s Los Angeles Jews consistently supported legislation for

fair employment practices (FEPC), struggled against housing discrimination,[88] and worked to dismantle quota systems in university
admissions and fraternities.[89] Wyman supported the FEPC bill introduced in the council by Roybal after state legislative and referendum
attempts failed, but it, too, did not pass. A bill in the Los Angeles
County Board of Supervisors met a similar fate. Ironically, persistent
Jewish support for FEPC singled them out as a white ethnic group in
Los Angeles, where the white majority opposed the legislation. The
list of speakers favoring FEPC at the city council hearing reveals how
the issue drew minorities together into exactly the coalition Springer
had imagined. Jews sent representatives from the L.A. Jewish Community Council, ADL, Jewish Labor Committee, and AJCommittee.
African Americans from the Urban League and NAACP spoke, as did
representatives of the Community Service Organization for Mexican
Americans and members of the Japanese-American Citizens League.
Nonethnic support came from labor and two Christian groups,
women in the YWCA and the Church Federation of Los Angeles.[90]

Successful advocacy of FEPC brought Jews into the political mainstream in the many eastern and midwestern states that adopted the
program, while the unsuccessful efforts of Los Angeles Jews set them
apart from the Anglo majority. Yet Jews pursued their own political
interests despite a lack of receptivity in Los Angeles. They found in
political activism an important source of public identity and collective
consciousness, one that defined what it meant to be Jewish in L.A.
For migrants who had uprooted themselves from their homes and
neighborhoods to seek opportunity under the sunny skies of California, ethnic politics provided crucial familiar landmarks in otherwise
unmarked territory. Jews defined the boundaries of their group identity even as they built bridges through political activity to other Angelenos. The creation of Democratic party clubs on the west side, in
Beverly Hills, Hollywood Hills, Pacific Palisades, Santa Monica, and
the San Fernando Valley secured Jewish allegiances. The clubs
grounded Jewish politics in a social context and provided members
with a feeling of camaraderie and a sense of common purpose. The
clubs activated newcomers as newcomers activated the clubs, while
giving old-timers a base of operation.[91]

Politics thus helped recently arrived Jews to participate in a
Jewish community of Los Angeles even as it offered a vehicle to

transform that community's relationship to the larger whole. It gave L.A. Jews a way to blend their allegiances as well as to define their identity in the postwar decade.[92] And when the pall of the cold war began to lift in 1958, Jews found themselves well situated to carry their politics successfully into the Los Angeles public arena.[93]

In state elections that year Jews could glimpse the potential rewards. Stanley Mosk, the former head of the L.A. Jewish Community Council, ran a successful campaign for attorney general on the Democratic ticket with the support and help of Rosalind Wiener Wyman. One observer noted that old-timers considered the electioneering "one of the most frenetic demonstrations of bigoted conduct on the part of some candidates and their partisans, never before paralleled in this area." Vicious religious and ethnic slurs tarred Mosk; he was smeared as a communist, and a campaign truck was painted with such slogans as Remember the Jew Traitors Rosenberg and Vote Jew Zionist If You Vote for Moskovich. Yet Mosk ran a strong race, winning one hundred thousand more votes than Pat Brown did in his successful bid for governor. The Democratic sweep of state offices and the legislature finally brought FEPC to California, a victory Jews had struggled to achieve since the end of the war. That year also marked the beginning of a different two-party system in California, one closer to the political system Jews knew from their upbringing in the Northeast and Midwest. In 1958 candidates had to list their party affiliations when running in the primaries, and voters chose only members of their own party. In a sense the two-party system started from scratch after the abolition of cross-filing.[94]

The political centrality of Israel for Jews received recognition in a tight contest between two liberal city council members for a seat on the County Board of Supervisors. Both men made political capital of recent visits to Israel to portray themselves as staunch supporters of the state and champions of Jewish rights. These ethnic appeals to Jewish voters led to "a great deal of moaning and wailing" at the Community Relations Committee meeting by individuals embarrassed that Jews had been singled out for recognition as Jews and that Jewish votes were being solicited by an appeal to Jewish concern for Israel. Despite the embarassment of some, the committee took no action. In 1958 California voters also rejected by a two-to-one margin a proposition designed to rescind the tax exemption of parochial schools.

The religious attacks on Catholics by those favoring the proposition prompted the Southern California Board of Rabbis to enter the political fray with a statement opposing the proposition. The rabbis' decision to express themselves on political issues involving social principles and their willingness to stand for their right to do so when criticized by some lay congregational leaders suggested that significant segments of Los Angeles Jewry had moved substantially beyond Magnin's nonethnic interpretation of Judaism.[95]

By contrast, Rosalind Wiener Wyman's decision to abandon public housing—the moral issue of her first campaign that had attracted Jewish voters—in favor of using the land to construct a baseball stadium for the Dodgers marked the pragmatic limits of ethnic politics. In choosing the Dodgers over public housing, she rejected not only the liberal political concerns of many of her constituents that helped define them as Jews but also minority coalition politics. It signified, too, the first flowering of Jewish loyalties to their city of choice.[96] Wyman's support for the controversial stadium led to threats upon her life and her loss of a segment of Jewish liberal voters. But she justified her change of opinion by an appeal to a larger vision of Los Angeles. "It was the first time this city ever unified for *anything*," she reflected. "We were so divided and dispersed. We had something that was our own." The site, embroiled in litigation and controversy, held the promise of giving the sprawling city an identity and paving its entry into the major leagues. The deep identification of Brooklyn with the Dodgers suggested that Los Angeles, too, could achieve the same renown, the same commonality of purpose and culture, if the baseball team moved to the city. The Dodgers would give L.A. a symbolic national presence and perhaps even the sense of *achdut*—unity—that Jews valued so highly. Sandy Koufax's growing fame as a pitcher—he won several Cy Young awards after moving with the Dodgers to L.A.—surely helped to cement the loyalties of Jewish fans.[97]

Jews achieved their political solidarity by excluding several of their own from the community and by placing Israel at the center of communal concern. On the ethnically diverse American scene, Zionism was "a relatively easy product to sell," Nussbaum observed. Since many minorities maintained "a first-class relationship" to their original country, Jewish support for Israel meshed comfortably into the American way. The new understanding of many Los Angeles Jews was that Americanism included not only support for and identification with Israel but other expressions of intensive Jewish identity. Parochial school education, once deemed un-American by the L.A. Jewish Community Council, found support within Jewish politics by the end of the 1950s. A Reform rabbi and Zionist, Nussbaum openly advocated a Reform day school in every large American city for "the gifted child" because it fit the American pattern. Although a minority voice, Nussbaum confidently predicted in 1963 the future triumph of the Hebrew day school. By contrast, Jewish support for interculturalism, so strong in the war's aftermath, gradually waned during the postwar decade as its most outspoken adherents became tainted by their association with the radical left.[98]

Although over a decade of intense political activity failed to erase all significant political divisions among Jews, by the 1960s the dividing lines had blurred so that a political profile emerged in L.A. Most observers labeled the profile liberal. Although useful in comparing Jews with others, this label obscures important conservative elements that became an integral part of Los Angeles Jewish political culture, differentiating it from the ethnic politics of eastern Jews who did not migrate and from the earlier faith of Jewish Angelenos.

As Los Angeles Jews confronted the issues of the postwar decade, they tried to recapture that moment of solidarity that had characterized their politics before the cold war's onslaught. Facing outsiders who did their best to smear Jews as communists and fellow travelers, Jews struggled to define their own political identity, to determine the boundaries of their community, to mark both Jewish distinctiveness and a vision of an inclusive Americanism that was good for Jews. They sought to find in politics a common faith to be shared by all believers, while newcomers tried to pursue the familiar ethnic politics they had known at home. Eventually, Jewish political behavior encompassed both a chastened faith and elements of an indigenous ethnic politics.

In the years after World War II, Jews in Los Angeles championed a politics that defined them as a visible white minority in a volatile and rapidly growing society. A diverse group of migrants, Los Angeles Jews discovered in politics a Jewish identity to share with each other. As they established the parameters of acceptable political behavior by drawing upon the Jewish ethnic politics they had known, they defined the boundaries of their public community. These efforts to create a viable politics initially isolated Jews in Los Angeles, as they had in Miami, because both cities were in the beginning inhospitable milieus. As a result, politics served Jews first as a vehicle of identity and only later as one of integration, reversing the process characteristic of the large multiethnic cities of the Northeast and Midwest. Because such issues as equal-opportunity legislation failed to resonate among other white Angelenos, their advocacy by Jews acquired a symbolic character and defined Jewish interests as different from those of other white Americans. In New York or Chicago many white Americans, children and grandchildren of immigrants, supported such legislation with Jews, recognizing the stake they had in creating a more open, egalitarian, and democratic society. Thus, the style and substance of California and Florida politics transformed the meanings of Jewish politics even as Jewish participation contributed to changing the urban political culture of Miami and Los Angeles.

8
Israel as Frontier

History cannot happen—that is, men cannot engage in purposive group behavior—without images which simultaneously express collective desires and impose coherence on the infinitely numerous and infinitely varied data of experience.

—Henry Nash Smith
Virgin Land

On the morning of July 1, 1945, as the fighting in the Pacific continued, Shepard Broad and Julius Fligelman met in the New York City penthouse apartment of Rudolf Sonneborn, the millionaire industrialist. Broad had left Miami and Fligelman had traveled from Los Angeles for the special, secret conference with David Ben Gurion and Eliezer Kaplan, the feisty labor Zionist leaders of the Yishuv. Sitting in Sonneborn's elegant living room in the sweltering summer heat, Broad and Fligelman discovered what they shared with the fifteen other wealthy American Jewish lawyers and businessmen gathered on that hot day. Dedicated Zionists, each desired to implement the Zionist program to rescue survivors of the Holocaust and establish a Jewish commonwealth. Ben Gurion called the meeting to discover just how committed these men were and whether the Yishuv could count on them to help win a difficult struggle for statehood. Specifically, Ben Gurion and Kaplan wanted to determine if they could depend on American Jews to back the Jews of Palestine in case war broke out with the Arabs after the British left.[1]

In Broad's view, the issue of rescue and statehood depended on the mettle and character of the Jews of Palestine. So he turned to Ben Gurion and asked: "What is a Palestinian Jew like?" Ben Gurion responded with a question of his own: " 'Were you ever in Iowa? . . . Visualize that you come up to the door of a farmer in Iowa, you knock on the door, and he comes and says, "Yes, my good man, what can I do for you?" And you tell that farmer, "Listen here, this farm doesn't belong to you. Get off right away!" ' " Ben Gurion paused, then asked, " 'You know what the farmer will do?' I said 'No, tell me.' He says, 'He would shut the door, go back in the kitchen, get a shotgun, and he'd come out, aim the shotgun at you and say "Will you repeat it?" ' " Broad responded: "I wouldn't have enlisted in the effort if I thought that on this end you had the kind of people who didn't have the courage to fight for their independence, because I would have felt that this would be a futile effort."[2]

The character of the new Jew in Palestine, so similar to the frontier American farmer, proved to be crucial to convince "most of us who were there to respond to any and every reasonable need that Ben Gurion might have in terms of furthering the establishment of the State." No people ever won its freedom without shedding blood, Ben Gurion told them, and this seemed logical to the assembled group. Fligelman remembered that "at the conclusion of the day's deliberations we were deeply impressed with the gravity of the situation facing the Jews of Palestine and by the integrity and the consummate statesmanship and ability of Ben Gurion." The men pledged their support for the secret, illegal struggle to rescue survivors and bring them to Palestine.[3]

Reuven Dafni arrived several months later, one of four emissaries sent by the Haganah to raise money to buy arms and ships.[4] Dafni was a particularly good choice. Tall, dark, and handsome, with a thin mustache, he reminded contemporaries of Errol Flynn. He not only looked like a dashing hero but was one. In 1944 Dafni and other Palestinian Jewish paratroopers had parachuted behind enemy lines in Hungary in a bold but doomed effort to rescue Hungarian Jews from extermination. Dafni discovered in Miami and especially Los Angeles an eagerness to embrace the new Palestinian Jew. He spoke "in very hush-hush parlor meetings for men only." He told the men about the Haganah's efforts to bring illegal Jewish immigrants to Palestine. His own military exploits and good looks enhanced his persuasive eloquence. Dafni soon realized the masculine appeal of secret meetings. "Many American Jews," he learned, "were willing to give a lot of money to be able to say to their wives that they can't come with them to the meetings, it's so secret that they can't tell them."[5]

Dafni "especially made an attempt to get into Hollywood, to get the film crowd involved, not only because there was the money in it, but for many other reasons." Although he failed to reach wealthy producers, he moved several of the younger men. Those at the beginning of successful careers, and especially left-liberal writers, directors, and producers, found his message and presence powerful. Such men as directors Fred Zinnemann and Jules Dassin, writers Carl Foreman and Michael Blankfort, and producer Dore Schary opened doors for Dafni and helped him penetrate the Hollywood "wall." Dafni recalled that "we eventually became very good friends."[6] In Hollywood, the town of images, Dafni instantly personified the ideal type of young Jew as a fearless man of action. Even before Israel's declaration of independence, Dore Schary told the annual January meeting of the Bay Cities' Jewish Community Council that the Haganah would give the world a new picture of the Jew during the coming year. Schary assured his listeners that this image would evoke their pride. He anticipated that "it will picture us as fighting men—men fighting for peace and security in the homeland." Schary's simple but profound and unalloyed identification with the new Jew suggests how deeply Dafni touched Jews eager to reassert themselves in the wake of the Holocaust and its painful passive imagery. A small group of Jews in the motion picture industry would do their best to help Israel by dramatizing its story and heroes for Americans.[7]

Dafni's presence and appeal inspired a handful to use their moviemaking skills to help convey the Zionist message. Among the first was Zinnemann. A native of Austria, he arrived in the United States in 1929, before the rise of Hitler. His parents, however, died in the Holocaust while waiting for American visas to leave Austria. In 1946 Zinnemann went to Europe to investigate the possibility of shooting a film that might awaken Americans to the horrors of the war.

The Search used case histories of war orphans in a story that linked them to an American soldier. Zinnemann shot the film in Germany on location, something rarely done in Hollywood at the time. The experience brought him face to face with the Jewish tragedy and with the illegal process of rescue. When the State of Israel was established in May 1948, Dafni obtained a visa for Zinnemann to visit despite the war then raging. Zinnemann later recalled,

> Enormous events were impending; after the experience of the UN Displaced Persons' camps in Germany I felt a strong need to witness what was going to happen next, and perhaps to make a film continuing the style of *The Search*. . . . We saw history made before our eyes; we saw it but could hardly believe it. . . . In the end nothing came of the plan to make a picture. What we had seen was so much larger than life it would have looked like pure propaganda. No one would have believed it.[8]

Zinnemann thought that the magnitude of the events surrounding the creation of the State of Israel transcended the conventions of the silver screen. Yet despite difficulties the subject grabbed the imagination of certain Jews in the motion picture industry.

Robert Buckner considered the topic of rescue worthy of a fast-paced action movie. He filmed *Sword in the Desert* less than a year after Israel's establishment. "I've long felt that the news can be made dramatically entertaining," Buckner told an interviewer. Born in Virginia, Buckner worked as the London correspondent for the *New York World* during the 1920s, wrote short stories, and also lived in Palestine before coming to Hollywood in 1937, where he established himself as a screenwriter and producer. He wrote the screenplay and produced the picture at Universal Studios. The director, George Sherman, known for his many westerns, worked quickly and efficiently. Under Sherman's direction the film took only fifty days to produce at a cost of just over one million dollars. The cast had a "one world flavor" unusual even in Hollywood; the Jewish actor Jeff Chandler played the Palestinian underground leader. Because of nationalist criticism in England, Buckner kept the film under wraps during production.[9]

Buckner promoted the film as a plea to better understanding between peoples. This was the goal of the final scene, he emphasized in an interview. In that scene a Christmas carillon in a Bethlehem church rings out through the surrounding hills. But, he explained, first he had to show the bitterness and misunderstanding between Jews and British as a prelude to peace. Without the prelude there could be no peace. His technical consultant, a Palestinian Jew who fought in the war of independence, was less sanguine about the healing power of the film's final scene. "The Jews will like [the movie] very much," Baruch Diener concluded, but scenes of British soldiers being killed would probably evoke antagonism.[10]

Diener's assessment proved to be accurate. When the movie—about a group of illegal immigrants trying to evade capture by the British authorities in Palestine—was released in 1949, critics condemned it as one-sided. "Its frank idealization of the struggle of the Jews to invest their 'homeland' and its crude ridicule of the British are potentially disturbing in these times," wrote Bosley Crowther. During World War II Britain had been portrayed as America's heroic ally; it was not easy for Americans like Crowther to temper their pro-British sentiment in favor of the Jewish struggle for a state, especially in the new cold war context in which Britain again was a staunch American ally. He characterized the fights between the Jews and British as virtual cowboy-and-Indian affairs. This typical Hollywood portrayal of good guys and bad guys disturbed Crowther, who observed that the Jews emerged triumphant at the "humiliating expense" of the British soldiers. Finding it difficult to accept Jeff Chandler as the new Jewish hero because he was fighting the British, Crowther shifted his focus and complained that "the measure of excitement which Mr. Buckner and his people have achieved has been bought at the price of a thorough or fair illumination of the facts."[11]

A melodramatic action movie built around an extended chase, *Sword in the Desert* pits Jews against British. The Jews are clearly good guys in this movie—they are brave and bold, dedicated and determined, clever and honest, coming close to Schary's image of the new Jew. They are all soldiers, but reluctantly so, taking up arms to defend their homes, rescue refugees, and redeem their homeland. The British, by contrast, are cads—"pip-pip old chaps, killers, unmerciful policemen and Christmas choralists, all rolled into one."[12] The movie's heroine, an underground radio announcer predictably named Sabra (Marta Toren), voices the film's ideological message through her passionate radio addresses. Following the U.N. vote for partition, she firmly rejects British rule:

A great many of you, here and in England, are friendly toward us. You have told us in private that you have no heart for this job. But you have orders to obey. Well, so do we. You have occupied our country, deprived us of our home and of our freedom. So we must fight.

When she is captured, Sabra defiantly tells the British: "I am still a Jew and this is my country. You have no rights here, moral or legal, and therefore no authority over me."

The movie reinforces its "argument" via the plot device of an outsider reluctantly converted to the Jews' cause. Events raise the consciousness of an Irish-American ship captain inadvertently caught between Jews and British. Captain Dillon (Dana Andrews) dislikes Jews and holds stereotyped opinions about them. He has no sympathy for his illegal cargo's suffering during the war. "I'm an American," he explains. "This isn't my fight. Why be a sucker?" Dillon single-mindedly pursues his own agenda—retrieving his money and returning to his ship—and consistently betrays the Jews in the process. Finally, the British capture the illegals, hero, and captain. At this point the captain, doggedly trying to remain the outsider, must choose between the British and the Jews.

As the movie moves toward its climax, the British pressure Dillon into identifying Kurta, the underground leader. The scene is Christmas Eve with British soldiers sitting in camp singing carols. Dillon and the British officer stroll by a bare-branched tree, decorated for the holiday. When Dillon pauses to ask about it, the officer explains that "they call it the Judas tree." In case that might slip by the audience, he spells out the message: "According to the Bible, Judas hanged himself after the betrayal. The legend says it was a tree like this, hence the infamous name." This is enough even for the cynical Dillon, and he refuses to identify Kurta. Dillon suddenly sees his act of betrayal in religious terms, but when he is asked why he changed his mind, he answers: "I don't know why." "These people don't mean anything to you," the British press him. Then in a touch of hyperbole, "You're making the single greatest mistake of your life." "Maybe," he answers, "but I'm still going to have to shave this mug every day for the rest of my life. I wouldn't like what I saw."

The American rejects the British and throws in his lot with the Jews on the grounds of simple decency and self-respect. His decision immediately precedes the climax, a dramatic escape from the camp.

In the end Dillon affirms to Sabra, "I'll be back, too." These lines close the movie as Dillon and one of the underground leaders escape toward Bethlehem against the carillons Buckner thought would bring a message of peace. Dillon's change of heart on Christmas Eve emphasizes the holy character of the land and endows the Jews' nationalist efforts to rescue survivors and reclaim their homeland with spiritual meaning. These new Jews of the Holy Land, Dillon comes to realize, resemble their ancestors in Palestine more than Jews of the diaspora. *Sword in the Desert* appealed simultaneously to Christians and Jews as it recast a story of rescue into one of redemption.[13]

The movie treated the political realities of the postwar world as raw materials for a vision of Israel and its creation. It accepted a Zionist understanding of recent Jewish history. This interpretation justified the crucial need for a Jewish state by linking the destruction of European Jews to the necessity of rescuing refugees by bringing them to the only existing haven: their homeland in Palestine. It imagined the major players in the Jewish drama on the stage of world politics as Palestinian Jews, settlers and pioneers living in the land of Israel; the British, mandatory power and ruler over the Palestinians; and the refugees, European survivors of the Nazi death camps. Important but minor players included Americans, influential observer and power in the free world; American Jews, less influential observers but economically secure; and Arabs, fellow residents of Palestine who opposed Jewish immigration to the land. In the drama of the creation of the Jewish state, Palestinian Jews were heroes, seeking to rescue refugees from DP camps and bring them to their homeland through illegal immigration. The British emerged as villains, trying to thwart illegal immigration and prevent the establishment of a Jewish state. The DPs were objects of pity and suffering, who yet possessed a spark that could be kindled into a flame in their homeland. American Jews were helpful supporters (as were all freedom-loving peoples), Arabs were harmful opponents (but not as serious an enemy as the British), and Americans were bystanders to be wooed and enlisted on the side of liberation.

This drama of Israel's creation paralleled the American experience. It combined elements of the American revolution against the British with frontier settlement and the fight against Indians. Reduced to melodrama, this reading of postwar Jewish politics ignored the reality of bitter, fratricidal struggles among Zionist parties, especially between labor Zionists and Revisionists and their respective military arms, the Haganah and Irgun. Its themes were liberation and redemption, reenactment in secular terms of a religious message. Although rooted in Zionist understanding of recent Jewish history, the transformation of newspaper headlines into frontier visions of the creation of the Jewish state ultimately involved bypassing Zionism itself, especially American Zionist politics. Zionism involved more than idealism; as a complex nationalist movement it contained many competing ideological groups that often scorned each other's Zionist vision; occasionally they fought over both ends and means of achieving their goals.

The consensus adopted by the movies simplified the historical reality, giving it a single trajectory, idealizing its participants, and emphasizing its American resonance, as Ben Gurion's tale of the Iowa farmer had done. But in its focus on Palestine's frontier conditions, the drama of Israel's establishment had no room for offscreen events taking place in American living rooms, meeting halls, and synagogues or in Washington's corridors of power. Ironically, American Zionists played no role, not even a supporting one, in this American Jewish interpretation of Israel's creation. They appeared neither as important intermediaries with American leaders nor as vital Jewish figures rallying American Jews to support their brethren fighting the frontline battles. The vision departed significantly from historical reality.

During the first precarious months of Israel's existence, as it fought a war against Arab armies on all fronts, American Zionists were, indeed, best prepared to throw themselves into the fateful task of helping Israel survive the onslaught. Zealously Zionists raised funds, lobbied for political support, purchased arms and materiel and secretly shipped them to Israel, staged enthusiastic receptions for the first Israeli representatives to arrive in the United States, and gloried in the symbols of statehood. When Dafni returned to Los Angeles in the fall of 1948, he came as the first Israeli consul general to the city. Yet by the time he left three years later, Zionists found their hegemony as interpreters of Israel to Americans and American Jews undermined by their very success.[14]

As American Jews rallied to Israel's cause, they also grasped the power to project their visions upon historical reality, forming an attractive image of the meaning of the Jewish state that ignored any role for American Zionists. Ben Gurion, on the other hand, made it clear that Zionists belonged in Zion. The task of converting American diaspora Jews to the support of Israel belonged to Israelis; American Zionists were no longer needed in America even to generate enthusiasm for Israel among American Jews. Zionists could not easily disregard the prime minister's call to American Jews to come to Israel, or at least to send their sons and daughters to settle and build the new state. Nor could they summarily reject Ben Gurion's appeal for *aliyah*—immigration to Israel—as did the anti-Zionists.[15] Yet most American Zionists chose to remain in the United States.

American Zionists struggled to define themselves vis-à-vis American Jews and Israelis. Joseph Shane, an active fund-raiser in Los Angeles and a national chairman of the United Jewish Appeal by 1960, admitted, "I don't know what it takes to be a Zionist."[16] A dedicated supporter of the state, Shane saw Israel as a refuge, a haven that gave strength to the Jewish people. Although Zionists intensified and expanded their political roles within the American Jewish community, they found themselves gradually displaced by other, less ideologically committed interpreters of Israel, especially the fund-raisers. These manipulators of symbols crafted a new image of Israel that appealed to American Jews, drawing upon American myths in the process. Their success in raising funds contributed to the displacement of Zionist ideology. American Jews were fascinated by Israel, the first Jewish state in almost two thousand years, not by political struggles among labor Zionists, Revisionists, and religious Zionists. As American Zionists lost control over fund-raising, they similarly lost their ability to fashion popular and enduring myths about Israel.

Leaders of an independent state, Israelis felt free to draw upon wider circles of Jewish support and to bypass the internal political wrangling of American Zionists.[17] The decision to establish Israel bonds in September 1950 allowed a broader spectrum of Miami Jews to wrest Israel from the control of local Zionist leaders and thus hasten their decline as guardians of the Israeli myth-in-the-making. Israeli cabinet ministers, ambassadors, and military men and women graced the numerous bond rallies, dinners, meetings, and receptions and presented an Israel of mythic proportions that appealed to Miami Jews by addressing their desire for a homeland to redeem

Jews. Miami Jews projected their fantasies of Israel upon visiting Israeli emissaries, endowing them with heroic dimensions as creators of Jewish sovereignty. Israelis came to Miami to ask American Jews for money, encouraging a sense of partnership in the great task of state building. The proud new state of Israel loomed above all of the petty political intrigue and ideological debates that had plagued American Zionism. Through the purchase of bonds in a public forum designed to stimulate support for Israel, Miami Jews simultaneously invested in a permanent Jewish homeland and signified their identification with its Jewish heroes and heroines.

Israel bonds gave Miami Jews a direct, continuous, and powerful tie with the Jewish state and a concrete means of building the Jewish homeland. Increasingly Miami Jews responded to the message of the constant campaigns. Israel became their homeland, too, through their wholehearted investment in its economic future. Without strong ties to their new homes, Miami Jews preferred to purchase bonds that gave them a stake in a surrogate home. Although speakers often presented Israel as besieged, an island of democracy in a hostile sea, this imagery always accompanied an emphasis upon defense, action, and an aggressive preparedness. Jews in Miami could appreciate this response in other Jews, especially when those others were ready to face the dangers. Israel provided an arena to enact frontier visions Jews could not imagine pursuing in Miami. Israel offered them a future, a chance to help create a new Jewish society, and the power and glamour of statehood. Since they could not seize these perquisites in Miami or even in Miami Beach, they encountered little resistance to adopting Israel as the source of their redemption. Israel guaranteed the Jewish future, and bonds guaranteed Israel. The link was simple, the identification was direct. Bonds were a powerful vehicle to implement dreams.

Unlike the United Jewish Appeal's plea for tax-deductible contributions, only part of which went to the faction-ridden Jewish Agency to help Israel, bonds were sold as direct investments in Israel. No intermediaries stood between the state and American Jewish investors. Bondholders received interest on their investments from the State of Israel. "I moved over to Bonds because everybody moved over," Lou Boyar recalled. "We weren't fighting local—local didn't have Bonds. We honestly believed that the future of the Jewish people in Israel meant they have to be self-supporting. They have to earn enough money and they can't earn it unless they get investments." A bond purchase translated into exclusive support for Israel, not adherence to any local Los Angeles or Miami Jewish organizations.[18]

The shift away from local Zionist groups to direct investment was spurred partly by a series of exceptionally effective speakers who delivered Israel's message, beginning in the months following the U.N. vote for partition. They spoke, logically, as Palestinian Jews and appealed for support in their struggle for independence. Among the most effective was Golda Meir (Meyerson), who visited Miami in February 1948 as part of an impromptu fund-raising swing through American cities. When she entered a meeting room of the White House Hotel where forty hotel owners were holding their Central Jewish Appeal breakfast, excitement swept the room. "As if instructed by an invisible courier, the entire assemblage was on its feet, applauding," the local paper reported. "Miami Beach reminds me of Tel Aviv," Meir began, immediately establishing a direct connection between America and Zion. Only there was an important difference between the two: "Here one doesn't hear any shooting by day and by night." She went on to explain that the war had begun; it was not a war the Jews had chosen, "but the Mufti, friend and co-worker of Hitler during the World War, has refused to permit us to live in peace. . . . Great Britain is neutral—neutral between the attacker and the attacked." Jews could not even legally possess weapons to defend themselves under Britain's policy, she explained. "This is your war, too," Meir concluded. "But we do not ask you to guard the convoy. If there is any blood to be spilled, let it be ours. Remember, though, that how long this blood will be shed depends upon you."[19] Meir's compelling vision of collective responsibility, the continuing war against Hitler's minions in Arab dress, Britain's betrayal, and a fierce, determined Jewish heroism sparked Miami Jews to raise unprecedented sums to help secure the Jewish state.

Meir remembered Miami as "a good example" of her fundraising itinerary, methods, and rhetoric. "We started off with a breakfast meeting; then there was a luncheon in a nightclub, and in the evening we flew from Miami to Miami Beach for another meeting in the big hotel there. . . . At that hotel, although it was owned by a Jew, fundraising was forbidden." But the pressing needs of the fledgling Jewish state could not defer to such rules. If wealthy Jews on vacation were willing to come to a dinner, Meir had to appeal to them for their financial support. Although she did not necessarily expect an invitation to fund-raise, Meir nonetheless found the situation daunting. "I remember coming down to the patio, which was so beautiful, and thinking that this I couldn't take." As she looked at the audience, "I was sure they couldn't care less. I didn't eat a thing. I drank black coffee and smoked my cigarettes with tears in my eyes. I thought 'How can I, in this beautiful atmosphere, speak about what's happening at home.' . . . I was sure that when I got up to talk, they would all walk out." But Henry Morgenthau Jr. reassured her.[20] The former secretary of the treasury headed the United Jewish Appeal and was running the meeting. In fact, nobody walked out, and the evening dinner raised around one and a half million dollars in cash. As Meir recognized, "Not all of them were Zionists, but they all realized what was at stake." The single day in Miami netted between four and five million dollars.[21]

Miami Jews were not alone in the outpouring of money. In 1948 the United Jewish Appeal (UJA), a coalition of Zionist and non-Zionist organizations created on the eve of World War II to coordinate fund-raising on a national level, raised an enormous sum from American Jews in comparison to previous levels of giving. Fligelman remembered that "we all experienced a great exhilaration at being able to raise a total of over ten million dollars, which was unparalleled up to that time in the entire history of the city of Los Angeles." Miami Jews, like Los Angeles Jews, continued to give at a rate far above the pre-1948 standard because of the rapid growth of the community. In both cities, however, the amount of funds allocated to the UJA after the joint federation-UJA campaign failed to increase, due both to competing demands for moneys by other organizations (like synagogues that had delayed ambitious construction projects) and to a decline in the sense of urgency that surrounded the first year of statehood.[22]

In 1949 Miami Jews accepted an ambitious goal of raising a million dollars for the UJA, but the fund drive fell far short of its aim.[23] The following year fund-raisers lowered their sights, but they still failed to reach their self-imposed quota. Seeking stabilization, Miami's federation voted in 1951 on a precampaign allocation formula that affirmed the primacy of Israel's needs over local ones. This decision to divide the expected funds to be raised gave 58 percent of the first million dollars raised to UJA to be used to help Israel. The remaining 42 percent went to local and national Jewish organizations.[24] Miami was one of the first cities to make a precampaign commitment to the UJA, a sign of Zionist strength within the federation. The Los Angeles Jewish Community Council did not vote for a precampaign formula, with 60 percent going to UJA, until 1953 when Zionists captured a majority of the council seats.

The UJA had raised impressive funds, but its basic charitable structure, combining support for Israel's needs with aid to local and national organizations, meant that its component parts were often in an uneasy truce. When fund-raisers could not reach their UJA quotas, this truce often erupted into open battles between Zionists and non-Zionists over division of the moneys. The decision to inaugurate a campaign for Israel bonds designed to generate money exclusively for Israel occurred against this background of stabilizing or declining contributions to the UJA. In the spring of 1951, the Israeli minister of trade and industry visited Miami to initiate planning for the bond campaign. Two members of the local professional fund-raising staff of the federation left to work for bonds. The federation's executive director ruefully recognized the "friendly competition" and Israeli leaders' preference for bonds, despite the comparative superiority of the UJA. Israel's decision to back the bond drive meant not only competition for funds but also the development of an unmediated relationship by American Jewish bond purchasers with the State of Israel. Rather than helping Israel through a contribution to Miami's Central Jewish Appeal, which provided funds to local and national American Jewish organizations as well, Miami Jews now possessed a vehicle of direct support of the state.[25]

When Golda Meir returned to Miami in 1951 as Israel's minister of labor, she came to speak at a local Salute to Israel bond rally. Two thousand turned out to hear her. Meir's effective oratory produced the "miracle of Miami": the sale of over $500,000 of bonds in the first ten days of the drive. This sum came close to the total annual Miami contribution to the UJA.[26] Before the year ended—a year that included several bombings of Miami synagogues—Miami Jews purchased over a million dollars of bonds. They responded warmly to an array of rallies and concerts and to speeches by such Israelis as Avraham Harman and Abba Eban. In February the State of Israel honored Joseph

Cherner for his role in the bond drive. Henry Morgenthau Jr., now the national head of Israel bonds, came down for the luncheon, which featured the black entertainer Lena Horne. Yacov Shapiro, Israel's first attorney general, represented the young state at the event. The press billed the affair as the first time Israel had paid "official tribute" to an American citizen.[27]

In 1952 Miami Jewish leaders sought to replicate the success of the initial year. They repeated the parade of Israeli visitors to Miami on behalf of bonds. "In those days everybody was coming to America," Herbert Friedman recalled. "Anybody who came from Israel and who spoke with an accent was a great attraction." In January the Chief Rabbi of Tel Aviv arrived; Golda Meir returned in March. This time over four thousand crowded the Miami Beach auditorium to hear her speak. Gershon Agron, editor of the *Jerusalem Post*, followed in April, and in June Moshe Sharett, Israel's foreign minister, came. As 1952 drew to a close, a final "big day" for bonds was scheduled. The Florida Power and Light Company dedicated its downtown window on Northeast Second Street off Flagler to a special display honoring Miami Jews' efforts in behalf of the Jewish democracy. The mural depicted a background montage documenting the progress of Israeli industry, agriculture, and port facilities. In the foreground stood an American Jewish man and woman jointly watering the flower of the newly flourishing land.[28]

The image of nurturing the economy of the new state reflected nicely the sense of partnership the bond campaigns inspired among Miami Jews. They saw bonds as a form of patriotic investment in the State of Israel, just as the purchase of United States Liberty Bonds represented an investment in the future of America. Coming only a few years after intensive bond drives in the United States during World War II, Israel bond campaigns evoked similar altruistic sentiments. Morgenthau's presence as head of Israel bonds reinforced a sense of continuity with his years as secretary of the treasury, when he orchestrated the successful hoopla surrounding U.S. savings bonds. Both investments combined elements of patriotism and faith, fused American and Jewish experience, and suggested a pleasing parallel between the national struggles of the United States and Israel. Yet purchasers also understood that the bonds were in fact redeemable with interest. Unlike contributions to the Central Jewish Appeal, bond purchases could not be written off as charity. Indeed, by the mid-1950s Miami Jews increasingly gave Israel bonds as payment on their pledges to the Central Jewish Appeal.[29]

Solicitation of bonds often occurred within a festive and heroic milieu, unlike requests for UJA funds, which tended to stress Jewish suffering, misery, and the needs of rescue and rehabilitation. The differing appeals for money amplified the contrast between a bond investment versus a charitable contribution. In 1952, in response to Israel's critical need for cash, the Central Jewish Appeal answered an emergency request from the UJA by borrowing $200,000 from local banks. Similarly, during the Suez crisis in 1955 and 1956, local Miami leaders raised over $500,000 in emergency funds through loans. By contrast, after the Sinai campaign, the Israel bonds organization sent over a number of Israeli military heroes, including Ezer Weizman, then the fighter-wing commander of the Israeli Air Force, and Mordecai Gur, at that time a battalion commander of Nahal paratroopers.[30]

Miami Jews saw Weizman as the personification of the "indomitable spirit of the Jewish State and its people." Ten years later Weizman recapitulated Dafni's success. Weizman had already appeared briefly on television, interviewed by Edward R. Murrow in a *See It Now* program on Israel and Egypt. Murrow asked Weizman, standing beside an old warplane, how he managed with such obsolete aircraft. Weizman admitted he would like high-speed aircraft and that it was difficult to shoot down the new Egyptian planes. The discussion then turned to how few minutes and seconds it took to fly over Israel. For American Jews watching the program, Weizman broadcast a clear message of heroism, danger, and need, a message reiterated when he appeared before Miami Jews in person. Weizman and Gur, like Dafni in 1946, represented the living reality of the new Jew who had risen out of the ashes of the destruction of European Jewry.[31]

In fact, bond drives generated mutual interaction of Israelis and American Jews. A sabra (a native-born Israeli), Gur recalled that his bond trip "was the first time I saw Jews living outside Israel. It was the first time I saw American Jews and understood what it meant to be one." Gur's visits up and down the East Coast, from Miami to Montreal, affected him. "For the first time I felt a part of the Jewish world which was a new phenomenon for me." Bonds engendered a mutual sense of belonging shared by American Jews and Israelis, albeit one unconnected to Zionism. Gur "didn't feel there was any difference between those who considered themselves Zionists and those who did not." He thought that involvement in Jewish and pro-Israel activity was crucial, not membership in a Zionist organization.[32]

By 1958 competition of bond campaigns with local federation fund-raising for Israel eased in Miami. Bond leaders accorded recognition to important figures in the federation as coworkers on behalf of Israel by including them on the dais at public events. Indeed, by 1958 Miami's bond campaign achieved such prominence that it could afford a generous gesture. Bond drives even entered Miami synagogues with great success. Appeals to purchase of bonds made from pulpits during the High Holidays signaled Israel's centrality for Miami Jews. Synagogues normally reserved the High Holiday appeal for funds to those needed to help cover congregational expenses. By urging the purchase of bonds instead, congregations implicitly gave Israel's needs priority over their own. "The sale of bonds is the closest tie between Israel and Judaism during the High Holy Days," affirmed Miami's rabbis. Not all rabbis accepted the consensus, of course. Narot rejected the plea that he urge congregants to purchase bonds from the pulpit of Temple Israel, and the congregation's lay leaders agreed. By 1958 Temple Israel stood apart from Miami synagogues in its refusal to support bonds from the pulpit.[33]

Israel became the spiritual home of most Miami Jews. They raised record amounts during the High Holidays in the other Miami congregations. Sales of over $700,000 in 1958 placed Miami among the top three cities in the United States. In January 1959 and again in 1960, Miami received recognition as the leading American city for its ever-increasing rate of bond purchases. That year the head of the UJA attacked Miami Jews for their "negligence" and long record of "sluggish giving" to the city's "major philanthropy." Miami failed to support adequately the Central Jewish Appeal. The city ranked lowest of the largest Jewish cities in funds raised annually for the UJA and the federation. The contrast between Miami's low standing in the UJA with its prominence in selling bonds underscored Israel's significance for uprooted Miami Jews.[34]

Los Angeles Jews working in Hollywood possessed an even more powerful tool to mobilize and sustain support for Israel. In the dozen years following the establishment of the State of Israel, a handful of

Jewish writers, directors, and producers transformed ideological rhetoric into compelling images, Zionist politics into Israeli national myths, Middle Eastern history into an American epic.[35] After Buckner's *Sword in the Desert*, two other producers filmed Israel's story. One of them created a fiery, romantic image that seized the American imagination; like the burning bush, it burned but was not consumed.[36] This vision derived from a powerful book written by a newcomer to Los Angeles, Leon Uris. Both the book, *Exodus*, and its movie version helped make Israel into a frontier myth, a staple of American Jewish popular culture.

Exodus, a movie in the form of a current event, became possible due to structural changes in Hollywood's famed industry. After World War II the motion picture industry had cause to be nervous: Hollywood studios were whiplashed by divergent forces, including political and legal attacks and the rapid rise of television. Anticommunist investigations coincided with antitrust prosecution designed to force large studios to divest their control over either production, distribution, or exhibition. The studios chose to give up their control of theaters and to impose a form of self-censorship. Without the security of block booking and the bulk of the first-run theaters' income that control of the theaters had afforded, studios abandoned the contract system and turned increasingly to distributing and financing independently produced films. "It isn't generally understood," noted Stanley Kramer, among the first of the successful postwar independents, "that for the most part the producer, on the American scene at least, does have the dream. It is his concept and he is the one who brings the elements together," he explained. "He selects the piece of material, chooses a director, and sometimes works with the writers. He follows the shooting very closely, edits the films and then, in effect, sells the film."[37]

As opportunities for independent producers increased in the 1950s, so did possibilities of turning the drama of Israel's creation into a feature film. Figures like Stanley Kramer, one historian observed, became powers in the industry overnight as studios vied to lease space to them. Each movie became autonomous, and individual films were produced for specific rather than for general audiences. Even with the new opportunities, Jews had to overcome a fairly strong industry bias against making movies on Jews and Jewish issues. With rising antisemitism in the 1930s, Jews had gradually disappeared from the screen. Established studio heads contended that no one wanted to see a movie about Jews. Neil Gabler argues that "Hollywood was itself a means of avoiding Judaism, not celebrating it." Projects involving Jews "often got lost in ambivalence and unresolved feelings about Judaism." The Nazis' slaughter of European Jewry raised the consciousness of some politically engaged Jews and Gentiles. Ideologically self-conscious, they turned to the "social problem film" to explore potentially subversive issues. The conjunction of changing attitudes in a changing industry loosened constraints about making movies on Jews and Jewish issues.[38]

Only producers with liberal leanings saw the creation of Israel as a potential moral drama and a potential hit. In the postwar period three Hollywood producers, all of them independents—Robert Buckner, Stanley Kramer, and Otto Preminger—filmed Israel's story. They imagined Israel's struggle for freedom as an extension of their own liberal credo. Thus, their movies endowed Israel with a spiritual significance that incorporated central values of American Jews' liberal creed.

After Buckner's modest success Stanley Kramer took up the challenge of shooting Israel's story. Born and raised in New York City, Kramer came to Hollywood in 1933 upon graduation from New York University. Although hired initially as a writer, based on his journalism experience at college, he quickly lost that position. "I was nineteen and I found myself in Hollywood and I had lived in New York all my life. If I had had the fare to go back at the time, I would have, but I didn't." Kramer learned the movie business by working at an array of jobs at MGM. During the war he served in the Army Signal Corps. In 1947 he invited several army buddies into a company to make films and began his career as an independent producer, what he described as "a self-styled originator and quadruple-threat man who can move in several directions at the same time and wind up the day's work by expertly sweeping out the studio after everyone else has gone home." He recognized that "to make a place for himself the independent producer has to *add* something to the industry's output." Kramer added through his subject matter, often topical social issues that reflected his liberal politics. In 1951 he signed an agreement with Columbia Pictures that gave his independent company production freedom in return for a commitment to make thirty films in four years. The movies he made at Columbia, including *The Juggler*, about a severely disturbed DP in Israel, were "terrible financial disasters," except for *The Caine Mutiny*, which bailed him out. Kramer then left Columbia and made a deal with United Artists to direct and produce.[39]

A common interest in Israel brought Kramer together with Michael Blankfort, who wrote both the novel and screenplay of *The Juggler*. Born and raised in New Jersey, Blankfort left a career as a professor of psychology to work in the theater. During the 1930s he joined such communist writers as Mike Gold in writing plays about labor struggles. Blankfort then came to Hollywood as a screenwriter, but he also wrote novels, including one on the Spanish Civil War. During the war he served in the Marine Corps. The destruction of European Jewry moved him to explore his Jewish identity; he discovered Zionism. He fell under the spell of Shlomo Bardin and actively supported Bardin's efforts to build the Brandeis Camp Institute in Los Angeles. A friend of Dafni, Blankfort visited Israel in the early years of statehood and came away with a profound commitment to the Zionist cause, seeing it as "a popular revolution."[40]

For both the Jewish writer Blankfort and the Gentile director Edward Dmytryk, one of the Hollywood Ten, *The Juggler* represented the cause of Israel, a progressive cause—perhaps also a safe one—in a time of fear in Hollywood. "I did that film in order to see Israel, a country that was . . . doing wonderful things for the world," Dmytryk recalled. The male lead, Kirk Douglas, who knew some Hebrew, saw a different Israel. Douglas noticed that "there was extreme poverty; food was rationed." But he found it "wonderful, finally, to be in the majority."[41]

Like Kramer's previous films on postwar problems, *The Juggler* focuses upon a single individual whose alienation has reached psychopathic proportions. The movie refers directly to the physical and psychological destruction that the Nazis wreaked on the Jews, although it offers no visual images of the camps. Kirk Douglas's portrayal of a damaged man—a sick soul—elicited criticism. Some thought it "doubtful whether the adventures of a psychopath, however pitiable, are quite the right glass through which to view modern Israel." Others criticized the movie more harshly: "What might have been a film about Israel becomes a film about a neurotic rehabilitated by Stanley Kramer." Yet the link between survivors and state could not be ignored. Israelis, intrigued by the first Hollywood feature to be filmed in the new nation,[42] thought that the story about a man thrust into Israel by fate, without any idealistic preparation, was "a true problem," the case of hundreds of thousands of recently arrived refugees. Several years later Kramer returned to the subject of the Holocaust when he directed *Judgment at Nuremberg*. *The Juggler* approaches the Holocaust from an explicitly Jewish perspective. Although the movie exposes the devastating impact of the Holocaust upon one Jew, it also portrays Israel as the Jews' heroic response to Hitler's destruction.[43]

The Juggler explores the problem of homelessness by following one survivor's efforts to escape his brutalized past in the Jewish homeland. Hans Muller, a juggler born in Munich, fears enclosed spaces and the police. He arrives in Israel but immediately tries to flee his new homeland. Hans knows only the suffering and "outsiderness" of a Jew. He is a stranger to Israel—the land, its people, and its language. An accident outside a kibbutz allows Hans to meet the beautiful blond sabra Yael (Milly Vitale). Blankfort's screenplay describes Hans's first waking vision of the new Jewish woman, the Israeli: "The sun, pouring through the open door, frames her body, and brightens, in a kind of halo, the blondness of her hair. She is beautiful. Her face, however, does not get the sun, and is in partial shadow."[44]

A key scene of identification midway through the movie juxtaposes the agony of homelessness with the promise of coming home. But faced with the human wreckage of the Holocaust, Yael's Zionist message is muted. The scene occurs in an abandoned Arab village overlooking the verdant Hulah valley.[45] Hans reluctantly reveals his true identity to Yael after she unintentionally uncovers the numbers tattooed on his arm. "Why do you hide the fact that you were in a concentration camp?" she asks. Hans answers by describing the crowded cell where "they told me my wife and children had been burned in their ovens." He wanted to die and then begged to live. "I learned that day that terror can become stronger than grief." When Yael urges him not to blame himself, Hans admits his guilt for his wife's and daughters' deaths. "I didn't think they could touch me," he says. "I was their hero. . . . I could have left Germany at any time, taken my wife and children to safety. But no, no, not me. I was above it all." He laughed at his friends' warnings. "Who's a Jew? I'm a German." He waited "until it was too late. . . . Now, if a dog were to lick my heart, he would die of poison." As Hans begins to juggle, Yael urges him to stay at the kibbutz, his home. Hans responds bitterly, "A home is a place you lose." This is the second time in the movie that Hans has uttered this sentence. He knows that Jews have neither home nor homeland. They have lost both in the devastation of World War II. Yael decisively rejects this, insisting, "That's not true." The scene ends with their embrace.

This central scene of identification reveals how *The Juggler* affirmed the Zionist position: Israel was the Jewish homeland, the only true home for survivors. During their second love scene Yael, the sabra, the new Jew, redeems Hans, the sick survivor, the diaspora Jew. After dancing a hora around the evening campfire, Yael and Hans leave the circle. Hans lies down on the ground; Yael sits beside him. "What can I do to make you accept this place, this country, this home?" she asks. After Hans answers in a noncommittal fashion, Yael takes the offensive. "I've been taught to have hope. I want a husband, children, to build a good home, in a good country." Here Yael combines the traditional woman's dream of marriage and children with the frontier vision of building the land and the nation. Although Hans responds that "half a heart doesn't make for a full love," that he can't promise anything but the moment, he yields to her.

The Juggler reaffirmed convictions of Miami and L.A. Jews that survivors belonged in Israel, the one Jewish home and homeland. Its vision of rebirth amid pioneering struggles offered solace to Jews who had uprooted themselves from their homes. As permanent tourists, Jews in Miami and L.A. peered into the distance for a redeeming image of a homeland with which they could identify. Israel promised to heal the wounds of the Holocaust not only for survivors, who had suffered as grievously as Hans, but also for American Jews, who had observed the disaster from afar. If Yael could win Hans, who pretends at several points in the movie to be an American from Hollywood, then the fair and beautiful Israel surely could capture the hearts of American Jews.

Two years after the *The Juggler* appeared, Dore Schary decided to try to make a movie on Israel. Like Kramer, Schary wore his social conscience on his sleeve; unlike Kramer, Schary assumed a position of leadership within the Jewish community. Schary was a political liberal, a committed Jew involved in Jewish communal activities, and a supporter of Israel. He grew up in Newark, the son of immigrant parents who ran a kosher catering hall. "I spoke *mama loshen* (i.e., Yiddish) with my grandparents," he recalled, "and . . . I feared to break the fast on Yom Kippur and would wait dutifully on the last day of Pesach for the sun to hide beyond the roof of the school before running into the bakery to buy a Charlotte Russe and break the anguish of the long week without *chumitz* (leavened bread)." Like Kramer, Schary came to Hollywood as a writer from New York in the 1930s and learned the industry by doing various writing jobs. He was promoted to head of production at RKO in 1947, a reward for having produced a series of profitable quality B movies at MGM. In 1948 he moved back to MGM as chosen successor to Louis B. Mayer. Although Schary did not visit Israel until 1957, its establishment moved him deeply. When Leon Uris approached MGM with a proposal to write a novel on Israel that would then become a movie, he received a commission.[46]

Uris grew up in Baltimore in a secular, radical Jewish home. He enlisted in the Marine Corps a month after Pearl Harbor at the age of seventeen. At the end of the war, he landed in San Francisco. "Like most writers and most human beings, I hated the war," Uris recalled, "but unlike most modern novelists, I did not hate the men who fought the war, and I believed in what I was fighting for." Following the popular success of his novel *Battle Cry*, he moved with his family to Encino to write the screenplay for Warner Brothers. In 1955 MGM gave him an advance for a novel on the creation of the Jewish state that would become the basis of a movie. Uris went to Israel in March 1956 to research the book and logged thousands of miles conducting interviews, taping notes, and shooting photographs. When the Sinai campaign interrupted his research, he covered the war as a correspondent. "It was a revelation to me," he told an interviewer, "when I was researching *Exodus* in Europe and in Israel. And the revelation was this: that we Jews are not what we have been portrayed to be. In truth, we have been fighters." Like Zinnemann, Uris saw Jewish history made as he watched; like Schary, he discovered the new Jew and proudly identified with this hero. Unlike Schary,

Uris saw his own image reflected back in the vision of the new Jew; unlike Zinnemann, he thought he could capture the drama in an epic novel of Israel's creation.[47]

Exodus became a best seller a month after publication in 1958 and stayed on the charts for an entire year, including nineteen weeks as number one. "Word-of-mouth made it a favorite first among Jewish readers in New York, then slowly among Jews and Gentiles in other large cities, finally in towns where Jews are as scarce as Mormons." Its vision of the creation of the State of Israel influenced an entire generation of American Jews. One critic credited Uris with seeing "the total picture of the creation of Israel as a shattering, overwhelming historic event." Another noted that the novel's major characters "stand in roughly the same relation to the reality of Israel as Scarlett O'Hara, Rhett Butler, and Ashley Wilkes do to the American Civil War and Reconstruction South. Like *Gone With the Wind*," Joel Blocker observed, "*Exodus* shows a scrupulous regard for the small facts of history, but sacrifices genuine historical complexity for the sake of the epic-sized image." Veteran American Zionists were appalled, however, at how Uris transformed Zionist idealism into "sentimentality and sensationalism." Writing in the Zionist monthly *Midstream*, Joel Carmichael complained that "the extraordinary feat of setting up the state of Israel, the culminating point in the self-sacrifice of generations of idealists, is utterly trivialized by the pro-Israel sentimentality Uris's *Exodus* has done so much to fortify."[48]

Carmichael's complaint echoed among other Jewish critics; many tried to understand why *Exodus* so captured the American Jewish imagination. Frank Cantor observed in the left-wing magazine *Jewish Currents* that "while dealing ostensibly with Israel, *Exodus* is actually an *American* book, which portrays Israel *through American eyes*." American Jews want to read this novel "because it seems to tell them *a new kind of story* about *a new kind of Jew*." These new Jews are the ones "who have stopped running, hiding, scheming or pretending. They are Jews who fight, who die, who love and who *triumph*." Indeed, they resemble Ben Gurion's Iowa farmer, that captivating image of American frontier heroism. One Israeli correspondent bluntly wrote that the hero, "Ari Ben Canaan is not a Jew . . . [but] the very ideal of true blue American manhood [or] . . . the stereotype of the Anglo-Saxon white Protestant."[49]

Blocker saw a real danger in Uris's vision. "A strong element of anti-Semitism . . . predisposes the Gentile to think of Israel in non-Jewish terms," Blocker wrote. "He readily identifies with the new kind of Jew, the Hebrew; perhaps he is relieved of a certain measure of guilt he previously felt because of dislike of the Jew." Blocker's analysis explained the reaction of a U.S. State Department official speaking to a Jewish reporter.

> *Exodus* revealed what I suspected. The State of Israel is a remarkable revival of the ancient Hebrew nation. . . . They have gotten over their Jewishness and become a new people, a reincarnation of old Hebrews. I have sympathy for the Israelis like Ari Ben Canaan in *Exodus*. . . . In fact, Israel is a nation of farmers and fighters, real people. They are not like the Jews here who are so materialistic and money-mad, the Miami Beach crowd. The Israelis are so different from the Jews.[50]

Philip Roth saw an even darker side to this notion "that you don't have to worry about Jewish vulnerability and victimization after all, the Jews can take care of themselves." He speculated that Gentiles liked *Exodus* because "the burden that it is working to remove from the nation's consciousness is nothing less than the memory of the holocaust itself, the murder of six million Jews, in all its raw, senseless, fiendish horror."[51]

Exodus's compelling power drew American Jews to visit the scene of the historic events. One reporter noted that an American couple who had planned a summer vacation in Europe received a copy of *Exodus* at their bon voyage party. By the time they reached Switzerland, they had read the book and decided to change their entire itinerary to visit Israel. "Israelis are reported to have regarded Uris's book as a bonanza pure and simple; it is supposed to have made a substantial contribution to Israel's desperately needed revenues." Ben Gurion remarked that "as a piece of propaganda, it's the greatest thing ever written about Israel." But other Israelis regarded it with embarrassment. "We thought we had about convinced the world we were just normal human beings, until *Exodus* came along," one complained. Most Israelis kept their distress to themselves. Tour guides found that American visitors "keep asking them where is this or that village they read about in *Exodus*, or where this battle was fought." Responding to an interest that rivaled the Bible as background literature for a visit to Israel, tourist companies introduced an Exodus Tour that took the visitor through the scenes in the novel.[52]

Among the American Jews captivated by *Exodus* was the producer Otto Preminger. The movie imagery that offended some critics of *Exodus*—Dan Wakefield wrote that the novel was "written in Vista-Vision"—grabbed him. Although movie conventions made sense in a novel originally destined to be a screenplay, when Uris returned to Los Angeles, he found that MGM had shelved the project. While Uris was reporting on the Sinai campaign, Schary was fired from his position at MGM. With Schary's departure, support for the project disappeared. Nonetheless, Uris went ahead and wrote the novel. At this point Preminger made his move.[53]

A Jewish refugee from Nazism, Preminger immigrated to the United States in 1935 from Vienna, where he had directed plays. He worked briefly in Hollywood and then returned to the theater in New York. In 1943 he came back to making movies for Twentieth Century Fox. Frustrated with the way "the whole studio works within the border lines of the tastes and personalities of the studio heads," Preminger left Fox to become an independent producer in 1951. Like Schary's and Kramer's, Preminger's liberal politics appeared in his choice of subjects to film, often topics considered taboo. His decision to release *The Moon Is Blue* without the Production Code seal of approval spurred a revision of the code that lifted the ban on the treatment of such topics as drug traffic, abortion, prostitution, and kidnapping. The novels that attracted his attention portrayed real adventures of exceptional individuals, included a large cast of characters, and examined one or two great moral questions. But Preminger regularly discarded the author's themes and point of view because they rarely fit his own political inclinations.[54]

Preminger read Uris's novel in manuscript and offered to purchase the film rights to *Exodus* from MGM for seventy-five thousand dollars (the amount MGM had paid). According to Preminger, he put the fear of an Arab boycott of all MGM films into the mind of Joseph Vogel, the head of MGM. "You can't afford an Arab boycott but I can," Preminger recalled telling Vogel. "Since I'm an independent producer, they can't hurt me too much." Preminger's seed of fear bloomed, and he bought the rights in 1957 for what was a small sum, given the subsequent popularity of the novel that rivaled *Gone with the Wind* in sales. Preminger then turned to Arthur Krim of United Artists for money to do the movie. Krim was an ardent supporter of Israel, and his wife, Mathilde, had worked as a research scientist at the Weizmann Institute. Subsequently Preminger contacted the veteran Zionist Meyer Weisgal, now head of the Weizmann Institute, to serve as his guide to Israel and through its bureaucracy.[55]

Not only did Preminger buy the film rights, he also rejected Uris as scriptwriter, though Uris had written screenplays before, including those for *Gunfight at OK Corral* and his own earlier novel, *Battle Cry*. Uris did write a first treatment. "I very quickly realized he couldn't write it," Preminger recalled, "at least not the way *I* wanted it." Preminger's vision of the movie *Exodus* differed radically from Uris's point of view in the novel. Preminger wanted to make "an American picture, after all, that tries to tell the story, giving both sides a chance to plead their side." He worked hard to balance his characters, including a British general sympathetic to Jews to contrast with an officer who is "frankly anti-Semitic." Preminger explained, "We tried to make this [antisemitism] humorous and entertaining."[56] Uris found antisemitism neither humorous nor entertaining. Like Buckner, Uris had portrayed the British as the enemy.

Instead of Uris, Preminger turned, as Kramer had, to one of the Hollywood Ten who was not Jewish. Preminger hired the black-listed writer Dalton Trumbo and worked with him to shape a screenplay quite different from Uris's novel. In fact, Preminger and Trumbo were criticized for having "considerably temporized in exposing the adversaries." Others disagreed, complaining that "the film unequivocally blames the Arabs, absolutely absolves the Jews." *Time* magazine also resented the sympathetic portrayal of the Irgun, claiming that "the picture goes on to sanctify the Jewish terror." The review concluded that "the kind of blind hatred that excuses the Jewish terror was also used to excuse the Nazi extermination camps." To add to the controversy surrounding the movie, Preminger decided to give Trumbo credits in his own name on the finished movie.[57] Preminger's announcement of the decision before the filming began helped to break the blacklist. The movie symbolically marked the end of the painful postwar era of anticommunist investigations. When it was released, American Legion pickets protested the picture, having previously criticized both Preminger and Kramer for hiring "Soviet-indoctrinated artists."[58]

Exodus draws upon its predecessors but outdoes all of them in scope, drama, complexity, and production values. The movie evokes the Bible in its title and sweep and extraordinary length (over three and a half hours). Critics have seen the movie as a variant on American westerns and war movies or as a modernized version of the Biblical epics of Cecil B. DeMille. Lester Friedman calls it "a Hollywood Western played out in the desert instead of on a prairie, a tale of brave men overcoming the dangers of a wild frontier to bring law, order, and civilization to a new land."[59]

Exodus was a landmark for American Jews because of its wild box office appeal. Of the three movies on Israel, only *Exodus* was a major financial success. When it opened in December 1960, *Exodus* had the largest advance sale of any movie to date, some $1.6 million. The picture, with a production budget of $3.5 million, grossed $13 million. Like the novel on which it was based, *Exodus* was extraordinarily popular. Both Uris and Preminger sold their frontier vision of Israel to millions. American Jews enjoyed the movie and welcomed its portrait of Israel, in part because so many Americans accepted the Israel they saw on the screen. John Stone, then the Jewish community's man in the industry, reported: "What the picture shows to the world—and that's the important thing—is Jewish heroism in their [*sic*] struggle for freedom." "The glory of the Jewish military man," writes Friedman, "wipes away the shame of the Jew as victim, implying that what happened in Germany will never occur again because now, at long last, the Jew can defend himself." By drawing upon the western genre familiar to Americans, *Exodus* gave Israel a persona. The movie placed the figurative white hat on Israel's head, endowing the state and its leaders with good guy status. *Exodus* spoke powerfully to American Jewish ethnic self-consciousness.[60]

In a crucial scene Preminger cast Israel's meaning as the Jewish homeland in terms of a symbolic American Jewish ethnicity. At the heart of the scene is an emphatic statement by the hero that "people are different." He delivers the banal but revealing statement as something of a manifesto that must be accepted eventually by the heroine (despite her initial rejection of it). Hardly a complex idea, the notion that people are different carried significant ideological freight, especially for American Jews in 1960.

The scene occurs midway through the movie when the handsome hero (played by Paul Newman), Ari Ben Canaan—literally, Ari the son of Canaan, the ancient Gentile term for the land of Israel—pulls off the road to show Kitty, the pretty blond American Christian nurse (Eva Marie Saint), the valley of Jezreel and Mount Tabor. The movie has already shown Ari to be a laconic soldier and fighter, clever underground organizer, and audacious leader of men. Now he appears as a *moreh derech* (guide), an interpreter of the land and *Tanach* (Hebrew Bible) to the American outsider. Pointing to the peaceful scene below, Ari reminds Kitty of the story of Deborah calling her troops and Barak to battle. Kitty remembers the biblical tale that she undoubtedly learned in a Presbyterian Sunday school in Indiana. Ari quotes *Tanach* to set forth his claim to the land: Jews first came to this valley thousands of years ago. Then, eschewing a subtlety inappropriate to the movies and Hollywood, Ari spells out the Zionist history lesson for Kitty (and all Americans, in case they hadn't understood): "I just wanted you to know that I'm a Jew. This is my country." Ari's defiant statement to the American nurse echoes Sabra's similar response to the British in *Sword*.

Kitty replies that she understands (after all, she is a smart American woman). She then goes on to express the universalist American creed of equality: "All these differences between people are made up. People are the same no matter what they're called." Kitty's rejoinder sounds like an ADL educational pamphlet prepared for Brotherhood Week, a popular observance in Eisenhower's America that Jews strongly supported. But Ari answers her as the new Jew, the post-Holocaust Jew, the Jew who lives in his own land and fights for his freedom, the Jew so secure in his Jewishness and sense of purpose, a hero of such integrity, that he can befriend all who respect him. As a Jew rooted in Israel, the land of his birth, he deals equally with Arab and Englishman, even with feuding father and uncle, personifications of the Haganah and Irgun. "Don't ever believe it," he tells Kitty. "People are different. They have a right to be different. They like to be different. It's no good pretending that differences don't exist. They do. They have to be recognized and respected." A bold statement for a Jew to make to an American audience in 1960!

Unlike Sabra's remarks to the British or *The Juggler's* painful scene of identification, *Exodus* challenged directly the familiar credo of many American Jews. Ari's forthright defense of the right to be different rejects the values of "ambivalent American Jews" and identifies the new Israeli Jew with a proud assertive creed of Jewish differentness. As Miami Jews had done through the purchase of

Israel bonds, two Los Angeles Jews imagined in Ari an Israeli hero who eschews any pandering for Gentile approval. This frontier vision projected an alternative to the path taken by most Los Angeles Jews seeking acceptance and integration into American society as well as recognition and respect for Jewish group survival.[61] Although *Exodus* projects intermarriage as the future of Kitty and Ari's relationship, it also assures the audience that Ari will not lose his ethnic distinctiveness. Nor, by the way, will Kitty. Ari will remain a Jew; there can be no doubt in any viewer's mind. When Kitty will come to love and accept him, she will love and accept him as a Jew.

Before the movie ends, Ari chooses the American, the good Gentile, and tells her to come with the Jews. Their struggle for a state of their own is any righteous Gentile's battle, and Ari welcomes those, especially Americans, who offer the hand of friendship and love. Kitty's eventual acceptance of Ari signifies the acceptance of Israel by Americans; her embrace of the new Jew suggests the possibility of accepting those Jews who identify with Israel. These Gentiles find Israelis appealing because they are exactly the ones who neither need nor desire Gentile approval.

In an interview during the movie's shooting, Eva Marie Saint admitted to an identification with the character Kitty. "I know the type of person she is because I was like her myself once," Saint explained. "Ten years ago I had many misunderstandings about people and certain unconscious prejudices. When I heard people voice these things I rebelled inside but said nothing and did nothing although I felt I should." She understood the "passive anti-Jewish point of view." Making the movie, Saint discovered that she felt "like I'm part of history—a history I had nothing to do with but I have a compassion for." She hoped that "if I can involve the audience, perhaps change someone's prejudice to understanding, it will all be to the good." When the reporter responded that Kitty never existed but is merely a prototype, Saint answered, "Women like her did. She's real to me."[62] This sense of reality appeared on the screen and helped to make *Exodus* so convincing.

Preminger sought to portray conflict between Jews and Arabs from an American viewpoint, showing both sides of the issue. Newspapers reported that the film script was altered "to remove material objectionable to Arabs." Despite these changes both Newman and Preminger received threatening letters at their Haifa hotel. Perhaps in response to Arab criticism, *Exodus* carefully presents its representative Arab in a most favorable light.[63] Unlike the novel, the movie holds out the hope of eventual fellowship of Jew and Arab because it makes the German Nazi adviser of the Mufti the instigator of actual violence, echoing Golda Meir's speech to Miami Jews. Thus, the onus is lifted from Arabs, who followed the wrong leaders with their bad advisers, while the Jews' fight against Arabs becomes a struggle against surrogate Nazis.

In subordinating the conflicts of Jews with Arabs and British, *Exodus* emphasizes instead the theme of brothers at war in a common land. In the process the movie portrays complexities within Jewish politics. Ari's most difficult task is to reunite the feuding factions of his own family. But he cannot overcome the implacable anger between the two brothers, his uncle, Akiva (David Opatoshu), head of the Irgun, and his father, Barak (Lee J. Cobb), a Haganah leader. Each adheres passionately to his Zionist ideology. Ari comes to seek an alliance of Irgun and Haganah to fight the British, their common enemy. Akiva opposes the alliance; he is unwilling to renounce terrorism. Violence is the midwife of nations, he explains to Ari. Barak will not countenance terrorism, and he will not forgive his brother for being a terrorist. Ari bridges only imperfectly the chasm between the brothers and their ideologies. By portraying both brothers as good men, *Exodus* suggests that both ideologies, political parties, and military organizations—labor Zionism and Revisionism, Mapai and Herut, Haganah and Irgun—are ultimately reconcilable because both are right. Despite the absence of reconciliation on the screen, the movie smoothes out a profound division among Jews, creating consensus in support of Israel.

Preminger noted with approval that he angered both representatives of the Labor government and their Revisionist opponents. "You do not want to rewrite the script," he told the Labor representatives, "you want to rewrite history!" In his autobiography Preminger recalls telling Golda Meir, Ben Gurion, and Moshe Dayan that Israel would not "have emerged as a nation without the terrorists. I don't like violence but that is unfortunately the truth. The British would never have given in without the high pressure from the radical element."

Menachem Begin on the other hand objected that the movie didn't give the Irgun enough credit.[64]

Exodus ends with the Jews going off to fight for their independence against the Arabs, not the British. The penultimate scene is a joint funeral: Karen, a Jewish teenage refugee, is buried next to the Arab *mukhtar* of the neighboring village, Ari's boyhood friend. Both have been killed by Nazi-led Arabs. Ari gives the funeral oration, expressing the hope that the living will have peace, not just the dead. He concludes with an oath: "I swear . . . that the day will come when Arab and Jew will share in peaceful life in this land that they have always shared in death." The film's last word is "Shalom," the only Hebrew spoken in the movie. *Exodus* depicts the destruction of Arab-Jewish friendship, identifying it as the price paid for the creation of the Jewish state. But the movie also subverts its own theme of reconciliation. Dov (Sal Mineo), the angry young survivor of Auschwitz and dedicated terrorist, whose love for Karen held out the promise of rebirth, refuses to shovel earth on the common grave. Filled with hatred, he will not mourn.[65]

The destruction of European Jewry and struggle for a Jewish state shook the world of many American Jews. The process of postwar reconstruction involved repairing their damaged identity as a people herded to their deaths, as well as rescuing refugees and lobbying for a Jewish state. For a few Los Angeles Jews in the motion picture industry, movies provided a vehicle to articulate their new self-consciousness as American Jews and to project a frontier vision, provided they could find a sufficiently popular subject. Israel's creation gave these Jews their chance, and on the third try, with *Exodus*, they enjoyed a remarkable success. The cinematic Israel addressed postwar dilemmas, but it refocused them for the silver screen. It gave Jewish and Gentile Americans a hero to root for and to identify with, if only while they sat in the darkened movie theater. The plucky little Jewish state fighting for its freedom became a Hollywood legend. And possibly because Gentile Americans momentarily identified with the screen Israel, American Jews considered going even further: They let the movie image blur the distinction between imagination and reality, "between us and them."[66] The anthropologist Hortense Powdermaker observed that "audiences tend to accept as true that part of a movie story which is beyond their experience."[67] Given

Israel's distance from most American Jews, accepting the screen image for many represented a giant step toward reverentially incorporating Israel into their Jewish self-consciousness.

Committed Zionists disliked the new, popular image of Israel that captured the American imagination. Trying to explain Israel's transformation into a romantic legend, Carmichael looked for the sources of Uris's success as "a social phenomenon, perhaps even a syndrome." He blamed the postwar growth of a pro-Israel piety on the character of American culture and on the loss of Zionist influence. "[The] general vulgarization of Jewish life for the past decade has been forcefully attested to by the withering away of Zionist idealism," he wrote, "and its replacement by the conformist pro-Israel piety of bond drives, souvenir hunting, tourism to Israel, chauvinistic *schmaltz* and all the other manifestations of communal allegiance devoid of spiritual content." The popularity of Israel's screen image found "its niche within the larger phenomenon of the dilution of ideals, judgement and taste that has become a hallmark of mass culture in Twentieth Century America." Carmichael bemoaned what he saw to be the outcome of this transformation of Zionism into "insipidity and simple-mindedness." "Sentimentality and sensationalism have replaced organic identification, and Jews are left clinging to attitudes and slogans in place of traditions, ideas, and beliefs," he concluded.[68]

Carmichael's complaints convinced only a handful; pioneering visions of Miami and Los Angeles Jews proved too compelling to resist. The furthest removed from any identification with long-rooted communities, Los Angeles Jews produced the most powerful slogans and images that simplified and symbolized Jewish life. Fashioned out of their own experience and need, their mythic vision of Israel was accessible, heroic, uplifting. It promised redemption, a way to be Jewish in America with pride. Those who knew Israel well—Israelis and American Zionists—often were disturbed by the distortion, but few sought to challenge Israel's new popularity by producing alternative images. Instead, Uris entered the lecture circuit. Miami's Central Jewish Appeal featured him as the key speaker inaugurating its 1959 fund-raising drive. El Al, Israel's national airline, sponsored a tour of Israel in 1961 that followed in Preminger's footsteps, stopping at the places he had made famous on film. Ernest Gold's theme music for the movie acquired lyrics and became a popular song. Pat Boone crooned, "This land is mine, God gave this land to me!"[69]

The reverential embrace of Israel sparked by the creation of a screen legend did not reach one significant segment of the American Jewish population: its New York intellectuals. A 1961 symposium on "Jewishness and the Younger Intellectuals" in *Commentary* magazine produced remarkably ambivalent comments about Israel and no expressions of pro-Israel piety despite a specific question inquiring if the respondent felt "any special connection with the State of Israel."[70] Although one writer admitted that "at the time of the Sinai campaign I felt a distinct physical elan: a sense of victory," he immediately concluded, "even Israel, however, cannot save us."[71] Removed from American popular culture—usually defined as mass culture—the intellectuals were largely removed as well from Israel. Carmichael's Zionist idealism failed to touch them, as Zionism as a political movement had failed to reach an older generation during the Depression.[72] Unlike most American Jews, intellectuals usually ignored Israel, either as a mundane reality or romantic legend. Those Jewish writers who did not trek to Hollywood but turned to Jewish topics often produced satire, not heroism. In 1959, the year after Uris published *Exodus*, Philip Roth published his first book, a collection of short stories and a novella, *Goodbye Columbus*. Its portrait of nouveau riche Jews provoked laughter in many and outrage in the established Jewish community. Few were prompted to find "pride in their Jewishness" as they had in *Exodus*. The contrast between East and West, center and periphery, civilization and frontier appeared vividly in this juxtaposition of high versus popular culture.[73]

Preminger's *Exodus* produced an enduring image of Israel and its Jews.[74] Israel entered the popular American Jewish imagination as a romantic screen legend. The story of its creation became part of the fantasies of American Jews. In its legendary form Israel became the redemptive homeland of American Jews, and Israelis their heroic Jewish alter egos. For over a decade nothing significantly challenged this frontier vision. Indeed, it could be argued that so many American Jews responded so quickly to the crisis of May–June 1967, not just because it awakened dormant fears of another holocaust, but also because Israel had become such an integral part of their self-consciousness. In an uncanny fashion newspaper headlines appeared to follow a Hollywood script. First came three weeks of increasingly unendurable tension: removal of UN peacekeeping troops, sealing the Straits of Tiran, mobilizing of Egyptian and Syrian forces on the border, massing of tanks and guns poised for invasion, inflammatory threats of destruction by Arab leaders, refusal of any Western nation to raise its voice or lift its hand to help Israel. By the beginning of June, Israel stood completely alone—as a Hollywood hero should stand—against the massed military might of the entire Arab world. Then, in six brilliant, tension-filled days, the Israeli military not only single-handedly fought off the Arab armies of Egypt, Syria, and Jordan, but reunited Jerusalem, recaptured the Sinai, and doubled the territory of the state. In the Six-Day War Israel miraculously lived up to its legend. Image and reality fused; Israel redeemed its promise, and heroic visions became living history.

Produced by three very different men, the three movies on Israel helped to transform Zionist ideology into pro-Israel piety. These movies gave recent Jewish history a palpable reality of mythic dimensions as they transmuted the rhetoric of Zionist politics into rallying cries of heroes. The Jews who produced the movies adopted without reservations the Zionist message of statehood as the solution for survivors. Here was the answer to Hitler's destruction of European Jews: the creation of a screen Israel that was larger than life. Philip Roth saw this and found it disturbing. "One week *Life* magazine presents on its cover a picture of Adolf Eichmann; weeks later, a picture of Sal Mineo as a Jewish freedom fighter," he wrote. "A crime to which there is no adequate human response, no grief, no compassion, no vengeance that is sufficient seems, in part then, to have been avenged."[75] The movies helped raise Israel into an object of veneration for American Jews—indeed, into a screen legend. As Hollywood had done with countless stars, so it did with Israel: It took the mundane reality of a small, poor state struggling to absorb hundreds of thousands of destitute immigrants and remade it into a living romance.

This imagined Israel displaced New York as the source of authentic Jewish culture for Los Angeles and Miami Jews. Israel offered itself as an attractive new love. Distant and exotic, a young country of pioneers and soldiers, Israel was utterly unlike the New York that Jews knew so well. American Jews projected upon Israelis the image of a new Jew nurtured in the soil of the recently recovered homeland, a Jew who bore an uncanny resemblance to the heroic American pioneer farmer. This new Israeli Jew created on the screen and paraded upon the podium of countless bond rallies—unafraid, outspoken, and rooted—possessed vision and purpose, the drive and dimensions of heroism.

Israel's arrival on the world scene coincided with the efforts of Miami and Los Angeles Jews to seek roots and forge an identity for themselves. Israel beckoned to them; Israel suggested the possibility of rebirth. Having recently uprooted themselves and turned their backs upon the homes of their youth, newcomers proved particularly receptive to the drama of Israel because it let them come to terms with their Jewishness. Distance placed few restraints upon their imagination. Through Israel they seized the opportunity of fashioning anew the substance of an American Jewish identity. Israel allowed them to reimagine home and roots in an alternative homeland. Israel even became American Jews' insurance policy, despite its precarious political and economic situation. In Los Angeles and Miami, Jews projected heroic dreams onto the new state. These frontier visions—of pioneering, striking roots, building a new home, and defending it against enemies—spoke to their specific situation as newcomers as well as to their need to define themselves as American Jews in a post-Holocaust age.[76] Israel entered their consciousness first through its commitment to rescue survivors. But Jews in Miami and Los Angeles secured Israel's place by transforming rescue into a promise of redemption.

9
The New American Jew

As opposed to more established areas of the country, where
one tends to fall into a ready-prepared pattern, in California one can and must build one's own life. Hence the pride
and confidence that are noticeable in so many Californians
by adoption. They have confronted the strangeness of the
West and they have conquered it: out of bits and pieces of
the new and the old they have constructed their lives on a
pattern that is all of their own devising.

—H. STUART HUGHES
"California—The America to Come," *Commentary*, May 1956

The United States has been a country animated by the idea that the
American dream could be realized through an act of self-creation. In
the aftermath of World War II, American Jews seized upon America's
endless promise to reinvent themselves. After the Holocaust they
claimed the mantle of leadership of a two-thousand-year-old diaspora,
and they affirmed their solidarity with Israelis, their contemporary
cousins living in the sovereign Jewish state. During the first decades
of the American century, they culled their American experiences to
fashion a Jewish way of life. America, as ever, held out the possibility
of rebirth. "We all felt the world was our oyster and California was the

leading edge," recalled one migrant to Los Angeles in a piquantly un-kosher mixed metaphor.[1] Jews setting out after the Dream, a new kind of life in Miami and Los Angeles in the postwar era, often succeeeded handsomely. Some, of course, merely fled what they considered to be an oppressive past and jettisoned their Jewish identity. But many oth-ers reinvented themselves as American Jews. They chose the palm tree paradises of the South and West, and they chose to live as Jews in their new American heaven. A few self-consciously sought to reimag-ine an authentic American Jew, an un-self-conscious blend of Ameri-can promise and Jewish fulfillment. Of those who spurned the lure of Miami and Los Angeles, mocking its shallow popular Jewish culture, only a few did so because they championed an elite Judaism that rejected American mores. Even some of these Orthodox and intellec-tual naysayers packed their bags and moved in the 1970s, tempted by the possibility of enjoying a life of both leisure and Jewish commit-ment that the first newcomers had created.

Most Miami and Los Angeles Jews accepted a halfway covenant: Born into Judaism, they acknowledged its periodic obligations.[2] Their arrangement challenged those who insisted that such compromises led to decline, that a bland, positive, upbeat, and affirming Judaism that placed few demands upon its adherents would not sustain future generations.[3] Many Jews in Miami and Los Angeles did just what committed ideologues said could not be done: They lived as American Jews where few distinctive markers set them apart from their Chris-tian neighbors, they embraced a Jewish identity derived less from tra-dition than from personal choice, they forged bonds of community in political support for Israel, and they continued unabashedly to remake themselves. A dynamic framework bulging with promise and opportu-nity enveloped Jewish newcomers; they made their choices surround-ed by affluence and captivated by self-fulfillment. Those Jews who came to Miami and Los Angeles and decided to remain Jews wanted it all. They wanted to be Jews under the American sun, the best of both worlds, the chance to live as Jews in a free society. To borrow from the Puritan past, Jews encountered their wilderness and discovered their errand in postwar Miami and Los Angeles. As they planted congrega-tions, built communities, and forged collective bonds, they fashioned a Jewish way of life focused upon the individual and responsive to the rapidly changing experiences of the present.

Starting over in a new city promised not only rebirth but also many options of youth and its freedoms. Moving to Los Angeles meant a fresh beginning. The city's natural beauty constantly reminded newcomers that they had entered a world of seemingly limitless possibilities. In L.A. and Miami, Jews enjoyed a leisure life that suggested a continuous sabbath. Even the elderly discovered an unexpected energy and ease permeating their mundane routines. Daily activities themselves acquired a freshness from being situated in such an exotic environment. Many interpreted their move into new hotels or apartments as a sign of rediscovered youth. "I see many funny and silly things here often because many people desire to appear young and not old," I. B. Singer admitted. Jews discarded the clothes and furniture of the cold northeastern cities for those bright colors and lightweight alternatives appropriate to Miami's sunny skies. Visible external symbols corresponded to a changing inner reality that found expression in forms of Jewish life that appeared only tenuously connected to past traditions, such as the program of Jewish "ritual observance" (modeled on Weight Watchers) of Conservative Temple Beth Ami in Reseda. The goal, potential members were assured, was "not to make them become any more Jewish than what they will be comfortable with."[4]

The loss of conventional Jewish constraints and their replacement by an array of alternatives continually amazed outside observers. Bruce Phillips found a greater diversity of congregations in Los Angeles than in any other city and a greater tolerance of difference. "We thought we were the leading edge of social and racial tolerance," one newcomer admitted. The number of Jewish possibilities continued to increase as the Jewish population grew throughout the 1960s and 1970s. It reached 440,000 by 1970 in Los Angeles and exceeded half a million by 1980; in Miami there were 230,000 Jews by 1970 and a peak population of almost 290,000 five years later. Even substantial numbers of Orthodox Jews, both centrist and pietist, were among the newcomers. The visible presence of their synagogues and schools, kosher shops and religious bookstores contributed to Jewish diversity. "On the West Coast," observed Shlomo Cunin, director of the Lubavitch Hasidic movement in Los Angeles, "particularly in L.A., the people are very wild, very open minded. . . . People are not fixed in their ways, they are searching."[5]

Despite the changing numbers and types of migrants, the dynamic—the centrality of individual choice—remained constant. Unlike the situation in northeastern and midwestern suburbs, where pressures to conform to established patterns of Christian religious behavior encouraged Jews to build and join synagogues, the situation in L.A. made Jews feel free to follow their own inclinations. In New York the success of Jewish ethnic politics even led to closing the public schools on the High Holidays, thus eliminating the choice of whether or not one should attend school on those holy days. In Miami and L.A. the decision remained a personal one to be made by each individual.[6]

Migration placed the individual at the center of Jewish collective endeavor and transformed community activity. Entrepreneurship generated action; showmanship launched communal projects. Individual Jews supported Israel, joined a synagogue, or participated in Jewish politics, not due to the weight of tradition or any collective compulsion, but because each one saw some personal meaning in the act. "In a society based upon the legitimacy of individual expressions of identity and the affirmation of individual personality development, there is a constant emphasis upon the full and frank acceptance of oneself and one's origins and roots." Although Jews established communal institutions in Miami and Los Angeles that appeared superficially similar to those in other cities, the characteristic agent of Jewishness became the singular individual. This process anticipated changes that eventually would overtake most American Jews. Writing in the 1980s, Charles Liebman observed that for many American Jews "personal choice is endowed with spiritual sanctity and is in all cases (contrary to past tradition) considered more virtuous than performing an act out of one's sense of obedience to God."[7]

During the postwar decades such freedom—typical of newcomers to Miami and L.A.—did not yet characterize most American Jews. In 1960 Nathan Glazer and Daniel Patrick Moynihan found many Jews in New York City still living lives bounded by a visible ethnicity. Their neighborhoods, occupations, and educations constrained them and made their Jewishness less a matter of choice than of birth, upbringing, and experience. New York Jews, aware of where they stood in the urban world, still pursued a politics of self-interest, seeking through their votes to free teachers from working on the High Holidays, not just as an expression of ethnic identity, but because many Jewish teachers would otherwise be penalized if they observed them. Similarly New York Jews encouraged the city and state to build middle-income housing, not just to affirm their domestic liberalism, but because many Jews needed such apartments. However, some behavior visible among newcomers to Miami and L.A. in the postwar decades appeared on the suburban frontier by the mid-1960s. Examining a wealthy Chicago suburb, the sociologist Marshall Sklare observed that "the modern Jew selects from the vast storehouse of the past what is not only objectively possible for him to practice but subjectively possible for him to 'identify' with."[8]

As suburban American Jews began to resemble Jews in Miami and L.A., differences between the two leisure cities on the ocean sharpened. The maturation of a local, native-born generation of Jews as well as the influx of new immigrants endowed Los Angeles and Miami with some familiar ethnic attributes that Jews associated with metropolitan life in the Northeast and Midwest. In the 1960s and 1970s the enormous migration of elderly Jews turned Miami into the preeminent retirement center, especially after new hotel construction slowed. In addition, immigration of Cubans to the city radically changed its character. Reporters commented on the widely available rich, dark coffee rather than on the bagels with a spot of cream cheese. In the 1970s and 1980s the huge influx of immigrants to Los Angeles, not just from Mexico and South America but also from many Asian nations, similarly transformed that city. Mike Davis called it a "city of quartz," evoking a "junkyard of dreams"; David Rieff dubbed it the "capital of the third world." Both emphasized how contemporary Los Angeles, a multiethnic immigrant metropolis, differed from the white Protestant urban society that Jews had discovered during the postwar era.[9]

The cities changed, yet retained the allure of ease and opportunity. They continued to entice newcomers, setting Jews in Miami and Los Angeles apart from their less mobile relatives. Rootlessness and nostalgia pulled this new generation of newcomers together as had been the case for postwar migrants. In the 1980s Jeffrey Silber encouraged a group of uprooted Jews from the Bronx to form the Bronx Alumni Arts Council. The council published a newsletter to keep its members in touch. In its second issue the comedian Carl Reiner explained that

"*Geshmak* [delicious] is the quality everyone from the Bronx has. When one of us says 'hello,' you know we're from the Bronx." In 1985 over eight hundred showed up at the first annual Bronx festival in Beverly Hills to participate in festivities on the grounds of El Rodeo School. This second-generation *landsmanshaft*, or hometown society, also sponsored such activities as a street-games festival. In the middle of Los Angeles—the city of freeways, not sidewalks—these former New Yorkers taught their children how to play stickball and hopscotch in an effort to transmit and preserve their hometown culture. The council raised money as well to help rebuild their devastated borough, and they sponsored seventy arts scholarships to give a few lucky Bronx kids a chance to escape the Bronx. In all its grittiness, the Bronx remained home (though one could not go back again), as Los Angeles, in all its loveliness, was not.[10]

Alongside the newcomers, by the 1970s a native-born local generation of Los Angelenos and Miamians had reached maturity, ready to take its place within established organizations. By the 1980s there were even examples of second-generation Miamians and Los Angelenos, children whose parents had been born and bred in these cities of newcomers. The presence of a native-born local generation started a new process of communal transformation in Miami and Los Angeles. Their Jewish society grew closer in some ways to the older Jewish worlds of the Northeast and Midwest. The arrival of a new rabbi at Temple Beth Sholom after Leon Kronish suffered a debilitating stroke reveals the influence of this more rooted generation. The lay leadership deliberately looked not for an innovative builder but for a *heymish* rabbi who would focus his energies upon the intimate world of the temple. Even in his physical appearance the new rabbi represented a radical alternative to Kronish. Short and chubby, Rabbi Gary Glickstein exuded a casual buoyancy that contrasted vividly with the tall, slim Kronish's elegance and wit. Congregants were no longer insecure newcomers without a well-established temple, and they asserted authority and rootedness through their choice of a spiritual leader.

Yet L.A. and Miami remained a place for innovation where the ambitious few could experiment with the experience of Jewish living. In his mid-forties Isaiah Zeldin took the risk of setting out on his own; he decided to use his enormous entrepreneurial talents to build an empire. With a handful of devoted followers, he created the Stephen

S. Wise Temple in 1964. Zeldin developed a wide variety of Jewish educational settings for all ages, from infants and toddlers to grandparents. "We take you from the sperm to the worm," joked a temple official. Within five years of its founding, the Stephen S. Wise Temple schools enrolled 4 percent of all Jewish children in Los Angeles religious schools, drew 250 regularly to its adult education classes, sent 15 children from its Hebrew high school to Israel, and generated enough enthusiasm among its teenagers that many lingered at the temple after Friday night services to dance Israeli folk dances until midnight. Zeldin also began a bus service to bring to the temple his increasingly far-flung congregants, from Fairfax to Pacific Palisades and from Northridge to North Hollywood. Narot had initiated a similar practice in Miami when he realized that his membership, like Miami's Jewish population, lived scattered half in the town and the other half in the Beach.[11]

Zeldin kept emphasizing to his congregants, as Bardin had done to his followers, the critical importance of participation for understanding and commitment. "Our goal here is to help them feel as comfortable about their Jewishness as they do about being Americans," he explained. "Judaism becomes an integrated way of life rather than a compartmentalized life experience relegated to Friday night services." Programs were open to nonmembers; as a result, often 60 percent joined the temple by the end of a session. By the mid-1970s the temple had over twelve hundred members; ten years later they numbered ten thousand.[12]

The key lay in education, "a pillar of our congregation life. . . . Our goal is to have every member of every family in at least one program of Jewish study," Zeldin explained. Zeldin kept on expanding the types of educational programs available to reach as many people as possible, taking as his starting point his congregants' needs, both potential and actual. He adopted most of the earlier innovations, including summer camping, a holiday workshop series that ran for the entire year, and special programming for teenagers. Then he added some innovations of his own by responding to requests and by encouraging individual initiative. These new programs included a parenting center for infants and mothers, a Daddy and Me program for toddlers and fathers, and a group for widows and widowers with small children, in addition to extensive family-life programs for the single, adoptive, intermarried, and remarried parent. Finally, Zeldin embarked on an ambitious day school venture, entering a field that most synagogues had avoided due to its cost. He plunged energetically into a form of education rejected by most Reform rabbis as parochial and inappropriate to American society.[13]

By the 1970s Zeldin was not alone. Other ambitious rabbis saw the possibilities in a day school. Valley Jewish Community Center (which later adopted the more Jewish name Adat Ari El) also started a day school, as did Lehrman at Temple Emanu-El. Even Bardin wanted to establish a high school, albeit one modeled on the elite New England private boarding academies. These changes, introduced by newcomers like Zeldin or Harold Schulweis when he moved to Encino to become rabbi of Temple Valley Beth Sholom, actually represented continuity with innovations associated with Los Angeles's boomtown past and open opportunities that produced a new American Jew.[14]

In Miami and Los Angeles, Judaism increasingly acquired aspects of Protestant individualism: the search for personal meaning to be found through experience and an emphasis on an individual's voluntary affirmation. Unlike the family-centered Judaism of the northeastern suburbs, with its overlapping circles of primary group ties where synagogue participation involved "simultaneously a gathering of kin, neighbors, fellow-workers, and leisure-time friends," the Judaism of the Jews of Miami and, especially, Los Angeles focused upon the individual and her peer group.[15] The individual Jew chose her faith and expressed it through her politics and values. Such a faith called for celebrations of annual holidays with friends and family—surrogate or actual—as well as observance of life cycle events. This new Jewish faith also espoused a number of cardinal tenets. Among these was belief in Israel as homeland and holy land, a nation to be supported and cheered, a land where frontier visions could be fulfilled, a country peopled by a new breed of Jews. American Jews accepted as a sacred trust the duty to defend, upbuild, support, and celebrate Israel. Despite its focus on individual affirmation, this Judaism articulated a belief in Jewish peoplehood, a collective responsibility for the fate of other Jews.[16]

Perhaps most important, the new "folk Judaism" blurred traditional gender distinctions in its emphasis upon the centrality of experience. By focusing upon a Jewish experience of the sabbath or holiday observance or a trip to Israel, Jews not only appealed to personal feelings but also sanctified doing over learning, action over belief, behavior over understanding, emotion over intellect. Such an emphasis reflected what had traditionally been within the woman's sphere. Women lived a home-centered Judaism and knew what to do, not because they had studied sacred texts, but because of accumulated experiences. Yet since few Jews in Los Angeles or Miami could recall such familial experiences, they turned to Jewish schools, camps, and synagogues to provide an emotional and spiritual encounter with Judaism in an intensive form. Out of this experiential emphasis came occasionally a desire to study and learn, as well as motivation to continue to affirm a Jewish identity.

Finally, this new American Judaism warmly adopted those ideals deemed central to American society, especially democratic pluralism and a commitment to "prophetic" universal principles of justice. Such a popular faith did not particularly condemn intermarriage, since Judaism could be voluntarily chosen and there were, in fact, many ways to be Jewish. Being a Jew gradually ceased to be a matter of birth and inheritance, of family constraints and collective guilt. Jewishness became instead an aspect of one's identity that is periodically relevant, a source of joy and occasional solidarity, a subtle marker distinguishing one as a particular type of American. Gradually, other American Jews who did not move to Miami and L.A. came to adopt many of the same values and attitudes, especially as the individualism and mobility of American society eroded traditional urban Jewish communities.

In the face of obvious change, Jewish experiences in Miami and Los Angeles suggest remarkable continuity. At the moment in the postwar era when America really opened up to Jews—in part because Jews fought hard for an end to discrimination—many Jews in Miami and Los Angeles opted, without much ambivalence, for Jewish continuity. Indeed, by supporting Israel and fighting for civil rights they reinforced their differentness from their Christian neighbors but not from other American Jews. Yet they also transformed Judaism, their dissenting non-Christian religion, into an individualist faith that increasingly resembled dominant forms of American Protestantism. Thus, as they chose to continue to identify as Jews, they recast Jewish religious and ethnic culture of the urban Northeast and Midwest into a bricolage of individual faith, voluntary association, politics, morals, life cycle occasions, and symbolic cultural fragments.

Few observers of American Jewish life found much to cheer in these Jews in Miami and L.A. who reconstructed Judaism and reinvented themselves. Beginning in the mid-1960s, a series of increasingly dire predictions regarding the American Jewish future, in contrast to more upbeat self-assessments of the postwar era, captured the attention of American Jews.[17] "Young Jewish men and women are threatening the future of Judaism with their ever-increasing tendency to marry and raise their children outside the faith," wrote a *Look* reporter. "And, slowly, imperceptibly, the American Jew is vanishing." This was not the first, nor would it be the last, of such predictions. The 1964 *Look* article focused discussions from the Catskills to St. Louis over tensions between "the twin commitments to social acceptance and group survival." It signaled the end of the postwar era.[18]

Looking for the American Jew in the nation's metropolitan centers—the Jew Americans had come to know and recognize—*Look*'s reporter missed the new American Jew. How indeed was he to recognize that the American Jew was now the suntanned one with the open shirt and the flashy jewelry? What made this devotee of the good life any different from other Americans similarly situated? From the contemporary observer's perspective it was difficult to notice the distinctive signs, to see the mezuzah or Magen David on the gold chain, to note that suntanned faces filled pews at Friday night services or thronged to a rally for Israel. Astute observers remarked on the changing folk patterns of American Jews, the new shape being given their holidays, the changing status of women. They observed the commodification of popular Jewish culture and the singular role Israel occupied in the American Jewish imagination. A few grasped the new significance of politics for American Jews as an arena of solidarity rather than conflict. But most remembered only how it had been in their childhood and knew that that world had vanished forever.[19]

Life in Miami and Los Angeles assuaged the agony of ambivalence. Pursuit of integration and a nondiscriminatory society led Jews to understand their very distinctiveness as a separate group within that society. Conversely, their wholehearted support of Israel as the symbol of their separateness produced an unanticipated measure of integration into their chosen cities. Thus, Jews in Miami and Los Angeles naturally turned toward a liberal politics of sentiment focused upon Israel. They abandoned such political ideologies as communism and anti-Zionism, which fostered intra-Jewish conflict, for a form of politics that united Jews as Jews. A few Los Angeles Jews even tried to export their exuberant embrace of the right to be different, with its romantic projection of the Israeli, as an icon of the new Jew.

The portrait offered by demographers of American Jews in the last decade of the twentieth century suggests that if Jews in Los Angeles and Miami did not always succeed in exporting their popular Jewish culture, they did at least indicate the path most American Jews eventually would follow. Contemporary American Jews resemble in many ways the pioneering postwar generation of Miami and Los Angeles: Israel is central to their politics and religion; ethnicity is so attenuated that most Jews no longer describe themselves in ethnic terms; intermarriage is widespread, yet paradoxically the Jewish spouses still think of themselves as Jews; divorce approaches the 20 percent characteristic of Miami Beach parents in the 1960s; liberalism continues to be the political faith of most American Jews, though its substance is far removed from a politics of self-interest; and peer-group structures characterize much Jewish organizational activity. In 1990 American Jews present an extraordinary profile of an exceptionally affluent and well-educated group with a distinctive brand of liberal politics and weak ties to any version of religious faith. American Jews are almost as likely to marry Gentiles as Jews. American Jews have become overwhelmingly American, most with American-born parents and grandparents. Many are three, four, and even five generations removed from their immigrant origins. Even their geographic distribution approaches the American pattern. Along with their fellow Americans, Jews have moved in such large numbers to the West and South that these regions surpass the Midwest in Jewish population. Only 40 percent of American Jews still live in the Northeast, the section that historically held the majority of American Jews.[20]

Yet Jews deviate from the American norm in important ways, despite the apparent convergence in their behavior and high rates of intermarriage. As the demographer Barry Kosmin observes, "The Jews are too old, too well-educated, too liberal, too secular, too metropolitan, too wealthy, too egalitarian, too civic-minded to be normal Americans when compared to the overall U.S. population."[21]

Kosmin's list is instructive. It suggests that Jewish distinctiveness now derives less from facts of birth than from a series of choices Jews have made. These choices include where to live (in urban areas), how many children to have (very few, usually not more than two), what education to obtain (college degrees for almost 90 percent and graduate degrees for at least a third), what occupations to enter (the professions and management levels of business), what politics to pursue (liberalism), and which values to espouse (egalitarianism, secular humanism, and civic-mindedness). Most Jews identify themselves as members of a cultural group—the least clearly defined of the choices available in the survey; only a minority affiliate with synagogues and observe the many public and private rituals of Judaism.

Those who read these statistics as a premonition of doom might look again at the Jews of Los Angeles and Miami of thirty years ago. Having arrived at the future ahead of most American Jews, Los Angeles and Miami Jews offer a useful index of where the future may well lead. Writing in the 1970s, Moses Rischin, historian of Jewish immigrants in New York City, called the Jewish way of life in Los Angeles "problematic"; "post-Judaic" and "post-secular," it was "remote even from an earlier sub-culture of Jewishness" and was sustained neither by traditional religious patterns nor by a vigorous secular ethnicity.[22] Rischin's description of Los Angeles Jews now seems to apply more generally to all American Jews. Yet in the thirty years since the postwar era came to an end, Los Angeles and Miami Jews have not vanished but have persisted and even flourished. The chosen cities have continued to attract thousands of newcomers. Even Jews from the promised land of Israel have discovered L.A.'s opportunity and Miami's vacation world. Israeli newcomers begin a process of reinventing themselves similar to the one Jewish migrants embarked upon when they first arrived in the booming postwar years.

How did American Jews, who had experienced discrimination and prejudice in the years prior to World War II, acquire the freedom to choose to be Jews? How did the distinctive Jewish pattern emerge, linking wealth and education with political liberalism, secularism, and a steadfast commitment to Israel? The possibility of a new Jewish synthesis emerged from changes in the United States following World War II. For Jewishness to become a matter of choice, the subtle and not-so-subtle barriers of discrimination in education, housing, and employment had to be dismantled. Prejudice against Jews had to lose its respectability. Jews had to work at opening society before they could thrive in it and fashion an American Judaism appropriate to such a free milieu. Only then could they discover the "crisis of freedom": the opportunity offered by an increasingly open society to intermarry and the challenge it presented to maintain Jewish distinctiveness and collective continuity.[23] Because they chose their cities, Jewish newcomers to Miami and L.A. encountered the promise and challenge of America ahead of their less mobile relatives.

Yet in many ways the Jewish worlds of Los Angeles and Miami can be seen as the offspring of Jewish New York, Chicago, Philadelphia, and Boston and of the more modest Jewish communities of such cities as Omaha, St. Louis, Milwaukee, Cleveland, Newark, Baltimore, and Detroit. More specifically, Los Angeles is a product especially of Chicago and the midwestern cities, while Miami is clearly a child of New York and the northeastern cities. As Jewish New York, Chicago, and Philadelphia represent continuity with a European past because they were created by immigrants from the cities and towns of eastern Europe, so Jewish Miami and Los Angeles represent continuity with an American past as the creations of Jews from northeastern and midwestern cities. American Jews produced in the postwar era a second generation of urban communities, offspring of the first generation. It was, perhaps, a very American thing to do: sending off sons and daughters, and even grandfathers and grandmothers, to settle Miami and Los Angeles in quest of opportunity and leisure, freedom and security. Yet even as their adventure transformed them and their chosen cities, it opened new possibilities for the American Jewish future.

Notes

Abbreviations Used in Notes

AAJE   American Association for Jewish Education
AJA   American Jewish Archives
AJC   American Jewish Committee
AJHS   American Jewish Historical Society
CLSA   Commission on Law and Social Action
HUC-JIR   Hebrew Union College-Jewish Institute of Religion
ICJ   Institute of Contemporary Jewry
JCA   Jewish Centers Association (Los Angeles)
JFC   Jewish Federation Council of Los Angeles
JTS   Jewish Theological Seminary
LAJCC   Los Angeles Jewish Community Council
UCLA   University of California, Los Angeles
UJA   United Jewish Appeal
YIVO   YIVO Institute for Jewish Research

Preface

1. Alexander F. Miller, "Oral Memoirs," *"Not the Work of a Day"*: *Anti-Defamation League of B'nai B'rith Oral Memoirs*, 5 (New York: Anti-Defamation League of B'nai B'rith, 1987), 22–24.
2. The conference proceedings were published in *Shades of the Sunbelt*, ed. Randall M. Miller and George E. Pozzetta (New York: Greenwood Press, 1988).

Chapter 1. On the Threshold

1. The American Jewish Committee, American Jewish Congress, Jewish Labor Committee, Agudah Israel, and the Friends of Jewish Palestine, as well as the YIVO Institute and Hadassah, had research institutes devoted to Jewish postwar problems. Nonetheless, there was public Jewish apathy. Abraham G. Duker, *Political and Cultural Aspects of Jewish Post-War Problems* (New York: American Jewish Committee, 1943), 3–4, 13. See also Max Gottschalk and Abraham G. Duker, *Jews in the Post-war World* (New York: Dryden Press, 1945), 75–100, 170–182; "Annual Report of the American Jewish Committee," especially "Statement of Views," "Address of the Honorable Joseph M. Proskauer," and "Report of the Chairman of the Overseas Committee," by George Z. Medalie, in *American Jewish Year Book* 45 (1943): 608–9, 641–42, 646–50.

2. Isaac Bashevis Singer, "My Love Affair with Miami Beach," in *My Love Affair with Miami Beach* (New York: Simon & Schuster, 1991), vi, v.

3. Seymour Samet to Eleanor Ashman, memo re: MIAMI, U.S.A., 1 December 1955, Florida/Miami (44–62), Box 10, General 13, Geographic/Domestic, AJC, YIVO.

4. The Los Angeles reality approached these perceptions: in 1940 there were 1,160,000 cars, or 2.4 persons per vehicle; single-family houses occupied 31 percent of city land, compared to 2 percent for multiple-family dwellings. Robert Fishman, *Bourgeois Utopias* (New York: Basic Books, 1987), 177.

5. Of the 1,412,480 acres of Dade County, 64,245 were farmlands, over two thirds under cultivation; *Guide to Miami and Environs*, 74.

6. Jean Paul Sartre, "American Cities," in *The City*, ed. Alan Trachtenberg, Peter Neill, and Peter C. Bunnell (New York: Oxford University Press, 1971), 202; Fishman, *Bourgeois Utopias*, 155; *Guide to Miami and Environs*, 3.

7. Deborah Dash Moore, "Social History of American Judaism," in *Encyclopedia of the American Religious Experience* (1987), I: 295; Vivian Gornick, "There Is No More Community," *interChange* 2 (Apr. 1977): 4.

8. The wealth of memoir literature by second-generation New York Jews attests to this. For example, Alfred Kazin, *A Walker in the City* (New York: Harcourt Brace Jovanovich, 1951), and Norman Podhoretz, *Making It* (New York: Random House, 1967), on Brownsville; Jerome Weidman, *Fourth Street East* (New York: Random House, 1970), Samuel Chotzinoff, *A Lost Paradise* (New York: Knopf, 1955), and Charles Reznikoff, *Family Chronicle* (New York: C. Reznikoff, 1963), on the Lower East Side; Kate Simon, *Bronx Primitive* (New York: Viking Press, 1982), and Irving Howe, *A Margin of Hope* (New York: Harcourt Brace Jovanovich, 1982), on the East Bronx; Ronald Sanders, *Reflections on a*

Teapot (New York: Harper & Row, 1972), on Flatbush. There is a less extensive list of memoirs on the other cities.

9. Gerson Cohen, "The Scholar as Chancellor," in *Creators and Disturbers*, ed. Bernard Rosenberg and Ernest Goldstein (New York: Columbia University Press, 1982), 217; Ira Rosenwaike, *Population History of New York City* (Syracuse: Syracuse University Press, 1972), 100–112.

10. Victor Gotbaum, "The Spirit of the New York Labor Movement," in *Creators and Disturbers*, 246; Grace Paley, "The Writer in Greenwich Village," in *Creators and Disturbers*, 289–90; Simon, *Bronx Primitive*, 39; Irving Howe, "The New York Intellectuals," in *Decline of the New* (New York: Horizon Press, 1970), 216–217.

11. Irving Howe, "The Way Things Were," *interChange* 2 (February 1977): 8; Irving Howe, "The Range of the New York Intellectual," in *Creators and Disturbers*, 264 (emphasis in the original).

12. Nat Hentoff, *Boston Boy* (New York: Knopf, 1986), 4, 17, 19; Alan Brinkley, *Voices of Protest* (New York: Vintage Books, 1983), 206.

13. Peter Binzen, "A Place to Live," *Philadelphia Jewish Life 1940–1985*, ed. Murray Friedman (Ardmore, Pa.: Seth Press, 1986), 186, quote on 186; Irving Cutler, "The Jews of Chicago," *Ethnic Chicago*, ed. Melvin G. Holli and Peter d'A. Jones (Grand Rapids: William Eerdmans, 1984), 92, 99.

14. Rentals also allowed Jews to use their capital for business investment or to invest in education for their children.

15. Jay Leyda's film *Bronx Morning* captures these patterns.

16. June Sochen, *Consecrate Every Day* (Albany: SUNY Press, 1981), 50–74; Hannah Kliger, ed., *Jewish Hometown Associations and Family Circles in New York* (Bloomington: Indiana University Press, 1992), 35; Abraham J. Karp, "Overview: The Synagogue in America," in *The American Synagogue*, ed. Jack Wertheimer (Cambridge: Cambridge University Press, 1987), 13–23.

17. Jacob Katzman, *Commitment* (New York: Labor Zionist Letters, 1975), 70.

18. Stephen D. Isaacs, *Jews and American Politics* (Garden City: Doubleday, 1974), 156; Henry L. Feingold, *The Politics of Rescue* (New Brunswick: Rutgers University Press, 1970), 298–304.

19. E. Digby Baltzell, "Foreword," in *Philadelphia Jewish Life 1940–1985*, x; Maurice J. Karpf, *Jewish Community Organization in the United States* (New York: Bloch Publishing, 1938), 166–67; Howe, "Range," 281.

20. Andrew R. Heinze, *Adapting to Abundance* (New York: Columbia University Press, 1992), 68–85; Arthur Liebman, *Jews and the Left* (New York: John Wiley & Sons, 1979), 261–62; Deborah Dash Moore,

At Home in America (New York: Columbia University Press, 1981), ch. 3; Susan A. Glenn, *Daughters of the Shtetl* (Ithaca: Cornell University Press, 1990), 177–182.

21. Maxwell E. Greenberg, "Oral Memoirs," in *"Not the Work of a Day":* *Anti-Defamation League of B'nai B'rith Oral Memoirs* (New York: Anti-Defamation League of B'nai B'rith, 1987), II: 8–9.

22. Greenberg noted that the first Jewish lawyer accepted at the L.A. law firm of O'Melveny and Myers was Richard Sherwood, who had changed his name from Shapiro. Greenberg, "Oral Memoirs," II: 28–29.

23. Nathan Perlmutter, *A Bias of Reflections* (New Rochelle: Arlington House, 1972), 103–4; Conversation with Martin Dash, 9 November 1992; Seymour Graubard, "Oral Memoirs," in *"Not the Work of a Day,"* II: 21–22; Paul Jacobs, *Is Curly Jewish?* (New York: Vintage Books, 1973), 127–28.

24. S. C. Kohs, "Jewish War Records of World War II," *American Jewish Year Book* 47 (1946): 167; I. Kaufman, *American Jews in World War II* (New York: Dial Press, 1947), I: 349. This represented an average rate of participation.

25. Quoted in Moses Kligsberg, "American Jewish Soldiers on Jews and Judaism," *Yivo Annual of Jewish Social Science* 5 (1950): 264; quoted in Marianne Sanua, "From the Pages of the *Victory Bulletin,*" *YIVO Annual* 19 (1990): 308.

26. Quoted in Sanua, *"Victory Bulletin,"* 318 (emphasis in the original).

27. Greenberg, "Oral Memoirs," II: 10; Gotbaum, "Labor Movement," 249; Kligsberg, "Jewish Soldiers," 258; Kimberg quoted in *Jewish Youth at War,* ed. Isaac E. Rontch (New York: Marstin, 1945), 105; Uris quoted in *Jewish Youth,* ed. Rontch, 225.

28. Eisen quoted in *Jewish Youth,* ed. Rontch, 43; Paris quoted in *Jewish Youth,* ed. Rontch, 147; Kligsberg, "Jewish Soldiers," 62.

29. Morris Adler, "The Chaplain and the Rabbi," *Reconstructionist* 11 (6 Apr. 1945): 11; Edward T. Sandrow, "Jews in the Army," *Reconstructionist* 10 (17 Mar. 1944): 15.

30. Kligsberg, "Jewish Soldiers," 263, 265; Sandrow, "Jews in the Army," 17.

31. Martin Peppercorn, Oral History Interview, 20 July 1977, 4, Oral History of the UJA, Oral History Archive, ICJ, Hebrew University; Gotbaum, "Labor Movement," 250–51.

32. Irving Heymont, *Among the Survivors of the Holocaust* (Cincinnati: American Jewish Archives, 1982), 25, 109.

33. Jacobs, *Is Curly Jewish?* 133; Howe, "New York Intellectual," 285; Kligsberg, "Jewish Soldiers," 260.

Community, Dade County Development Department, Table II, Population, 3.

9. I am relying for Jewish population estimates on the demographer Ira Sheskin's work, which modifies older, less reliable estimates. In 1944 the Population Survey Committee of the Greater Miami Jewish Federation estimated the Jewish population of Greater Miami (Dade County) at 29,000, with 16,000 on the Beach. Given the difficulty of determining who is a resident in Miami, it must be emphasized that population figures are only estimates. Ira M. Sheskin, "Demographic Study of the Greater Miami Jewish Community, Summary Report" (June 1984), typescript, 4–7. See also Adrienne Rebecca Millon, "The Changing Size and Spatial Distribution of the Jewish Population of South Florida," M. A. thesis, University of Miami, 1989, 53.

10. Another nickname was "Iowa's port city." The statistics tell a slightly different story. In the prewar period the leading states sending migrants to Los Angeles were New York (10%), Illinois (10%), Texas (8%), Missouri (7%), and Oklahoma (6%). This differed from the leading states sending migrants to California: Oklahoma, Texas, Missouri, Illinois, and New York. Eshref Shevky and Marilyn Williams, *The Social Areas of Los Angeles* (Berkeley: University of California Press, 1949), 26–27.

11. "Characteristics of the Population," *The Researcher: Annual Review Number (Revised)* 12:1–2 (First Quarter 1954): 5, in Box 50, folder L.A. Chamber of Commerce, California Ephemera Collection 200, UCLA library. DeGraaf's figures are higher: African Americans were 6.5 percent of the Los Angeles population in 1940 and 10.7 percent in 1950; DeGraaf, "Negro Migration," 188.

12. McNally, *Catholicism*, 100, 112; *United States Census of Population in 1960—Florida* I: 2, C-D (Washington, D.C.: U.S. Government Printing office, 1961), 11–294.

13. Sidney Goldstein, "American Jewry, 1970: A Demographic Profile," *American Jewish Year Book* 72 (1971): 37–38.

14. Vance Packard, *A Nation of Strangers* (New York: David McKay, 1972), 7–8. Although both the prewar (1937) and postwar (1960) distribution of Jews by state and region produces only a modest rank of 4 on an index of dissimilarity, this rises to a high of 9 for states and 8 for regions when migration patterns are charted for the years 1937–1960. Ira Sheskin, "The Migration of Jews to Sunbelt Cities," 12–13, unpublished paper in author's possession; Peter L. Halvorson and William M. Newman, *Atlas of Religious Change in America 1952–1971* (Washington: Glenmary Research Center, 1978), 12.

15. The Jewish population in the South rose from 330,000 in 1937 to 486,000 in 1960, and Miami's growth accounted for 132,000 of the increase. Similarly, Los Angeles accounted for 300,000 of the increase

from 219,000 in 1937 to 598,000 in 1960 in the West. In the following decade, Los Angeles accounted for 64 percent of the regional increase, and Miami accounted for only 29 percent of the regional increase; computed from Sheskin, "Migration of Jews," tables 1, 3, 5.

16. Benjamin Leftgoff, Mark Itelson, interviews with author, 14 July 1989; Erich Rosenthal, "This Was North Lawndale," *Jewish Social Studies*, 12 (April 1960): 74; Nathan Perlmutter, "Oral Memoirs," in *"Not the Work of a Day,"* I: 26.

17. Isaac Bashevis Singer, "My Love Affair with Miami Beach," in *My Love Affair With Miami Beach*, (New York: Simon & Schuster, 1991), v–vi; Murray Getz, interview with author, 14 July 1989. Perlmutter also found the palm trees enticing; Oral History, 16.

18. Bruce Henstell, *Los Angeles* (New York: Knopf, 1980), 185; Robert Fishman, *Bourgeois Utopias* (New York: Basic Books, 1987), 178–79.

19. Gerald D. Nash, *The American West Transformed* (Bloomington: Indiana University Press, 1985), quote on 14, 35–36.

20. *Guide to Miami and Environs*, 6, 80, quote on 75; Seymour Samet to Eleanor Ashman, memo, re: MIAMI, U.S.A., 1 December 1955, Florida/Miami/Chapter (44–62), Box 10, General 13, Geographic/Domestic, AJC, YIVO; Rheinhold P. Wolff, "Case Studies in South Florida Manufacturing Industries" (Coral Gables: University of Miami, 1963), 1–6, 20–23.

21. McNally, *Catholicism*, 72; City of Miami, *Golden Anniversary 1896–1946*, 34, 11, Rosen files; David R. Goldfield, *Promised Land* (Arlington Heights: Harlan Davidson, 1987), 5–6.

22. Singer, "My Love Affair," vii. I appreciate the insight of Joel Schwartz in distinguishing the two migration streams.

23. Paul Sperry, interview with author, 7 March 1989; "Reactions of Los Angeles Chapter to *A Fresh Look at Anti-Semitism in Your Community*," 16 April 1958, California/Los Angeles Chapter (52–62), Box 10, General 13, Geographic/Domestic, AJC, YIVO.

24. Benjamin Perry, Isidore Rosenthal, Lenny Gottlieb, interviews with author, 14 July 1989.

25. Fred Massarik, "Report," (1959), 20; Peter Antelyes, conversation with author, 20 September 1991.

26. The gross statistics were $243 million for Miami (of which $170.5 million went to Miami Beach) and $457.8 million for Southern California; *Selling Vacations on Miami Beach*, Miami Beach Hotel Owners Association (Miami Beach, 1949), 3–4, Rosen files.

27. Advertisement, 3 January 1960, quoted in *New York Times*, 4 August 1968: 8; Fran Denner, conversation with author, 19 March 1991; Nathan Glazer, "Notes on Southern California," *Commentary*, 28 (July 1959): 106.

28. Stephen Birmingham, "The Florida Dream," *Holiday* 34 (Dec. 1963): 62; Nathan Perlmutter, interview, 22 June 1967, Rosen files.
29. Shafter, "Miami," 19; Singer, "My Love Affair," vii; "Florida Jewry: 1763–1990," in *Mosaic: Jewish Life in Florida*, ed. Henry Alan Green and Marcia Kerstein Zerivitz (Miami: Hallmark Press, 1991), 21; see also ads in *Jewish Spectator* 12 (Mar. 1945): 26, and 13 (Nov. 1947): 33; Carson, "Miami Beach," 24.
30. *Guide to Miami and Environs*, 158; Ralph G. Martin, "Big Rush to the Sun," *Newsweek*, 17 January 1955: 71; Polly Redford, *Billion-Dollar Sandbar* (New York: E.P. Dutton, 1970), 244; Alexander F. Miller, "Oral Memoirs," in *"Not the Work of a Day,"* V: 23–26, quote on 24; Russell Baker, "Miami Beach and the Politicians," *New York Times*, 4 August 1968, I: 1.
31. Albert Fried, *The Rise and Fall of the Jewish Gangster* (New York, 1980), 244. Fried points out that Italian mobsters made the same trek for the same reasons. *The Kefauver Committee Report on Organized Crime* (New York: Didier, 1951), 11–14, 161; Carson, "Miami Beach," 23–24; Koretzky, interview; Narot, interview; Joseph Rappaport to Moshe Davis, 22 February 1955, Rosen files; Redford, *Sandbar*, 226.
32. Redford, *Sandbar*, 240; Ralph Blumenthal, "Miami Beach Fights to Regain Its Superstar Billing," *New York Times*, 17 June 1979, section 10: 1, 7; Seymour Samet, "Report," December 15, 1957–February 15, 1958; Reports, Florida/Miami Chapter, 1959-1958-1957, Box 10, General 13, Geographic/Domestic, AJC, YIVO.
33. Patricia Erens, *The Jew in the American Cinema* (Bloomington: Indiana University Press, 1984), 229–230, notes that the film, starring Frank Sinatra, changed the Jewish family of the stage production into an Italian one; Carson, "Miami Beach," 4; Miller, "Oral Memoirs," V: 23–26.
34. Massarik, "Report," (1953), 22; Fred Massarik, "The Jewish Population of Los Angeles," *Reconstructionist* 18 (28 Nov. 1952): 13; Manheim Shapiro, *The Bayville Survey*, Summary Statement (1961), n.p.
35. The vast postwar internal migrations carried one out of four to new homes every five years. Americans migrated across the continent in astonishing numbers. Their restlessness modified the sectional character of the United States and laid the foundation for a major shift in national politics. Carl Abbott, *The New Urban America* (Chapel Hill: University of North Carolina Press, 1987), 24–30, 39–40; A. Russell Buchanan, *The United States and World War II* (New York: Harper & Row, 1964), II: 323.
36. Mike Singer, David Moretzky, Alex Bratman, interviews with author, 14 July 1989.
37. Fred Massarik, "A Report on the Jewish Population of Los Angeles 1968" (Jewish Federation-Council of Greater Los Angeles), Table II.

38. Letter to editor, *California Jewish Voice*, 6 August 1954: 5; Arthur Rosichan, interview, June 1965, Rosen files; *Guide to Miami and Environs*, 9–10; Harriet Sadoff Kasow, interview with author, 5 May 1992.
39. Martin Rosenbaum, interview with author, 14 July 1989, and subsequent letter, October 1992; Ben Perry, interview with author, 14 July 1989, and subsequent letter, October 1992. Ben and Florence's immediate family eventually joined them in Los Angeles. Sy Bram, interview with author, 17 July 1989.
40. Bram, interview; Sperry, interview.
41. Nathan Glazer and Daniel Patrick Moynihan, *Beyond the Melting Pot* (Cambridge: M.I.T. Press, 1963), 93–95.
42. David P. Varady, "Wynnefield: Story of a Changing Neighborhood," in *Philadelphia Jewish Life 1940–1985*, 167–182; Albert I. Gordon, *Jews in Suburbia* (Boston: Beacon Press, 1959), 10; Rosenthal, "This Was North Lawndale," 67; Gottlieb, interview.
43. Quoted in Barbara Myerhoff, *Number Our Days* (New York: E.P. Dutton, 1978), 46; Michael Wiener, interview with author, 14 July 1989; Bernard Finkelstein with Albert Rosen, "Socio-Economic Diagnostic Study of the South Shore of Miami Beach, Florida," Welfare Planning Council of Dade County, Florida (November 1968), 2, AJC Library; Anton Lourie and Elizabeth Frank, "Report on interviews held with prospective candidates for the proposed Home for Aged German-Jewish Emigres in Los Angeles, California" (July 1955), 3, Max Weinreich MSS, YIVO.
44. David Moretzky, Seymour Hacken, interviews with author, 14 July 1989; Max Holland, *When the Machine Stopped* (Boston: Harvard Business School Press, 1989), 7–16
45. In 1940 Los Angeles had a higher proportion of its population aged sixty-five and older than the nine other largest cities in the United States. The median age in L.A. was 33 compared to 29 for the U.S. Los Angeles had 8.5 percent of its population 65 and over, compared to 5.8 percent for Chicago, 5.5 percent for Cleveland, 4 percent for Detroit, and 5.6 percent for New York City. Morris Zelditch, *Survey Report: Care of the Jewish Aged, Los Angeles, California* (New York: Council of Jewish Federations and Welfare Funds, 1948), 5–6 in Miscellaneous file, Aged, Archives of Jewish Community Library, JFC.
46. "Miami Beach Senior High School Evalution 1967–68," Report of School and Community Committee, 16–17, Rosen files.
47. Michael Sossin, interview with Gladys Rosen, 7 June 1966, Rosen files; Andrew Kazdin, conversation with author, December 1991. Sossin System, Inc. reported over $2 million in revenues for 1968–69. Catering to the aged was a profitable business. Redford, *Sandbar*, 270.
48. Fred Massarik, "Final Report, Hollywood-Los Feliz Study 1959," 7–8, Histories File, JCA, Archives, Jewish Community Library, JFC; Lynn

Craig Cunningham, "Venice, California: From City to Suburb," Ph.D. diss., UCLA, 1976, 133–34, 173–78.

49. Cunningham, "Venice," 133–34, 173–78; Myerhoff, *Our Days*, 11, quote on 6.

50. Massarik, "Population," *Reconstructionist*, 13; Fishman, *Bourgeois Utopias*, 178; Henstell, *Los Angeles*, 185–86, 200; Vorspan and Gartner, *Jews of Los Angeles*, 233–35.

51. Vorspan and Gartner, *Jews of Los Angeles*, 233–36; Harry Brown in *The Hollywood Screenwriters*, ed. Richard Corliss (New York: Avon Books, 1971), 250; *California Jewish Voice*, 28 June 1946, 13 May 1949, 13 April 1945; Bud and Ellie Hudson, interview with author, 11 July 1989.

52. In 1945 the United Jewish Welfare Fund received its first two gifts of $50,000 each, one from the builders Harry Mier and Haskell Kramer of Sales Builders, Inc., and the other from Hollywood, David Factor and Max Firestein of the cosmetics firm Max Factor. *California Jewish Voice*, 13 April 1945; Vorspan and Gartner, *Jews of Los Angeles*, 233–36.

53. Michael Kanin, Oral History Memoir, 91; Michael Singer, interview with author, 14 July 1989.

54. Massarik, "Report," (1959), 22; Vorspan and Gartner, *Jews of Los Angeles*, 235. Bram's family firm used to name the streets after the people from whom they bought the land. "They loved that because it was a way of perpetuating their name in that area," he remarked. Bram, interview. Ben Leftgoff, Mark Itelson, interviews with author, 14 July 1989.

55. Gladys Rosen, draft chapter; Irving Lehrman "Historical Review of Annotated Card Bibliography of the South Florida Jewish Community," DHL, JTS, 1957, 76; Redford, *Sandbar*, 273; Malvina W. Liebman and Seymour B. Liebman, *Jewish Frontiersman* (Miami Beach, n.d.), 49.

56. Shepard Broad, interview, 28 April 1964; Rosen files.

57. Its population was 296 in 1950 when housing development began; the numbers increased to 3,900 by 1964 after extensive construction. *Metropolitan Miami, Dade County, Florida: Reflections of a Growing Industrial Community*, 3. There are many newspaper articles on Broad; see, for example, *Miami Herald*, 14 October 1951: G-1; 7 August 1952; 8 August 1952: 2-B; 10 August 1952: 14-A; 29 January 1954.

58. Keys to Growth: Metropolitan Miami (Dade County Development Department, n.d.), 5; Birmingham, *Holiday*, 75; Thomas J. Wood, "Dade County: Unbossed, Erratically Led," *Annals of the American Academy of Political and Social Science* (May 1964): 66; Miami Beach Chamber of Commerce Statistical Review (1955), 3; Edward Sofen, *The Metropolitan Miami Experiment* (Bloomington: Indiana University Press, 1963), 22; *Jewish Floridian*, 11 April 1969; Max Orovitz, interview with Gladys Rosen, n.d.; Redford, *Sandbar*, 256.

59. Fred Massarik, "A Report on the Jewish Population of Greater Miami," National Jewish Population Study, Report #6, Council of Jewish Federations and Welfare Funds, n.d. [1970], 31, AJHS; Redford, *Sandbar*, 255–256; Finkelstein and Rosen, "Diagnostic Study," 81.

60. Herbert Abrams, interview with author, 12 July 1989; Shimon Orenstein, interview with author, 19 July 1989.

61. Alex Bratman, Michael Wiener, interviews with author, 14 July 1989.

62. Sonia Klein Roberts, conversation with author, November 1989; Shafter, "Miami," 20.

63. A number of Jewish chicken farmers who were attracted by the agricultural opportunities proved to be the exception. Jews came to the San Gabriel Valley largely from New York and Chicago, with smaller percentages from such cities as Detroit, Newark, Cleveland, and St. Louis. Charles Zibbell, "A Preliminary Study of the Jewish Community of San Gabriel Valley California" (1948), typescript, 14–17, Miscellaneous Files, Archives, Jewish Community Library, JFC. "Reactions of Los Angeles Chapter to *A Fresh Look at Anti-Semitism in Your Community*," 16 April 1958, California/Los Angeles Chapter (52–62), Box 10, General 13, Geographic/Domestic, AJC, YIVO.

64. Rosenthal, "Lawndale," 67–82; Kenneth Jackson, *Crabgrass Frontier* (New York: Oxford University Press, 1985), 238–43.

65. Glazer, "Notes," 104–5.

66. Marshall Sklare and Joseph Greenblum, *Jewish Identity on the Suburban Frontier* (1967; rpt. Chicago: University of Chicago Press, 1979), and Sidney Goldstein and Calvin Goldscheider, *Jewish Americans: Three Generations in Jewish Community* (Englewood Cliffs: Prentice-Hall, 1968), indicate continuities as well as changes.

67. Herbert Gans, "Park Forest: Birth of a Jewish Community," *Commentary* 11 (Apr. 1951): 330–39, and "Progress of a Suburban Jewish Community," *Commentary* 23 (Feb. 1957): 113–22; Paula Hyman, "From City to Suburb: Temple Mishkan Tefila of Boston," in *A History of the American Synagogue*, ed. Jack Wertheimer (Cambridge: Cambridge University Press, 1987), 188–192, 201–202.

68. Bruce A. Phillips, lecture at conference on Jews in Los Angeles, UCLA, 6 May 1990; *California Jewish Voice*, 3 July 1953: 6.

69. Wiener interview, 14 July 1989.

70. Jacob Sonderling, Sermon no. 5 at the Embassy Auditorium, Los Angeles, Yom Kippur 1946; typescript, Small Collections, AJA.

71. Broad, interview, Rosen files.

Chapter 3. Permanent Tourists

1. Bram Goldsmith, Oral History Interview, 26 July 1979, 3, Oral History of the UJA, Oral History Archives, ICJ, Hebrew University.

2. Neil Sandberg, *Jewish Life in Los Angeles* (Lanham, Md.: University Press of America, 1986), 19; Glazer, "Notes," 104.

3. James Q. Wilson, "A Guide to Reagan Country," *Commentary*, May 1967, 39; David Rieff, *Los Angeles* (New York: Simon & Schuster, 1991), 48; Richard Lehan, "The Los Angeles Novel and the Idea of the West," in *Los Angeles in Fiction*, ed. David Fine (Albuquerque: University of New Mexico Press, 1984), 31. Wilson notes that in 1936 40 percent of the church membership was Catholic and only 26 percent of the Protestants in L.A. belonged to nonfundamentalist churches.

4. Paul Skenazy, "Behind the Territory Ahead," in *Los Angeles in Fiction*, 95; editorial, *California Jewish Voice*, 13 April 1945; Nathan Perlmutter, Oral History, 15, Oral History of the AJC, William E. Wiener Oral History Library; Nathan Perlmutter, *A Bias of Reflections* (New Rochelle: Arlington House, 1972), 69.

5. Isidore Rosenthal, interview with author, 14 July 1989.

6. Martin Rosenbaum, interview with author, 14 July 1989; Gloria Shulman Blumenthal, "Boyle Heights: L.A.'s Lower East Side," *Davka*, October 1973: 8; Marvin Zeidler, interview with author, 22 July 1989.

7. George J. Sanchez, "Jews Among the Others: An Exploration of Multiethnic Life in Boyle Heights, 1920–1960," 6–10, paper given at conference on Jews in Los Angeles, UCLA, 6 May 1990; Zeidler, interview.

8. Robert Gerstein, "Recollections of My Early Childhood in Boyle Heights," *Davka*, October 1973: 9.

9. Blumenthal, "Boyle Heights," 9; Sanchez, "Jews Among the Others," 14; Gerstein, "Recollections," 9; Gerald Faris and Skip Ferderber, "Fairfax: Lower East Side of the West," *Los Angeles Times*, 18 February 1973, part 9.

10. Rosalind Wiener Wyman, " 'It's a Girl': Three Terms on the Los Angeles City Council, 1953–1965, Three Decades in the Democratic Party, 1948–1978," 15–16, an oral history conducted 1977–1978 by Malca Chall, Regional Oral History Office, The Bancroft Library, University of California, Berkeley, 1978, Courtesy of The Bancroft Library; Faris and Ferderber, "Fairfax;" Bertram Gold, interview with author, 12 October 1989; Bruce A. Phillips, lecture at conference on Jews in Los Angeles UCLA, 6 May 1990.

11. These figures are taken from Bruce A. Phillips, "Los Angeles Jewry," in *American Jewish Year Book* (1986), 163, Table 2C, who modifies slightly the numbers produced by Fred Massarik. The shift to the San Fernando Valley continued in the 1960s, so that by 1970 it held 26 percent of the Jews. See also Eshref Shevky and Marilyn Williams, *The Social Areas of Los Angeles* (Berkeley: University of California Press, 1949), 50–56, 73; Fred Massarik, "A Report on the Jewish Population of Los Angeles" (1959), 11–13, in AJC Library.

12. "The Pressman Tapes" (interview), *Davka*, October 1973: 19–20; computations based on figures in Massarik, "Report" (1959), 8, 8A.

13. Samuel Kohs, "The Jewish Community of Los Angeles," *Jewish Review* II (July–Oct. 1944): 117–119. Kohs estimates 40 percent in clerical and sales, 24 percent proprietors and managers, 11 percent in crafts, 10 percent professional and semiprofessional. For a sense of the range of occupations and the amount of moneys contributed to the city's major Jewish fund-raising campaign, see United Jewish Welfare Fund of the Los Angeles Jewish Community Council, *Liberation Year Book* (1945), 98–106, Benjamin F. Platt MSS Coll. 929, Box 5, Special Collections, UCLA.

14. Clancy Sigal, "Hollywood During the Great Fear," *Present Tense*, 9 (Spring 1982): 46; Ted Thomas, interview with author, 13 July 1989; Julius Epstein, talk at conference on Jews in Los Angeles, UCLA, 6 May 1990.

15. Max Nussbaum, "Jews in the Motion Picture Industry," *Reconstructionist* 18 (28 Nov. 1952): 25–26, quote on 25; Vorspan and Gartner, *Jews in Los Angeles*, 269; Tom Tugend, "The Hollywood Jews," *Davka* 5 (Fall 1975): 6.

16. Massarik, "Report" (1959), 20–25. These trends continued for another decade, so that by 1968 a third of the Jews of Los Angeles were professionals or semiprofessionals and another third worked in service businesses. Massarik, "Report" (1968), Table 25, 26.

17. Reuben Dafni, Oral History Interview, 16 March 1979, 3, Oral History of the UJA, Oral History Archives, ICJ, Hebrew University.

18. Kohs, "Jewish Community," 87.

19. *California Jewish Voice*, 23 November 1945; Bertram Gold, "Report on Los Angeles" (1949), 2, AJHS; "Prospectus Jewish Center Needs in Los Angeles" (December 1946), prepared by Jack Berman and Meyer Fichman, n.p., in Jewish Community Library, JFC.

20. Peter M. Kahn, "Jewish Education in Los Angeles," *California Jewish Voice*, 9 September 1947.

21. William Zuckerman, "Revolt Against New York (A Letter from Los Angeles)," *Jewish Exponent*, 7 March 1952: 29.

22. Leonard Sperry, "The Development of Program in the Los Angeles Chapter," papers read at Chapter Leaders Workshop, 16 April 1959, California/Los Angeles Chapter (52–62), Box 10, General 13, Geographic/Domestic, AJC, YIVO; Maxwell E. Greenberg, "Oral Memoirs," *"Not the Work of a Day,"* I: 25.

23. Cover letter accompanying memo re: YMHA, 2 March 1967, Rosen files; Martin Peppercorn, Oral History Interview, 20 July 1977, 26–27, Oral History of the UJA, Oral History Archives, ICJ, Hebrew University; Rabbis Rutchik and Solomon Schiff, interviews, n.d., Rosen files.

24. The Miami Beach Jewish Center offered a special twenty-five dollar membership plan for tourists known as the Sabbath Service Admission

Card. Minutes of the Executive Meeting, Miami Beach Jewish Center, 20 November 1951.

25. Memo re: YMHA, 2 March 1967, Rosen files; Ephraim Gale, interview, n.d., Rosen files.

26. Robert Sherrill, "Miami Beach: The All-Too-American City," *New York Times Magazine*, 4 August 1968: 7–8; Jon Nordheimer, "Florida's Defeat of Gambling Seen as Measure of Maturity," *New York Times*, 18 November 1987: 8.

27. Toby Shafter, "Miami: 1948," *Jewish Frontier* 15 (Jan. 1948): 19–20.

28. Shafter, "Miami," 19–20; Polly Redford, *Billion Dollar Sandbar* (New York: E. P. Dutton, 1970), 262, 267; Isaac Bashevis Singer, "My Love Affair with Miami Beach," in *My Love Affair with Miami Beach* (New York: Simon & Schuster, 1991), vii–viii.

29. Shafter, "Miami," 19–20; Irving Lehrman, "Historical Review of Annotated Card Bibliography of the South Florida Jewish Community" (DHL, JTS, 1957), 70.

30. One survey of the area estimated that 35 percent of those living alone and 17 percent of the households with two people were living at or below the poverty line in 1968. Bernard Finkelstein and Albert Rosen, "Socio-Economic Diagnostic Study of the South Shore Area of Miami Beach, Florida," Welfare Planning Council of Dade County, Florida (November 1968), 82. See also Adrienne Rebecca Millon, "The Changing Size and Spatial Distribution of the Jewish Population of South Florida" (MA thesis, University of Miami, 1989), 81–82; Redford, *Sandbar*, 262.

31. Memo re: YMHA, 2 March 1967, and report, Rosen files; Morris Janowitz, *Judaism of the Next Generation* (Miami: Rostrum Books, 1969), 44, Table 4.3.

32. Memo re: YMHA, 2 March 1967, Rosen files; Massarik, "Report" [1970], 15–17.

33. The *Valley Jewish News*, 21 April 1950, estimated that there were over one hundred city clubs—*landsmanshaftn*—at that time in Los Angeles as well as over forty state societies in the general community (or one for almost every state in the union). The 1950 *Jewish Community Directory of Greater Los Angeles* (Los Angeles Jewish Community Council) lists fifty-five traditional *landsmanshaftn* and thirty-four of the new ones. In Nearprint Box, Geography, Los Angeles Jewish Community Council, AJA. *California Jewish Voice*, 17 January 1947. Max Vorspan and Lloyd P. Gartner, *History of the Jews of Los Angeles* (Philadelphia: Jewish Publication Society, 1970), 227–28, note that many local Jewish papers retained their subscribers in Los Angeles.

34. *California Jewish Voice*, 25 March 1949, 3 October 1952, 25 April 1949; letter to the editor from Mrs. William Ehrlich, *California Jewish Voice*, 6 June 1952, 4.

35. *California Jewish Voice*, 13 June 1947; 20 February 1948; 17 July 1948 for Buffalo, New York, picnic; 19 December 1947; 12 March 1948.
36. The papers regularly listed meetings of the clubs. See, for example, *California Jewish Voice*, 3 February 1950 for announcements of Los Angeles Buffalo Club, Rochester, New York, Club, and Cleveland Club; and 10 February 1950 for announcements of Chicagoans of California, Cincinnati Social Club, Boston Club, and Minneapolis-St. Paul Benevolent and Social Club.
37. Even those who didn't make it to high school used the neighborhood and its clubs as the basis for a type of *landsmanshaft*. See, for example, Jon Nordheimer, "Far From Brooklyn and Youth, the 'Dux' Hold Court Again," *New York Times*, 18 March 1987. Bud Hudson, interview with author, 10 July 1989.
38. *California Jewish Voice*, 4 February 1949, 12 January 1951. I appreciate the insight of Michael Ebner regarding the meanings of such associations for their members.
39. *California Jewish Voice*, 2 July 1948, 20 October 1950.
40. *California Jewish Voice*, 14 October 1949, 10 October 1952, 22 April 1949: 7. Announcements for Purim dances appeared annually in the press; see, for example, *California Jewish Voice*, 11 March 1949 for Boston Club and New York Friendship Club; 3 March 1950 for Buffalo Club and Cleveland Social Club; letter to the editor from Arnold Mintzer, *California Jewish Voice*, 14 October 1949; M. Shalit, "In Los Angeles" [Yiddish], *California Jewish Voice*, 7 October 1949: 8; *Temple Emanu-El Review*, 14 September 1956.
41. Lazarus Axelord, "A Gallup Poll on Los Angeles Jewry?" *California Jewish Voice*, 12 January 1951; letter to the editor from Thomas Novak, *California Jewish Voice*, 6 March 1953.
42. Southern States Region, Miami Excerpt from Regional Analysis, 25 July 1958, Council of Jewish Federations and Welfare Funds, AJHS; Arthur Rosichan, interview, June 1965, Rosen files; cover letter to memo re: YMHA, 2 March 1967, Rosen files; Harry Simonoff, *Under Strange Skies* (New York: Philosophical Library, 1953), 313; Judith Nelson Drucker, quoted in *Jewish Times*, Howard Simons (Boston: Houghton Mifflin, 1988), 144; Louis Shub, Oral History, 22 January 1981, 24, quote on 41, Oral History of the AJC, William E. Wiener Oral History Library, AJC.
43. Seymour Philips, interview with author, 14 July 1989.
44. Mark Itelson, interview with author, 14 July 1989; "Manual of Leadership Chaim Weizmann Jewish Community Center" (June 1954), JCA, Chaim Weizmann Jewish Community Center, Histories File, Archives, Jewish Community Library, JFC.
45. Itelson, interview; Joseph Shane, Oral History Interview, 16 June 1977,

1, 12, Oral History of the UJA, Oral History Archives, ICJ, Hebrew University; Herbert Abrams, interview with author, 12 July 1989.

46. Walter S. Hilborn, "Reflections on Legal Practice and Jewish Community Leadership: New York and Los Angeles, 1907–1973," 102, quote on 69, an oral history conducted 1973 by Malca Chall, Regional Oral History Office, The Bancroft Library, University of California, Berkeley 1974, Courtesy of The Bancroft Library; Myrtle Karp, Oral History Interview, 15 March 1976, quotes on 5, 30, Oral History of the UJA, Oral History Archives, ICJ, Hebrew University.

47. Rabbi Paul Dubin to Gladys Gewirtz, 30 June 1955, Congregation Bnai Israel, Synagogues File, Archives, Jewish Community Library, JFC.

48. This was Samuel Gach's characterization. *California Jewish Voice*, 24 August 1945.

49. The best history of Los Angeles Jews is Vorspan and Gartner, *Jews of Los Angeles*. Hilborn contends that the first board of the LAJCC was, with few exceptions, all drawn from Temple Wilshire and hardly representative of Los Angeles Jewry. This changed gradually during the war years. Hilborn, "Reflections on Legal Practice," 171.

50. Irwin Soref, "The Jewish Community of Los Angeles in Retrospect," *Reconstructionist* 18:15 (28 Nov. 1952): 12; *Judge Harry A. Hollzer, 1880–1946*, Los Angeles Jewish Community Council (1946), 5–10.

51. *California Jewish Voice*, 27 December 1946, 7 September 1951, letter to the editor, 7 September 1951.

52. Charles Zibbell, "The Los Angeles Jewish Community Council," *Reconstructionist* 18:15 (28 Nov. 1952): 21–22; William Bruck, Oral History Interview, 12 July 1979, 14, Oral History of the UJA, Oral History Archives, ICJ, Hebrew University.

53. In 1944 these included eight synagogues (a majority Orthodox), branches of the Workmen's Circle, B'nai B'rith, American Jewish Congress, Jewish War Veterans, National Council of Jewish Women, a number of Zionist groups including the Zionist Organization of America, Mizrachi, the Labor Zionist Farband, Hadassah, Pioneer Women, and the local Y, Jewish Social Service Bureau, and the coordinating Greater Miami Jewish Federation. "Population Survey," 2, Council of Jewish Federations and Welfare Funds, AJHS.

54. Manheim S. Shapiro to A. Harold Murray, 28 December 1954, Visits, Florida/Miami Chapter (44–62), Box 10, General 13, Geographic/Domestic, AJC, YIVO; Arthur S. Rosichan, Executive Director, Greater Miami Jewish Federation, report to Executive Committee, at Special Meeting held at Algiers Hotel, 6 April 1960, 3, in AJHS.

55. Manheim Shapiro to A. Harold Murray, memo re: Miami, 28 December 1954, Visits, and S. H. Bucholtz's Report #14 on Greater Miami, 28

July 1944, Visits in Florida/Miami (44–62), Box 10, General 13, Geographic/Domestic, AJC, YIVO.

56. Seymour Samet to Eleanor Ashman, memo re: MIAMI, U.S.A., 1 December 1955, Florida/Miami/Chapter (44–62), and Manheim S. Shapiro to A. Harold Murray, 28 December 1954, Visits, Florida/Miami Chapter (44–62) in Box 10, General 13, Geographic/Domestic, AJC, YIVO.

57. Moshe Davis, Oral History Interview, 14–15; Dafni, Oral History, 2.

58. *California Jewish Voice*, 9 February 1945; Arthur Hoffnung, "History of the University of Judaism," ed. Steven Lowenstein, 25.

59. Abraham P. Gannes, "Five Years of the Bureau of Jewish Education of Miami" (July 1950), introduction, 8–10, Rosen files.

60. Herbert Passameneck's survey of Jewish community centers documents the substantially higher salaries of most workers. See Herbert Passameneck, "Study and Evaluation of the Jewish Centers Association and Constituent Centers of Los Angeles, California" (February 1947), 61, in JCA, Histories file, Jewish Community Library, JFC.

61. Bertram Gold, Oral History, 22–35, Oral History of the AJC, William E. Wiener Oral History Library, AJC. Gold returned thirteen years later to New York as executive director of the American Jewish Committee.

62. Alexander M. Dushkin, "Survey of Jewish Education in Los Angeles, California" (1944), 1–5, 84, Archives, Bureau of Jewish Education, Histories File, Jewish Community Library, JFC.

63. *California Jewish Voice*, 15 September 1944.

64. Dushkin, "Survey," 25–26; "Jewish Education in Los Angeles, A Report by the Bureau of Jewish Education," Los Angeles Jewish Community Council (1951), 4, Bureau of Jewish Education, Histories File, Archives, Jewish Community Library, JFC.

65. Samuel Dinin, "The Role of the Bureau in the Community," in *Twenty-fifth Jubilee Book*, ed. Jacob Gurev, Hebrew Teachers Federation of Los Angeles and Vicinity (Los Angeles, 1956), n.p., Archives, Hebrew Teachers Federation, Histories File, Legal Size, Box 1, Jewish Community Library, JFC; Rabbi Dubin, interview, Interview Folder, Los Angeles [probably 1955], ˙I-75, Box 24, AAJE, National Study: Community Studies, AJHS.

66. Dinin, "The Role of the Bureau," n.p.; Report of Jewish Education Study Commission: LAJCC Board of Directors, 1958–59, 1–4, Bureau of Jewish Education, Histories File, Archives, Jewish Community Library, JFC; President, Hebrew Teachers Federation, ". . . Who enabled us, and sustained us, and brought us to this time," n.p. [Hebrew], in *25th Jubilee Book*.

67. Gannes, "Five Years," 4–8, 10–13.

68. Gannes, "Five Years," 4–8, 10–13; Louis Schwartzman, *Seventeenth*

Annual Report, Bureau of Jewish Education, Miami, Florida (July 1961–1962), n.p., Rosen files.

69. Miami Beach Chamber of Commerce, Statistical Review (1955), 1, Rosen Files; Arthur S. Rosichan, Report, 4, Rosen files; Peppercorn, Oral History, 26–27.

70. M. William Weinberg, interview with author, 16 March 1991.

71. Ronald Kronish, interview with author, 3 March 1992. Perlmutter shared his assessment, see Perlmutter, "Oral Memoirs," in *"Not the Work of a Day,"* I: 37. Harriet Sadoff Kasow, interview with author, 5 May 1992.

72. Dena Kaye, American Jewish Committee Annual Meeting, 14 May 1977, 6, Oral History Library Panel Session, William E. Wiener Oral History Library, AJC; Judith Nelson Drucker, in *Jewish Times*, 143.

73. Fay Kanin, Oral History Memoir, 15 July 1980 and 20 August 1980, 45–48, quote on 45, William E. Wiener Oral History Library, AJC.

74. *California Jewish Voice*, 9 January 1953; "Hebrew Language Offered in Public High Schools," *BJE Newsletter* (June 1965); Robin Rheingold, interview with author, 20 July 1989.

75. Drucker, in *Jewish Times*, 141; Minutes of Education Committee of the American Jewish Committee, 29 May 1956, Reports, Florida/Miami Chapter, Box 10, General 13, Geographic/Domestic, AJC, YIVO. The Surf Club and Bath Club, as well as Indian Creek and La Gorce clubs, continued to exclude Jews in the 1960s. Charlotte Curtis, "Miami: A Youthful City of Indeterminate Social Standing and a Great Deal of New Money," *New York Times*, 2 Feb. 1965, 24.

76. Seymour Samet, "Report," September-October 1957, Reports, Florida/Miami Chapter, 1959–1958–1957, and Minutes of Executive Committee Meeting, 2 June 1955, Reports, 1955, Florida/Miami Chapter, in Box 10, General 13, Geographic/Domestic, AJC, YIVO; Sadoff Kasow, interview.

77. Meeting of the Greater Miami Rabbinical Association, 7 October 1953, 1/19, 185, Jacob S. Kaplan MSS, AJA; David Hudson, interview with author, 20 July 1989; *Bulletin of the Valley Jewish Community Center*, 15 February 1949.

78. David Hudson, Robin Rheingold, and Judith Kantor interviews with author, 20 July 1989.

79. Joseph Roos, the CRC executive, wrote to the superintendent of schools explaining the difficulty for Jewish teachers and students and urging him to consult the religious calendar to avoid similar problems in the future. The board of rabbis expressed regret and urged Jewish parents, teachers, and students "to maintain a high measure of self-discipline and community self-respect by not attending schools sessions" on the opening

days. See Joseph Roos to Ellis A. Jarvis, 21 April 1958, and Resolution of Board of Rabbis of Southern California, 21 April 1958, in Communal Issues, Jews and Judaism, California/Los Angeles (51–59), Box 10, General 13, Geographic/Domestic, AJC, YIVO. See also Annual Reports of Jewish Community Council of the Bay Cities, 21 January 1948, and Minutes of Executive Board Meeting, 27 October 1960, Jewish Community Council of the Bay Cities, Histories File, Archives, Jewish Community Library, JFC.

80. *California Jewish Voice*, 5 September 1947; Executive Committee Meeting, Minutes, 14 October 1959, Committees and Officers, Executive, Florida/Miami Chapter (52–61), Box 10, General 13, Geographic/Domestic, AJC, YIVO.

81. Executive Committee Meeting, Minutes, 23 December 1957, Committees and Officers, Executive, Florida/Miami Chapter (52–61), Box 10, General 13, Geographic/Domestic, AJC, YIVO; conversation with Alan Weisbard, 13 November 1991.

82. Sadoff Kasow, interview; Hudson, interview. David remembered the date: "It was June, at the end of school, I think Frank Sinatra had married Mia Farrow right about then."

83. The following material is drawn from "Miami Beach Senior High School School Evaluation 1967–68," Report of the School and Community Committee, Rosen files. The questions were asked of the students in all three grades, tenth through twelfth. Total responses vary slightly but most totals equalled 1,680. Folklore maintained that 90 percent of the student body was Jewish. By the mid-1960s this had probably dropped to 80 percent. Fifteen percent of the students were Cuban (i.e., born in Cuba), but these numbers undoubtedly included quite a few Jews. Perlmutter, "Oral Memoirs," I: 37, tells a story of his daughter coming home and saying, "Daddy, we have so many Cubans in class, and they have such funny names, Menendez, Mendorez, Gonzales." Then she added: "But some of them have American names, Goldstein and Schwartz." Estimates suggested that there were 3,500 Cuban Jews in Miami by the mid-1960s, most of them living on Miami Beach, in the South Beach section and in the North Shore area between 62nd and 95th streets. Seymour Liebman, "Cuban Jewish Community in South Florida," in *American Jewish Year Book* (1969), 243.

84. Kronish, interview.

85. Of the fathers, 23 percent were professionals, 27 percent managers and proprietors, and 18 percent in sales. These figures, reported by the students, correspond to the communal survey estimates.

86. The house parties under Jewish youth group auspices were subsequently banned after severe criticism in the press, by parents, and by the Dade

County Board of Public Instruction. *Temple Israel of Miami Bulletin*, 27 April 1956; Kronish, interview.

87. Howard I. Friedman, Oral History, 18 December 1980, 58, Oral History of the AJC, William E. Wiener Oral History Library, AJC.

88. Friedman, Oral History, 8–9; Sandberg, *Jews of Los Angeles*, 131.

89. Peter Medding argues that American Jews in the postwar era created a "community of shared identity." Within this community ethnicity became segmented but linked to the core of personality. He writes, "In the community of shared identity continuity is deemed to be dependent upon the actions of the members of the group themselves." Thus, "ensuring continuity is no longer a matter of faith, it has become a question of politics." Peter Medding, "Segmented Ethnicity and the New Jewish Politics," in *Studies in Contemporary Jewry* III (New York, 1987), 30–31.

Chapter 4. Seeking Religious Roots

1. Letter to the editor of the *Los Angeles Times* in 1970, quoted in Stephen J. Sass, "Southern California," *Present Tense*, 9 (Spring 1982): 33.

2. I am grateful for insights regarding characteristics of L.A. rabbis to Wolfe Kelman, who oversaw the placement of Conservative rabbis in the postwar era. Wolfe Kelman, interview with author, 5 March 1988. Bruce Phillips, lecture at conference on Jews in Los Angeles, UCLA, 6 May 1990.

3. Marc Lee Raphael, *Profiles in American Judaism: The Reform Conservative, Orthodox, and Reconstructionist Traditions in Historical Perspective* (San Francisco: Harper & Row, 1984).

4. Quoted in "The Jews of Los Angeles: Pursuing the American Dream," *Los Angeles Times*, 29 January 1978.

5. "Yarmulke comes from Poland to Brooklyn to Los Angeles. It's Brooklynese and Polish. Since the founding of the State of Israel it's become kind of a badge to some Jews." Edgar F. Magnin, "Leader and Personality," an oral history conducted 1972–1974 by Malca Chall, 10, Regional Oral History Office, The Bancroft Library, University of California, Berkeley, 1975. Courtesy of The Bancroft Library.

6. Irving Lehrman quoted in Paul S. George, "An Enduring Covenant" in *Event of the Decade* (1988), 19; Albert Lewis to Maurice Eisendrath, 30 December 1952, General Correspondence, 1/7, Box 212, Albert M. Lewis MSS, AJA.

7. *Temple Beth Sholom Bulletin*, 10 December 1948; Report of Leon Ell, Membership Committee, 24 April 1945; Minutes of Meeting of Board of Directors of Temple Emanu-El, 21 August 1958. Lehrman and Kronish studied at Wise's Jewish Institute of Religion; Narot learned

from Wise during the years Narot served as rabbi in Atlantic City. See Joseph R. Narot, "First Teachers in Last Resorts," *CCAR Journal*, Winter 1978: 46–47.

8. He also frequently attended the Brooklyn Jewish Center, one of the foremost and innovative Conservative synagogue centers in the borough, to hear the preaching of its rabbi, Dr. Israel Levinthal. Irving Lehrman, "The Sermon," in *In the Name of God* (New York, 1979), 216.

9. *Center Review*, 23 September 1943: 4; Helen Goldman, telephone conversation, 10 January 1993; Michael A. Meyer, "A Centennial History," *Hebrew Union College-Jewish Institute of Religion at One-Hundred Years*, ed. Samuel E. Karff (Hebrew Union College Press, 1976), 150, 159.

10. George, "An Enduring Covenant," 9–78. Unless otherwise noted, material is drawn from this commissioned history.

11. This was the first sabbath observed in the new synagogue building. *Center Review*, 21 October 1948: 3.

12. Elaine Glickman, interview with author, 19 March 1991.

13. Lehrman found the architect Charles Greco, who had designed a large synagogue in Cleveland. George, "An Enduring Covenant," 19; Polly Redford, *Billion Dollar Sandbar* (New York: E. P. Dutton, 1970), 274.

14. The board of directors unanimously voted to give Lehrman life tenure in January 1951, less than ten years after his arrival. *Center Review*, 19 January 1951: 5.

15. Glickman, interview; quote from George, "An Enduring Covenant," 48.

16. See, for example, *Center Review*, 15 October 1947 and 5 October 1951. By 1952 the *Review* reported many more girls enrolling in the more intensive Hebrew department of the school, rather than just in the once-a-week Sunday school; 19 September 1952. See also *Jewish Center Review*, 8 May 1953 and 17 September 1954.

17. In 1961–62, after more than a decade of exhortation, there were still over twice as many boys (194) as girls (74) enrolled in the afternoon Hebrew school. Girls, on the other hand, dominated the Sunday school, 155 to 91. Louis Schwartzman, *Seventeenth Annual Report*, Bureau of Jewish Education, Miami, Florida (July 1961–1962), n.p., Rosen files.

18. *Jewish Center Review*, 17 October 1952.

19. *Jewish Center Review*, 4 December 1953; Glickman, interview.

20. Lehrman had convinced the congregation to eliminate *shnoddering*, which was considered undignified, but those who were given an *aliyah* were expected to announce their contribution from the *bima*. The men leading the congregation did not want to forgo this traditional source of synagogue income. See "President's Report" in the *Review*, 7 April 1948, and Minutes of the Executive Committee Meeting, 14 November 1954.

21. *Jewish Center Review*, 11 January 1952; Irving Lehrman, "The 'Power of Prayer,'" in *In The Name of God*, 197. Graham did invite Lehrman to speak at the 1961 Crusade held in the Miami Beach Convention Center. George, "An Enduring Covenant," 61.

22. See *Temple Emanu-El Review*, 17 September 1954, 10 December 1954, 17 December 1954, 24 March 1955, 31 March 1955, 5 September 1956.

23. Glickman, interview.

24. I appreciate Richard Cohen's insights on the multiple meanings of ritual objects. For an early perceptive discussion see Abraham G. Duker, "Emerging Culture Patterns in American Jewish Life," *Publications of the American Jewish Historical Society* 39:4 (June 1950), 351–88.

25. *Jewish Center Review*, 7 December 1951, 3 December 1954.

26. *Temple Emanu-El Review*, 19 October 1956, 4 January 1957, 8 March 1957, 22 March 1957, 9 September 1957.

27. Letter from Morris Berick to officers and members of Temple Beth Sholom, 27 March 1946, Minutes of Temple Beth Sholom; History in Minutes of the Beth Sholom Center, 6 April 1942; Temple Beth Sholom, *Twentieth Anniversary, 1942–1962*, Jubilee Book and Calendar (1962–63), n.p.; Minutes of the First General Meeting of the 1944–45 Season, 8 November 1944, in Minutes of Temple Beth Sholom.

28. See instructions in temple etiquette, *Beth Sholom Bulletin*, 11 February 1949; also Maxine Kronish Snyder, "My Father and My Family: Growing Up Jewish," in *Towards the Twenty-First Century: Judaism and the Jewish People in Israel and America*, ed. Ronald Kronish (Hoboken: KTAV, 1988), 332; report of Leon Ell, Membership Committee, Minutes of Meeting of Board of Directors of Beth Sholom Center, 24 April 1945.

29. Constitution, n.d., in back of Minutes of Temple Beth Sholom. The Miami Beach Jewish Center also changed its name to Temple Emanu-El, but not until 1954.

30. He didn't actually purchase them, and when he returned, he thought "out loud" about using another prayer book. However, the religious committee did order the prayer books, although the temple declined for several years to join the UAHC because of the vehement opposition of one member who thought that such membership would label it Reform. See letter from Morris Berick, 27 March 1946. On the UAHC issue see Minutes of Meeting of Board of Directors of Temple Beth Sholom, 27 December 1945, 22 January 1948, 29 January 1948, 9 March 1950.

31. See Minutes of Special Meeting of Board of Directors of Temple Beth Sholom, 29 January 1949; also, Minutes of Regular Meeting of Board of Directors of Temple Beth Sholom, 24 May 1945, 6 August 1945, 27 December 1945, 21 March 1946, 22 January 1948, 9 March 1950.

32. *Temple Beth Sholom Bulletin*, 10 December 1948. Kronish actually

anticipated an American Union of Liberal Synagogues that would absorb Conservative, Reform, and unaffiliated into a renascent *klal yisroel*.

33. In this case Kronish argued that the congregation should follow the pattern of the State of Israel. There are interesting theological implications of such an argument, but Kronish did not discuss them. Minutes of Regular Meeting of Board of Directors of Temple Beth Sholom, 17 March 1949. See also an earlier argument in *Temple Beth Sholom Bulletin*, 15 September 1947. "Since Palestine is now THE CENTER of our spiritual and cultural life, and can safely be said to determine the norm of Jewish existence, as a gesture of Jewish solidarity, we deem it important to follow the Palestinian custom."

34. Ronald Kronish, interview with author, 2 March 1992; Minutes of Meeting of Board of Directors of Temple Beth Sholom, 1 October 1945.

35. *Temple Beth Sholom Bulletin*, 14 March 1947, 23 May 1947, 14 January 1949, 17 September 1948, 1 September 1947.

36. Minutes of General Membership Meeting, 27 March 1946, Minutes of Temple Beth Sholom; *Temple Beth Sholom Bulletin*, 17 September 1948; Minutes of the Regular Meeting of the Board of Directors of Temple Beth Sholom, 20 October 1949.

37. *Temple Beth Sholom Bulletin*, 5 December 1947, 14 January 1949, 4 April 1947.

38. Maxine Kronish Snyder, "My Father and My Family," 329.

39. Included in *Temple Beth Sholom Bulletin*, 17 October 1947.

40. *Temple Beth Sholom Bulletin*, 17 September 1948; *Jewish Center Review*, 16 November 1951.

41. Biographical details and quotes from Joseph R. Narot, "The Meaning of My Life," in *High Holy Day Sermons Preached at Temple Israel of Greater Miami, 1969/5730*, Joseph R. Narot and Steven B. Jacobs (n.d.), 1–5.

42. Narot's concern to expand the membership appears regularly in Minutes of the Meeting of the Board of Trustees of Temple Israel of Miami, 6 November 1951, 4 December 1951, 6 May 1952, 11 November 1952, 10 August 1953, 12 October 1954. See also Joseph R. Narot, "The Earnestness of Being Important," in *Letters to My Congregation* (1959–60), 3.

43. The sisterhood did open a gift shop. Minutes of the Meeting of the Board of Trustees of Temple Israel of Miami, 4 December 1951.

44. For example, in the matter of synagogue ritual, Temple Israel only had mourners stand to say kaddish, the traditional practice. Narot convinced the board to have the entire congregation stand for the kaddish, an innovation of classical Reform. Minutes of the Meeting of the Board of Trustees of Temple Israel, 9 September 1952, for reaffirmation of earlier

policy; Minutes of the Regular Meeting of the Board of Trustees of Temple Israel of Greater Miami, 9 February 1959, for the change.

45. Joseph R. Narot, "What I Believe About Bar Mitzvo," in *An Introduction to a Faith* (Miami, n.d.), n.p., and "Bar Mitzvo Again—Once Over Heavily," in *Letters to My Congregation* V (Miami, 1962), 2; Minutes of the Regular Meeting of the Board of Trustees of Temple Israel of Miami, 12 September 1955, 14 February 1955; Joseph R. Narot, *Letters to My Congregation* (Miami, n.d. [1960?]), *An Introduction to a Faith* (Miami, n.d. [1961?]), *A Primer for Temple Life* (Miami, n.d.), "Do I Protest Too Much?" in *Letters to My Congregation* (Miami, n.d.), 15.

46. See Joseph R. Narot, "Horse Races, Barber Shops, and Reform Judaism," in which he defends his decision to go to the races and get his hair cut on the sabbath. *Letters to My Congregation* V, 34.

47. Morris Janowitz, *Judaism of the Next Generation* (Miami: Rostrum Books, 1969), 37, Table 3.2.

48. Magnin, Oral History, 27.

49. Magnin, Oral History, 85, 89; Neal Gabler, *An Empire of Their Own* (New York: Crown, 1988), chapter 8.

50. Magnin, Oral History, 126–27, 186 (emphasis in the original), 56, 53.

51. Magnin, Oral History, 259. Wilshire Boulevard Temple introduced a High School department and a Hebrew department, the former requiring additional study after confirmation and the latter requiring more intensive study for two and a half more hours per week. In 1960 the Academy School for gifted children was started, an even more intensive program in religious education. The academy enrolled thirty children in its first year and required attendance three days each week. See Wilshire Boulevard Temple, President's Annual Report (1961), 3, Wilshire Boulevard Temple, Box 841, George Piness MSS, AJA.

52. The account is drawn from Alfred Wolf and Dan Wolf, "Wilshire Boulevard Temple Camps, 1949–1974," in *Wilshire Boulevard Temple Camps*, ed. Alfred Wolf (Los Angeles: Wilshire Boulevard Temple, 1975), 5–17, quote on 5, Los Angeles, Wilshire Boulevard Temple Camps, Nearprint Box—Geography, AJA. *Bulletin of the Valley Jewish Community Center*, 6 December 1946.

53. Wolf and Wolf, "Wilshire Boulevard Temple Camps," 6.

54. Wolf and Wolf, "Wilshire Boulevard Temple Camps," 8.

55. Tom Redler quoted in Wolf and Wolf, "Wilshire Boulevard Temple Camps," 17.

56. One needed to be a temple member to send one's child to camp. Occasionally this requirement generated resentment. Ellie Hudson, interview with author, 10 July 1989.

57. See Jenna Weissman Joselit, ed., *A Worthy Use of Summer: American*

Jewish Summer Camping, 1900–1950 (Philadelphia: National Museum of American Jewish History, 1993).
58. Jacob Sonderling followed a similar path. He founded the Society for Jewish Culture that offered dramatic lectures in worship and "conservative reform." Vorspan and Gartner, *Jews of Los Angeles*, 235.
59. *Bulletin of the Valley Jewish Community Center*, 3 January 1947, 21 March 1947, 28 March 1947, 18 April 1947.
60. The account, unless otherwise noted, is drawn from Cynthia and Robert Rawitch, *The First Fifty Years, Adat Ari El* (North Hollywood, 1988), quote on 55.
61. *Bulletin of the Valley Jewish Community Center*, 3 October 1947, 10 October 1947, 5 December 1947.
62. Quoted in Rawitch and Rawitch, *Adat Ari El*, 9.
63. Biography of Irma Lee Ettinger by Elaine Brown, *Adat Ari-El Yearbook* (1981), n.p.; *Bulletin of the Valley Jewish Community Center*, 24 October 1947. For other explanations of Conservatism, see 31 October 1947, 7 November 1947, 21 November 1947.
64. Wise quoted in Rawitch and Rawitch, *Adat Ari El*, 56; *Bulletin of the Valley Jewish Community Center*, 24 October 1947, 1 December 1948.
65. *Bulletin of the Valley Jewish Community Center*, 1 November 1951, 1 January 1949, 15 September 1951.
66. *Bulletin of the Valley Jewish Community Center*, 1 January 1949, 1 June 1950.
67. Quoted in Rawitch and Rawitch, *Adat Ari El*, 70–71.
68. Fred Massarik, "The Jewish Population of Los Angeles: A Panorama of Change," *Reconstructionist* 18:15 (28 Nov. 1952): 14.

Chapter 5. Spiritual Recreation

1. *California Jewish Voice*, 15 September 1944; Simon Greenberg, interview with author, 1 November 1989.
2. Moshe Davis, interview with Arthur Hoffnung, June 1985.
3. I appreciate the insight of Aryeh Goren regarding L.A.'s image.
4. Quoted in Shlomo Bardin, "The Brandeis Camp Institute," *Jewish Education* 17: 5 (June 1946): 27.
5. As the political scientist Peter Medding argues, "Personal feelings have been invested with heightened significance because they are the language and common denominator of shared identity, while ethnic roles have become a matter of personal choice and definition." Peter Medding, "Segmented Ethnicity and the New Jewish Politics," in *Studies in Contemporary Jewry* III (Oxford: Oxford University Press, 1987), 27. He continues, "The community of shared identity is also characterized by the increased significance of non-systematically articulated and

non-text-centered elements of Jewish ethnicity, which are maintained without being related to the needs of logical or theological consistency. Since roles are performed and customs observed by virtue of individual choice and voluntaristic group decisions, external environmental influences become a major source of legitimation."

6. Mordecai M. Kaplan, *Judaism as a Civilization: Toward a Reconstruction of American Jewish Life* (1934, rpt.; Philadelphia: Jewish Publication Society, 1981).

7. Mordecai M. Kaplan, *A University of Judaism—A Compelling Need* (New York: United Synagogue of America, 1946), 5, 10.

8. Kaplan, *A University of Judaism*, 3, 10.

9. Mordecai M. Kaplan Diary entry, 18 April 1945, quoted in Arthur Hoffnung, "History of the University of Judaism," ed. Steven M. Lowenstein, 8, typescript, University of Judaism; Davis, interview with Hoffnung, June 1985.

10. Hoffnung, "History," 4–5, 9–10; Davis, interview with Hoffnung, June 1985.

11. Wanger headed the motion picture division in the 1946 campaign. *California Jewish Voice*, 10 May 1946.

12. Dore Schary, *Heyday* (Boston: Little, Brown, 1979), 267. Wolfe Kelman described Pressman as a showman rabbi. Wolfe Kelman, interview with author, 5 March 1988. Moshe Davis, Oral History Interview, 10.

13. Edgar F. Magnin, "Leader and Personality," an oral history conducted by Malca Chall, 139, Regional Oral History Office, The Bancroft Library, University of California Berkeley, 1975, courtesy of The Bancroft Library; Simon Greenberg, interview with author, 1 November 1989; Hoffnung, "History," 24–25.

14. Alfred Wolf to Alfred Gottschalk, 8 June 1979, correspondence of Rabbi Wolf and Dr. Alfred Gottschalk, Los Angeles: College of Jewish Studies, Histories File, AJA; Greenberg quoted in Hoffnung, "History," 26.

15. Samuel Dinin, "Reconstructionism and the Future of Jewish Life in Los Angeles," *Reconstructionist* 18:15 (28 Nov. 1952): 16–17; letters from Simon Greenberg, 27 and 28 February 1947 and 17 March 1947, quoted in Hoffnung, "History," 29–30, 34.

16. Report of Simon Greenberg to Louis Finkelstein, 4 March 1947, quoted in Hoffnung, "History," 35–36.

17. The extensive press coverage of gangster Mickey Cohen was also enlisted as an argument; Finkelstein said the *Times* told him, when he protested the headlines, that when the Jews produced other news, the papers would cover it. Greenberg, interview, 1 November 1989.

18. Simon Greenberg, "Some Reflections," *Women's League for Conservative Judaism* 58:4 (Summer 1988): 22.

19. Hoffnung, "History," 89.
20. Samuel Dinin, "University of Judaism: A Description and Evaluation of Present Schools and Programs and a Projection of Future Plans and Programs," August 1968/5728, typescript, 4, 13; Greenberg, interview, 1 November 1989.
21. Hoffnung, "History," 43–45; Minutes of the Executive Committee Meeting of the Board of Overseers, 28 October 1952, 1 July 1952; Davis, Oral History, 18.
22. Estaire Koplin, "Graduation to What?" *Siyum Hazman* (1952), University of Judaism, Histories File, Archives, Jewish Community Library, JFC.
23. Hoffnung, "History," 131–32.
24. He didn't realize at the time that he was also taking a 30 percent cut in pay. Max Vorspan, interview with author, 19 July 1989.
25. *Jewish Community Bulletin* (San Francisco), 29 August 1947, in Scrapbooks, House of the Book Library, Brandeis-Bardin Institute; Hoffnung, "History," 132–33.
26. The department heads included Mario Castelnuovo-Tedesco for music, Stephen Kayser in aesthetics, Joseph Young in the visual arts, and Zemach in theater.
27. Kaplan quoted in Hoffnung, "University of Judaism," 132; see also 133–35. The School of the Arts did not survive, however. It was closed in 1972 because of accreditation problems and the lack of charismatic leadership.
28. Dinin, "University of Judaism," 11.
29. Hoffnung, "History," 27–28.
30. Albert Lewis to Maurice Eisendrath, 30 December 1952, General Correspondence, 1/7, Box 212, Albert M. Lewis MSS, AJA; Uriah Engelman, "National Study: Community Series, Los Angeles" (AAJE, 1956), Table, n. p., in Box 24, ˙I-75, AAJE, AJHS.
31. Announcement of Courses for Adult Education and Religious School Teacher Training, Box 1, College of Jewish Studies, AJA.
32. Robert L. Katz to Alfred Wolf, 12 December 1947, Box 1, College of Jewish Studies, AJA; Nelson Glueck to Haskell W. Kramer, 4 June 1948, Box 1, College of Jewish Studies, AJA.
33. *B'nai B'rith Messenger*, 28 June 1985; Isaiah Zeldin, "Report on West Coast School, 1953–54," Box 30, California School #4, 1953–54, HUC-JIR, Office of the President, Correspondence-General, 1953–54, AJA.
34. Michael A. Meyer, "A Centennial History," *Hebrew Union College-Jewish Institute of Religion at One Hundred Years*, ed. Samuel E. Karff (Cincinnati: Hebrew Union College Press, 1976), 192–93; Solomon B. Freehof to Earl Morse, 31 December 1957, California School, Box 57, HUC-JIR, AJA; Zeldin, "Report on West Coast School, 1953–54."

35. Isaiah Zeldin to Nelson Glueck, 18 November 1954, and Isaiah Zeldin, "Report on Los Angeles College of Jewish Studies," 16 September 1954, Box 36, California School, #6, 1954–55, HUC-JIR, Office of the President, Correspondence-General 1954–55, AJA; Meyer, "Centennial History," 193–94.

36. Meyer, "Centennial History," 193–94, 275.

37. Nelson Glueck to Robert P. Goldman, 16 December 1957, California School, Box 57, HUC-JIR, AJA; Isaiah Zeldin to Maurice Eisendrath, memo re: Advantages to Separation of the Two L.A. Schools, 10 December 1957, California School, Box 57, HUC-JIR, AJA; Louis A. Chase to Earl Morse, 2 January 1958, California School, Box 57, HUC-JIR, AJA.

38. Isaiah Zeldin, remarks, Executive Committee Meeting, 10 December 1957, Box 212, Office of the President, Board of Governors, Reports and Minutes of Meetings, HUC-JIR, AJA; Meyer, "Centennial History," 195.

39. Alfred Gottschalk, Zeldin's successor, eventually led the California School to a site and relationship with the University of Southern California, where he was taking his graduate degree. Before construction began on the new building in 1970, the College of Jewish Studies rejoined the California School as its School of Education and Jewish Studies. Gottschalk also used his position as head of the California School to launch himself into the presidency of the Hebrew Union College–Jewish Institute of Religion. Meyer, "Centennial History," 195.

40. Bardin, "The Brandeis Camp Institute," 27.

41. Shlomo Bardin, interview with Jack Diamond, 2 February 1958 and 20 May 1958, III:7, in House of the Book, Brandeis-Bardin Camp Institute; *California Jewish Voice*, 8 August 1947; B.C.I. *Masterbooks*, 1947, 1952, Brandeis-Bardin Institute; Bardin, "The Brandeis Camp Institute," 27.

42. Shlomo Bardin, interview with Jack Diamond, 11 February 1958 and 20 May 1958, in House of the Book, Brandeis-Bardin Institute.

43. Shlomo Bardin to Mrs. Moses Epstein, 31 July 1942, House of the Book, Brandeis-Bardin Institute; *Hancock Herald*, 22 July 1943, in scrapbooks, House of the Book, Brandeis-Bardin Institute.

44. *Hancock Herald*, 5 August 1943; Bardin, interview, 11 February 1985 and 20 May 1958, III:10; Wolfe Kelman, interview with author, 5 March 1988.

45. Bardin, interview III: 9–10; *Masterbook*, BCI West (1952).

46. Bardin, interview III:13; Irma Lee Ettinger, interview with author, 6 July 1989.

47. Irma Lee Ettinger was one of the first to receive a scholarship from Los Angeles. Ettinger, interview, 6 July 1989.

48. *Hancock Herald*, 22 July 1943; Moshe Davis, Oral History, 7.

49. *California Jewish Voice*, 22 November 1946, 28 February 1947, 7 March 1947.
50. *California Jewish Voice*, 8 August 1947; *Star–Free Press*, 19 July 1947, in Scrapbooks for 1947–48, House of the Book, Brandeis-Bardin Institute.
51. *California Jewish Voice*, 29 August 1947; David Sokolov, "Brandeis Camp Gives Youth Direction," *Jewish Post*, 20 October 1949; Ettinger, interview, 6 July 1989.
52. Chava Scheltzer to Lev [Abe] Herman, 24 September 1946, S32/1205, 1 June 1946–30 September 1946, 10235/62, Youth Matters, U.S.A. [Hebrew], Central Zionist Archives; see also Shlomo Bardin to Abe Herman, 1 September 1945, in which he describes the kind of *shaliach* he desires: "young men from rural settlements or colonies who, in their very appearance, personify the new Palestine. . . . The ability to sing and dance, and particularly to convey the spirit via singing and dancing, are very essential. With all this, they cannot be partisans in a political party sense. They must be broad enough to include all Palestine, with all its groups and factions." S32/536, Central Zionist Archives.
53. Summary of Activities of the Brandeis Youth Foundation, n.d., House of the Book; Ettinger, interview, 6 July 1989; Sokolov, "Brandeis Camp Notes," *Jewish Post*, 27 October 1949, in Scrapbooks.
54. Bruce Powell, "The Brandeis-Bardin Institute: A Possible Jewish Model for Multicultural Education," Ph.D. diss., University of Southern California, 1979, 134.
55. Rosalyne Eisenberg quoted in Maurice Zigmond to Rabbi Theodore H. Gordon, 1 April 1948, included with cover letter to Members of the National Youth Commission from Shlomo Bardin, 26 April 1948, F25/162, Central Zionist Archives; David Sokolov, "Brandeis Camp Gives Youth Direction," *Jewish Post*, 20 October 1949, in Scrapbooks; Ettinger, interview, 6 July 1989; quoted in Gene N. Levine, *An Adventure in Curing Alienation* (Summer 1971), 25–26.
56. A 1971 survey found 68 percent women and 32 percent men over the course of three decades. However, in the early years during World War II, there were as many as 190 women to 10 men. Levine, *Adventure*, 9.
57. Ramon F. Berger, "An Aliyah to the Brandeis Camp Institute," ed. Graenum Berger (Santa Susana, 1968), n.p.; Bardin, interview, 11 Febuary 1958 and 20 May 1958, II:5.
58. Graenum Berger, "An Aliyah to the Brandeis Camp Institute," (Santa Susana, 1968), n.p.; Bardin, interview, III:12; *Masterbook*, BCI West, 1952.
59. Minutes of the Meeting of the Board of Governors of the Brandeis Youth Foundation, 26 September 1951, House of the Book, Brandeis-Bardin Institute; Minutes of Meeting of National Board of Brandeis

Youth Foundation, 23 February 1953, House of the Book, Brandeis-Bardin Institute.

60. Kelman, interview, 5 March 1988; Minutes of Meeting of the Brandeis Camp Institute of the West, 7 June 1952, House of the Book, Brandeis-Bardin Institute; on scripts, Minutes of Meeting of Members of Brandeis Youth Foundation in Los Angeles, 15 April 1953, House of the Book, Brandeis-Bardin Institute.

61. Ettinger, interview, 6 July 1989; Fay Kanin, Oral Memoir, 57–58, William E. Wiener Oral History Library, AJC.

62. Max William Bay, Oral History Interview, 25 July 1979, 4, 8, Oral History of the UJA, Oral History Archives, ICJ, Hebrew University; Ted Thomas, interview with author, 13 July 1989.

63. See Members of Board of Directors, 1954; Minutes of Meeting of the Executive Committee of the Brandeis Youth Foundation, 7 June 1953, House of the Book, Brandeis-Bardin Institute. Bardin also dreamed of establishing a Jewish prep school, thereby returning to his initial field of activity as a pedagogue in Haifa, but he never succeeded in raising the funds necessary for such an ambitious venture.

64. Walter S. Hilborn, "Reflections on Legal Practice and Jewish Community Leadership: New York and Los Angeles, 1907–1975," 216, an oral history conducted by Malca Chall, Regional Oral History Office, The Bancroft Library, University of California, Berkeley, 1974. Courtesy of The Bancroft Library.

65. *San Francisco Jewish Tribune*, 14 September 1947, in Scrapbooks; Edward Meltzer quoted in *B'nai B'rith Messenger*, 6 August 1948; Steve Broidy, Oral History Interview, 27 July 1979, 2–3, Oral History of the UJA, Oral History Archives, ICJ, Hebrew University.

66. Jacob I. Hurvitz, *Brandeis Camp Institute* (New York, n.d.), quotes on 11–12, House of the Book, Brandeis-Bardin Institute; Bardin, interview, VI:1.

67. Editorial, *California Jewish Voice*, 16 July 1948.

68. Powell, "The Brandeis-Bardin Institute," 120.

69. Charles S. Liebman is one of the most astute observers of changes in American Jewish religious life; see his "Ritual, Ceremony and the Reconstruction of Judaism in the United States" in *Studies in Contemporary Jewry* VI (Oxford: Oxford University Press, 1990), 272–83; for another recognition of changes in American religion, see Phillip E. Hammond, "Religion and the Persistence of Identity," *Journal for the Scientific Study of Religion* 27:1 (1988): pp. 1–11.

Chapter 6. Politics in Paradise

1. *Jewish Floridian*, 5 April 1946, 8 June 1951, 5 October 1951, 12 October 1951, 14 December 1951. The last bombing came just two days after explosions at the segregated Carver Village housing project. *Jewish Floridian*, 7 December 1951.
2. Burnett Roth, interview, n.d., Rosen files; Gladys Rosen, "Community Relations: 1945–1960 Post-War Period," 2, paper in author's possession.
3. *Jewish Floridian*, 27 June 1947, 24 June 1949; Polly Redford, *Billion Dollar Sandbar* (New York: E. P. Dutton, 1970), 222.
4. Enforcement was another problem. Signs remained on the beach through the 1950s. Survey of Resort Discrimination by Anti-Defamation League reported in *Jewish Floridian*, 29 April 1960: 11C; see also 10 November 1950.
5. *Jewish Floridian*, 29 June 1951, 29 April 1960. On the impact of the new Jewish owners, see, for example, *Jewish Floridian*, 29 August 1947, which reported that the formerly restricted New Surf Hotel at 89th and Surfside was taken over by a Cleveland group with Charles Goldberg as managing director.
6. Peter Medding, "Segmented Ethnicity and the New Jewish Politics," in *Studies in Contemporary Jewry* 3 (New York, 1987), 32–34.
7. Blacks were 15 percent of the residents, 9 percent of the registered voters, and 5 percent of the actual voters. Thomas J. Wood, "Dade County: Unbossed, Erratically Led," *Annals of the American Academy of Political and Social Science*, May 1964: 67.
8. Seymour Samet, Oral History Interview, 65, Oral History of the AJC, 1981, William E. Wiener Oral History Library, AJC.
9. In his masterful study of southern politics, V. O. Key noted that "Florida is not only unbossed, it is also unled. Anything can happen in elections, and does." V. O. Key, *Southern Politics* (New York: Vintage Books, 1949), 82.
10. In 1960 Miami Beach even voted to secede from Dade County and set up a separate county of Greater Miami Beach, but the legislation enabling such action was never presented to the Florida legislature. Edward Sofen, *The Metropolitan Miami Experiment* (Bloomington: Indiana University Press, 1963), 161. Wood, "Dade County," 65.
11. Wood, "Dade County," 65–69.
12. Aronovitz resigned due to ill health. *Jewish Floridian*, 25 November 1955.
13. Wood, "Dade County," 65–69; *Jewish Floridian*, 20 November 1953.
14. The absence of any comments in the records of the various Jewish defense organizations on the problem of Jewish gangsters and their control of the gambling syndicate contrasts with explicit concern over the extravagant behaviour of nouveau riche Jews visiting the Beach hotels.

15. Lawrence H. Fuchs, *The Political Behavior of American Jews* (Glencoe: The Free Press, 1956), 77–78, quote on 99; Samuel Lubell, *The Future of American Politics* (New York: Harper & Row, 1965), 198.

16. Leonard Dinnerstein, *America and the Survivors of the Holocaust* (New York: Columbia University Press, 1982), 101.

17. Melvin I. Urofsky, *We Are One!* (Garden City: Doubleday, 1978), 24–30, chap. 3; Dinnerstein, *Survivors*, 6–8; editorial, *Jewish Floridian*, 2 November 1945.

18. Melvin I. Urofsky, *American Zionism from Herzl to the Holocaust* (Garden City: Doubleday, 1976), 394–95. Urofsky notes that Kaufmann proved to be a disappointment. Shepard Broad, Oral History Interview, 10 April 1977, 2, Oral History of the UJA, Oral History Archives, ICJ, Hebrew University; Harry Simonoff, *Under Strange Skies*, (New York: Philosophical Library, 1953), 317–18.

19. Broad, Oral History, 6, 9.

20. *Miami Beach Sun Tropics*, 25 April 1945, Rosen files; *Jewish Floridian*, 27 April 1945; Gladys Rosen, "The Zionist Movement," 4, Rosen files.

21. *Jewish Floridian*, 12 July 1946, 19 July 1946.

22. For more detail, see chapter 8.

23. Broad, Oral History, quote on 3, 20–21.

24. *Jewish Floridian*, 16 May 1947. Six months later, in response to the U.N. vote on partition, the paper editorialized: "We are on the eve of an era in which the Jews of Palestine and the Jews of America will determine the rate of Jewish immigration and Jewish development in the Jewish State" (5 December 1947).

25. The biblical verse to sound the shofar to proclaim the Jubilee year. See *Encyclopedia Judaica* 14: 1443.

26. *Jewish Floridian*, 1 June 1951, 15 November 1948, 21 May 1948.

27. Robert Rosen argues that Broad rested his career as a "lawyer emissary" on demonstrating his divided loyalties, not on overcoming them as suggested by the conventional interpretation of the lawyer emissary. Robert Rosen, "Jews and Corporate Legal Practice," paper given at Conference on Jews and the Law in the United States, 14–17 November 1991, University of Wisconsin, Madison, 11.

28. *Jewish Floridian*, 17 June 1949, 19 August 1949. Smathers's bill was fairly comprehensive: It included those who took part in the fighting between 15 September 1947 and 31 January 1949.

29. *Jewish Floridian*, 1 February 1946, 25 June 1948.

30. *Jewish Floridian*, 6 November 1953. The men involved in the hotel venture included Dan Ruskin, Max Orovitz, Samuel Friedland, Lewis Stein, Sam Stein, Samuel Blank, and I. L. Mintzer. On Israel entering the sacred calendar, see *Temple Emanu-El Review*, 25 April 1958, 8 May 1959, where Israel shared billing with a Mother's Day sabbath. Speech

of Joseph Weidberg, 28 May 1953. Weidberg was both a Zionist and chair of the local American Jewish Committee chapter. Fund Raising/Joint Defense Appeal, Florida/Miami (46–61), Box 10, General 13, Geographic/Domestic, AJC, YIVO.

31. *Jewish Floridian*, 14 December 1951, 3 April 1953, 4 July 1952.
32. Samuel Gach, "In the Know," *California Jewish Voice*, 18 January 1952: 1–2 (emphasis in the original); editorial, *California Jewish Voice*, 18 January 1952.
33. *Jewish Floridian*, 21 March 1952; background material for Miami Chapter, n.d. [probably March 1952], Rosen files; Irving M. Engel to Baron de Hirsch Meyer, draft of letter, n.d. [probably 25 March 1952], Rosen files.
34. The AJCommittee's first two chairs were both members of ADL. Joseph Weidberg, who succeeded Meyer, was on the executive committee of ADL at the same time that he was president of AJCommittee. Joseph Weidberg to George Talianoff and Leonard Abess, 17 February 1954, Communal Organizations/AJC-ADL, Florida, Miami, (1953–58), Box 10, General 13, Geographic/Domestic, AJC, YIVO.
35. Deborah Dash Moore, *B'nai B'rith and the Challenge of Ethnic Leadership* (Albany: SUNY Press, 1981), 130–31; MacIver File, Greater Miami Jewish Federation, Rosen files. Both ADL and American Jewish Committee withdrew from NCRAC after it accepted the MacIver report with its criticism of duplication. Irving M. Engel to Baron de Hirsch Meyer, n.d. [probably 25 March 1952], Rosen files; M. C. Gettinger to Morris Klass, 16 January 1951, Greater Miami Jewish Federation, 1947 Census, Miami (1950–60), Rosen files; Abraham G. Duker, *Jewish Community Relations: An Analysis of the MacIver Report* (New York: Jewish Reconstructionist Foundation, 1952), 9–14.
36. Leo Robinson, "AJCommittee Serves Miami," n.d. [probably 1958–59], Rosen files; Nathan Perlmutter, Oral History Interview, 27, Oral History of the AJC, William E. Wiener Oral History Library, AJC; Bertram Gold, Oral History Interview, 26, Oral History of the AJC, William E. Wiener Oral History Library, AJC.
37. Jacobs continues his account with a description of the Jewish Labor Committee, American Council for Judaism, and the American Zionist Council. Paul Jacobs, *Is Curly Jewish?* (New York: Vintage Books, 1965), 140–41.
38. B'nai B'rith did have a separate women's division, B'nai B'rith Women, but it possessed far fewer numbers than the men and suffered from second-class status. Moore, *B'nai B'rith*, 183–84.
39. Seymour Samet to A. Harold Murray, 18 August 1955, Fund-Raising, Florida/Miami (55–61), and Seymour Samet, "Report," May 1955,

Reports, 1955, Florida/Miami Chapter, in Box 10, General 13, Geographic/Domestic, AJC, YIVO.

40. Manheim Shapiro to A. Harold Murray, memo re: Miami, 28 December 1954, Visits, Florida/Miami (44–62), Box 10, General 13, Geographic/Domestic, AJC, YIVO.

41. Reinhold P. Wolff and David K. Gillogly, *Negro Housing in the Miami Area* (Miami: University of Miami, 1951), 3, 14; Toby Shafter, "Miami: 1948," *Jewish Frontier* 15:1 (January 1948): 20; Seymour Samet to Max Birnbaum, 23 December 1952, Communal Issues/Public Accommodations, Florida, Miami (52–62), Box 10, General 13, Geographic/Domestic, AJC, YIVO.

42. Seymour Samet to Max Birnbaum, 3 November 1952, Communal Issues/Public Accommodations, Florida, Miami (52–62), and Seymour Samet to Manheim Shapiro, 26 August 1953, Communal Issues/Public Accommodations, Florida, Miami (52–62), Box 10, General 13, Geographic/Domestic, AJC, YIVO.

43. Seymour Samet to Manheim Shapiro, 13 May 1953, Communal Issues/Public Accommodations, Florida, Miami (52–62), and Seymour Samet to Manheim Shapiro, 26 August 1953, Communal Issues/Public Accommodations, Florida, Miami (52–62), Box 10, General 13, Geographic/Domestic, AJC, YIVO.

44. Seymour Samet to Manheim Shapiro, 13 May 1953, Communal Issues/Public Accommodations, Florida, Miami (52–62), Box 10, General 13, Geographic/Domestic, AJC, YIVO.

45. Seymour Samet to Morris Kertzer, 8 June 1956, Communal Issues/Housing, Florida, Miami (51–62), Box 10, General 13, Geographic/Domestic, AJC, YIVO.

46. Seymour Samet to Morris Kertzer, 8 June 1956, Communal Issues/Housing, Florida, Miami (51–62), Box 10, General 13, Geographic-Domestic, AJC, YIVO; Leo Mindlin, "During the Week As I See It," *Jewish Floridian*, 8 June 1956; Orr quoted in Seymour Samet to Ed Lukas, 10 September 1956, Committees and Officers, Executive, Florida/Miami Chapter (52–61), Box 10, General 13, Geographic/Domestic, AJC, YIVO. Orr lost the primary two years later after he strongly supported school desegregation in the Florida legislature.

47. Raymond A. Mohl, "Blacks, Jews, and the Civil Rights Movement in Miami, 1945–1960," paper presented at annual meeting of the Southern Historical Association, November 1992.

48. *Jewish Floridian*, 5 October 1956, 1 July 1955, 23 August 1957; Samet, Oral History, 42.

49. Ronald Kronish, interview with author, 3 March 1992; *Jewish Floridian*, 29 August 1960.

50. Seymour Samet to Ira Gissen, 26 March 1958, and Seymour Samet to Ed Lukas, 29 September 1959 Communal Issues/Integration, Florida, Miami (1952–62), Box 10, General 13, Geographic/Domestic, AJC, YIVO. The owner of Burdine's was on the national Executive Board of the AJCommittee. "There seems to have developed on the part of the Burdine's people the attitude that I and possibly the AJC are working as an arm of CORE in attempting to get them to change their practices," Samet noted with frustration.

51. Seymour Samet to Ann Wolfe, 17 April 1958, Communal Organizations, Florida/Miami (53–61), Box 10, General 13, Geographic/Domestic, AJC, YIVO; *Jewish Floridian*, 4 April 1952, 2 December 1949. The physician was Dr. Aubrey Warren Henry.

52. That most of these Jews were also radicals and many had been communists further complicated the matter.

53. Characterization of Woloth and Stern quoted in Mohl, "Blacks, Jews," 37. See also 37–43. Seymour Samet to Ed Lukas, 29 September 1959, Communal Issues/Integration, Florida/Miami (53–59), Box 10, General 13, Geographic/Domestic, AJC, YIVO. There was another irony not commented upon by Samet; namely, that the choice of the small Jewish-owned store, which had a branch in Miami's black neighborhood, instead of a large chain generated dissension within CORE's ranks, since many of its white sit-down protesters were Jews. Raymond Mohl, conversation with author, 28 December 1992.

54. This was an AJCongress initiative. The congress also helped get a $10,000 Field Foundation grant to revive the almost moribund DCCCR so that Miami would have nonsectarian auspices to sponsor integration. Statement by the American Jewish Congress, Local Programs and Activities, March 1959, Greater Miami Jewish Federation Community Relations File, Miami (1950–60), Rosen files. The AJCommittee sponsored a similar program by forming a Citizens Committee for Better Schools to urge the state legislature to pass a bill that would give each locality the right to make its own decision on whether to desegregate. Seymour Samet to Max Birnbaum, 2 April 1959, Communal Issues/Integration, Florida, Miami (1953–59), Box 10, General 13, Geographic/Domestic, AJC, YIVO.

55. Seymour Samet to Ed Lukas, 11 September 1956, and Seymour Samet to Max Birnbaum, 23 March 1956, Communal Issues/Integration, Florida, Miami (1953–59), Box 10, General 13, Geographic/Domestic, AJC, YIVO.

56. ADL supported the Southern Regional Council. *Jewish Floridian*, 12 March 1948; Steven F. Lawson, "The Florida Legislative Investigation Committee and the Constitutional Readjustment of Race Relations,

1956–1963," in *An Uncertain Tradition*, ed. Kermit L. Hall and James W. Ely, Jr. (Athens, Ga.: University of Georgia Press, 1989), 296–299.

57. Some came because they thought the meeting would discuss the recent Supreme Court decision, *Brown v. Board of Education.* They were ruled out of order. A. J. Kaplan to George Talianoff, 19 July 1954, Communal Organizations/AJC-ADL/Joint Committee on Civil Liberties, Florida, Miami (54), Box 10, General 13, Geographic/Domestic, AJC, YIVO.

58. Seymour Samet to Manheim Shapiro, 29 July 1954, Communal Organizations/AJC-ADL/Joint Committee on Civil Liberties, Florida, Miami (54), and Burnett Roth to George Talianoff, 25 August 1954, Communal Organizations, Florida, Miami (1953–61), in Box 10, General 13, Geographic/Domestic, AJC, YIVO.

59. Seymour Samet to Manheim Shapiro, 24 September 1954, Communal Organizations/AJC-ADL/Joint Committee on Civil Liberties, Florida, Miami (54), and Seymour Samet to Manheim Shapiro, 26 March 1954, Reports, 1954, Florida/Miami Chapter, and Seymour Samet to Ed Lukas, 16 November 1954, Reports, 1954, Florida/Miami Chapter, in Box 10, General 13, Geographic/Domestic, AJC, YIVO. Not all took this approach. Maurice Carroll, director of the Jewish Cultural Center, appealed a Miami court order to answer questions about Communist party activities prior to his naturalization in Philadelphia in 1928. Seymour Samet to Ed Lukas, 12 April 1955, Reports, 1955, Florida/Miami Chapter, in Box 10, General 13, Geographic/Domestic, AJC, YIVO.

60. "A Guide to Agency Policy Representing the View of the Presidents of Federation and. . . ," Communal Organizations/AJC-ADL/Joint Committee on Civil Liberties, Florida, Miami (54), Box 10, General 13, Geographic/Domestic, AJC, YIVO.

61. Seymour Samet to Ed Lukas, 27 September 1954, Communal Organizations/AJC-ADL/Joint Committee on Civil Liberties, Florida, Miami (54), Box 10, General 13, Geographic/Domestic, AJC, YIVO.

62. Samet, Oral History, 12–15; *Miami News*, 3 July 1958, in Communal Organizations, Florida, Miami (1953–61), Box 10, General 13, Geographic/Domestic, AJC, YIVO; Sam Cohen to Benjamin B. Rosenberg, 25 February 1958, enclosure of statement, Greater Miami Federation Old Files, A–D, Miami (1950–60), Rosen files.

63. The full name of the committee was the Florida Legislative Investigation Committee. For a discussion of its history, see Lawson, "Florida Legislative Committee," 296–325.

64. Haskell L. Lazere to Rabbi Leon Kronish et. al., 6 March 1958, and "AJ-Congress warns Johns Committee still 'dangerous,'" press release from Haskell Lazere, American Jewish Congress, Communal Organizations/

AJC-ADL, Florida, Miami (1953–58), Box 10, General 13, Geographic/ Domestic, AJC, YIVO. Lazere wrote Pfeffer that Toby Simon, one of the sharpest critics of Jewish community-relations agencies in Miami, told Lazere when he first came down "that no Jewish agency would have the guts to publicly criticize the activities of the Johns Committee. When the Congress did go after the Johns Committee, I got a lengthy letter of apology from Simon along with his dues." Haskell Lazere to Leo Pfeffer, 25 November 1960, Resnick files, CLSA, American Jewish Congress library.

65. ADL was trying to oppose the link between anticommunism and antisemitism championed by white racists. *Jewish Floridian*, 18 August 1950.

66. *Miami Herald*, 17–19 March 1958; *Miami News*, 18 March 1958.

67. Nathan Perlmutter, "Bombing in Miami: Anti-Semitism and the Segregationists," *Commentary* 25 (June 1958): 500, quote on 503; Samet, Oral History, 15–16; transcript of proceedings before the subcommittee on Community Relations of the Greater Miami Jewish Federation, 5 March 1959 (AJCongress), 9 March 1959 (ADL), 11 March 1959 (AJCommittee), 55–56, Greater Miami Jewish Federation, Community Relations File, 1950–60, Rosen files; Haskell Lazere, Oral History, 71, Oral History of the AJC, William E. Wiener Oral History Library, AJC.

68. Easter assembly program, Miami Senior High School (1960), Resnick files, CLSA, American Jewish Congress library.

69. Seymour Samet to Manheim Shapiro, 16 April 1954, and Seymour Samet to Malvina Liebman, 27 December 1957, Communal Issues: Religion and Schools, Florida/Miami (48–61), Box 10, General 13, Geographic/Domestic, AJC, YIVO.

70. Seymour Samet to Manheim Shapiro, 2 August 1955, and American Jewish Committee, "What Advice Shall We Give Our Miami Chapter Concerning the Distribution of Gideon Bibles in the Public Schools of Miami, Florida?" for meeting of Civil Rights and Civil Liberties Committee, 1 September 1956, and memo re: Proposed Teaching of Religion in Miami Schools, 15 December 1955, and Statement of Ad Hoc Committee on Religion and the Public Schools, 23 January 1956, in Communal Issues: Religion and Schools, Florida/Miami (48–61), Box 10, General 13, Geographic/Domestic, AJC, YIVO.

71. Seymour Samet to A. Harold Murray, 20 April 1960, Communal Issues: Religion and Schools, Florida/Miami (48–61), Box 10, General 13, Geographic/Domestic, AJC, YIVO.

72. Haskell Lazere prepared a long memo outlining the chronology of the case because, after it came to court, it aroused bitter intramural Jewish arguments. His account is confirmed by material in AJCommittee records. The following draws upon Lazere except where otherwise indicated. Memo to Congress Staff from Haskell L. Lazere, re: Background

Information on Miami Law Suit, 23 December 1960, Resnick files, CLSA, American Jewish Congress library. See also Haskell L. Lazere to Leo Pfeffer, 18 August 1959, Resnick files, CLSA, American Jewish Congress library.

73. Naomi W. Cohen, *Jews in Christian America: The Pursuit of Religious Equality* (New York: Oxford University Press, 1992), 192, notes that "disagreement arose over principles and tactics, but much sprang from sheer jealousy." See 192–197 for a clear overview of the case and internal Jewish interagency conflict. File memorandum: Meeting of executive committee and other interested parties to hear Mr. Leo Pfeffer, n.d. [probably May 1960], Greater Miami Jewish Federation, Religion in Public School file, Miami (1950–60), Rosen files; Leo Pfeffer to Will Maslow, 22 December 1960, Resnick files, CLSA, American Jewish Congress.

74. Transcript of proceedings before the subcommittee on Community Relations of the Greater Miami Jewish Federation, 5 March 1959 (AJCongress), 9 March 1959 (ADL), 11 March 1959 (AJCommittee), Greater Miami Jewish Federation, Community Relations File, 1950–60, Rosen files. In 1956 Pfeffer had looked into the Nashville Bible-reading case of *Carden v. Bland* but declined to get involved. The arguments of the local leadership that Jews were a tiny minority of the population and that it would be inappropriate for "the People of the Book" to oppose Bible-reading carried weight with AJCongress. Correspondence quoted in Frank J. Sorauf, *The Wall of Separation* (Princeton: Princeton University Press, 1976), 46.

75. Form letter, "Dear Rabbi," signed by Burnett Roth and Stuart Simon, and accompanying memo, Burnett Roth to Nathan Perlmutter, memo re: Conference concerning survey of religious practices in the Dade county public school system, 23 November 1959, in Communal Issues: Religion and Schools, Florida/Counties/Dade (53–60), Box 10, General 13, Geographic/Domestic, AJC, YIVO.

76. Plaintiffs' Memorandum on the Facts, Leo Pfeffer, Counsel, Resnick files, CLSA, American Jewish Congress library.

77. Quoted in Sol Rabkin, memo to ADL Regional Offices, 2 August 1960, Resnick files, CLSA, American Jewish Congress library.

78. Lazere, Oral History, 75; Sorauf, *Wall*, 280; Haskell L. Lazere, "Historic Fight for Religious Liberty," *Congress Bi-Weekly* 27:12 (22 August 1960): 10.

79. Haskell L. Lazere to Leo Pfeffer, 17 May 1960, Resnick files, CLSA, American Jewish Congress library; Seymour Samet to A. Harold Murray, 16 June 1961, Communal Issues: Religion and Schools, Florida/Miami (48–61), Box 10, General 13, Geographic/Domestic, AJC, YIVO; Haskell L. Lazere to Leo Pfeffer, 12 September 1960, Resnick files, CLSA, American Jewish Congress library.

80. Sidney M. Aronovitz to Kenneth Oka, 15 August 1960, Greater Miami Jewish Federation Old Files, M–Z, Miami (1950–60), Rosen files; Haskell L. Lazere to Leo Pfeffer, 12 September 1960, Resnick files, CLSA, American Jewish Congress library.
81. Seymour Samet to A. Harold Murray, memo re: The Chamberlin Case—Miami, 16 June 1961, Communal Issues: Religion and Schools, Florida/Miami (48–61), Box 10, General 13, Geographic/Domestic, AJC, YIVO; Haskell L. Lazere to Congress Staff, 23 December 1960, Resnick files, CLSA, American Jewish Congress library.
82. "Decision in Miami: How the Court Ruled on Religion in the Schools," brochure by American Jewish Congress, from article in *Congress Bi-weekly* by Richard Cohen, Rosen files; Seymour Samet to A. Harold Murray, 16 June 1961, re: The Chamberlin Case—Miami; Committees and Officers, Executive, Florida/Miami Chapter (52–61), Box 10, General 13, Geographic/Domestic, AJC, YIVO.
83. Opinion in the Supreme Court of Florida, 29 January 1964, 4, Chamberlin files, CLSA, American Jewish Congress library; Sorauf, *Wall*, 160, 217.

Chapter 7. Choosing Sides

1. "Shlomo Gach Endorses," *California Jewish Voice*, 31 May 1946.
2. The most articulate and persistent advocate was Mordecai M. Kaplan. See his *Judaism as a Civilization* (1934, rpt.; New York: Schocken, 1967) and *The Future of the American Jew* (New York: Reconstructionist Press, 1948). For a brief discussion of the origins, purposes, and characteristics of Jewish Community Councils, see Isaac Franck, "The Changing American Jewish Community," in *The Tercentenary and After*, ed. Eugene Kohn (New York: Reconstructionist Press, 1955), 38–42. Daniel Elazar, *Community and Polity* (Philadelphia: Jewish Publication Society, 1976), discusses the common forms of Jewish communal organization in the United States.
3. Max Vorspan and Lloyd P. Gartner, *History of the Jews of Los Angeles* (Philadelphia: Jewish Publication Society, 1970), 264–68; *California Jewish Voice*, 1 December 1944, 26 January 1945.
4. Vorspan and Gartner, *Jews of Los Angeles*, 200–202.
5. Ezra Mendelsohn, *Towards Modern Jewish Politics* (New York: Oxford University Press, 1993), chap. 6–7; for the period of the popular front and war years, see Larry Ceplair and Steven Englund, *The Inquisition in Hollywood* (Garden City, N.Y.: Doubleday, 1980), chap. 2–6; Michael Blankfort, *The Strong Hand* (Boston: Little, Brown, 1956), 4–5.
6. Vorspan and Gartner, *Jews of Los Angeles*, 201, note that "the perusal of an evenly divided group declaring for the presidential candidates in

1940 tends to show that the more recently arrived Jews generally favored Roosevelt; earlier settlers seemed to prefer Willkie."

7. Isaiah Terman, report of visit to Los Angeles, 14–15 December 1945, Visits, California/Los Angeles (45–62), Box 10, General 13, Geographic/Domestic, AJC, YIVO; Edgar F. Magnin, "Leader and Personality," an oral history conducted 1972–1974 by Malca Chall, 250–52, quote on 210, Regional Oral History Office, The Bancroft Library, University of California, Berkeley, 1975. Courtesy of The Bancroft Library.

8. Halliwell charts a decline in interest group politics and ethnic politics and an increase in what he calls culture politics, e.g., antisubversives, antiobscenity laws; Michael John Halliwell, "California Politics: Key Statewide Contests and Issues, 1958–1966," Ph.D. diss., UCLA, 1974, x.

9. James Q. Wilson, "A Guide to Reagan Country," *Commentary*, May 1967: 40; Paul Jacobs, *Is Curly Jewish?* (New York: Vintage, 1965), 196; *California Jewish Voice*, 22 June 1945. Warren's stand probably reflected the pressure of state oil interests.

10. Carey McWilliams, *Southern California Country* (New York: Duell, Sloan & Pearce, 1946), 312–13; Halliwell, "California Politics," 149–50; Wilson, "A Guide to Reagan Country," 39; Earl Warren, *The Memoirs of Earl Warren* (Garden City, N.Y.: Doubleday, 1977), 155–160. In fact, in 1946 Warren ran for the governorship with both the Democratic and Republican nominations (240). H. Stuart Hughes, "California—The America to Come," *Commentary* 21:5 (May 1956): 457–59.

11. Helen L. Jones and Robert F. Wilcox, *Metropolitan Los Angeles: Its Governments* (Los Angeles: The Haynes Foundation, 1949), chap. 1–3. In 1952 Douglas MacArthur and his Christian Nationalist party polled equal percentages of votes in Los Angeles precincts that had split between Democrats and Republicans in 1948. Samuel Lubell to Fred Schreiber, 2 July 1954, Communal Issues, California/Los Angeles (45–62), Box 10, General 13, Geographic/Domestic, AJC, YIVO.

12. The American Jewish Conference admitted the JPFO in 1944 as a member despite the threat of the Jewish Labor Committee to withdraw. The American Jewish Congress admitted the JPFO in May 1945, based upon the wartime cooperation. Jeffrey M. Marker, "Communism and Liberalism in the Jewish Community," M.A. thesis, University of Maryland, 1976, 24–25; Vorspan and Gartner, *Jews of Los Angeles*, 269–72.

13. Arthur Liebman, *Jews and the Left* (New York: John Wiley & Sons, 1979), 311; Samuel B. Gach, "National Cleavage Reflected Locally," *California Jewish Voice*, 15 June 1945.

14. *California Jewish Voice*, 16 March 1945, 14 December 1945.

15. Lawrence Bloomgarden, Field Report, 6–13 August 1945, Visits, California, Los Angeles (45–62), Box 10, General 13, Geographic/Domestic, AJC, YIVO; Vorspan and Gartner, *Jews of Los Angeles*, 265; Magnin,

"Leader and Personality," 151; Simon Greenberg, interview with author, 1 November 1989; Henry Montor, Oral History Interview, 15 April 1976, 21, Oral History of the UJA, Oral History Archives, ICJ, Hebrew University.

16. Ceplair and Englund characterize the Hollywood Independent Citizens Committee of the Arts, Sciences and Professions as a popular front group that contained communists and fellow travelers but whose leadership in 1946 was in the hands of liberals and left-wing Democrats. The latter two groups left HICCASP after losing a bitter fight over whether to endorse Will Rogers, Jr., an anticommunist liberal, or Ellis Patterson for a Senate seat later in 1946. See *The Inquisition in Hollywood*, 227–29, 237–39.

17. *California Jewish Voice*, 21 June 1946, 6 September 1946.

18. Samuel Lubell, *The Future of American Politics* (New York: Harper & Row, 1965), 102–3. Lubell notes (197) that all five precincts that Wallace carried in Los Angeles were Jewish and that Jewish supporters of Wallace in Los Angeles resembled his Jewish voters in the Bronx: Both lived in rapidly changing neighborhoods into which Negroes had started to move, and both were hurt by postwar inflation.

19. Lawrence Bloomgarden to A. Harold Murray, 10 May 1955, California/Los Angeles Chapter (52–62), Box 10, General 13, Geographic/Domestic, AJC, YIVO.

20. Otto Friedrich, *City of Nets* (New York: Harper & Row, 1987), 303–7; "In the Know," *California Jewish Voice*, 24 October 1947.

21. Quoted in John Cogley, *Report on Blacklisting* (New York: Fund for the Republic, 1956), I:22; Victor Navasky, *Naming Names* (New York: Viking Press, 1980), 83.

22. Melvin I. Urofsky, *We Are One!* (Garden City: Doubleday, 1978), 151; *California Jewish Voice*, 15 August 1947; Jacob Sonderling, Sermon #3, 16 September 1947, Sermons by Rabbi Jacob Sonderling for Rosh Hashanah and Yom Kippur 1947, Small Collections, AJA; Reuven Dafni, Oral History Interview, 16 March 1979, 6, Oral History of the UJA, Oral History Archives, ICJ, Hebrew University.

23. *California Jewish Voice*, 19 September 1947, 3 October 1947. The Hollywood Arts, Sciences and Professions Council of the Progressive Citizens of America produced the plays with Blankfort.

24. Walter S. Hilborn, "Reflections on Legal Practice and Jewish Community Leadership: New York and Los Angeles, 1907–1973," an oral history conducted in 1973 by Malca Chall, 129, Regional Oral History Office, The Bancroft Library, University of California, Berkeley, 1974, Courtesy of The Bancroft Library; Louis Boyar, Oral History Interview, 14 March 1976, 8, Oral History of the UJA, Oral History Archives, ICJ, Hebrew University.

25. Maurice J. Karpf to John Slawson, 19 June 1945, John Slawson to Maurice J. Karpf, 18 July 1945, Maurice J. Karpf MSS, 196, Box 1, 1/2, AJC, AJA.

26. Clancy Sigal, "Hollywood During the Great Fear," *Present Tense* 9 (Spring 1982): 47.

27. The CRC's predecessor was established in 1932 because of the need for a local committee to act against Nazi and antisemitic groups in Los Angeles. The committee gathered information on these hate groups and turned it over to several government agencies. Mendel Silberberg served as chair of this Community Committee, which had an "uptown" branch for movie people.

28. Joseph Roos quoted in Navasky, *Naming Names*, 110; Jacobs, *Is Curly Jewish?* 111; Lawrence Bloomgarden, Field Report, 6–13 August 1945, Visits, California, Los Angeles (45–62), Box 10, General 13, Geographic/Domestic, AJC, YIVO; Maxwell E. Greenberg, "Oral Memoirs," "*Not the Work of a Day*," II: 23–24.

29. Lillian Hellman took a different tack. Despite an upbringing as a Jew, she characterized her morals as following "ideals of Christian honor." Letter written to HUAC quoted in Cogley, *Report*, 101.

30. Navasky, *Naming Names*, 109–12; Sigal, "Hollywood During the Great Fear," 48.

31. Gang credits George Piness, president for many years of the Wilshire Boulevard Temple, for helping him get along with Silberberg. Martin Gang, Oral History, 42–43, 79, Oral History of the AJC, William E. Wiener Oral History Library, AJC.

32. Navasky characterizes Gang as a "collaborator." See *Naming Names*, 98–108, for his discussion of Gang's activities as a "clearance" lawyer.

33. Ceplair and Englund, *Inquisition*, 329; Martin Gang, Oral History, 77–81. Vorspan and Gartner, *Jews of Los Angeles*, 263, characterize CRC policy as "neutrality."

34. Frederick Schreiber to Manheim Shapiro, 16 April 1954, Reports, 1954–1953–1952, California/Los Angeles, Box 10, General 13, Geographic/Domestic, AJC, YIVO. In 1954, when Tenney was defeated in his reelection bid, his campaign included attacks on ADL as "the Jewish Gestapo."

35. See director's report in Minutes of the Annual Board Meeting, Soto-Michigan Jewish Community Center, 15 March 1949; and Minutes of Board Meeting of Soto-Michigan Jewish Community Center, 14 September 1948, JCA, Histories File, Archives, Jewish Community Library, JFC.

36. Lawrence Irell to Leslie Cramer, 19 October 1948, including exhibit A and B, JCA, Histories File, Archives, Jewish Community Library, JFC; Minutes of the Board Meeting, Soto-Michigan Jewish Community

Center, 22 October 1948. Among the letters of support were several from UOPWA locals. On membership loss, see Minutes, 14 December 1948 in JCA, Histories File, Archives, Jewish Community Library, JFC.

37. Letters of support in Minutes of Board Meeting of Soto-Michigan Jewish Community Center, 22 October 1948; membership loss and Welfare Federation letter in Minutes, 14 December 1948, JCA, Histories File, Archives, Jewish Community Library, JFC. The IWO was placed on the attorney general's list in 1947; Liebman, *Jews and the Left*, 312. Sam Bates to Lester Cramer, 14 December 1948, in Soto-Michigan Jewish Community Center Minutes, JCA, Histories File, Archives, Jewish Community Library, JFC.

38. Marker, "Communism and Liberalism," 25, 28; Naomi W. Cohen, *Not Free to Desist: The American Jewish Committee 1906–1966* (Philadelphia: Jewish Publication Society, 1972), 346–356.

39. Jacobs, *Is Curly Jewish?* 161; Report of the Special Committee to Study Jewish Community Council Institutional Members, 11 March 1949, revised and approved by Community Relations Committee, 18 March 1949, Communal Organizations, Jewish Community Council, California/Los Angeles (37–61), Box 10, General 13, Geographic/Domestic, AJC, YIVO.

40. Minutes of the Staff Meeting, 20 June 1950, Communal Organizations, Jewish Community Council, Community Relations Committee, Minutes, California/Los Angeles (49–54), Box 10, General 13, Geographic/Domestic, AJC, YIVO; *California Jewish Voice*, 25 March 1949; see also 15 April 1949; Minutes of Board of Soto-Michigan Jewish Community Center, 13 June 1950, JCA, Histories File, Archives, Jewish Community Library, JFC; Minutes of Meeting of Board of Directors, Beverly-Fairfax Jewish Community Center, 26 June 1950, 24 July 1950, Nathan Hurvitz MSS, 100, Box 1, Folder 7, JCA, May–August 1950, AJA; S. B. Gach, "In the Know," *California Jewish Voice*, 18 March 1949.

41. Charge by the Jewish War Veterans against the Jewish Peoples Fraternal Organization, 14 March 1950, Communal Organizations, Jewish Community Council, California/Los Angeles (37–61), Box 10, General 13, Geographic/Domestic, AJC, YIVO; Fred Reynolds, *California Jewish Voice*, 14 July 1950; letter to the editor from Abraham Held, Jewish Labor Committee, *California Jewish Voice*, 21 July 1950; S. B. Gach, "In the Know," *California Jewish Voice*, 21 July 1950, 11 August 1950.

42. Max Mont to Isaiah Terman, 30 August 1950, memo re: Los Angeles Ordinance for Registering Communists, Communal Issues, California/Los Angeles (45–60), Box 10, General 13, Geographic/Domestic, AJC, YIVO; "Report of the Membership Committee," Member's Kit for Seventeenth Annual Meeting of the Los Angeles Jewish Community Council, 28 January 1951, 49–51.

43. Quoted in column by Abraham Protes, *California Jewish Voice*, 12 March 1948; *Congress Bulletin* 3:3 (May-June 1948).

44. The CRC provided funds to help establish the Community Service Organization to address problems within the Mexican community. Jews saw the CSO as a potential coalition partner in politics that could help achieve such common goals as FEPC. Minutes of Meeting, Subcommittee on CSO, 31 August 1950, Committees and Officers, California/Los Angeles Chapter (44–62), Box 10, General 13, Geographic/Domestic, AJC, YIVO.

45. Chapter Leaders Workshop, 16 April 1959, California/Los Angeles Chapter (52–62), and Minutes of the Labor Advisory Committee of the American Jewish Committee, 15 February 1949, Committees and Officers, California/Los Angeles Chapter (44–62) and Report of visit of Isaiah Terman to Los Angeles, 14–15 December 1945, Visits, California, Los Angeles (45–62), in Box 10, General 13, Geographic/Domestic, AJC, YIVO.

46. The executive and administrative committees of the American Jewish Congress voted to expel JPFO from national and local branches in the spring of 1949. Marker, "Communism and Liberalism," 39–40.

47. *California Jewish Voice*, 28 October 1949; S. B. Gach, "In the Know," *California Jewish Voice*, 11 November 1949, 2 February 1951; see also 8 June 1951 on the lawsuit the locals instituted.

48. "Statement of Principles and Policies," adopted by board of trustees of the Jewish Centers Association, 10 March 1949, Nathan Hurvitz MSS, 100, 1/5, Los Angeles, JCA (1949), AJA.

49. Soto-Michigan's board voted to invite Alvin Wilder and Carey McWilliams to speak despite reservations expressed by the CRC. However, the board also decided to refuse the rental request of the Eastside Council for Rent Control. Minutes of Board of Soto-Michigan Center, 10 October 1950, 13 February 1951, JCA, Histories File, Archives, Jewish Community Library, JFC.

50. Herbert Morris Biskar, "A History of the Jewish Centers Association of Los Angeles with Special Reference to Jewish Identity," D.S.W. diss., University of Southern California, 1972, 69; Minutes of Meeting of Board of Directors, Beverly-Fairfax Jewish Community Center, 22 August 1949, Nathan Hurvitz MSS, 100, 1/5, Los Angeles JCA, AJA; Minutes of the Board Meeting, Soto-Michigan Community Center, 13 June 1950, JCA, Histories File, Archives, Jewish Community Library, JFC; *Digest of Public General Bills*, 81st Congress, 1st session, Final Issue (Washington: Library of Congress, 1949), 106.

51. Milton Malkin, "Report of Center Director to Board Meeting," 13 September 1950, Nathan Hurvitz, MSS, 100, 2/1, Los Angeles, JCA (September–December 1950); AJA, Minutes of Board Meeting of Soto-

Michigan Center, 12 April 1950, JCA, Histories File, Archives, Jewish Community Library, JFC.

52. This was the characterization of the anticommunist American Jewish Committee. Fred Schreiber to Manheim Shapiro, 20 March 1950, Communal Issues: Housing, California/Los Angeles (47–62), Box 10, General 13, Geographic/Domestic, AJC, YIVO. In an interview with Bertram Gold, 12 October 1989, he confirmed the left-wing and liberal character of the board.

53. Bertram Gold, interview with author, 12 October 1989; Minutes of Meeting of Board of Directors, Beverly-Fairfax Jewish Community Center, 23 May 1949, 1/5, and Report of Center Director to Board Meeting, 24 April 1950, Minutes of the Board of Beverly-Fairfax Jewish Community Center, 17 December 1951, 2/4 (September–December 1951), and Report of Center Director to Board Meeting, 29 May 1950, Minutes of Adult Education and Forum Committee Meeting, 11 May 1950, Beverly-Fairfax Jewish Community Center, 1/7, in Nathan Hurvitz MSS, 100, JCA, AJA.

54. Minutes of Meeting of Board of Directors, Beverly-Fairfax Center, 23 October 1950, Nathan Hurvitz MSS, 100, 1/7, JCA (May–August 1950), AJA; Ceplair and Englund, 100–104, 228, 438; Milton Malkin, "Report of Center Director to Board Meeting," 13 September 1950, Nathan Hurvitz MSS, 100, 2/1, JCA (September–December 1950), AJA.

55. Jacobs, *Is Curly Jewish?* 169 (emphasis in the original).

56. Louis Warschaw to Bernard Levin, 20 March 1951, Minutes of Board Meeting, Beverly-Fairfax Jewish Community Center, 30 April 1951, Nathan Hurvitz MSS, 100, 2/3, JCA (January–August 1951), AJA. The debates, which explicitly address whether communists, fellow travelers, and fascists should be allowed to speak on noncontroversial subjects, appear in several center contexts. For a particularly full discussion, see Minutes of the Board Meeting, Beverly-Fairfax Jewish Community Center, 17 December 1951, Nathan Hurvitz MSS, 100, 2/4, JCA, AJA.

57. Minutes of the Board Meeting, Beverly-Fairfax Jewish Community Center, 17 December 1951, Nathan Hurvitz MSS, 100, 2/4, JCA (September–December 1951), AJA. The federation backed the JCA's position of not inquiring into the political beliefs of staff. Minutes of the Board of Soto-Michigan Jewish Community Center, 27 November 1951, JCA, Histories File, Archives, Jewish Community library, JFC.

58. Minutes of the Board of Soto-Michigan Jewish Community Center, 14 February 1950, 13 March 1951, JCA, Histories File, Archives, Jewish Community library, JFC; Report of Center Director to Board Meeting, 20 February 1950; Milton Malkin, Report of Center Director to Annual Meeting, 8 March 1950, 4, Beverly-Fairfax Jewish Community Center,

Nathan Hurvitz MSS, 100, 1/6, JCA, AJA. See also *California Jewish Voice*, 24 March 1950, 31 March 1950, 7 April 1950; Seymour Soroky to Nathan Weisman, 13 October 1953, memo re: Communist Activity Among Social Workers, Communal Issues, California/Los Angeles (45–62), Box 10, General 13, Geographic/Domestic, AJC, YIVO; Biskar, "Jewish Centers Association," 76; Bertram Gold, "Report on Los Angeles" (27 July 1949), 8; Herbert Passameneck, "Study and Evaluation of the Jewish Centers Association and Constituent Centers of Los Angeles California" (February 1947), 55, 58, in JCA, Histories File, Archives, Jewish Community library, JFC.

59. Minutes of the Board of Soto-Michigan Jewish Community Center, 27 November 1951, JCA, Histories File, Archives, Jewish Community library, JFC; letter to the editor from Leo Zimmerman, *California Jewish Voice*, 21 December 1951.

60. Minutes of the Board of Soto-Michigan Center, 27 November 1951, 8 January 1952, and Resolution from the Menorah Center Board, Minutes of 10 July 1952, in Minutes of Soto-Michigan Jewish Community Center, JCA, Histories File, Archives, Jewish Community library, JFC.

61. Minutes of the Board of Soto-Michigan Jewish Community Center, 9 September 1952, JCA, Histories File, Archives, Jewish Community library, JFC.

62. The JCA also excluded any representative of Yiddish cultural interests. Minutes of the Board of Beverly-Fairfax Jewish Community Center, 25 May 1953, Nathan Hurvitz MSS, 100, 3, JCA (May–Sept. 1953), AJA.

63. Minutes of the Board of Beverly-Fairfax Jewish Community Center, 27 April 1953, Nathan Hurvitz MSS, 100, 3, JCA (Jan.-Apr. 1953), AJA; Bertram Gold, interview with author, 12 October 1989. Gold described the process as complementary: a desire to clean house, on the one hand, and an attempt to attract the Beverly Hills crowd, on the other. On Jewish cultural concerns, see, for example, Anne Pollock, "Report on Education Program," 1 February 1955, Westside Jewish Community Center, Nathan Hurvitz MSS, 100, 4/1, JCA, AJA. Pollock points out (2): "It is important for members of our Cabinet to be aware that we recognize that the Jewish purpose of our agency finds expression in each of our classes and activities."

64. Frederick Schreiber to Manheim Shapiro, 27 January 1953, Communal Organizations, Jewish Community Council (37–61), and Executive Committee Meeting Minutes, 11 February 1953, Reports (1954–1953–1952), and Report of the Resolutions Committee to the Nineteenth Annual Meeting of the Los Angeles Jewish Community Council, 25 January 1953, Communal Organizations/Jewish Community Council Resolutions Committee (53–57), and Frederick Schreiber to Nathan Weisman,

Report, 31 March to 31 May 1953, Reports (1954–1953–1952), in California/Los Angeles, Box 10, General 13, Geographic/Domestic, AJC, YIVO.

65. S. B. Gach, "In the Know," *California Jewish Voice*, 29 February 1952 emphasis in the original. *California Jewish Voice*, 29 February 1952, 7 March 1952, 14 March 1952 (emphasis in the original).

66. One of the doctors called before HUAC "declared that he is a Jew, and that the Jews are opposed to the methods used by the committee." Monthly Report, October 1952, Reports, California, Los Angeles (1954–1953–1952), Box 10, General 13, Geographic/Domestic, AJC, YIVO. The three physicians were Murray Abowitz, Richard W. Lippman, and Alexander E. Pennes. *California Jewish Voice*, 25 January 1952.

67. Report of the Resolutions Committee to the Annual Meeting of the Los Angeles Jewish Community Council, 25 January 1953, Communal Organizations, Jewish Community Council, Resolutions Committee, California/Los Angeles (53–57), Box 10, General 13, Geographic/Domestic, AJC, YIVO.

68. The Jewish Labor Committee and the American Jewish Committee wanted to get the Yikuf (Yiddish Kultur Farband), a Yiddish culture organization on the attorney general's list, and the Southland Jewish Organization, a left-wing group, removed from the L.A. Jewish Community Council. Monthly Report, August 1955, Reports (52–60), and Executive Board Meeting Minutes, 18 November 1956, Reports, 1956–1955, in California/Los Angeles Chapter, Box 10, General 13, Geographic/Domestic, AJC, YIVO.

69. Report of the Resolutions Committee to the Annual Meeting of the Los Angeles Jewish Community Council, 25 January 1953, Communal Organizations, Jewish Community Council, Resolutions Committee (53–57), and Frederick Schreiber to Nathan Weisman, Report, 30 September 1953–28 February 1954 and 1 March–30 June 1954, Reports (1954–1953–1952), and Report of the Resolutions Committee to the Twenty-second Annual Meeting, 29 January 1956, Reports, 1956–1955, in California/Los Angeles Chapter, Box 10, General 13, Geographic/Domestic, AJC, YIVO.

70. Report of the Resolutions Committee to the Twenty-third Annual Meeting, 27 January 1957, Communal Organizations, Jewish Community Council, Resolutions Committee, California/Los Angeles (53–57), Box 10, General 13, Geographic/Domestic, AJC, YIVO.

71. The San Francisco Board of Education rejected the program because of the votes of two Jewish board members.

72. Edith Swerdlow to I. M. Prinzmetal, 28 November 1949, memo re: Interim Report on Survey of Released-Time Program in the Los Angeles City School District, and Fred Herzberg to Lawrence Bloomgarden, 9

March 1948, in Communal Issues: Religion and Schools, California/Los Angeles (43–60), Box 10, General 13, Geographic/Domestic, AJC, YIVO; *California Jewish Voice*, 26 January 1945; *Bulletin of the Valley Jewish Community Center*, 24 January 1947.

73. Rabbi Rudolph Lupo served as the Jewish representative on the supervisory Interfaith Committee. Los Angeles City Board of Education, "Revised Communication of the Committee of the Whole, no. 1," Auxiliary Services Division, 18 August 1949, Communal Issues: Religion and Schools, California/Los Angeles (43–60), Box 10, General 13, Geographic/Domestic, AJC, YIVO.

74. Naomi W. Cohen, *Jews in Christian America* (New York: Oxford University Press, 1992), 140–146; memo to the files from Edith Swerdlow, 19 August 1949, Communal Issues: Religion and Schools, California/Los Angeles (43–60), Box 10, General 13, Geographic/Domestic, AJC, YIVO.

75. A. L. Wirin was the lawyer. He was also one of the few to oppose the deportation of Japanese during the war. Frederick Schreiber to David Danzig, 12 August 1949, Communal Issues: Religion and Schools, California/Los Angeles (43–60), Box 10, General 13, Geographic/Domestic, AJC, YIVO.

76. Theodore Leskes to John Slawson, 30 August 1949, Communal Issues: Religion and Schools, California/Los Angeles (49–60), and Program Survey Committee Minutes, 22 April 1949, Committees and Officers, Program Survey (49–50), in California/Los Angeles, Box 10, General 13, Geographic/Domestic, AJC, YIVO.

77. Report of the Resolutions Committee to the Twenty-first Annual Meeting of the Los Angeles Jewish Community Council, 30 January 1955, and Report of the Resolutions Committee to the Twenty-third Annual Meeting, Los Angeles Jewish Community Council, 27 January 1957, in Communal Organizations, Jewish Community Council Resolutions Committee, California/Los Angeles (53–57), Box 10, General 13, Geographic/Domestic, AJC, YIVO.

78. Sol Rabkin and Theodore Leskes to CRC offices, ADL offices, AJC offices, 9 December 1952, Communal Issues: Religion and Schools (43–60), and Background Memorandum for CRC Discussion, 23 March 1956, Reports (1955–56), and Frederick Schreiber to Nathan Weisman, Report, 31 March – 31 May 1953, Reports (1954–1953–1952), and Frederick Schreiber, Bi-Monthly Report, 26 April–25 June 1957, Reports, in California/Los Angeles, Box 10, General 13, Geographic/Domestic, AJC, YIVO; "Ban on Nativity Plays in Schools Provokes Anti-Jewish Propaganda," Jewish Telegraphic Agency, 10 April 1957.

79. The rationale in support cited the psychological value for the Jewish child and the importance of intercultural education as an antidote to potentially divisive Christmas celebrations. Opponents argued that the

issue involved interreligious activity and that this emphasized differences. Seymour Soroky and Haskell Lazere to Clarence Fielstra, 4 May 1953, Communal Issues: Religion and Schools, California/Los Angeles (43–60), Box 10, General 13, Geographic/Domestic, AJC, YIVO.

80. Frederick Schreiber to Nathan Weisman, Report, 1 January–28 February 1953, Reports (1954–1953–1952), and Executive Board Meeting Minutes, 14 May 1956, Reports (52–60), and Background Memorandum for CRC Discussion, 23 March 1956, Reports (1955–56), in California/Los Angeles Chapter, Box 10, General 13, Geographic/Domestic, AJC, YIVO.

81. Herman Silver was the last Jew to serve on the city council, from 1896 to 1900. S. B. Gach, "In the Know," *California Jewish Voice*, 24 April 1953.

82. Frederick Schreiber to Nathan Weisman, Report, 31 March–31 May 1953, Reports (1954–1953–1952), California/Los Angeles, Box 10, General 13, Geographic/Domestic, AJC, YIVO.

83. Rosalind Wiener Wyman, " 'It's a Girl': Three Terms on the Los Angeles City Council, 1953–65, Three Decades in the Democratic Party, 1948–1978," an oral history conducted 1977–1978 by Malca Chall, 23, Regional Oral History Office, The Bancroft Library, University of California, Berkeley, 1978. Courtesy of The Bancroft Library.

84. S. B. Gach, "In the Know," *California Jewish Voice*, 24 April 1953; Wyman, Oral History, 14.

85. Seymour Soroky to Nathan Weisman, Report, 1 June – 30 September, 1953, Reports (1954–1953–1952), California/Los Angeles, Box 10, General 13, Geographic/Domestic, AJC, YIVO; Wyman, Oral History, 50.

86. Wyman, Oral History, 50.

87. *California Jewish Voice*, 15 February 1957, S. B. Gach, "In the Know," 3 April 1953; Bi-Monthly Report, September–October 1957, Reports, California/Los Angeles, Box 10, General 13, Geographic/Domestic, AJC, YIVO.

88. This issue generated intra-Jewish conflict, specifically between the majority that supported public housing and antidiscrimination statutes and a handful of influential Jewish builders. Despite threats from the builders to withhold contributions, the CRC and LAJCC took public stands favoring unsegregated public housing. Neither body succeeded, however, in getting the Jewish builders who discriminated against Mexicans and Japanese to cease their practices. Frederick Schreiber, Monthly Report, Los Angeles, February 1952, Reports (1954–1953–1952), California/Los Angeles, Box 10, General 13, Geographic/Domestic, AJC, YIVO.

89. An ADL survey of regional schools found only four (12%) that asked no questions regarding race, religion, color, or national origin on their

application forms. Two were in the Los Angeles area, San Bernadino
Junior College and Santa Monica City College. *California Jewish Voice*,
25 February 1949.

90. On FEPC, see *California Jewish Voice*, 6 January 1950, 10 March 1950,
12 November 1954; on housing, see 30 May 1952; Frederick Schreiber,
Monthly Report, January 1956, February 1956, Reports, 1956–1955,
California/Los Angeles, Box 10, General 13, Geographic/Domestic, AJC,
YIVO; Wyman, Oral History, 75. For Roybal's role see: Reports, May
1955, California, Los Angeles (1956–1955), Box 10, General 13, Geo-
graphic/Domestic, AJC, YIVO. Labor included representatives from the
Steel Workers Union, CIO, AFL, Central Labor Council, Building
Trades Council. Fred Schreiber to Manheim Shapiro, 10 January 1958,
Communal Issues/Employment, California/Los Angeles (49–58), Box
10, General 13, Geographic/Domestic, AJC, YIVO.

91. Wilson, "A Guide to Reagan Country," 43–44. Wilson identifies young
Jews, intellectuals, persons transplanted from the East, and older California radicals as those most attracted to the clubs. The categories are
not necessarily mutually exclusive and Jews could be found in each.

92. Peter Medding, "Segmented Ethnicity and the New Jewish Politics,"
makes a similar point, 31. "Segmented Jewish ethnicity . . . has two major concerns: identity and continuity. Because group activity is necessary to secure these in pluralist societies, politics became increasingly
significant with regard both to respect—the group's capacity to win acceptance of its identity—and to power—the capacity to influence those
outcomes which will affect or determine continuity."

93. Fernando J. Guerra and Dwaine Marvick argue that the "Jewish take-
off" in Los Angeles electoral politics occurred in the 1970s, when Jews
moved beyond ethnic districts to win twenty-two positions. "Ethnic Of-
ficeholders and Party Activists in Los Angeles," in *ISSR Working Papers
in the Social Sciences*, Los Angeles, University of California, vol. 2, no.
12 (1986–87), 5–8.

94. Brown was running against a popular Republican governor. The Democrats controlled the state assembly (48–32) and the state senate
(27–13). Frederick Schreiber, Bi-Monthly Report, 16 October–15 December 1958, California/Los Angeles, Box 10, General 13, Geograph-
ic/Domestic, AJC, YIVO; Wyman, Oral History, 51; Halliwell, 150.

95. This was Proposition 16; Proposition 18, to outlaw the union shop, was
also defeated. Halliwell, 150–51; Frederick Schreiber, Bi-Monthly Report, 15 April–15 June 1958, and 16 October–15 December 1958, Reports, 1958, California/Los Angeles, Box 10, General 13, Geographic/
Domestic, AJC, YIVO. The rabbis had not been silent during the cold
war. The board passed a resolution condemning loyalty oaths for faculty
in the University of California.

96. In the 1960s Jews began to build public cultural institutions for the city, but sports came before music, art, and theater.

97. Wyman, 50, 75–76, 88–90, quote on 90 (emphasis in the original), Thomas S. Hines, "Housing, Baseball and Creeping Socialism: The Battle of Chavez Ravine, Los Angeles, 1949–1959, *Journal of Urban History* 8:2 (February 1982), 123–143. See also Raymond E. Wolfinger and Fred I. Greenstein, "The Repeal of Fair Housing in California: An Analysis of Referendum Voting," *The American Political Science Review* 62:3 (September 1968), 753–789.

98. Max Nussbaum, interview, 12 July 1963, n.p., Jerusalem, Israel, Biographies File, AJA.

Chapter 8. Israel as Frontier

1. Leonard Slater, *The Pledge* (New York: Simon & Schuster, 1970), 21–27; Julius Fligelman, Oral History Interview, 1 August 1979, 8, Oral History of the UJA, Oral History Archives, ICJ, Hebrew University.

2. Shepard Broad, Oral History Interview, 10 April 1977, 25, Oral History of the UJA, Oral History Archives, ICJ, Hebrew University.

3. Broad, Oral History, 3; Fligelman, Oral History, 8.

4. The other three were General Dori, Ze'ev Shind and Minna Ben-Zvi. In 1947 Teddy Kollek came, and Dafni returned in 1948. Dafni credits Marie Syrkin, who prevailed upon Golda Meir, for his being chosen, as well as his ability to speak English. Reuven Dafni, Oral History Interview, 16 March 1979, 1, Oral History of the UJA, Oral History Archives, ICJ, Hebrew University.

5. Isaac Imber, conversation with author, November 1992; Marie Syrkin, *Blessed Is the Match: The Story of Jewish Resistance* (Philadelphia: Jewish Publication Society, 1976), 33–39; Dafni, Oral History, 1–2.

6. Dafni's recollection is confirmed by Fred Zinnemann in his autobiography. See Fred Zinnemann, *An Autobiography: A Life in the Movies* (New York: Charles Scribner's Sons, 1992), 76. Quote from Dafni, Oral History, 6.

7. Dafni, Oral History, 3; Minutes of Annual Meeting of Jewish Community Council of the Bay Cities, 21 January 1948, Jewish Community Council of the Bay Cities, Histories File, Archives, Jewish Community library, JFC.

8. Zinnemann, *Autobiography*, 76.

9. Elizabeth Pallette, "Inspired by the Headlines," *New York Times*, 12 June 1949: II, 5–6.

10. Ibid.

11. Bosley Crowther, "On Taking Sides," *New York Times*, 28 August 1949: II, 1; *New York Times*, 23 August 1949; Bosley Crowther, review of *Sword in the Desert, New York Times*, 25 August 1949, 20.

12. Crowther, review of *Sword*, *New York Times*, 25 August 1949, 20.

13. An informal survey of a few Americans who remembered the movie indicated that Jews identified the film with Jeff Chandler and Christians with Dana Andrews.

14. Dafni, Oral History, 7.

15. Melvin I. Urofsky, *American Zionism from Herzl to the Holocaust* (Garden City: Doubleday, 1976), 259, 266–70.

16. Joseph D. Shane, Oral History Interview, 16 June 1977, 2, quote on 9, Oral History of the UJA, Oral History Archives, ICJ, Hebrew University.

17. S. Ilan Troen, "The 'American' Social-Economic School: The Reports of Elwood Mead and Robert Nathan," paper presented at conference on Envisioning Israel, Ben-Gurion University, 15 June 1993. Troen details Nathan's influential role in initiating the idea of Israel bonds, 16–18. See also Henry Morgenthau III, *Mostly Morgenthaus: A Family History* (New York: Ticknor & Fields, 1991), 411.

18. Louis Boyar, Oral History Interview, 14 March 1976, 5–6, Oral History of the UJA, Oral History Archives, ICJ, Hebrew University; Morgenthau III, *Morgenthaus*, 418.

19. *Jewish Floridian*, 13 February 1948. The dramatic article was written by Milton Malakoff, the public relations person for the UJA in Miami.

20. Morgenthau told Meir that it was his first visit to Miami.

21. Golda Meir, Oral History excerpt, *American Jewish Memoirs: Oral Documentation*, ed. Geoffrey Wigoder (Jerusalem, 1980), 85–87.

22. Fligelman, Oral History, 5; Minutes of the Board of Governors, Greater Miami Jewish Federation, 30 December 1952, Rosen files; Max Vorspan and Lloyd P. Gartner, *History of the Jews of Los Angeles* (Philadelphia: Jewish Publication Society, 1970), 270–271.

23. Only $1,101,000 was raised, so the UJA contribution was $530,000, or 53 percent of the total for 1949. *Jewish Floridian*, 13 January 1950.

24. The formula was worked out with the aid of UJA top brass, including Henry Montor. *Jewish Floridian*, 26 January 1951.

25. *Jewish Floridian*, 13 April 1951, 6 April 1951, 14 September 1951; Morgenthau III, *Morgenthaus*, 420.

26. In 1950 UJA received $583,487 from the CJA fund-raising; *Jewish Floridian*, 5 January 1951. The goal had been $810,000; *Jewish Floridian*, 13 January 1950.

27. *Jewish Floridian*, 18 May 1951, 16 November 1951, 25 May 1951, 14 September 1951, 30 November 1951, 1 February 1952.

28. Herbert Friedman, Oral History Interview, 7 December 1975 and 22 February 1976, 41, Oral History of the UJA, Oral History Archives, ICJ, Hebrew University; *Jewish Floridian*, 14 March 1952, 11 January 1952, 25 April 1952, 6 June 1952, 12 December 1952.

29. Minutes of the Executive Committee, Miami Jewish Federation, 23 April 1956, Rosen files; Morgenthau III, *Morgenthaus*, 418.

30. Minutes of Executive Committee, Greater Miami Jewish Federation, 26 February 1952, 22 March 1955, Rosen files; *Jewish Floridian*, 22 June 1956.

31. *Jewish Floridian*, 15 June 1956; "See It Now," 13 March 1956, at Jewish Museum's Broadcast Archives.

32. Mordecai Gur, Oral History Interview, 24 June 1979, 1–7, Oral History of the UJA, Oral History Archives, ICJ, Hebrew University.

33. Editorial, *Jewish Floridian*, 9 May 1958 and 1 June 1956; Minutes of the Executive Committee of the Board of Trustees of Temple Israel, 1 July 1958.

34. *Jewish Floridian*, 31 October 1958, 22 January 1960, 19 February 1960. The figures represented a significant decline for Miami's CJA fund-raising. In 1956 a survey of eighteen large cities in the United States and Canada indicated that only Miami and Cleveland exceeded the total funds raised in 1948, the peak year for contributions. *Jewish Floridian*, 10 August 1956.

35. For the difference in Zionist propaganda presented as dramatic pageant compared to a focus upon Israel as myth, see Atay Citron's dissertation on Ben Hecht's two pageants, "We Shall Never Die" and "A Flag Is Born," produced in 1943 and 1946, respectively, by the American arm of the Irgun: "Pageantry and Theatre in the Service of Jewish Nationalism in the United States, 1933–46," New York University, 1989, 276–421.

36. The movie's logo included flames licking at raised, clenched fists, one of which held a gun.

37. Thomas Schatz, *Old Hollywood/New Hollywood* (Ann Arbor: UMI Research Press, 1983), 170–72; Stanley Kramer, "Politics, Social Comment, and My Emotions," *Films and Filming*, June 1960: 7.

38. Neil Gabler, *An Empire of Their Own* (New York: Crown, 1988), 300–302, quote on 300; Schatz, *Old Hollywood*, 174, 186.

39. "Stanley Kramer," in *Directors at Work*, ed. Bernard Kantor, Irwin R. Blacker, Anne Kramer (New York: Funk & Waynalls, 1970), 178; Stanley Kramer, "The Independent Producer," *Films in Review* II: 3 (March 1951): 1, 4 (emphasis in the original); Roy Newquist, *A Special Kind of Magic* (New York: Rand McNally, 1967), 27.

40. Quoted in Patricia Erens, *The Jew in American Cinema* (Bloomington: Indiana University Press, 1984), 217.

41. Dmytryk quoted in Erens, 216, see also 217; Kirk Douglas, *The Ragman's Son* (New York: Simon & Schuster, 1988), 203–4.

42. Approximately 40 percent of the scenes were shot in Israel. The interiors were done in Hollywood because of the lack of proper equipment in Israel. Donald Spoto, *Stanley Kramer, Film Maker* (New York: G. P. Putnam's Sons, 1978), 141.

43. Otis Guernsey, Jr., quoted in Spoto, *Stanley Kramer*, 143; Bernard Dick, *Radical Innocence* (Lexington: University Press of Kentucky, 1989), 153; Dana Adams Schmidt, "Charting the Trail of the 'Juggler' in Israel," *New York Times*, 23 November 1952, II: 5.

44. Michael Blankfort, *The Juggler*, revised final draft, 10 July 1952, 85. Columbia Production # 8091 (The Stanley Kramer Company, Inc.), in Stanley Kramer MSS, Collection 161, Box 5, UCLA Special Collections.

45. The site itself suggests that perhaps Hans is right: Home is a place you lose. Once home to Arabs, the village now implicitly points to their homelessness.

46. Dore Schary, "What Judaism Means to Me," in *The Golden Land*, ed. Azriel Eisenberg (New York: Thomas Yoseloff, 1964), 476. Lester D. Friedman, *Hollywood's Image of the Jew* (New York: Frederick Ungar, 1982), 190–91, and Erens, *Jew in American Cinema*, 217–18, offer slightly different accounts of the movie's genesis.

47. Uris quoted in "Leon Uris," in *Something About the Author*, ed. Anne Commire (Detroit: Gale Research Company), 49: 189; Friedman, *Hollywood's Image of the Jew*, 190; Uris quoted in Philip Roth, "Some New Jewish Stereotypes," in *Reading Myself and Others* (New York: Farrar, Straus, Giroux, 1975), 138.

48. Seth S. King, "'Exodus' and Israel," *New York Times*, 4 October 1959, sec. II, part 2, 1, 8; Harold U. Ribalow, "A Look at the 'Israel Novel,'" *Congress BiWeekly*, 25 December 1961, 19; Joel Blocker, "Fantasy of Israel," *Commentary* 27 (1959): 539; Joel Carmichael, "The Phenomenal Leon Uris," *Midstream*, Autumn 1961: 89.

49. Frank Cantor, "A Second Look at *Exodus*," *Jewish Currents*, November 1959: 20–21 (emphasis in the original); and Yehuda Lev, "Letter from Israel," *Sentinel*, 3 April 1959, quoted in Cantor, 40.

50. Blocker, "Fantasy," 541; as reported by Milton Friedman in *Rochester Jewish Ledger*, 17 July 1959, quoted by Cantor, "A Second Look at *Exodus*," 40.

51. Philip Roth, "Some New Jewish Stereotypes," 145–46.

52. Quoted in "'Exodus' and Israel," *New York Times*, 4 October 1959, sec. II, part 2, 1, 8; Carmichael, "Phenomenal Leon Uris," 89.

53. Dan Wakefield, "Israel's Need for Fiction," *Nation* (11 April 1959), 318; Dore Schary, *Heyday* (Boston: Little Brown, 1979), 3.

54. Quoted in Gerald Pratley, *The Cinema of Otto Preminger*, International Film Guide Series (New York: A.S. Barnes, 1971), 66; Schatz, *Old Hollywood*, 186; Jacques Lourcelles, *Otto Preminger*, Cinema d'Aujourdui (Paris: Editions Seghers, 1965), 61.

55. Otto Preminger, *Preminger: An Autobiography* (Garden City, N.Y.: Doubleday, 1977), 165–66; Friedman, *Hollywood's Image*, 190.

56. Quoted in Pratley, *Cinema of Otto Preminger*, 133–35.

57. Trumbo had just finished the script for *Spartacus*, another epic film, which may account for some of the epic qualities of *Exodus*.

58. Bosley Crowther, Review of *Exodus*, *New York Times*, 16 December 1960, 44; *Time*, 19 December 1960, 69; *New York Times*, 20 January 1960, 1; 10 February 1960, 42; 22 December 1960, 16. The criticism of Kramer was for hiring Nedrick Young, under the pseudonym of Nathan Douglas, to write the screenplay of *The Defiant Ones*. Douglas/Young won an Academy Award for the movie in 1959 after the Motion Picture Academy of Arts and Sciences dropped its anticommunist ban as "unworkable and unpractical."

59. Friedman, *Hollywood's Image*, 192.

60. Friedman, *Hollywood's Image*, 192–93, 263, quote on 192; Willi Frischauer, *Behind the Scenes of Otto Preminger* (London: Michael Joseph, 1973), 195, on gross; Preminger, *Preminger*, 166, on budget; Stone quoted in Erens, *Jew in American Cinema*, 219.

61. Charles Liebman, *The Ambivalent American Jew* (Philadelphia: Jewish Publication Society, 1973), vii; Lothar Kahn observes in "The Magic of *Exodus*," *Congress Bi-Weekly*, 30 March 1959, 16, that "Not one of Uris' characters has either qualms about, or quarrels with his Jewishness."

62. Joe Hyams, "Miss Saint Happy in *Exodus* Role," clipping, 14 June 1960, in *Exodus* file, David Matis collection, Steven Spielberg Jewish Film Archives, Hebrew University.

63. *New York Times*, 11 May 1960.

64. Preminger quoted in Frischauer, *Behind the Scenes*, 195; Preminger, *Preminger*, 169.

65. Critics praised Mineo's portrait of Dov, a young Holocaust survivor. Like Douglas, Mineo plays a damaged, sick soul. But Dov's embrace of violence suggests that the military discipline of hatred learned by training as a terrorist and the release that comes from fighting back is more therapeutic than just the love of a woman and a return to the homeland. Perhaps revenge can redeem the shame of victimization.

66. "Movies," the critic Molly Haskell writes, "blur the distinction between us and them, between imagination and reality. They deal in myth, thus redemption." Molly Haskell, "Is It Time to Trust Hollywood?" *New York Times Book Review*, 28 January 1990: 36.

67. Hortense Powdermaker, *Hollywood, the Dream Factory* (Boston: Little, Brown, 1950), 13.

68. Carmichael, "Phenomenal Leon Uris," 90.

69. *Jewish Floridian*, 19 December 1958; Stephen J. Whitfield, "Value Added: Jews in Postwar American Culture," in *Studies in Contemporary Jewry*, 8 (New York: Oxford University Press, 1992), 77–79; *Forward*, 16

April 1961, 7, carried a full-page El Al ad filled with pictures from the movie for a 16-day Exodus-tour of Israel.

70. "A Symposium: Jewishness and the Younger Intellectuals," *Commentary*, April 1961: 306, questions on 311. For examples of ambivalence, see Irving Feldman, 321, Enoch Gordis, 324, Andrew Hacker, 327, John Hollander, 331, Michael Maccoby, 341. There were also a handful of expressions of straightforward commitment, e.g., Elihu Katz, 335, Herbert Gold, 323, Robert Lifton, 340.

71. The quote is from Joseph Kraft, "A Symposium," *Commentary*, 336. For a similar statement, see Edgar Rosenberg, 350. "I must have shared with many Jews an instinctive and altogether Byzantine sense of triumph at the news of the Israeli blitzkrieg. But I feel no political ties whatever to the State of Israel."

72. Alexander Bloom's book on the New York Jewish intellectuals, *Prodigal Sons: The New York Intellectuals and Their World* (New York: Oxford University Press, 1986); does not even include Zionism or Israel in the index. Midge Dector, writing in *Commentary*, admitted that she adamantly refused to read *Exodus* for two years but when she did pick it up, she couldn't put it down. "Popular Jews," *Commentary*, October 1961: 358.

73. On the response of the Jewish community, see Philip Roth, "Writing About Jews," in *Reading Myself and Others*, 149–69. Quote of Uris in letter to Whitfield on responses received to *Exodus*, in "Value Added," 8:78.

74. Erens, *Jew in American Cinema*, 220.

75. Philip Roth, "Some New Jewish Stereotypes," 146.

76. Urofsky, *We Are One*, 240–41.

Chapter 9. The New American Jew

1. Quoted in Robert Reinhold, "California, Land of Crises, Mingles Despair and Hope," *New York Times*, 31 July 1992: A14.

2. Werner Sollors, *Beyond Ethnicity: Consent and Descent in American Culture* (New York: Oxford University Press, 1986), chap. 7, esp. 230–36.

3. Arthur Hertzberg, *The Jews in America: Four Centuries of an Uneasy Encounter* (New York: Simon and Schuster, 1989), 388, argues that "American Jewish history will soon end."

4. I. B. Singer, interview, in *My Love Affair with Miami Beach* (New York: Simon & Schuster, 1991), 2; quoted in Charles S. Liebman, "Ritual, Ceremony and the Reconstruction of Judaism in the United States," *Studies in Contemporary Jewry*, 6 (New York: Oxford University Press, 1990): 276.

5. Bruce Phillips, Lecture at conference on Jews in Los Angeles, UCLA, 6 May 1990; quoted in Reinhold, "California, Land of Crises," A14; Steven Huberman, "Demographic Highlights of the Los Angeles Jewish Community" (Los Angeles: Jewish Federation Council of Greater Los Angeles, 1987), Table 1: n.p.; Ira M. Sheskin, "The Changing Geographic Distribution of the Jewish Population in Dade County," *Florida Jewish Demography*, ed. Ira M. Sheskin, 4: 1 (1 December 1990); Cunin quoted in Neil Reisner, "Rabbinical Movers and Shakers," *Present Tense* 9 (Spring 1982): 44.

6. Marshall Sklare and Joseph Greenblum, *Jewish Identity on the Suburban Frontier: A Study of Group Survival in the Open Society* (Chicago: University of Chicago Press, 1967), 44.

7. Peter Medding, "Segmented Ethnicity and the New Jewish Politics," *Studies in Contemporary Jewry* 3 (Oxford: Oxford University Press, 1987): 29; Liebman, "Ritual, Ceremony and the Reconstruction of Judaism," 275.

8. Nathan Glazer and Daniel Patrick Moynihan, *Beyond the Melting Pot* (Boston: MIT Press, 1963), 137–80; Sklare and Greenblum, *Jewish Identity*, 48.

9. David Rieff, *Going to Miami* (New York: Penguin Books, 1988), 36; Mike Davis, *City of Quartz* (New York: Vintage Books, 1992), chap. 7; David Rieff, *Los Angeles: Capital of the Third World* (New York: Simon & Schuster, 1991).

10. Robert A. Masullo, "The Flavor of the Bronx, The Taste of the Bronx," *Bronx Times*, Summer 1985: 1; *Bronx Times*, Summer 1985: 2; see also 2: 2 (Fall Winter 1987): 3. "A punchball game was organized on the loading dock of the Clothing Mart which was a realistic setting for a game which was usually played on city streets."

11. *B'nai B'rith Messenger*, 28 June 1985; Isaiah Zeldin, "Thoughts on the Installation of Officers," *Amarim* (May 1969); "Rabbi's Message," in *Once upon A Mountaintop: The Story of the Stephen S. Wise Temple*, Fred Plotkin et al. (Los Angeles, 1989), 52; Minutes of the Meeting of the Board of Trustees of Temple Israel, 4 March 1952, 10 January 1955, 14 March 1955.

12. *B'nai B'rith Messenger*, 28 June 1985.

13. Isaiah Zeldin, "Rabbi's Message," *News and Views* (October 1964); *Once upon a Mountaintop*, chap. 10, 14; Reisner, "Rabbinical Movers and Shakers," 45.

14. On Schulweis, see Neil Reisner, "Encino and Harold Schulweis," *Present Tense* 9 (Spring 1982): 37–39.

15. Phillip S. Hammond, "Religion and the Persistence of Identity," *Journal for the Scientific Study of Religion* 27:1 (1988): 2. Hammond is discussing

American Christianity, but his observations ring true for American Judaism.

16. Charles Liebman and Steven Cohen call this "historical familism." *Two Worlds of Judaism: The Israeli and American Experiences* (New Haven: Yale University Press, 1990), chap. 2.

17. Most notably, Will Herberg's influential *Protestant, Catholic, Jew.* There were also several considerably more gloomy predictions, e.g., Nathan Glazer, *American Judaism* (Chicago: University of Chicago Press, 1957); Herbert Gans, "American Jewry: Present and Future," *Commentary*, May 1956, 422–430, and "The Future of American Jewry: Part II," *Commentary* and the debate between Oscar Handlin and Jacob Marcus, "The Goals of Survival: What Will U. S. Jewry Be Like in 2000?" in *National Jewish Monthly*, May 1957: 4–6, 32–33.

18. Thomas B. Morgan, "The Vanishing American Jew," *Look*, 5 May 1964. See also articles by Irving Spiegel in the *New York Times*, 19 April 1964: 44; 22 April 1964: 44; 30 April 1964: 25; 28 June 1964: 36.

19. See, for example, Charles Liebman, *The Ambivalent American Jew* (Philadelphia: Jewish Publication Society, 1973); Gans, "American Jewry: Present and Future," 427–429; Abraham G. Duker, "Emerging Culture Patterns in American Jewish Life," *Publications of the American Jewish Historical Society* 39:4 (June 1950), 351–388.

20. *Highlights of the CJF 1990 National Jewish Population Survey*, Council of Jewish Federations (New York: Council of Jewish Federations, 1991), 10, 13–14, 25–26.

21. Barry A. Kosmin, "Exploring and Understanding the Findings of the 1990 National Jewish Population Survey," 6, paper prepared for the Sidney Hollander Colloquium, Wilstein Institute, July 7–10, 1991.

22. Moses Rischin, Foreword to *The Jews of Los Angeles, 1849–1945*, ed. Sara G. Cogan (Berkeley: Western Jewish History Center, Judah L. Magnes Memorial Museum, 1980), viii.

23. Morgan, "The Vanishing American Jew," *Look*.

Selected Bibliography

Major Manuscript Sources

American Jewish Archives:
  Hebrew Union College–Jewish Institute of Religion papers
  Nathan Hurvitz papers
  Maurice J. Karpf papers
American Jewish Historical Society:
  National Jewish Welfare Board papers
  American Association of Jewish Education papers
  Council of Jewish Federations and Welfare Funds papers
Archives of Jewish Community Library, Jewish Federation Council
  Jewish Centers Association, Histories file
YIVO Institute for Jewish Research
  American Jewish Committee papers, Domestic files

Major Oral History Sources

Bancroft Library, Regional Oral History Office
Columbia University Oral History Archives
Institute of Contemporary Jewry, Hebrew University:
  Oral History of the United Jewish Appeal
William E. Wiener Oral History Library, American Jewish Committee

Selected Sources

Abbott, Carl. *The New Urban America: Growth and Politics in Sunbelt Cities*. Chapel Hill: University of North Carolina Press, 1987.

Allman, T. D. *Miami: City of the Future*. New York: Atlantic Monthly Press, 1987.

Bardin, Shlomo. "The Brandeis Camp Institute." *Jewish Education* 17, 5 (June 1946): 26–27.

Berman, Aaron. *Nazism, the Jews and American Zionism 1933–1948*. Detroit: Wayne State University Press, 1990.

Biskar, Herbert Morris. "A History of the Jewish Centers Association of Los Angeles with Special Reference to Jewish Identity." D.S.W. Thesis, University of Southern California, 1972.

Blankfort, Michael. *The Strong Hand*. Boston: Little, Brown & Co., 1956.

Carmichael, Joel. "The Phenomenal Leon Uris." *Midstream* (Autumn 1961): 86–90.

Carson, Ruby Leach. "Forty Years of Miami Beach." *Tequesta: The Journal of the Historical Association of Southern Florida* 15 (1955): 3–27.

Ceplair, Larry, and Steven Englund. *The Inquisition in Hollywood: Politics in the Film Community 1930–1960*. Garden City, N.Y.: Anchor Press, 1980.

Citron, Atay. "Pageantry and Theater in the Service of Jewish Nationalism in the United States, 1933–1946." Ph.D. diss., New York University, 1989.

Cogley, John. *Report on Blacklisting*. New York: Fund for the Republic, 1956.

Cohen, Naomi W. *Jews in Christian America: The Pursuit of Religious Equality*. New York: Oxford University Press, 1992.

Cunningham, Lynn Craig. "Venice, California: From City to Suburb." Ph.D. diss., University of California, Los Angeles, 1976.

Davis, Mike. *City of Quartz: Excavating the Future in Los Angeles*. New York: Vintage Books, 1990.

Davka 5, 3 (October 1973): 4–51.

Dawidowicz, Lucy, and Leon J. Goldstein. *Politics in a Pluralist Democracy: Studies of Voting in the 1960 Election*. New York: Institute of Human Relations Press, 1963.

Dick, Bernard F. *Radical Innocence: A Critical Study of the Hollywood Ten*. Lexington, Ky.: University Press of Kentucky, 1989.

Didion, Joan. *Miami*. New York: Pocket Books, 1987.

Douglas, Kirk. *The Ragman's Son*. New York: Simon & Schuster, 1988.

Erens, Patricia. *The Jew in American Cinema*. Bloomington: Indiana University Press, 1984.

Fine, David, ed. *Los Angeles in Fiction*. Albuquerque: University of New Mexico Press, 1984.

Fishman, Robert. *Bourgeois Utopias: The Rise and Fall of Suburbia*. New York: Basic Books, 1987.

Friedman, Lester D. *Hollywood's Image of the Jew*. New York: Frederick Ungar Publishing Co., 1982.

Friedman, Murray, ed. *Philadelphia Jewish Life 1940–1985*. Ardmore, Pa.: Seth Press, 1984.

Friedrich, Otto. *City of Nets: A Portrait of Hollywood in the 1940s*. New York: Harper & Row, 1987.

Frischauer, Willi. *Behind the Scenes with Otto Preminger*. London: Michael Joseph, 1973.

Gabler, Neil. *An Empire of Their Own: How the Jews Invented Hollywood*. New York: Crown, 1988.

George, Paul S. "An Enduring Covenant: Temple Emanu-El of Greater Miami 1938–1988." In *Event of the Decade, Temple Emanu-El of Greater Miami Tribute Album*, 9–78. Miami, 1988.

Glazer, Nathan. "Notes on Southern California." *Commentary* 28 (July 1959): 100–107.

Glazer, Nathan, and Daniel Patrick Moynihan. *Beyond the Melting Pot: The Negroes, Puerto Ricans, Jews, Italians and Irish of New York City*. Cambridge, Mass.: M.I.T. Press, 1963.

Goldfield, David R. *Promised Land: The South since 1945*. Arlington Heights, Ill.: Harlan Davidson, 1987.

Gordon, Albert I. *Jews in Suburbia*. Boston: Beacon Press, 1959.

Halliwell, Michael John. "California Politics: Key Statewide Contests and Issues, 1958–1966." Ph.D. diss., University of California, Los Angeles, 1974.

Hammond, Phillip E. "Religion and the Persistence of Identity." *Journal for the Scientific Study of Religion* 27, 1 (1988): 1–11.

Hecht, Ben. *A Child of the Century*. New York: Simon & Schuster, 1954.

Henstell, Bruce. *Los Angeles: An Illustrated History*. New York: Knopf, 1980.

Hentoff, Nat. *Boston Boy*. New York: Knopf, 1986.

Heymont, Irving. *Among the Survivors of the Holocaust: The Landsberg DP Letters of Major Irving Heymont, United States Army*. Cincinnati: American Jewish Archives, 1982.

Holland, Max. *When the Machine Stopped: A Cautionary Tale from Industrial America*. Boston: Harvard Business School Press, 1989.

Howe, Irving. *A Margin of Hope: An Intellectual Autobiography*. New York: Harcourt, Brace, Jovanovich, 1982.

Hughes, H. Stuart. "California—The America to Come." *Commentary* 21 (May 1956): 454–460.

Isaacs, Stephen D. *Jews and American Politics*. Garden City, N.Y.: Doubleday, 1974.

Jackson, Kenneth. *Crabgrass Frontier: The Suburbanization of the United States*. New York: Oxford University Press, 1985.

Jacobs, Paul. *Is Curly Jewish?: A Political Self-Portrait Illuminating Three Turbulent Decades of Social Revolt—1935–1965*. New York: Vintage Books, 1965.

Janowitz, Morris. *Judaism of the Next Generation*. Miami: Rostrum Books, 1969.

Kanfer, Stefan. *A Journal of the Plague Years*. New York: Atheneum, 1973.

Kaplan, Mordecai M. *A University of Judaism: A Compelling Need*. New York: United Synagogue of America, 1946.

Katzman, Jacob. *Commitment*. New York: Labor Zionist Letters, 1975.

Key, V. O. *Southern Politics in State and Nation*. New York: Vintage Books, 1949.

Kligsberg, Moses. "American Jewish Soldiers on Jews and Judaism." *YIVO Annual of Jewish Social Science* 5 (1950): 256–265.

Kohs, Samuel. "The Jewish Community of Los Angeles." *The Jewish Review* 2 (July–October 1944): 87–126.

Lawson, Steven F. "The Florida Legislative Investigation Committee and the Constitutional Readjustment of Race Relations, 1956–1963." In *An Uncertain Tradition: Constitutionalism and the History of the South*, ed. Kermit L. Hall and James W. Ely, 296–325. Athens, Ga.: University of Georgia Press, 1989.

Liebman, Arthur. *Jews and the Left*. New York: John Wiley & Sons, 1979.

Liebman, Charles. *The Ambivalent American Jew: Politics, Religion and Family in American Jewish Life*. Philadelphia: Jewish Publication Society, 1973.

————"Ritual, Ceremony and the Reconstruction of Judaism in the United States." *Studies in Contemporary Jewry* 6 (1990): 272–285.

Lourcelles, Jacques. *Otto Preminger*. Paris: Editions Seghers, 1965.

Lubell, Samuel. *The Future of American Politics*. New York: Harper & Row, 1965.

May, Lary. *Screening Out the Past: The Birth of Mass Culture and the Motion Picture Industry*. New York: Oxford University Press, 1980.

Mazur, Edward. "Jewish Chicago: From Diversity to Community." *Ethnic Chicago*, ed. Melvin G. Holli and Peter d'A. Jones, 69–108. Grand Rapids: William B. Eerdmans, 1984.

McNally, Michael J. *Catholicism in South Florida 1868–1968*. Gainesville: University of Florida Press, 1982.

Medding, Peter Y. "Segmented Ethnicity and the New Jewish Politics." *Studies in Contemporary Jewry* 3 (1987): 26–48.

Medved, Michael, and David Wallechinsky. *What Really Happened to the Class of '65?*. New York: Random House, 1976.

Meyer, Michael A. "A Centennial History." In *Hebrew Union College–Jewish Institute of Religion at One Hundred Years*, ed. Samuel E. Karff, 1–283. Cincinnati: Hebrew Union College Press, 1976.

Millon, Adrienne Rebecca. "The Changing Size and Spatial Distribution of the Jewish Population of South Florida." Master's thesis, University of Miami, 1989.

Mulcahy, Patrick Herbert. "Urban Social and Spatial Structure: A Case Study of Los Angeles Voting Patterns, 1960–1968." Ph.D. diss., University of California, Los Angeles, 1971.

Myerhoff, Barbara. *Number Our Days*. New York: E. P. Dutton, 1978.

Nash, Gerald D. *The American West Transformed: The Impact of the Second World War*. Bloomington: Indiana University Press, 1985.

Navasky, Victor. *Naming Names*. New York: Viking, 1980.

Newquist, Roy. *A Special Kind of Magic*. New York: Rand McNally, 1967.

Perlmutter, Nathan. *A Bias of Reflections: Confessions of an Incipient Old Jew*. New Rochelle, N.Y.: Arlington House, 1972.

————"Bombing in Miami: Anti-Semitism and the Segregationists." *Commentary* 25 (June 1958): 498–503.

Phillips, Bruce A. "Los Angeles Jewry: A Demographic Portrait." *American Jewish Year Book* (1986): 126–194.

Powdermaker, Hortense. *Hollywood, The Dream Factory: An Anthropologist Looks at the Movie-Makers*. Boston: Little, Brown & Co., 1950.

Pratley, Gerald. *The Cinema of Otto Preminger*. New York: A. S. Barnes & Co., 1971.

Preminger, Otto. *Preminger: An Autobiography*. Garden City, N.Y.: Doubleday, 1977.

Present Tense 9, 3 (Spring 1982): 28–48.

Rawitch, Cynthia, and Robert Rawitch. "The First 50 Years, Adat Ari El." North Hollywood, Calif.: 1988.

Reconstructionist 18, 15 (28 November 1952): 8–32.

Redford, Polly. *Billion-Dollar Sandbar: A Biography of Miami Beach*. New York: E. P. Dutton, 1970.

Rieff, David. *Going to Miami: Exiles, Tourists, and Refugees in the New America*. New York: Penguin Books, 1987.

————*Los Angeles: Capital of the Third World*. New York: Simon & Schuster, 1991.

Rontch, Isaac E., ed. *Jewish Youth at War: Letters from American Soldiers*. New York: Marstin Press, 1945.

Rosenberg, Bernard, and Ernest Goldstein, eds. *Creators and Disturbers: Reminiscences by Jewish Intellectuals of New York*. New York: Columbia University Press, 1982.

Rosenthal, Erich. "This Was North Lawndale: The Transplantation of a Jewish Community." *Jewish Social Studies* 12, 2 (April 1960): 67–82.

Sandberg, Neil C. *Jewish Life in Los Angeles: A Window to Tomorrow*. Lanham, Md.: University Press of America, 1986.

Sanua, Marianne. "From the Pages of the Victory Bulletin." *YIVO Annual* 19 (1990): 283–330.

Schary, Dore. *Heyday*. Boston: Little, Brown, 1979.

Schatz, Thomas. *Old Hollywood/New Hollywood: Ritual, Art, and Industry*. Ann Arbor, Mich.: UMI Research Press, 1983.

Shafter, Toby. "Miami: 1948." *Jewish Frontier* 15 (January 1948): 18–20.

Shapiro, Manheim S. *The Bayville Survey of Jewish Attitudes*, American Jewish Committee, New York, 1961.

Sheskin, Ira M. "The Changing Geographic Distribution of the Jewish Population in Dade County." In *Florida Jewish Demography*, ed. Ira M. Sheskin. 1 December 1990.

Shevky, Eshref, and Marilyn Williams. *The Social Areas of Los Angeles*. Berkeley: University of California Press, 1949.

Silk, Mark. *Spiritual Politics: Religion and America since World War II*. New York: Simon & Schuster, 1988.

Simon, Kate. *Bronx Primitive*. New York: Viking, 1982.

Simons, Howard. *Jewish Times: Voices of the American Jewish Experience*. Boston: Houghton, Mifflin, 1988.

Singer, Isaac Bashevis. "My Love Affair with Miami Beach." In *My Love Affair With Miami Beach*, ed. Richard Nagler. New York: Simon & Schuster, 1991.

Sklare, Marshall, and Joseph Greenblum. *Jewish Identity on the Suburban Frontier: A Study of Group Survival in the Open Society*. Chicago: University of Chicago Press, 1979.

Sofen, Edward. *The Metropolitan Miami Experiment*. Bloomington: Indiana University Press, 1963.

Sontag, Susan. *On Photography* New York: Anchor Books, 1990.

Sorauf, Frank J. *The Wall of Separation: The Constitutional Politics of Church and State*. Princeton: Princeton University Press, 1976.

Sorin, Gerald. *The Nurturing Neighborhood: The Brownsville Boys Club and Jewish Community in Urban America, 1940–1990*. New York: New York University Press, 1990.

Spoto, Donald. *Stanley Kramer, Film Maker*. New York: G. P. Putnam & Sons, 1978.

Uris, Leon. *Exodus*. Garden City, N.Y.: Doubleday, 1958.

Urofsky, Melvin I. *American Zionism from Herzl to the Holocaust*. Garden City, N.Y.: Anchor Books, 1976.

———*We Are One!: American Jewry and Israel*. Garden City, N.Y.: Anchor Press/Doubleday, 1978.

Vorspan, Max. "Los Angeles." *Midstream* (February 1969): 43–48.

Vorspan, Max and Lloyd P. Gartner. *History of the Jews of Los Angeles*. Philadelphia: Jewish Publication Society of America, 1970.

Warren, Earl. *Memoirs of Earl Warren*. Garden City, N.Y.: Doubleday, 1977.

Whitfield, Stephen J. "Value Added: Jews in Postwar American Culture." *Studies in Contemporary Jewry* 8 (1993): 68–84.

Wilson, James Q. "A Guide to Reagan Country: The Political Culture of Southern California." *Commentary* (May 1967): 37–45.

Wolf, Alfred, and Dan Wolf. "Wilshire Boulevard Temple Camps, 1949–1974." In *Wilshire Boulevard Temple Camps: The first 25 years 1949–1974, A Personal History*, ed. Alfred Wolf, 5–17. Los Angeles: Wilshire Boulevard Temple, 1975.

Wolff, Reinhold P. *Case Studies in South Florida Manufacturing Industries*. Coral Gables: University of Miami, 1963.

Wolff, Reinhold P., and David K. Gillogly. *Negro Housing in the Miami Area: Effects of the Postwar Building Boom*. Miami: Bureau of Business and Economic Research, University of Miami, 1951.

Wood, Thomas J. "Dade County: Unbossed, Erratically Led." *Annals of the American Academy of Political and Social Science* (May 1964): 64–70.

Workers of the Writers' Program of the Work Projects Administration in the State of Florida. *Guide to Miami and Environs*. Northport, N.Y.: Bacon, Percy & Daggett, 1941.

Zinnemann, Fred. *An Autobiography: A Life in the Movies*. New York: Charles Scribner's Sons, 1992.

Index

Roosevelt, Franklin D., 8, 15, 57, 157–58, 191
Rootlessness, 62–63, 71, 94, 156, 267
Rose, Billy, 15
Rosemead, CA, 48
Rosen, Nig, 33
Rosenbaum, Marty, 37–38, 56
Rosenberg, Ethel, 173, 176, 207, 212, 213, 214
Rosenberg, Julius, 173, 176, 207, 212, 213, 214
Rosenthal, Erich, 28
Rosenthal, Isidore, 31, 56
Rosenwald, Lessing, 162
Rosenwald, William, 84
Rosenwald family, 63
Rosh Hashanah, 9, 88, 99, 103, 120, 221
Rosichan, Arthur, 76
Roth, Burnett, 154, 155, 156, 160, 173, 181
Roth, Philip, 250, 259, 260
Rothkopf, Louis, 33
Roybal, Edward, 205, 221, 222
Russian War Relief, 15

Sabbath, 93, 99, 109, 111, 112, 113, 119, 143, 147–48, 150, 270
Saint, Eva Marie, 253, 255
St. Louis, MO, 4, 37, 275
Samet, Seymour, 77, 156, 168–69, 184
Sandberg, Neil, 54, 91
San Fernando Valley, CA, 37, 42–43, 55, 56, 58, 66, 71, 84, 86, 94, 118, 222
San Gabriel Valley, CA, 48
San Juan, PR, 38
San Marino, CA, 48
Sans Souci hotel, 34
Santa Monica, CA, 38, 41, 84, 222
Sartre, Jean Paul, 3
Sax, George, 34
Saxony hotel, 34
Schary, Dore, 128–29, 148, 196, 229, 231, 247–49, 251
Scheltzer, Chava, 145
Schempp case, 185
Schools, 7, 78–83, 86–91, 190, 194, 222, 223–24, 225, 274; *see also* Higher education
demographics in, 90–91
Hebrew, 47, 78, 80, 82, 225, 270
in New York City, 78, 80, 81–82, 83, 266–67
parochial, 194, 223–24, 225

[Schools]
religious practices in, 87–89, 177–87, 216–19
segregation in, 169, 171, 172, 183, 186, 190
Sunday, 80, 82, 112, 115, 116, 135
Schulweis, Harold, 121, 270
Schwab, Oliver, 86
Schwartzman, Louis, 82
Search, The (film), 230
Sears, Roebuck stores, 63, 84, 205
Second-generation Jews, 66, 107, 268
Secularism, 70
Seder, 93, 103, 107
See It Now (television program), 241
Segregation, 6, 27, 155, 167
anticommunism and, 176, 177
in Los Angeles, 36
in Miami, 167–73, 182, 189, 199
in schools, 169, 171, 172, 183, 186, 190
Shabbat, 108, 142, 149, 151
Shabbat Shuva, 99
Shafter, Toby, 64–65
Shalo, Abe, 11
Shane, Joseph, 72, 235
Shapiro, Albert, 50
Shapiro, Chaim, 75
Shapiro, Harold, 50
Shapiro, Manheim, 76, 77
Shapiro, Yacov, 240
Sharett, Moshe, 240
Sharlin, William, 137
Shavuot, 106
Sheiner, Leo, 174
Shenandoah, 85
Sherman, George, 230
Sherry Frontenac hotel, 33
Shnoddering, 102
Shub, Louis, 71
Sierra Madre, CA, 218
Sigal, Clancy, 19, 59–60, 200
Silber, Jeffrey, 267
Silberberg, Mendel, 199–201, 214, 217
Simhat Torah, 69
Simi Valley, CA, 144, 148
Simon, Kate, 5
Simon, Stuart, 181
Sinai campaign, 241, 248, 251, 259–60
Sinai Temple, 131, 144
Sinatra, Frank, 197
Sinclair, Upton, 193
Singer, Isaac Bashevis, 2, 28, 30, 65, 265
Singer, Mike, 36, 43

Jewish Los Angeles
circa 1960

Simi Valley
Brandeis Camp Institute
Reseda
North Hollywood
California School of H.U.C.
Sherman Way
Van Nuys
Jewish Community Council
San Fernando Valley
Studio City
Reseda Blvd.
Paramount Studios
Hollywood Bowl
Vermont
Future site of University of Judaism & Stephen S. Wise Temple
Fairfax Ave.
Melrose
Ventura Blvd.
Encino
West Hollywood
Kosher Canyon
Mulholland Drive
Beverly
Wilshire Blvd. Temple
Woodland Hills
La Cienega
Beverly-Fairfax Jewish Community Center
Beverly Hills
Westwood
Temple Beth Am
Wilshire Blvd.
Olympic Blvd.
Pico
Hillcrest Club
Pacific Palisades
20th Century Fox Studios
Baldwin
Ocean Ave.
Venice
Santa Monica Pier
Venice Pier